CBASIC/CB86 with Graphics

Programming for Business

Harold Joseph Highland
Esther H. Highland

A Wiley Press Book

JOHN WILEY & SONS, INC.
New York • Chichester • Brisbane • Toronto • Singapore

To Rebecca Frances and Michael Joseph Highland

to whom the microcomputer does
not represent the world of the future

The manuscript for this book was written using a PeachText 5000 text editor. All programs were written and tested by the authors using CBASIC, CBASIC Compiler CB80, and CBASIC Compiler CB86. All computing was performed using Columbia Data Products microcomputers, an MPC-VP, and an MPC-1600, which permitted the use of both 8-bit and 16-bit software on a single machine. The graphics programs were developed and run on a Princeton Graphics System's HX-12 high resolution RBG color monitor.

Publisher: Judy V. Wilson
Editor: Theron Shreve
Managing Editor: Katherine Schowalter
Composition and Makeup: Cobb-Dunlop

Library of Congress Cataloging in Publication Data

Highland, Harold Joseph.
    CBASIC/CB86 with graphics: programming for business.
    Includes index.
    1. CBASIC (Computer program language) 2. Business—
Data processing. I. Highland, Esther Harris. II. Title.
HF5548.5.C14H54 1985   001.64'24   84-25740
ISBN 0-471-80226-3

85 86   10 9 8 7 6 5 4 3 2 1

Contents

What Is a Computer Language? . . Definition of Terms . . The CBASIC
Family . . The Structure of a Computer Program . . Your First Program
. . Compiling and Running a Program

Flowcharting Techniques . . A Sample Problem: Straight-Line
Depreciation . . Approaches to Problem Solving . . Further Reading

Constants and Variables . . Integer versus Real Variables . . Arrays . .
Mathematical Operators . . Intrinsic Arithmetic Functions

About the Authors

Dr. Harold Joseph Highland is Distinguished Professor Emeritus of the State University of New York, where he taught computer science, data processing, and microcomputing. In 1976 he received the Chancellor's Award for Excellence in Teaching. **Professor Esther H. Highland** is Professor Emerita of the City University of New York, where she taught statistics. Both had extensive business and writing experience prior to their teaching.

Between them they have written almost 30 books, several of which they did as co-authors. Some of their books have been translated into Japanese, German, French, Dutch, Finnish, and Hindustani. Both have had extensive experience as editors. Professor Highland has edited two encyclopedias as well as several books, and Dr. Highland has edited more than 20 volumes in the computing field. Dr. Highland's latest book, *Protecting Your Microcomputer System*, edited by Professor Highland, was published in 1984 by John Wiley & Sons.

Dr. Highland has been in computing for nearly 30 years and has worked with microcomputers since 1977. He has been director of two major computer centers. He was Fulbright Professor of Computer Science at Helsinki University of Technology and the University of Helsinki Medical School [Finland] and has taught and lectured at many universities in the United States, Canada, and Europe.

Since their retirement several years ago, they have been active in the computer field. They have done extensive magazine writing and editing in the microcomputer and computer security fields. Since 1980, Dr. Highland has served as Editor-in-Chief, and Professor Highland as Managing Editor, of *Computers & Security*, the official journal of the International Federation for Information Processing Technical Committee on security and protection in information processing systems, published by North-Holland Publishing Company of Amsterdam. Dr. Highland edits two journal that are published by the Association for Computing Machinery and is a National Lecturer for ACM. He is also a speaker at many national and international computing conferences.

Preface

CBASIC, as used in this book, is a *family name*. It refers not only to CBASIC, the non-compiler version of the language for 8-bit and 16-bit microcomputers, but also to CBASIC Compiler CB80 [8-bit] and CBASIC Compiler CB86 [16-bit].

Virtually all language manuals, whether written for mainframe or microcomputer users, do not meet the user's need. Manuals are written as reference guides for experienced programmers. Individuals who want to learn or have only a superficial knowledge of a language are often lost.

This book is both a textbook and a reference guide with detailed, step-by-step instructions. It is also an applications supplement illustrating the use of specific statements and functions in realistic programs. The book should be read sequentially by someone unfamiliar with programming; it can be consulted randomly by an experienced programmer.

WHY CBASIC?

Within a year after it was introduced in 1977 CBASIC became the most widely used commercial BASIC dialect for 8-bit microcomputers under CP/M. Somewhat later a compiler version, CBASIC Compiler CB80, was introduced and was widely accepted. The supremacy of CBASIC and CB80 was challenged with the advent of 16-bit microcomputers, additional operating systems, and the wide availability of some of the higher-level programming languages, COBOL, PL/1, and PASCAL in efficient form. The introduction of a 16-bit version of CBASIC and CBASIC Compiler CB86 that incorporates cursor control and graphics has again made this dialect a powerful microcomputer programming tool. There are versions of the language which operate under PC-DOS and MS-DOS as well as CPM/86.

There are several advantages for the programmer who uses CBASIC:

- CBASIC can be used with almost all the popular business-type microcomputers. Different compiler versions are available for 8-bit and 16-bit microcomputers and for many microprocessors. Thus a program developed for one machine is readily *transportable* to another microcomputer.
- Line numbers are *not* required on every line as is the case for other popular forms of BASIC.
- Variable names can be up to 31 characters in length and are *not* limited to single and double characters.
- Extended precision, 14-digit accuracy, in decimal arithmetic assures that fractional parts of dollar amounts will be exact. This is an advantage to anyone using CBASIC for technical and scientific work.
- Enhanced string processing is possible with the use of 11 built-in string functions permitting efficient use of memory.
- Simple file creation and handling statements permit random and sequential disk addressing.
- Assembly code ultilities can be easily interfaced with a CBASIC program.

CBASIC Compiler CB86 is a direct enhancement of CBASIC and offers many *additional* advantages.

- A *graphics package* is a part of CBASIC Compiler CB86 so that conventional business graphics can be programmed as an integral part of any CBASIC program.
- *Procedure names* rather than line numbers can be used.
- Programs can be used in a single-user, single-machine environment or in a multi-user, multi-machine environment without modification.
- Strings of any length up to 32,000 characters may be used, unlike other BASICs that limit strings to 255 characters.
- Cursor and screen controls are built-in, thereby making it easier to design input and output screens as well as hardcopy output.
- CBASIC Compiler is a native code compiler that allows separate modules to be written, tested, and then combined to create a complete program. This permits an efficient, modular, top-down approach to speed program writing and to make program maintenance easier.
- A compiled CBASIC program executes from eight to ten times faster than the same interpreted program.
- An executable version of a program provides computer security. It prevents making unauthorized changes in the program and copying source code.
- Multiple-key indexed files, similar to ISAM files, are supported in addition to sequential and random files. Such files speed searches and

retrieval of information and require the compatible package, *Access Manager*.
- CBASIC Compiler is also compatible with *Display Manager*, which eliminates the need for tedious formatting of console screen displays.
- Multiple-line functions, found in block-oriented languages, such as PL/1 and PASCAL, are fully supported.

Because of these features the CBASIC family, and particularly CBASIC Compiler CB86, is ideally suited as the prime language for business programming. It is easy to learn and simple for anyone knowing any dialect of BASIC to master in a short time.

ACKNOWLEDGMENTS

The authors would like to thank several individuals for their help in the development of this book.

- James Needham of Digital Research's Technical Support Department for his detailed review of the manuscript and for his technical support.
- Ms. Adrienne Hellman of Soft Stuff, Inc. for her review of the manuscript and her suggestions for the presentation of the programs.
- Donald Mills for producing the graphics printouts used in Chapter 15.
- Ms. Robin H. Zemble who did most of the text editing of the manuscript and many of the production chores associated with the preparation of this volume.

HOW TO USE THIS BOOK

This book is designed for all microcomputer users, ranging from those who are first learning to program, to those who already know another form of BASIC, and even to those who are familiar with CBASIC.

- If you are new microcomputers and unfamiliar with *any* programming language, you will find the book very detailed, written in step-by-step form, and replete with sample programs that enable you to get hands-on experience in programming methods. It is structured to introduce you to the most elementary techniques and to help you progress through the more advanced methods.
- If you already know some dialect of BASIC, this book will provide you with CBASIC's grammatical structure, an increased range of programming statements, and sample programs to illustrate differences between CBASIC and other forms of the language. It explains in detail the different methods of file handling, and introduces you to graphics programming as an extension of the language.

- If you are familiar with high-level languages, such as COBOL, PL/1, or PASCAL, this book offers you the foundations of CBASIC and contains illustrations of the power of advanced statements in this sophisticated language. It includes the use of graphics and emphasizes the basics of screen design for input and output and advanced methods of file manipulation.
- If you are already familiar with the older versions of CBASIC, you will find a complete review of the basic grammatical structures and many new statements which have been added to the language. You will also find details of built-in cursor control functions and built-in graphics capabilities.

A Flowchart for Using This Book

The accompanying flowchart is a compact, graphic guide to selecting the chapters that are relevant to your background and interests.

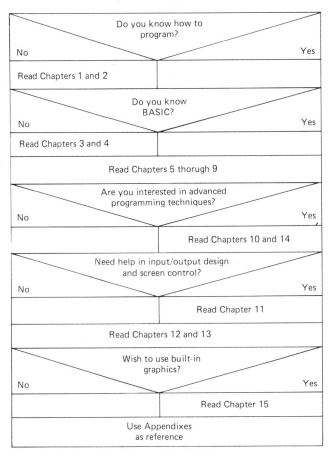

Language Coding Rules and Special Programming Notes

All programming statements and functions are fully illustrated and accompanied by special *Language Coding Rules* that are concisely explained. They are illustrated by sample programs. In addition, *Special Programming Notes* are included that contain tips for using the language statements and/or making programming easier and more efficient.

The Programs in the Book

This book contains 114 programs written and tested by the authors. It is strongly recommended, especially if you are unfamiliar with programming, that you enter many of these programs to obtain hands-on experience and reinforce your learning of the language coding rules.

The programs are written in either non-compiler or compiler form.

- If you are using non-compiler CBASIC, it is necessary to modify all the compiler versions in order to run them. The essential modifications are the use of suffixes with the variable names instead of declaration statements and the substitution of numbers for procedure names. In addition, in some of the advanced programs, there may be statements used which are not available in the non-compiler version.
- If you are using CBASIC Compiler CB86, you can run every program in this book without change.
- If you are using CBASIC Compiler CB80, some statements will have to be modified since they are not part of the set of statements for this version.

All programs are documented in detail in order to explain many of the statements included. Many of the more advanced programs can be used as *boilerplate programs*, that is, programs that can be easily modified to meet your specific needs.

The Programs on the Disk

Since many users will not want to take the time to enter all 114 programs and the necessary data files, there is a supplementary disk available for this book. In addition to the source code for all the book programs, the disk contains the data files used to illustrate and test specific programs. There are also six additional programs on the disk; these include advanced, menu-directed programs as well as convenient utility programs.

The Graphics Extension

The newer versions of CBASIC Compiler CB86 contain a built-in graphics extension package to enable you to incorporate graphs and charts as part of your CBASIC program. Chapter 15 contains 15 programs to help you understand how to use the graphics statements and functions. Also included are 16 illustrations of the output of the graphics programs.

A Reference Source

The six sections of the Appendix serve as a handy reference guide and supplement the very detailed index. In addition to several standard features, there is a complete guide to ASCII codes [all 256 characters], which is not readily found elsewhere. Also included is a convenient guide to conversion of strings-to-numbers and numbers-to-strings.

Harold Joseph Highland
Esther H. Highland

Directory of Programs, Figures, and Tables

Programs

(continues)

(continues)

(continues)

Figures

(continues)

Tables

LANGUAGE CODING IN THIS BOOK

The syntax or grammar of a computer language is rigidly defined so that the compiler can translate any user-entered statement unambiguously. Throughout this book we have included *LANGUAGE CODING RULES* that contain the essential elements of each CBASIC and CB86 statement and function available to the programmer. We follow conventional notation.

Boldface CAPS
Upper case or capital letters and any symbols in boldface are used to indicate those portions of statements that **must be entered** by the user **exactly** as shown.

< angle brackets >
Angle brackets indicate required **user-defined** data. Data enclosed in < > is defined by the programmer and special conditions are explained in the accompanying text.

[square brackets]
Square brackets indicate that the entry is **optional** and may be omitted by the programmer.

{ braces }
Braces are used where any portion of the statement is **optional and** may be **repeated** by the user as often as desired within the limits set by the compiler.

ABOUT THE PROGRAMS IN THIS BOOK

Each program in this book is identified for either non-compiler or compiler. This difference is critical *only* if you are using a non-compiler version of CBASIC.

1. Whether you use a non-compiler or compiler version:
   - modify the CLEAR.SCREEN statement to conform with your operating system *or* eliminate the CLEAR.SCREEN statements until some time later, *and*
   - the boldface type in the programs is for emphasis only.
2. With any **compiler** version, CB86, you can compile, link, and execute *all* of the programs in this book.
3. With the **non-compiler version**, CBASIC, you must remove the declaration of variables in compiler programs and add a terminal **$** to each string and a **%** to each integer variable. Also make certain that the statement or function is not reserved for compiler versions.

CHAPTER 1

Introduction to Programming in the CBASIC Family

BASIC is one of many computer languages. The name is an acronym for **B**eginners **A**ll **P**urpose **S**ymbolic **I**nstruction **C**ode. The language was developed in 1965 at Dartmouth College by J. Kemeny and T. Kurtz because they needed a computer language which was very simple to learn. Since then, there have been many changes made in the language so that today there are many dialects of BASIC.

BASIC is a high-level language, that is, it is similar to everyday language and is therefore easy to use. The computer does not understand a high-level language so that it is necessary to translate BASIC into a low-level language that can be executed by the computer or into machine-code which consists of a series of zeros and ones.

WHAT IS A COMPUTER LANGUAGE?

A computer language in many ways is similar to a human language, such as English, German, French, or Finnish. It consists of an alphabet, words, and sentences but uses technical terms for these components.

Character Set

The most elementary unit in any language is the alphabet. In English, for example, there are 26 letters, from A through Z. In Finnish, on the other hand, there are only 24 letters; there is no C, Q, W, or Z, but after the Y is Ä followed by Ö. Just as human alphabets vary, so do those used in computer languages. There are variations even within the dialects of the same computer language. In computing we call the alphabet a **character set**.

The character set of the CBASIC family consists of:

- 26 letters, from A through Z, used *both* as capitals and lower case
- 10 digits, from 0 through 9
- 7 mathematical symbols, such as +, =, −
- A set of special characters, such as $, ?, ! [Note that a *blank space* is a special character.]

Computer Words

We use the computer alphabet or character set to form words in a computer programming language as we do in human language. There are two types of words in non-compiler and compiler versions of CBASIC:

- First, there are **key words** which can be used only to instruct the computer to perform a specific task. For example, READ tells the computer to seek data in the program and "to read" it into its memory. Another example is RENAME which directs the computer to change the name of a file. These and other keywords, also known as **command** or **reserved words**, are part of the computer's normal vocabulary. [A list of the key or reserved words can be found in Appendix A.]
- Second, there are words that you can create to describe specific values which may change during a program. These are known as **identifiers** and are used in computer programs. In English we have rules about the sequence of letters; for example, "i before e except after c." Similarly, we have rules to form identifier words in a programming language.

Sentences

In everyday language we join various words according to grammatical rules to form sentences. We do the same in a computer language, and we call the sentences **statements**. In CBASIC non-compiler and compiler, as in other computer languages, there are two types of statements: executable and nonexecutable.

Nonexecutable statements provide information to the user or compiler but cause no program action. For example, a REM or remark statement serves as an internal memo within the program. The computer does not execute the statement since it has been instructed to ignore it. The END statement at the conclusion of a program lets both the reader and the computer know that nothing follows. It is another example of a nonexecutable statement.

Executable statements are processed by the computer. They perform specific tasks and control the flow of the program. For example, when the computer encounters a READ statement, it will seek the data to be read elsewhere in the program on a line which begins with the keyword, DATA. With a GOTO statement, the execution of the program will branch to the location indicated.

Although grammar rules in programming languages vary, there are certain similarities. If you know one dialect of BASIC, it is comparatively easy to learn another, and if you know BASIC, there is a larger family of languages that more or less follows similar rules.

It is important to remember that grammar rules must be rigidly followed. The computer has been programmed to accept correctly constructed statements so that it can distinguish between statements and between the elements within a statement. Despite its complexity and high speed, the computer does not know how to make subtle distinctions—it does only and exactly what it is told to do.

DEFINITION OF TERMS

Let us stop for a moment and define some basic computer terms.

- A **file** is either a computer program or a set of data such as accounts payable, payroll records, a mailing list.
- A **source program** is written by one or several programmers following the grammar and syntax rules established for a specific high-level computer language, such as CBASIC.
- A **compiler** is a computer program that translates the high-level source language program into either a machine-readable program that can be used directly by the computer or into an "intermediate" form.
- An **intermediate program** is a series of machine code programs that have been produced by a compiler which has checked a source program for grammar and other language rules.
- A **run-time interpreter** executes an intermediate program which has been generated by a compiler.
- A **library module** is a collection of subroutines [procedures] used when the computer runs a source program.
- A **link editor** is a program that joins the necessary portions of a library module to an intermediate program to form an object program.

- An **object program** is one which has been translated into machine-readable code and to which the necessary library programs have been added; it is directly executable by the computer.
- A **subroutine** or a **subprogram** as it is sometimes called, is a segment of a program that can perform a specific set of procedures. Subprograms reduce programming time and save memory space when the procedure is required at more than one point in the program.
- A **built-in function** or **intrinsic function** is a subprogram which is part of the compiler. It performs a specific procedure.

THE CBASIC FAMILY

The **CBASIC family** is one set of BASIC dialects which has been developed by Digital Research, Inc. This family, which includes both non-compiler and compiler versions, is available to operate with different:

- Operating systems: CP/M, MP/M, PC-DOS, MS-DOS, APPLE-DOS, and UNIX
- Bit-size configurations: 8- and 16-bit microcomputers
- Processors such as Z80, 8080, 8086, 8088, 68000, 6502, 80286
- Computers such as the IBM PC, IBM AT, IBM XT, DEC Rainbow, Apple II, Columbia MPC, COMPAQ, and most other 8-bit and 16-bit systems

As of early 1985 the following CBASIC versions were available:

- CBASIC
- CBASIC-86
- CBASIC-IBM PC
- CBASIC-DEC RAINBOW
- CBASIC-APPLE
- CBASIC COMPILER CB80
- CBASIC COMPILER CB86
- CBASIC COMPILER CB86 PC-DOS
- CBASIC COMPILER CB86 DEC
- CBASIC COMPILER CB86 APPLE
- CBASIC COMPILER CB86 MS-DOS
- CBASIC COMPILER 68K
- CBASIC COMPILER 80286

The relationship among these is shown in Table 1-1.

Although CBASIC [the non-compiler version] was developed in 1977 to work on 8-bit microcomputers under CP/M, there has been a rapid expansion of both non-compiler and compiler versions in the past few years.

TABLE 1-1   The CBASIC Family

	NON-COMPILER VERSION	COMPILER VERSION
8-bit computer	CBASIC	CBASIC COMPILER CB80
	CBASIC APPLE	CBASIC COMPILER APPLE
16-bit computer	CBASIC-86	CBASIC COMPILER CB86
	CBASIC-86 IBM PC	CBASIC COMPILER PC-DOS
	CBASIC-86 DEC	CBASIC COMPILER DEC
		CBASIC COMPILER MS-DOS
		CBASIC COMPILER 68K
		CBASIC COMPILER 80286

The versions operating under MS-DOS are not directly available from Digital Research but are provided by specific microcomputer manufacturers. The authors have been running CBASIC-86 and CBASIC COMPILER CB80 under CP/M, and also CBASIC COMPILER CB86 PC-DOS on a Columbia Data Products MPC 1600-1 and on a Columbia Data Products MCP-VP operating under MS-DOS. Graphics programs, covered in Chapter 15, were executed under PC-DOS.

NOTE: Throughout this book all references to CBASIC apply to all members of the CBASIC family. Differences between non-compiler and compiler versions will be noted.

The changes in BASIC over the years have been dramatic. For example, a popular version about a decade ago, which was used on mainframe computers, contained only 18 programming statements, four arithmetic operations, and had no built-in or intrinsic functions.

Today's **CBASIC** and **CBASIC-86** have:

- 48 programming statements
- 27 built-in or intrinsic functions
- 16 arithmetic and logical operators

Early versions of **CBASIC COMPILER CB80** and **CBASIC COMPILER CB86** had:

- 54 programming statements
- 35 intrinsic or built-in functions
- 16 arithmetic and logical operators

The newer **CBASIC COMPILER** versions for 16-bit microcomputers are available with GSX-86 Graphics Extensions and have additional intrinsic functions and additional statements, so that the Compiler versions, such as that for PC-DOS, now have:

- 79 programming and graphics statements
- 63 intrinsic functions
- 16 arithmetic and logical operators

CBASIC and CBASIC-86

CBASIC and **CBASIC-86** have two main components.

1. There is the compiler which translates the source program into an intermediate file. The source program name has two parts: the name of the program, and the file extension **BAS**, after a decimal point, **.BAS**. The compiler produces a file that has the program name, but instead of the **.BAS**, it now has the file extension **.INT**.
2. There is a run-time interpreter which runs or *executes* the **.INT** file.

CBASIC Compilers

The CBASIC compiler versions—CBASIC COMPILER CB80, CBASIC COMPILER CB86, and the other CBASIC COMPILERs—also have a two-phase system:

1. The compiler creates a relocatable file from the **.BAS** program. It is designated by the program name followed by **.REL** or **.OBJ** file extension for the 8-bit and 16-bit microcomputers, respectively.
2. By using the link editor, the relocatable file is linked with the necessary library routines to produce a new file. For example, it is the program name followed by **.COM** or **.CMD** when using CP/M80 and CP/M86 respectively. When using the CBASIC COMPILER CB86 for PC-DOS, the new file has the program name followed by **.EXE**. These are object programs that are directly executable so that all you need do to run them is to enter the program name immediately after a system's prompt.

THE STRUCTURE OF A COMPUTER PROGRAM

You can create a program for use with the CBASIC family by using the text editor that comes with your operating system. However, you may find it easier to use a stand-alone text editor. Most users have a text editor, such as

PEACHTEXT 5000, SPELLBINDER, EDIX, WORDSTAR, or VOLKSWRITER, as part of their microcomputer's software library.

✗   A computer program is a set of statements written in a computer language following specific grammar rules. **Program 1-1** calculates the amount to which $1,000.00 accumulates based on any given rate of interest for any number of compounding periods per year. It illustrates some programming techniques used in CBASIC and also shows some of the differences from other dialects. [**Note:** The numbers to the left of each statement are *not* part of the program but are used as references in the copy that follows.] Do not expect to understand the programs at this stage.

PROGRAM 1-1   **DEMO.BAS**   **[Non-Compiler]**

Demonstration Program for Compound Interest

Copyright 1984, 1985, Compulit, Inc.

```
 1|     REM    Sample Program to illustrate compound amount \
 2|            for $1000.00 with different compounding periods
 3|            CLEAR.SCREEN$ = CHR$(27) + CHR$(69) : REM CLEAR.SCREEN for CP/M 86
 4|     562    AMOUNT = 1000.00                    REM Starting principal
 5|            PRINT CLEAR.SCREEN$
 6|            INPUT "Enter annual interest rate as decimal .. "; RATE
 7|            INPUT "Enter number of compounding periods .... "; PERIODS
 8|            PERIOD.RATE = RATE / PERIODS
 9|            FOR K = 1 TO PERIODS
10|                    AMOUNT = AMOUNT + AMOUNT * PERIOD.RATE
11|            NEXT K
12|            INTEREST.RATE = RATE * 100
13|            PRINT:    PRINT "The amount is";
14|            PRINT USING "$$#,###.##"; AMOUNT;
15|            PRINT " when $1,000.00 is compounded"
16|            PRINT PERIODS; "times a year at"; INTEREST.RATE; "% interest."
17|            PRINT:  INPUT "Another run? ... [YES or NO] .......... "; ANS
18|            IF UCASE$(ANS) = "YES" THEN 562
19|            PRINT:  PRINT "Normal termination of the program."
20|            END
```

Some of the versions of CBASIC COMPILER CB86 do *not* include any command to clear the screen. This feature is both operating system and hardware dependent. How to clear the console screen, where it is not part of the compiler, is illustrated in different programs in the book. A detailed explanation of how to *clear the console screen* is given in Chapter 11.

Labels or Line Numbers

Unlike most other BASIC dialects, CBASIC does **not** require that each statement be preceded by a line number. Only those statements which are referenced within the program require a **label** [line 4 which is referenced in line 18].

The sequence of labels or statement numbers does **not** influence the order in which the statements are executed. The statements in a program are executed sequentially unless the program encounters a statement that causes it to branch to a specific label. [If the user of the illustrated program answers "YES" in line 17, the statement in line 18 returns program execution to label 562 or line 4.]

Rules for Forming Labels

- In CBASIC and CBASIC-86, a label consists of any set of digits, 0 through 9, and may be up to 31 digits long.
- A decimal point [.] may be embedded within a label. For example, 13 and 13.0 are treated as distinctly different labels.
- In CB80 and CB86 a label may include alphabetic as well as numeric characters but *must be started with a letter*, A through Z. Blank spaces and special characters, such as $ or #, may *not* be used. The label may be up to 31 characters long. [Also see page 35, "Additional Rules for Forming Variable Names."]
- If you use alphameric labels, be careful not to use the same set of characters for a line label and a variable name.

For users of the compiler versions: It is essential to follow an alphabetic label with a colon [:]. It is recommended that the label be placed on a line by itself and followed by a comment or remark to identify the label. This makes reading easy and simplifies program modification. For example:

```
PRINT.ROUTINE: \ Name and address print procedure

WRITE.TO.FILE: \ Write record on disk
```

Identifiers or Variable Names

CBASIC does **not** impose the severe restrictions of many other dialects in naming **identifiers**, the words used to specify a particular value in the program [lines 6–RATE, 7–PERIODS, and 12–INTEREST.RATE]. As many as 31 characters may be used to increase the readability of a program. For example, we could have used the identifier, NUMBER.OF.COMPOUNDING.PERIODS instead of PERIODS [line 7]. The identifier may also be very short, for example, N or NP.

In a long, complex program it would be difficult to remember the meaning of short identifiers, such as A, B2, I23X, or RPL. However, the use of long identifiers not only requires more key entry but also affects the time needed to compile the program. There is a trade-off between ease of reading a program and the time needed to enter and compile it.

Program Comments, Style, and Structure

Comments and blank lines may be included in a program to make it easier to read and follow. These lines start with **REM**, **REMARK**, or a backslash [\] [line 1]. A REM or a backslash [\] may also follow an executable statement, *but with the non-compiler versions, the backslash instead of REM following an executable statement will result in an error message.*

Continuation of a comment is possible if there is insufficient space on a single line. This is done by ending the line with a backslash [\] and continuing on the next line [lines 1 and 2]. *With the non-compiler version, the first comment line must start with a REM if the backslash [\] is used for continuation lines.*

An executable statement may be continued beyond a single line by ending each line with a backslash [\]. Some exceptions will be noted later.

LANGUAGE CODING RULE

A comment or remark in a program has the form:

    REM [statement]

or

    REMARK [statement]

or

    **** [statement]

- The comment or REM statement does not affect the size of the program compiled or executed.
- If the backslash, \, is used to indicate a remark, it may *not* be used on the same line to indicate a continuation of the remark. When a remark is continued using the \ at the end of the line, the line should begin with REM.

NOTE: We have used \ to designate a comment or remark in many programs used in this book.

For ease of reading, statement lines may be indented without affecting the compilation of a program [line 10].

Two or more statements may be written on a single line [lines 13 and 17] but they must be separated by a colon [:]. However, there are exceptions which will be noted as the statements are discussed.

It is good programming practice to write **END** [line 20] at the conclusion of a program. It is not essential since the compiler will automatically include it if it is omitted. However, it serves to assure any one who reads the program that no copy is missing.

An important advantage of CBASIC is that **alphanumeric strings**, as names, addresses, and similar data are called, can be read as part of a DATA statement in a program *without* beginning and ending with quotation marks as required in other dialects of BASIC.

A dollar sign has been printed in front of the numeric value computed by the program by using a special form of the PRINT statement [line 14].

Use of Upper and Lower Case Letters

Copy to be displayed on the screen or printed as hardcopy by the printer may be written in upper and lower case [lines 6, 7, 13].

CBASIC permits the user to enter the answer to an INPUT request [lines 6, 7] in either upper or lower case. An **intrinsic function**, a built-in subprogram, **UCASE$**, changes all lower case letters to upper case [line 18]. The user can answer the question in line 17 in upper case [YES] or lower case [yes] or even a combination [Yes] and the program would recognize all as equivalent to YES.

LANGUAGE CODING RULE

A source program is terminated with an END statement.

END

- The END statement is the last line of a program; the compiler will not read past the END statement.
- The END statement may not appear on the same line with any other statement.

The input and output from the program would appear on the screen as follows:

```
Enter annual interest rate as decimal ++ +08

Enter number of compounding periods ++++ 12

The amount is $1,083,00 when $1,000,00 is compounded
12 times a year at 8% interest+

Another run? +++ [YES or NO] ++++++++++ YES


Enter annual interest rate as decimal ++ +08

Enter number of compounding periods ++++ 365

The amount is $1,083,28 when $1,000,00 is compounded
365 times a year at 8% interest+

Another run? +++ [YES or NO] ++++++++++ NO

Normal termination of the program+
```

YOUR FIRST PROGRAM

Programming is best learned by doing. So, here is a simple problem to program.

1. Write down your house number.
2. Double it and add five.
3. Multiply by 50.
4. Add your age in years.
5. Add 365.
6. Subtract 615.
7. What happens?
8. You will find your house number at the left and your age at the right.

The following program steps are numbered to correspond to the list above. [The numbers are not part of the program.]

```
1. INPUT "ENTER YOUR HOUSE NUMBER"; HN
2. ANSWER = 2 * HN + 5
3. ANSWER = ANSWER * 50
```

```
4. INPUT "ENTER YOUR AGE"; AGE
   ANSWER = ANSWER + AGE
5. ANSWER = ANSWER + 365
6. ANSWER = ANSWER - 615
7. PRINT ANSWER
8. PRINT "HOUSE NUMBER IS ON THE LEFT; AGE IS ON THE RIGHT."
```

In practice, the eight steps would be combined into a shorter program with the arithmetic done in one line. The statement PRINT by itself will result in a blank line on the CRT when the program is run. This facilitates reading.

> **NOTE:** We have used upper case letters in the program for simplicity. It is **not** a requirement of the CBASIC family.

PROGRAM 1-2   **ANSWER.BAS**   **[Non-Compiler]**

First Program to Enter

Copyright 1984, 1985, Compulit, Inc.

```
INPUT "ENTER YOUR HOUSE NUMBER.........."; HN
PRINT
INPUT "ENTER YOUR AGE IN YEARS.........."; AGE
PRINT
ANSWER = (2 * HN + 5)* 50 + AGE + 365 - 615
PRINT ANSWER
PRINT
PRINT "HOUSE NUMBER IS ON THE LEFT; AGE IS ON THE RIGHT."
END
```

Enter this short program using a text editor; we will call the program ANSWER.BAS. The **.BAS** suffix is required in naming a program in all versions of CBASIC. Each line must be ended with a carriage return; this is a general rule in programming. Although the program is short it uses several commands and symbols, some of which will be explained later.

COMPILING AND RUNNING A PROGRAM

The procedures to compile and run a program are different for the compiler and non-compiler versions of CBASIC. All are included in the following illustration. We are using the latest versions of the compilers. Check your manual and disk directory if you are using older versions or future updates.

> **NOTE:** In the following copy as well as elsewhere in this book, the underlined characters are those which are typed by the operator at the keyboard and will appear on the screen. The system prompt, **A>**, and any computer responses are not underlined. A *carriage return*, a special key on the keyboard, is shown as <**CR**>.

Compiling the Program

After entering the program, exit from the text editor and return to the operating system. The screen will show **A>** or **A:** depending upon your computer's operating system. You are now ready to compile the program by entering:

```
          ¦  [CBASIC]      A>  CBAS2 ANSWER    <CR>
  8-bit   ¦
          ¦  [CB80]        A>  CB80 ANSWER     <CR>

          ¦  [CBASIC-86]   A>  CBASIC86 ANSWER    <CR>
 16-bit   ¦
          ¦  [CB86]        A>  CB86 ANSWER     <CR>
```

The computer will compile the program, and if you have made no typing errors, the following will appear on the screen if you are using CBASIC.

```
CBASIC COMPILER VER 2.08
    1:      REM  PROGRAM 1-2     ANSWER.BAS
    2:      INPUT "ENTER YOUR HOUSE NUMBER.........."; HN
    3:      PRINT
    4:      INPUT "ENTER YOUR AGE IN YEARS.........."; AGE
    5:      PRINT
    6:      ANSWER = (2* HN + 5)* 50 + AGE + 365 - 615
    7:      PRINT ANSWER
    8:      PRINT
    9:      PRINT "HOUSE NUMBER IS ON THE LEFT; AGE IS ON THE RIGHT."
   10:      END
NO ERRORS DETECTED
CONSTANT AREA:       8
CODE SIZE:         179
DATA STMT AREA:      0
VARIABLE AREA:      24
```

If you are using the other versions, you will find some slight differences. For example, if you have used CBASIC COMPILER CB86, the following will appear:

```
         ---------------------------------------------------
         CB86 CBASIC Compiler                    Version 1.0
         Serial No. PCB-000-00045    All rights reserved
         Copyright (c) 1982,1983  Digital Research, Inc.
         ---------------------------------------------------
    1:   0000h        REM   PROGRAM 1-2      ANSWER.BAS
    2:   0000h        INPUT "ENTER YOUR HOUSE NUMBER.........."; HN
    3:   001ah        PRINT
    4:   001dh        INPUT "ENTER YOUR AGE IN YEARS.........."; AGE
    5:   002eh        PRINT
    6:   0031h        ANSWER = (2* HN + 5)* 50 + AGE + 365 - 615
    7:   006dh        PRINT ANSWER
    8:   0076h        PRINT
    9:   0079h        PRINT "HOUSE NUMBER IS ON THE LEFT; AGE IS ON THE RIGHT."
   10:   0082h        END

end of compilation
no errors detected
code area size:     130        0082h
data area size:     148        0094h
common area size:   0          0000h
symbol table space remaining: 41116
```

No matter which version of CBASIC you have used, disregard everything but the error count. If an error is indicated, check your entries carefully and correct with a text editor. The only error you are likely to encounter at this stage is a **syntax error**, an error in grammar. For example, if when typing line 3 you omitted the first quotation mark:

```
INPUT ENTER YOUR HOUSE NUMBER..........."; HN
```

the display on the screen immediately below that line would read:

```
ERROR  SE  in Line 3 at Position 23.
```

The SE indicates a syntax error. There are many other errors that can be encountered during both the compile phase and run phase of a program. All error messages are listed in Appendix D and Appendix E. These include compile and run-time errors for non-compiler versions and compile, link and run-time errors for compiler versions. How to analyze and correct them will be covered more fully later.

Remember that grammar is much more important to the computer than to people. It will not, for example, accept a colon where it should find a semicolon. After any error has been corrected, recompile the program.

For Compiler Versions Only

[If you are using CBASIC or CBASIC-86, skip to the next section.]

For users of the Compiler version, it is now necessary to run the link editor which will join the necessary library functions to the intermediate program that has just been created. Do this by entering:

```
[CB80]                    A>   LK80 ANSWER        <CR>

[CB86]                    A>   LINK86 ANSWER      <CR>
```

This linkage will take place only if there is an ANSWER.REL program on the disk for CB80 or an ANSWER.OBJ program for CB86. The link editor cannot work directly on ANSWER.BAS. The output will vary somewhat depending upon the compiler, but for CB86 it would appear as:

```
-----------------------------------------------
LINK-86  Linkage Editor            Version 1.0
Serial No. PCB 000-00045    All rights reserved
Copyright (C) 1982,1983  Digital Research, Inc.
-----------------------------------------------
CODE      017A7
DATA      005B4

USE FACTOR:  .05%

-----------------------------------------------------------------------
```

The Compiler's link editor produces a new file, ANSWER.COM for CB80 or ANSWER.EXE for CB86 when using PC-DOS.

Running the Program

After you have successfully compiled the program with no errors [and it has been linked if you are using the compiler version], you are ready to run or *execute* the program. To do so enter:

```
         |   [CBASIC]      A>   CRUN238 ANSWER   <CR>
8-bit    |
         |   [CB80]        A>   ANSWER   <CR>

         |   [CBASIC-86]   A>   CRUN86 ANSWER    <CR>
16-bit   |
         |   [CB86]        A>   ANSWER   <CR>
```

Enter the data the program requests followed by <CR> each time. If your answer is not correct, check the program again. Did you omit both parentheses? Have you made a typographical error in the numbers? Such errors will not be caught when the program is compiled. The computer cannot tell that [+] was intended where [−] appears, and −356 is as valid a number to the microcomputer as 365, which is correct.

NOTE: Save the ANSWER.BAS program on your disk for future use. Variations of it will be used to illustrate programming methods later in the book.

Making a Back-up Copy

It is good programming practice to make a duplicate or **back-up** copy of any programs you write, or a copy of any data files you create later. The procedure to do this depends on the operating system.

If you have never made back-up disks refer to the appropriate section of your computer manual. Even though the programs are short at this stage, having a back-up disk will save you time in needless reentry if anything ruins the copy on the original disk you are using.

CHAPTER 2

Flowcharting and
Problem Solving

We have all had the experience of telling someone how to find the way to our home or the way to the post office.

Heading west on Southern State Parkway, take exit 13 northbound at Franklin Avenue. There is a traffic light at the next corner; turn left. You will be on a divided highway, Dutch Broadway. Proceed west for two miles until you reach the third traffic light at Central Avenue. Turn right, but if the street is closed to traffic because of repairs, continue west for one more block and then turn right. In either case, continue north two blocks until the first stop sign and turn left onto Croyden Lane. Drive until you are six blocks past the golf course; we're at the northwest corner.

These step-by-step instructions to perform a specific task are known as an **algorithm**.

Just as we could have drawn a map to show the way to our home, we can draw a special type of a map for any algorithm. First, several characteristics of the special map should be noted.

- *Special ovals* are used to indicate where to start and where to stop.
- *Rectangular boxes* are used to contain the instructions that must be followed.
- A *diamond-shaped box* is used at a decision point, where one must answer a question, that is, make a decision.
- *Arrows* are used to indicate the flow of instructions from one point to another until the procedure or algorithm has been completed.

17

```
        ┌─────────────┐
        │    START    │
        └─────────────┘
               │
               ▼
           ╱Heading╲
          ╱ west on ╲        NO
         ◇ Southern State ◇──────────────────┐
          ╲ Parkway? ╱                        │
           ╲       ╱                          │
            YES │                             │
               ▼                              ▼
        ┌─────────────┐              ┌─────────────┐
        │ Take exit 13│              │             │
        │ northbound at│             │  Get help!  │
        │ Franklin Avenue│           │             │
        └─────────────┘              └─────────────┘
               │                             │
               ▼                             ▼
        ┌─────────────┐              ┌─────────────┐
        │ Turn left at next│         │    STOP     │
        │ corner onto  │             └─────────────┘
        │ Dutch Broadway│
        └─────────────┘
               │
               ▼
        ┌─────────────┐
        │ Proceed west until│
        │ the third traffic light│
        └─────────────┘
               │
               ▼
           ╱  Is  ╲
          ╱Central Avenue╲   YES      ┌─────────────┐
         ◇ closed to  ◇──────────────▶│ Continue west for│
          ╲ traffic? ╱                │ one more block. │
           ╲       ╱                  └─────────────┘
            NO │                             │
               ▼◀────────────────────────────┘
        ┌─────────────┐
        │ Turn right and proceed│                    ┌─────────────┐
        │ until "Stop" sign. │              ╱Have╲   │             │
        └─────────────┘              ╱ you driven ╲  NO│ Continue driving│
               │                    ◇ six blocks ◇───▶│             │
               ▼                     ╲ past the golf╱  └─────────────┘
        ┌─────────────┐               ╲ course? ╱
        │ Turn left onto│──────────────▶ YES │
        │ Croyden Lane │                      ▼
        └─────────────┘              ┌─────────────┐
                                     │ STOP at northwest│
                                     │    corner   │
                                     └─────────────┘
```

FIGURE 2-1   Flowchart of a Simple Algorithm

We can use these symbols to provide instructions to reach our home [see **Figure 2-1**]. We can also use these symbols to show the procedures needed in preparing a business program for the computer. This special map used in computing is known as a **flowchart**.

FLOWCHARTING TECHNIQUES

A flowchart can show an overall view like a map of a city showing the highways around the city and the main streets in the city, or it can be detailed like a map showing each street in a specific neighborhood. A flowchart can provide an overall view of an accounts receivable and payable system or the details of a program to compute straight-line depreciation. The former is a *systems flowchart* and the latter a *program flowchart*.

A flowchart may be used for several purposes:

- It can provide an overall view of the approach to solving a specific problem, indicating what data has to be provided as input into the program, what computations have to be performed, and what output has to be stored on disk and/or printed.
- It can assist a programmer in detailing an intricate step-by-step procedure before writing any statements.
- It assures better communications between programmers, when more than one is working on the same job, or when one requests assistance from another.
- It can also help the programmer explain to the user what has to be done and why.

Although there have been modifications over the years in the shape of some of the symbols used in flowcharts, many programmers use those that conform to the International Organization for Standardization [ISO] draft. There are five basic ISO symbols: [1] beginning/ termination block, [2] input/ output block, [3] processing block, [4] decision block, and [5] flow arrows [see **Figure 2-2**].

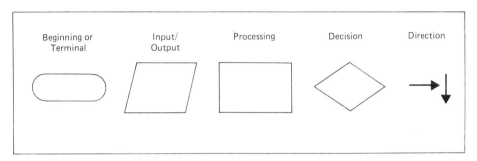

FIGURE 2-2   Fundamental Flowchart Symbols

A SAMPLE PROBLEM: STRAIGHT-LINE DEPRECIATION

To illustrate the use of a flowchart in programming, let us take a simple problem using the straight-line method of depreciation.

Prepare a program to compute straight-line depreciation for an item showing the years, annual depreciation, total depreciation to date, and book value at the end of each year.

All programming involves three phases, and most programmers use an **HIPO** [an acronym for **H**ierarchial **I**nput **P**rocessing and **O**utput] approach [see **Figure 2-3**].

1. *Input:* To produce the required program the following four data items must be obtained and entered: the current year, the cost of the item for which depreciation is being computed, the expected useful life of the item in years, and the salvage value of the item at the end of its useful life.
2. *Processing:* These calculations are necessary to process the data: annual depreciation, which is equal to the difference between the cost of the item and its salvage value, divided by the number of years of its useful life; cumulative depreciation, which is current annual depreciation plus the depreciation already accumulated; and book value at the end of the year, which is the previous year's book value less the annual depreciation.
3. *Output:* The appearance of the output is user dependent. If it is to be printed and presented to others, column headings, spacing between columns, and other features will have to be incorporated into the program. The visual impact of a computer printout or the CRT display is an important phase of programming and will be discussed in detail in Chapter 11, "The Design of Input and Output."

There are several approaches to writing the program, but for the present we will use the simple approach detailed below and shown in the accompanying flowchart [see **Figure 2-4**].

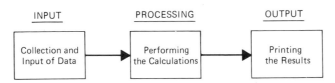

FIGURE 2-3   Hierarchical Input and Output Chart

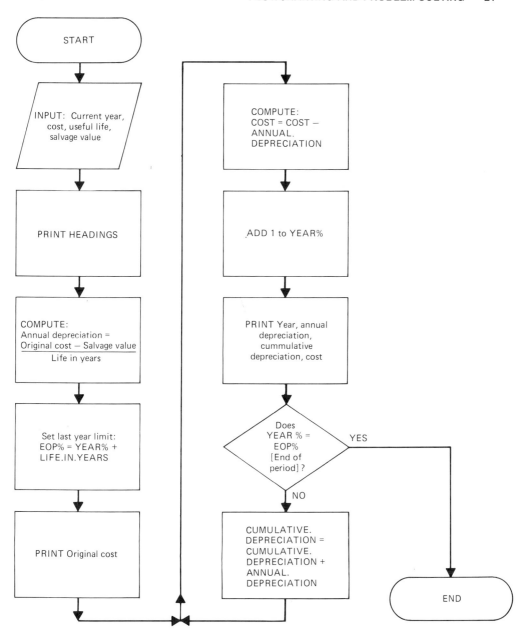

FIGURE 2-4   Flowchart for Straight-Line Depreciation

Step-by-Step Algorithm for Straight-Line Depreciation

1. Enter the four required data values.
2. Print the heads for the columns: year, annual depreciation, cumulative depreciation, and book value at end of the year.

3. Calculate the annual depreciation.
4. Define a control index which is equal to the sum of the current year and the useful life of the item in years. This value will end the calculation.
5. Set cumulative depreciation equal to the annual depreciation, which will be used for only the first year and then will be increased each year by annual depreciation.
6. Print current year and cost of item [or its initial book value].
7. Calculate the new book value by subtracting the annual depreciation from the previous year's book value.
8. Set year equal to previous year plus one.
9. Print year, annual depreciation, cumulative depreciation, and book value.
10. Determine if the value of year just printed is equal to the control index established in step 4.

   • If NO: let cumulative depreciation equal the cumulative depreciation plus the annual depreciation and return to step 7.
   • If YES: terminate computations and program.

The flowchart is a pictorial form of this step-by-step procedure. Once the flowchart has been prepared it is easy to write the necessary CBASIC statements to develop a working program, **Program 2-1**.

PROGRAM 2-1   **PRODVAL.BAS**   **[Non-Compiler]**

Calculation of Depreciation

Copyright 1985, Compulit, Inc.

```
\           Defining CLEAR.SCREEN for PC-DOS and MS-DOS
            CLEAR.SCREEN$ = CHR$(27) + "[2J"
            PRINT CLEAR.SCREEN$
            INPUT "       Enter current year ................... "; YEAR%
            INPUT "       Enter cost of item ................... "; COST
            INPUT "       Enter useful life of item in years ... "; LIFE.IN.YEARS%
            INPUT "       Enter salvage value of item ......... "; SALVAGE
            PRINT: PRINT: PRINT
            PRINT TAB(19); "Annual"; TAB(37); "Cumulative"; TAB(58); "Book Value"
            PRINT " Year"; TAB(16);"Depreciation"; TAB(37); "Depreciation"; \
                  TAB (56); "[End of Year]":    PRINT
            ANNUAL.DEPRECIATION = (COST - SALVAGE) / LIFE.IN.YEARS%
            EOP% = YEAR% + LIFE.IN.YEARS%
            CUMULATIVE.DEPRECIATION = ANNUAL.DEPRECIATION
            PRINT YEAR%, " ", " ", COST
10          COST = COST - ANNUAL.DEPRECIATION
            YEAR% = YEAR% + 1
            PRINT YEAR%, ANNUAL.DEPRECIATION, CUMULATIVE.DEPRECIATION, COST
            IF YEAR% = EOP% THEN 30
            CUMULATIVE.DEPRECIATION = CUMULATIVE.DEPRECIATION + ANNUAL.DEPRECIATION
            GOTO 10
30          END
```

SPECIAL PROGRAMMING NOTE

TO CLEAR THE SCREEN write a special statement in the program since only the PC-DOS compiler version contains a specific command to clear the console screen. The graphics version also has a **CLEAR** command, but without the graphics package, this deficiency can be overcome as shown in Program 2-1.

The statement depends on the operating system and whether you are using a monitor or a terminal. In any case, define "clear screen" early in a program.

- *With a monitor:* Using CP/M86, clearing the screen involves using two keys, the ESCAPE key and the upper case letter E. It is "translated" into CBASIC as:

CLEAR.SCREEN$ = CHR$(27) + CHR$(69)

Using a monitor under PC-DOS and MS-DOS, for example, the screen can be cleared with the statement:

CLEAR.SCREEN$ = CHR$(27) + "[2J"

- *With a terminal:* Refer to your terminal manual or check with the dealer to ascertain the correct code. The Hazeltine 1500, for example, under CP/M requires CONTROL and F to be pressed simultaneously. CONTROL F is translated as:

CLEAR.SCREEN$ = CHR$(06)

Whenever you wish *to clear the screen* in a program after CLEAR.SCREEN$ has been defined, include the statement:

PRINT CLEAR.SCREEN$

A more comprehensive treatment of this topic is included later in the book. See references in the Index.

To help you understand the translation of the flowchart into a computer program, we have added REM [remark statements] to Program 2-1 as shown in **Program 2-2**.

PROGRAM 2-2   **PRODVAL1.BAS**   **[Non-Compiler]**

Depreciation Program with REMS

Copyright 1985, Compulit, Inc.

```
\                Defining CLEAR.SCREEN for PC-DOS and MS-DOS
          CLEAR.SCREEN$ = CHR$(27) + "[2J"
          PRINT CLEAR.SCREEN$
REM              Input required values:  YEAR% is the current year; \
                 COST is cost of item to be depreciated;  LIFE.IN.YEARS% \
                 is expected useful life in years; SALVAGE is \
                 anticipated value of item at end of its useful life
          INPUT "           Enter current year ................... "; YEAR%
          INPUT "           Enter cost of item ................... "; COST
          INPUT "           Enter useful life of item in years ... "; LIFE.IN.YEARS%
          INPUT "           Enter salvage value of item .......... "; SALVAGE
          PRINT:  PRINT:  PRINT
\                Print of column headings
          PRINT TAB(19); "Annual"; TAB(37); "Cumulative"; TAB(58); "Book Value"
          PRINT " Year"; TAB(16);"Depreciation"; TAB(37); "Depreciation"; \
                 TAB (56); "[End of Year]":  PRINT
REM              Computation of annual depreciation, ANNUAL.DEPRECIATION \
                 Set up control index, EOP%; for first year set \
                 CUMULATIVE.DEPRECIATION equal to ANNUAL DEPRECIATION
          ANNUAL.DEPRECIATION = (COST - SALVAGE) / LIFE.IN.YEARS%
          EOP% = YEAR% + LIFE.IN.YEARS%
REM       Print first line of output: current year, YEAR%, and \
                 book value of item or its actual cost, COST
          PRINT YEAR%, " ", " ", COST
REM              Calculate new book value: subtract annual depreciation \
                 from cost.  Advance to next year by adding one to year \
                 Print a line which includes: year, annual depreciation, \
                 cumulative depreciation and book value
10        COST = COST - ANNUAL.DEPRECIATION
          YEAR% = YEAR% + 1
          PRINT YEAR%, ANNUAL.DEPRECIATION, CUMULATIVE.DEPRECIATION, COST
REM              Check to see is value of current year equals control index \
                 If YES go to 30; if NO continue
          IF YEAR% = EOP% THEN 30
REM              Compute new cumulative depreciation: add annual depreciation \
                 to cumulative depreciation; then go to statement #10
          CUMULATIVE.DEPRECIATION = CUMULATIVE.DEPRECIATION + ANNUAL.DEPRECIATION
          GOTO 10
30        END
```

The design of the output of a program is subjective; in all cases it should be easy to read and understand. The screen display and output of Program 2-1 would appear as follows:

```
          Enter current year ................... 1985
          Enter cost of item ................... 5000.00
          Enter useful life of item in years ... 5
          Enter salvage value of item .......... 500.00



                     Annual          Cumulative           Book Value
          Year     Depreciation      Depreciation        [End of Year]

          1985                                                5000
          1986         900              900                   4100
          1987         900             1800                   3200
          1988         900             2700                   2300
          1989         900             3600                   1400
          1990         900             4500                    500
```

If you are eager to work with your computer, enter and run the straight-line depreciation program using your own data. You can save time by omitting all comment or remark statements, the lines starting with a backslash [\].

Other Sample Flowcharts

For those interested in doing additional flowcharts, here are two problems. The answers are included at the end of this chapter.

1. Taylor & Farmer Ltd. maintains its inventory records on a floppy disk. The record for each item includes: item number, description of the item, cost price per unit, and quantity in stock. Prepare a flowchart for a report that lists each item's number, description, and dollar value, as well as the total value of all the inventory.
2. Rivers & Waters Inc. pays its hourly employees time-and-a-half for overtime after 35 hours. Prepare a flowchart for a program to calculate gross pay for each employee if the clerk enters: employee name, hourly rate of pay, and weekly hours worked, and the computer printout contains the employee's name and his/her gross pay.

Structured Programming and Flowcharts

One does not have to be in microcomputing long to realize that there is a lack of standardization. The traditional flowchart just presented has been losing favor because: [a] it is not truly standardized, and [b] the increased emphasis on structured programming has necessitated a change in flowcharting symbols. **Structured programming** is one of several methods designed to standardize and improve programming. Furthermore, many experienced programmers have found it tedious and time-wasting to prepare flowcharts. Instead they write their programs and later use the computer to draw the flowchart.

For years many people viewed each program as unique, and in industry it was difficult to assess the competence of individual programmers. Others, however, maintained that standardization is possible if each program is organized into distinct blocks or modules. This makes it easier to program, look for and find errors, and modify programs when required. Structured programming also makes it easier to have several people working on a program at the same time.

Let us turn back for a moment to the directions to get to my house [as shown in Figure 2-1]. When we arrive at Central Avenue we have to make a decision. If the street is open to traffic, we make a right turn. If it is closed to traffic, we proceed one more block west, and *then* make the right turn. The difference between the traditional flowchart and the structured programming flowchart [developed by Isaac Nassi and Ben Shneiderman] is shown in **Figure 2-5** for this segment of the flowchart.

Regardless of which type of flowchart is used or whether it is drawn before or after the program is written, it is a visual presentation of the particular method, or algorithm, used to solve the problem. Generally, there are several ways to approach and solve a given problem in programming.

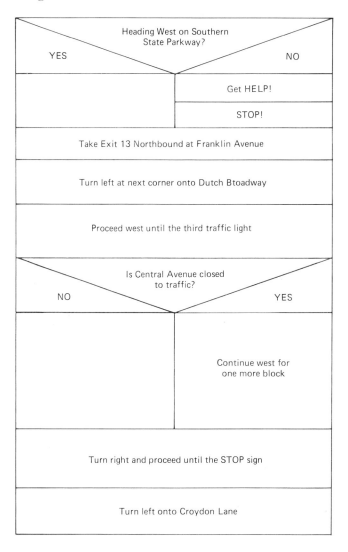

FIGURE 2-5   Nassi-Shneiderman Chart

APPROACHES TO PROBLEM SOLVING

Many books and articles have been written about how people think and solve problems and various approaches have been proposed. The behaviorists, such as B. F. Skinner, view problem solving as a relationship between stimulus and response, input and output. Other problem solving models are abstract generalizations to solve an unlimited group of problems. The information processing approach, influenced by the advent of the computer, emphasizes the process that occurs between input and output. It seeks to establish a pattern or algorithm for the problem solver, the programmer, to achieve a desired goal. It is, as Herbert Simon has put it, a "means-end analysis" that tries to discover the process that leads to the desired goal.

The Polya Approach

George Polya of Stanford University has devoted his career to an approach to problem solving and the way we think and has written numerous books on this topic. His classic approach involves four phases:

1. It is necessary to *understand* the problem. The way we look at the problem may require repeated changes of our point of view as we gain more insight into the problem and possible approaches to a solution.
2. It is necessary to develop a *plan* after we see how the various items are related and how the unknown items are related to those that are known.
3. We *execute* the plan developed to solve the problem.
4. We *review* the completed solution to determine its correctness and whether the plan truly solved the problem.

A Pragmatic Approach

Most problem solutions are based on past experience; such problems are solved by rote with few problem-solving techniques used. When we encounter a problem we have not seen before, we attempt to fit it into some category with which we are already familiar. Only when it fails to fit in are we truly faced with a problem-solving dilemma.

One solution is that proposed by Moshe Rubenstein in following a modified information processing approach. The simple model consists of four stages.

1. There is the initial planning. The problem solver decides upon all the input data elements required and, where possible, determines their interrelationships.
2. The problem solver *lists* the different approaches that can be used to solve the problem. This is particularly true in computer programming because the different language commands enable the programmer to structure his procedure differently.
3. There is the inspirational or decision stage in which the problem solver attempts to build an algorithm for the problem. If several approaches are possible a decision must be made based on time necessary to write a program, the complexity of data entry, and the time required for the program to be executed.
4. There is the verification stage. This involves checking to determine if the correct answers have been obtained, if the printout and/or CRT display are easily readable, and if the program has been run in the shortest or at least a reasonable time.

FURTHER READING

Those interested in how people think or how to solve problems should find the following books interesting:

James L. Adams: *Conceptual Blockbusting*. San Francisco: Freeman and Company, 1945.

George Polya: *How to Solve It*. Princeton NJ: Princeton University Press, 1974.

George Polya: *Mathematics and Plausible Reasoning*. Princeton NJ: Princeton University Press, 1954.

George Polya: *Mathematical Discovery: On Understanding, Learning and Teaching Problem Solving*. New York: John Wiley & Sons Inc., 1962.

Moshe F. Rubenstein: *Patterns of Problem Solving*. Englewood Cliffs NJ, Prentice-Hall, Inc., 1975.

Wayne A. Wickegren: *How to Solve Problems*. San Francisco: Freeman and Company, 1974.

Patrick H. Winston and Richard H. Brown, editors: *Artificial Intelligence: An MIT Perspective*. Cambridge MA: The MIT Press, 1975.

SOLUTIONS

Solution to Problem 1 on page 25.

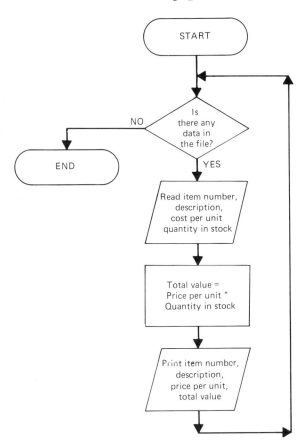

Solution to Problem 2 on page 25.

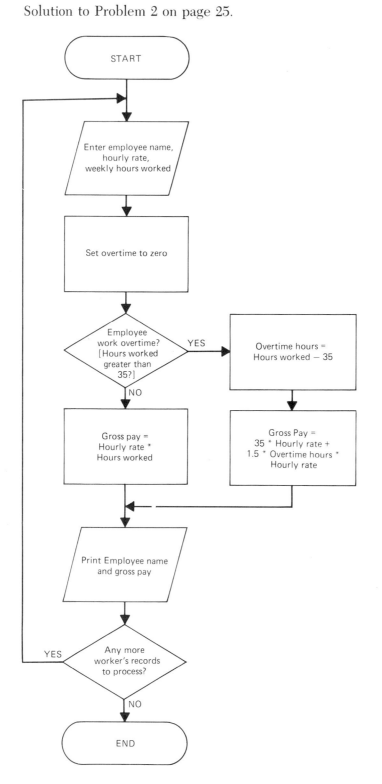

CHAPTER 3

Names, Numbers, and Arithmetic

We know from the two programs that you have entered and run that the computer manipulates arithmetic data. It adds, subtracts, multiplies, and divides. But the computer does more than manipulate numbers; it can also distinguish between words or data. The non-compiler and compiler versions of CBASIC use a set of special statements and **intrinsic** or **built-in functions** in order to manipulate data. The functions are short programs, which are part of the language. They are designed to provide the user with a quick way of performing a specific operation without writing a program to do it.

CONSTANTS AND VARIABLES

Data entered into the computer may be either constants or variables:

- A **constant** is a quantity with a fixed value that remains unchanged throughout the program.
- A **variable** is a quantity for which the value may change.

For example, if you plan to buy five computer ribbons but do not know the price, then:

COST = 5 * PRICE

The number 5 is a constant. Price is a variable for which the value will be determined by the store and cost is a variable for which the value will be determined by price.

Constants

The computer recognizes and processes constant data in both numeric and string form:

Numeric constants may be either:

- **Integers** or whole numbers [44, 620, 7] in the range from –32768 to +32767 under CBASIC. Two forms in addition to the usual decimal form may be used for integers, binary and hexadecimal. Although the computer stores numbers and does its calculations in binary arithmetic, this form is not used in business programming. Hexadecimal notation is used in some advanced programming methods.
- **Real** or **floating point**, which we are accustomed to call decimals [44.2, 620.542, 7.0]. These may contain up to 14 digits, a sign [+ or –], and must include an embedded decimal point. A real value containing more than 14 digits will be rounded to 14 digits. Larger numbers can be represented but they will not be accurate to more than 14 digits. This is not really limiting since 14 digits will allow accuracy up to but not including one trillion dollars with cents.

If a number is entered *without* a decimal point or if it *ends* with a decimal point it will be stored as an integer. If the decimal point is followed by one or more digits it is real. Thus:

20   is an integer;
20.   is an integer; but
20.0 is real.

Real numbers may also be used in **exponential format**, although this is not common in business programming. This form is useful for very large or very small numbers. The exponent consists of E, the sign of the exponent, which is optional for a positive value, and one or two digits. Thus, E+4 means move the decimal point four places to the right, and 2.3E+4 is equivalent to 23,000. Other examples are:

–3.68E+2 equivalent to –368
–3.68E–2 equivalent to –0.0368
 1.02E–5 equivalent to 0.0000102

In exponential form real numbers can range from 1.0E–64, or a decimal

point followed by 63 zeros and then a 1, to 9.9999999999999E62, or
9.9999999999999 followed by 49 zeros.

STRING constants may be **alphanumeric** [that is, they may include
numbers, letters, and any of the special symbols], but they must be enclosed
in quotation marks [with some exceptions which will be noted as they are
needed]. A set of adjacent quotation marks, " ", is a **null string**.

Program 1-2, ANSWER.BAS has several string constants in it. Each
INPUT statement is followed by a string, called a **string prompt**, enclosed in
quotation marks, for example, "ENTER YOUR HOUSE NUMBER." Each
phrase enclosed in quotation marks is a **string constant**.

The maximum length for a string constant is 255 characters all of which
must be on one "computer" line. The console screen holds only 80 characters
on a single line. However, if the string is longer than the screen size, it will
"wrap around"; that is, it will continue on the next line but without a carriage
return. To the computer, it is one line until either a <**CR**> is encountered
or the line contains 255 characters.

Neither the backslash [\] nor a <**CR**> is permitted inside the set of
quotation marks that enclose a string constant.

To print quotation marks within a string constant use a triple set. The
outer set encloses the entire string constant. The part to be printed with
quotation marks in the output is enclosed in a double set; each adjacent pair
of quotation marks results in one quotation mark in the output. For example,
the output of

```
PRINT "She said, ""The computer is down."""
```

is

```
She said, "The computer is down."
```

Variables and Their Identifiers

For the *non-compiler versions*, CBASIC and CBASIC-86, the final character identifies the type of data.

- A **string variable** name must end with $: NAME$, PHONE.NO$.
- An **integer variable** name must end with %: KEY%, PART.NO%.
- If neither of these symbols ends the identifier the computer assumes
  that the identifier is a **real variable**: SALES, NET.PAY.

The following is a summary of the six data types used in CBASIC and CBASIC Compiler:

	EXAMPLE OF	
DATA TYPE	VARIABLE	CONSTANT
Integer	PARTS%	5394
Real	PAY	6.09
String	NAME$	"YES"

Basic Rules

- An *integer variable* is an identifier with a % as the last character.
- An *integer constant* is a numeric value with *no* embedded decimal point [embedded commas are not permitted].
- A *real variable* is any identifier that does *not* end with either the % or $ symbol.
- A *real constant* is a numeric value with an embedded decimal point.
- A *string variable* is an identifier ending with a $.
- A *string constant* is any set of alphanumeric characters enclosed within quotation marks.

For the non-compiler versions of CBASIC the following are examples of identifiers used, some of which are valid and some are not. Try covering the right hand column and identifying the type [integer, real, string] for the valid ones and the reason why the others are invalid.

VARIABLE NAME	TYPE
NEW.WAGE.RATE	Real
#1645	Invalid; it does not start with a letter
NO.OF.CHECKS%	Integer
NET PAY	Invalid; it includes a blank space
ANSWER$	String
DAYS.IN.COURT%	Integer
K345	Real
CLIENT.NAME$	String

With the *compiler versions* you may ignore the % and $ symbols at the end of an integer variable or string variable identifier. You can declare the variables as integer, real, or string by using the following declaration statements:

`INTEGER  KEY, I, PART.NO`	Sets *KEY*, *I*, and *PART. NO* to integer.
`REAL  SALES, A, NET.PAY(30)`	Sets *SALES*, *A*, and *NET. PAY* to real.
`STRING  NAME, PHONE.NO`	Sets *NAME* and *PHONE. NO* to strings.

The declaration statements, STRING, INTEGER, and REAL, should be the initial executable lines of a program, prior to all other executable statements.

LANGUAGE CODING RULE

In using the compiler versions of CBASIC, it is possible to declare variables by using the INTEGER, REAL, and/or STRING statements, placed at the beginning of the program *before* any variable names are used. In programming code form, they would appear as:

INTEGER <identifier> { , identifier}

REAL <identifier> { , identifier}

STRING <identifier> { , identifier}

Additional Rules for Forming Variable Names

The other rules for forming **variable names**, also called **identifiers**, are the same for *all* versions of CBASIC.

- The first character must always be a letter.
- The remaining characters may be letters, numbers, or periods. Special characters such as @, #, &, $, etc. are not permitted.
- Blank spaces are not permitted. A period may be used to separate parts of a name. TODAYS DATE is *not* valid but TODAYS.DATE is valid. Simply running the two words together, TODAYSDATE, would negate the value of the realistic name.

- A maximum of 31 characters may be used for an identifier. If more than 31 characters are used the computer will disregard everything after the 31st character although it will pick up the identifying symbol at the end. But 31 characters should be adequate even for realistic names like TOTAL.DEBT or END.OF.MONTH.SUMMARY. Long identifiers take more storage space and more time to compile and execute.
- You may use lower case letters in string identifiers but they will be changed by the compiler to upper case letters unless otherwise instructed.
- A numeric variable is equal to zero and a string variable is a null string until given other values by the program.
- In *non-compiler* versions an identifier may not begin with **FN**, a combination which is reserved by the language for a special use.
- Do not use a **reserved word** as a variable name or alphanumeric label. There are differences between the reserved words for the non-compiler and compiler versions. To provide for transportability between different versions of CBASIC, do not use any of the words in the Reserved Word List [see Appendix A].

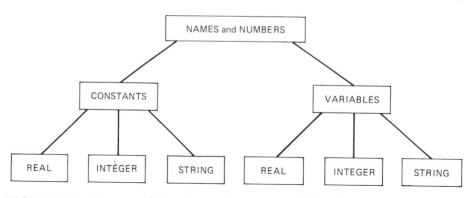

FIGURE 3-1   Names and Numbers—Constants and Variables

INTEGER VERSUS REAL VARIABLES

The use of integers where possible instead of real numbers speeds the execution of the program. It also uses less storage space but there is a limitation on the use of integers which should be noted. *CBASIC will accept and process integers only in the range of –32768 and +32767*. If during the calculation with integers a number outside this range is encountered the result will be negative and incorrect although no error message is produced.

An example is in Program 1-2, ANSWER.BAS. Although both house number and age in years are integers, the variable names were **HN** and

AGE, both of which indicate real values. If HN% and AGE% are used the result is a very large negative number.

If an **overflow** occurs with real numbers [a number is encountered which is larger than the machine can store] execution continues but a warning is printed. However, since the machine can store extremely large or small numbers between $1.0E-64$ and $9.9999999999999E+62$ an overflow would only occur in a normal business situation because of an error in programming or data entry.

ARRAYS

An **array** is an efficient way of organizing and processing a large amount of similar data, such as a list of employee names, customer addresses, number of units sold for each item produced. In its simplest form it is a **list** where each item has a number associated with it indicating its position in the list. The identifiers for array variables may be integer, real or string. If a string array is used, each element may have up to 255 characters.

There are two parts required when using an array variable.

1. The **DIM** or dimension statement tells the machine how much space to allocate to the variable. **DIM** is followed by the array name and a number in parentheses which indicates the maximum number of items which may be in the list. This is one more than the number itself because the first position in an array is the zero position; 50, for example, refers to the fifty-first cell in the array. An attempt to enter more than the indicated number will produce an error and stop program execution.

Examples are:

```
DIM ITEM.NO% (50)
```
The variable identifier is ITEM.NO% and the array can have up to 51 integer values in the list.

```
DIM CLIENT.NAME$ (75)
```
CLIENT.NAME$ is a string array which may have up to 76 items in it.

```
DIM WEEKLY.PAY (150)
```
WEEKLY.PAY identifies an array with up to 151 real values.

The space reserved for the array is determined as soon as the DIM statement is encountered and using a larger than necessary number wastes memory space. Until the elements in an array are given values they are stored as zero for numeric variables and null strings for string variables.

The DIM statement should be placed near the beginning of the program or at the beginning of the module in which the array is used. This is not a language requirement but when something goes wrong, as it often does, the location of this key statement will make error detection easier. The DIM statement must appear *before* the variable is used in a statement.

A DIM statement may dimension more than one array at a time. The three statements above could have been combined into:

```
DIM ITEM.NO%(50), CLIENT.NAME$(75), WEEKLY.PAY(150)
```

The DIM statement must be on a line by itself. Unlike most other statements in CBASIC it may not be combined with another statement on one line separated by a colon.

2. When the array variable is used in the program the form is illustrated by:

```
ITEM.NO% (I%)
```

In this case I% should be an integer constant or a variable for which the value is an integer. It represents the position of a particular item in the list. For example, it may be the second as in ITEM.NO%(1), or the tenth as in CLIENT.NAME$(9). The value of I% is frequently determined during program execution.

I% is called the **subscript** and an array variable is also referred to as a **subscripted variable.** *The first subscript in a CBASIC array is zero.* Since this is not the usual way to designate the first item in a list, many programmers use one [1] for the subscript of the first value and leave the zero position unused. There will still be space allocated to the position with subscript zero but not enough to be important if you are subscripting a single list.

ARRAY or LIST   MATRIX or TABLE

FIGURE 3-2   Array/List and Matrix/Table

Multidimensional Arrays

An array may include several lists; it can then be thought of as **multidimensional array**, or a **table** with rows and columns. A two-dimensional array would be used, for example, to record salesmen's names [list 1], commission rate [list 2], year-to-date sales [list 3]. For 50 salesmen, using the zero subscript for the rows and columns, it would be dimensioned by:

```
DIM SALES.COM$ (49, 2)
```

which allocates space for 50 rows for the number of salesmen and 3 columns [0, 1, 2] for name, rate, and sales.

A three-dimensional array is more difficult to visualize. It would be used, for example, to include salesmen's names, sales per month, and total sales per year for five years. Using the zero subscripts to prevent a large waste of space in this three-dimensional table, the dimension statement would be:

```
DIM SALES.RECORD$ (49, 11, 4)
```

The array may include data for 50 salesmen, for 12 months and for 5 years.

Multidimensional arrays occur often in business programming; programming is often simplified if the lists are treated as a multidimensional array rather than as different variables. This advantage is illustrated later in the chapters on sorting and advanced file handling.

Additional examples of valid **DIM** statements for multidimensional arrays are:

```
DIM CLIENT.NAME$ (50, 2)
```
Allows for 51 items with three entries for each; name, address, phone number.

```
DIM ACCT.RECORD (87, 4, 3)
```
May include 88 account numbers, 5 product numbers and sales for 4 years.

Several points should be noted here.

1. In the second illustration above, the identifier is a floating point number and is only valid if all the entries in the array are of this type. An integer will be stored as a real value. *All the parts of a multidimensional array must be in the same mode; the entire array is one variable.* In this illustration the product numbers would be indicated by numbers which could embed a decimal point but no other special symbols. The same applies to the account numbers.

LANGUAGE CODING RULE

Whenever you use an array or table, its structure is:

DIM { <variable name> (<subscript list>) }

The subscript list may be integer constants or integer variable names that have been previously set to a numeric value.
This statement must appear on a line by itself.
Multiple variable names and subscript lists must be separated by commas.

---

2. The waste of storage space if the subscript zero is not used is substantial. For each of the rows there is a space set aside for the zero subscript and this is also true for each of the columns. In all there are 1760 elements in this three-dimensional matrix but only 1044 spaces are used if we omit the zero cells.
3. Non-compiler CBASIC permits the use of the same identifier for a subscripted and a nonsubscripted variable. PAY$ and PAY$(I%) are different and valid but should *not* be used. The computer may not confuse them but the user probably will.

Ease in using subscripts is essential in business programming. For practice, locate the elements listed after the following two-dimensional array [**Figure 3-3**] without using the answer column. Use it only to check your answers. Note that the zero subscripts have been used and that, for example, row 3 refers to the row numbered 3, not the third row from the beginning.

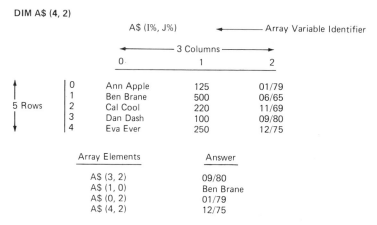

FIGURE 3-3   Illustration of Matrix Subscripts

MATHEMATICAL OPERATORS

There are three classes of mathematical operators which can be used to perform calculations; they are **basic arithmetic operators**, **relational operators**, and **logical** or **Boolean operators**. [Relational and Boolean operators are covered in Chapter 6.] The computer performs these mathematical operations in a specific sequence known as the **hierarchy of operations** as shown in **Table 3-1** on page 42.

The basic arithmetic operators are familiar to all of us although the computer symbols may be different.

OPERATION	COMPUTER SYMBOL
Addition	+
Subtraction	−
Multiplication	*
Division	/
Exponentiation	^

The computer performs its computations from left to right in the following order. Any calculation within parentheses is done first using this hierarchy of operators.

1. Exponentiation
2. Multiplication and division in the order written
3. Addition and subtraction in the order written

The successive steps are shown in the following illustration:

$$
\begin{array}{rccccc}
 & 15/(6 * 0.5) & + 12 & ^\wedge\ 2 & - 2 \\
= & 15/\ \ 3 & + 12 & ^\wedge\ 2 & - 2 \\
= & 15/\ \ 3 & + & 144 & - 2 \\
= & 5 & + & 144 & - 2 \\
= & & 149 & & - 2 \\
= & & & 147 &
\end{array}
$$

If the parentheses had been omitted the answer would have been 143.25.

$$
\begin{array}{rccc}
 & 15/6 * 0.5 & + 12\ ^\wedge\ 2 - 2 \\
= & 15/6 * 0.5 & + \ \ 144 \ - 2 \\
= & 2.5 * 0.5 & + \ \ 144 \ - 2 \\
= & 1.25 & + \ \ 144 \ - 2 \\
= & & 145.25 \ \ \ - 2 \\
= & & 143.25
\end{array}
$$

TABLE 3-1   Hierarchy of Operators

HIERARCHY	OPERATOR	DEFINITION
1	( )	Perform arithmetic within parentheses
2	^	Raise value to a power, exponentiation
3	* /	Do multiplication and division
4	+ −	Perform addition and subtraction
	RELATIONAL OPERATORS	
5		
	< or **LT**	Less than
	<= or **LE**	Less than or equal to
	> or **GT**	Greater than
	>= or **GE**	Greater than or equal to
	= or **EG**	Equal to
	<> or **NE**	Not equal to
	LOGICAL OR BOOLEAN OPERATORS	
6	NOT	
7	AND	See Chapter 6
8	OR	
9	XOR	

The Assignment Statement

As the name implies, the **assignment statement** gives, or assigns, a value to a variable. It has three parts: the variable identifier, an equal sign [=], and an expression. The value of the expression *on the right of the equal sign* [=] is assigned to the *variable on the left* and both must be either string or numeric. The use of a number and string in the same assignment statement will cause a mixed-mode error. It is important to note that the variable to which a value is given is *always* on the left side of the equal sign. A reversal of this order would result in an error message.

The following are examples of valid assignment statements.

```
INDEX% = INDEX% + 1

COST = PRICE + COMMISSION

NAME$ = "Sue Smart"
```

The assignment statement is also known as a **LET statement**. In CBASIC the use of the word **LET** is optional; avoiding its use saves entry time and makes the printed program look cleaner.

LANGUAGE CODING RULE

The structure of an *assignment statement* is:

[**LET**] <variable> = <expression>

The variable and the expression must *both* be the same data type, either numeric or string.

Arithmetic Statement

The most frequent use of the assignment statement is an arithmetic statement used to perform calculations. The **expression** may combine numeric constants and/or variables with mathematical operators and, when needed, instrinsic functions.

The line in Program 1-2, ANSWER.BAS, in which the calculation is performed is an arithmetic statement.

```
ANSWER = (2 * HN + 5) * 50 + AGE + 365 - 615
```

Numeric variable = Arithmetic expression

Other valid examples are:

```
COST = PRICE.PER.UNIT * NO.OF.UNITS

WIDTH = A + B - C / D

OVERTIME.PAY = (HOURS - 40.0) * RATE * 1.5
```

Although CBASIC will accept a combination of integers and real numbers in an arithmetic statement, it is better to keep all the identifiers in the expression in one mode. If the arithmetic expression contains both types, the integers will be converted to real numbers before the calculation is done. This has no advantage and wastes computer time.

The following is an example of a **mixed-mode expression**.

```
GROSS.PAY = 5 * HOURS.WORKED
```

Both identifiers, GROSS.PAY and HOURS.WORKED, are real numbers but 5 is an integer and should have been written as 5.0.

The mode in which the variable identifier is written will determine the form in which the answer is stored. An illustration is the case where the result of the calculation is required in integer form although the calculation is based on real numbers. [This is done in the Social Security System where payments are "rounded to the next lower dollar" or truncated.]

If we enter:

```
PAYMENT% = 1.074 * 545.50
```

the computer's answer is 586, a rounded integer, although the accurate answer with real values is 585.867. In business practice this would be rounded to 585.87 for dollars and cents.

The following are arithmetic statements which may be invalid or have expressions in mixed mode. Cover the right hand column and decide whether the statement is valid, whether or not the expression is in mixed mode, and in what form [integer or floating point] the result will be.

STATEMENT	DESCRIPTION
X = Y + Z	Valid; all real including result.
REC.NO% = REC.NO% + 1.0	Valid but mixed mode. Change 1.0 to 1. Result is an integer.
SALARY = SALARY$ + 1.45	Invalid; contains a string.
TOTAL = TOTAL% + CHECK%	Valid; expression is integer but result will be real.
K% = K% + REC.NO%	Valid; all integers including result.

A note on accuracy: Always check answers to a calculation. Many inexperienced programmers tend to accept any computer result as accurate but this is a faith without foundation. First check visually. Is this a possible answer to the problem? An obviously incorrect answer may be the result of an entry error such as a misplaced or omitted decimal point. Second, run the program with simple test data for which you have the correct answer. A program may compile and run with no error messages but a logic error is still possible.

Integer versus Real Identifiers in Business

Although arithmetic operations can be performed in integer mode, the user should be aware of one major drawback. If the variable and expression are all in integer form, addition, subtraction, and multiplication can be performed accurately within the range for integers, that is, between −32768 and +32767.

If division is performed, however, the resulting value will be truncated. For example, if we write:

```
JAY% = SUM% / NUMBER%
```

with SUM% = 14 and NUMBER% = 3, the answer for JAY% will be 4; the decimal portion, .6̄6̄6̄ has been truncated. Even though the answer is mathematically incorrect, integer division has its uses in special programming techniques when using lists and tables.

Difficulties may be encountered in early compiler versions when using integer division if the value of the denominator can be equal to zero when the program executes. Division by zero is undefined in mathematics, but with some compilers an incorrect value will be computed by the microcomputer, no error message will be given, and the program will continue processing.

In general you will find it helpful to use real values except for some special applications. First, business records involve dollars and cents which requires that you use a real value. Second, an integer has a more restricted range of values and it is likely that your calculations will at some time exceed 32767.

Integers can be used, for example, to indicate the number of items in inventory. However, if you wish to obtain the value of that inventory by multiplying the number of units by cost, the computer will do it but at a slower speed than if both values were real. A part number, on the other hand, can be an integer since it will not be used in arithmetic operations provided that it contains only numbers not letters, dashes, etc.

INTRINSIC ARITHMETIC FUNCTIONS

Intrinsic functions are short programs which are built-in as part of a computer language. Most have been designed for scientific use, but several of CBASIC's intrinsic functions are useful in business calculations.

The ABS Function

ABS function returns the absolute value of a numeric expression. The form is:

X = **ABS**(numeric expression)

If the value of the numeric expression is zero or positive this function does not change it. If the value of the numeric expression is negative it returns the value without the sign. In either case the value returned is real if the left hand variable is written in real form. If X% is used instead of X the result will be integer.

K   = ABS (2.1 - 4)   will give K = 1.9
K%= ABS (2.1 - 4)   will give K = 2, an integer and rounded.

LANGUAGE CODING RULE

The ABS function returns the absolute value of an expression or identifier.

<variable> = **ABS (**<numeric expression>**)**

FLOAT Function

This function changes an integer to a floating point number. The form is:

K = **FLOAT** (J%)

where K is the floating point number to which the integer J% has been converted. For example:

```
J% = 11
K = FLOAT (J%)
R = K / 3
PRINT K, R
END
```

In this illustration the value of K will be printed as 11 and R as 3.6666666666667. If we had divided J% by 3, the answer would have been 3.

INT and INT% Functions

There are three ways of changing a real value to an integer. One involves the use of the assignment statement and the other two are the **INT** and **INT%** functions.

LANGUAGE CODING RULE

The FLOAT function is used to convert an integer to a real value.

<real variable> = **FLOAT(**<integer variable>**)**

NOTE: FLOAT may also be used for one variable within an expression as:

<real variable> = <real variable> / **FLOAT(**<integer variable>**)**

If we write: I% = A where A = 29.6, the result will be A=30. The assignment statement rounds the real value to an integer.

The INT function returns the integer part of a real number; the decimal part is truncated, not rounded. The integer part is then stored as a *real* number. The form is:

Z = **INT** (K)

The INT% function also truncates the decimal and returns only the integer part of the real number. However, the integer is stored as an *integer*. The form is:

Z% = **INT%** (K)

The difference between the two function results is not apparent to the user as the following illustration shows. The difference is in the way the computer stores and handles the two results during subsequent program execution.

Z = INT (12.69 – 2.2)   returns Z   = 10

Z% = INT% (12.69 – 2.2)   returns Z% = 10

Determining If There Is a Decimal Remainder

We have just discussed two built-in functions, INT and INT%, that are designed to return the integer portion of a real value. There are times when it is useful to determine if a decimal portion of a value exists. CBASIC does not include any built-in function to perform this operation. However, this

---

LANGUAGE CODING RULE

The INT function truncates the fractional part of a real number and returns only the integer portion which is stored as real.

<real variable> = **INT(**<real variable>**)**

---

deficiency can be easily overcome by using both the ABS and INT built-in functions in a single line statement.

$$Y = ABS(X - INT(X))$$

The Y value will be zero if X is an integer, or a positive value no matter what the sign of X was originally and if there is a decimal remainder.

LANGUAGE CODING RULE

The INT% function truncates the decimal part of the real number, and stores the integer part as an integer.

<integer variable> = **INT% (** <real variable> **)**

CHAPTER 4

Simple Input/Output of Data

This chapter covers the elementary input/output statements with which data is entered in a program and results are either displayed on the CRT or printed. The input/output statements for data files are covered in Chapter 5.

Several related command statements and/or built-in functions useful in the input/output process are also covered.

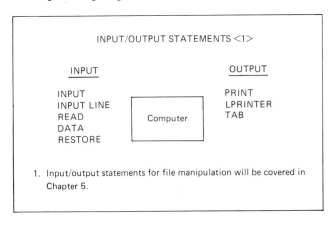

FIGURE 4-1   Input/Output Statements

DATA INPUT

There are three ways to input data from the console for a computer program:

1. The most elementary is by using the **assignment statement.**
2. The second way is with the **READ** and **DATA** statements, which are always used together.

3. The third way is by using the **INPUT** statement, which is preferred because of its flexibility.

The Input Statement

In Program 1-2 ANSWER.BAS we supplied the data to be used in the calculation by **INPUT** statements, for example:

```
INPUT "ENTER YOUR HOUSE NUMBER....."; HN
```

When you enter the number and <CR>, the carriage return, the computer assigns that number to the variable HN. "ENTER YOUR HOUSE NUMBER" is not required by the language but without this phrase, called a prompt, only a question mark [?] will appear on the screen and the user will have to know what value is required. Don't depend on remembering what the computer is asking for; put the prompt into the statement.

The essential parts of the grammar are the quotation marks around the statement you want to appear on the screen, that is, **the string constant**, the semicolon which follows it, and the name of the variable.

The INPUT statement is only one of the three ways of entering data into a program, but we will emphasize it throughout the book because it is the most useful way. It takes advantage of the interactive ability of the microcomputer [you and the machine talk to each other]. It permits the operator to decide what value to enter during program execution depending on the results which have been obtained thus far. It permits the program to be reused with different values with no change in the program itself.

For example, add the following lines to ANSWER.BAS before END and insert the number 10 at the beginning of the first line.

```
INPUT "DO YOU WANT TO TRY AGAIN?.. (YES/NO) ..."; AN$
IF AN$ = "YES" THEN 10
```

You can now run the program repeatedly and terminate it at will. If you enter YES in response to the prompt you will return to the beginning which is now line 10. If you enter NO the program will terminate. It is not necessary to enclose the string response to an INPUT request in quotation marks.

The INPUT statement may ask for more than one value in the same line. Thus, in ANSWER.BAS, the two INPUT statements could have been combined into:

```
INPUT "ENTER YOUR HOUSE NUMBER AND AGE....."; HN, AGE
```

You would then enter the two numbers separated by a comma and the computer would assign the first number to HN and the second to AGE. Although this is grammatically correct, it is generally not advisable. It has been found that computer users are more comfortable responding to one request at a time.

When assigning names to variables it is very important to match the identifying symbol at the end to the data type assigned to it. If, for example, you wrote an INPUT statement which said:

```
INPUT "ENTER YOUR NAME..."; NAME
```

and you responded with Jon Jones, the program would not execute. The computer would expect the variable NAME to represent a real number and would not accept a string. This is a *mixed-mode* assignment. NAME would have to be changed to NAME$ or with compiler versions NAME would have to be *declared* as a string.

Do not use a comma in any value you enter even if it is ordinarily written with a comma. The comma is a *separator* to the computer and may not be used when entering numeric data. For example, 4,639 would be interpreted as two numbers, 4 and 639. Similarly, entering Smith, Mary in response to an INPUT request would result in the computer considering the input as two variables. This limitation in the use of the comma can be overcome for string variables by the use of the INPUT LINE statement which follows this section.

Integer variables present two problems for the programmer:

1. If the value entered for assignment to an integer is real, the computer will truncate the decimal portion if it is less than .5, but it will round to the next higher integer if the decimal portion is .5 or greater. Thus, 11.49 entered for an integer variable would be stored as 11, but 11.50 would be stored as 12.
2. If the integer value is outside the allowable range [−32768 to +32767], an incorrect value will be assigned and the user will be given no warning.

Real variables do not create the same problems. If a real variable that exceeds the limits of CBASIC is entered by mistake, a warning message appears on the screen.

The INPUT LINE Statement

This form of the INPUT statement causes the computer to read all of the response as a single string. Its use is limited to string inputs to be assigned to

---

LANGUAGE CODING RULE

An INPUT statement is used to enter data from the console and assign the data to a variable. The form is:

INPUT [prompt string ;] < variable > { , variable }

- The variable[s] may be simple or subscripted string or numeric.
- The prompt must be a string constant enclosed in quotation marks. If a prompt string is used, the question mark [?] will be suppressed.
- If more than one variable is entered from the keyboard in response to a single INPUT statement, each variable must be separated from the next by a comma.
- No more than 255 characters may be entered in response to an INPUT no matter how many variables appear in the variable list. Any additional characters are ignored by the computer. Remember that commas between variables, quotation marks before and after each string, and even blank spaces are included in the character count.

---

a string variable and only one string variable may be entered with each **INPUT LINE** statement.

The response to the INPUT LINE prompt may *include commas;* the statement:

```
INPUT "ENTER YOUR COMPANY'S NAME.. "; LINE CO.NAME$
```

SPECIAL PROGRAMMING NOTE

To run any program repeatedly and to terminate the program at will, use the following:

INPUT "Do you wish to rerun the program? Enter YES or NO "; AN$
IF UCASE$(AN$) = "YES" THEN <label or statement number>

- The prompt string after **INPUT** should be included and may contain any wording you wish.
- After **THEN** enter the label or statement number to which the processing should return.
- The built-in function, **UCASE$** [see Chapter 8], is used to "trap" all possible replies. It will equate *YES, yes,* and *Yes* as well as other variations, such as *yES.*

---

may be answered with **Black, Greene, White & Co.** without producing an error.

The INPUT LINE statement will accept a null string as an input. If in response to the prompt, the carriage return is hit, this statement will accept the null string and continue. This is not true of the INPUT statement which requires that some key, even if only the space bar, be pressed before a carriage return. This is handy to keep data on the screen so that the user has time to read it.

LANGUAGE CODING RULE

To enter a string variable which contains a *comma* in response to an INPUT request, use:

   INPUT [prompt string ;] **LINE** <string variable>

NOTE: Only *one* string variable may be entered with an INPUT LINE statement.

The READ and DATA Statements

Another method of entering data is by using the **READ** and **DATA** statements so that the data is part of the actual program. Instead of the two **INPUT** statements in Program 1-2, ANSWER.BAS we could have written:

```
10    READ HN, AGE
      DATA 348, 23
```

SPECIAL PROGRAMMING NOTE

To keep copy on the screen to facilitate reading during the display of output, use the **INPUT LINE** statement as follows:

   INPUT "Press RETURN KEY to continue .... "; LINE REPLY$

Copy will be held on the CRT screen until the return key is pressed.

The two statements do not need to follow each other. In fact, when DATA statements are used, they are usually grouped together prior to the END statement or immediately after the program algorithm is finished.

When the computer finds the **READ** statement it looks for a **DATA** statement and assigns the first value to HN and the second to AGE. Every line of data must begin with **DATA**. If an instruction is added to return to the **READ** statement and more data is supplied, the program will pick up the third and fourth numbers, respectively, and assign them to HN and AGE and use them for the next calculation.

The program would appear as follows.

PROGRAM 4-1   **ANSWER1.BAS**   **[Non-Compiler]**

ANSWER.BAS with READ-DATA Statements

Copyright 1984, 1985, Compulit, Inc.

```
        PRINT "HOUSE NUMBER IS ON LEFT, AGE IS ON RIGHT"
        PRINT
10      READ HN, AGE
        IF HN = 0 THEN 20
        ANSWER = (2 * HN + 5) * 50 + AGE + 365 -615
        PRINT ANSWER
        PRINT
        GOTO 10
        DATA 348, 23, 962, 15, 0,0
20      END
```

The output would be:

```
HOUSE NUMBER IS ON LEFT, AGE IS ON RIGHT

34823

96215
```

The line after the **READ** statement and the 0,0 in the **DATA** statement have been added to terminate the program without an "out-of-data" error message. Without this statement and the use of the 0,0 [called a **trailer**] the computer keeps going back to **READ** looking for another set of values. This technique will be explained in detail in Chapter 6.

How to Enter Extensive Data Values

Multiple DATA statements can be used if there are too many values for a single DATA statement. There is a difference between the compiler and non-compiler versions of CBASIC when using multiple data lines.

Compiler versions permit the use of the backslash [\] continuation character so that it is not necessary to repeat "DATA" on each line. For example:

```
DATA 13, 26, 7, Rebecca Frances Highland, Princeton, 08540   \
10, 94, 11001, Han van Eybergen, Bijzonderheden, 100001   \
48, 54, 130426, Peter and Stephanie Smid, Hoorn, 207613
```

Non-compiler versions do *not* accept the use of the continuation mark [\] with a DATA statement. To enter multiple lines repeat "DATA" on each line; for example:

```
DATA 11, 69, Susan L. Solomon, Cheney, 99004, 12/22/84
DATA 41, 13, Michael Joseph Highland, Princeton, 08540, 11/22/84
DATA 46, 77, James H. Finch, Toronto, M5B1J3, 7/4/85
```

The language treats all the DATA lines as a single unit and concatenates or links together, the list of constants separated by commas. Thus, even if the values are read in pairs as in ANSWER.BAS, the data could be entered as:

```
DATA 456, 19, 3854, 23, 1130, 47, 562
DATA 66, 2842, 34, 9906, 7, 14, 14, 2861
DATA 28, 0, 0
```

Entering String Values

Unlike other versions of BASIC, it is *not* necessary to use quote marks around a string in a DATA statement in CBASIC. The quotation marks are accepted but not required. This makes entry simpler for anyone not familiar with data entry in BASIC. It also saves considerable keystrokes when an extensive list of string variables is used in DATA statements.

CBASIC will accept any of the following data statements where string constants are assigned to string variables:

```
DATA Judy and Tom Barta
DATA "Nana and Castor Lindqvist"
DATA HELI AND KLAUS RAHKA
```

Limitations of READ/DATA Statements

The READ/DATA method of entering data has much less flexibility than the INPUT statement. Although it is simple to provide for more than one

---

LANGUAGE CODING RULE

To include data as part of the program use *both* **READ** and **DATA** statements:

READ <variable name> { , <variable name> }
DATA <constant> { , <constant> }

- The READ statement sequentially assigns the constants in a DATA statement to the variables.
- The DATA statement must be the *only* statement on a line.
- Each constant must be of the same type as the variable to which it is assigned—an integer to an integer, a string to a string, a real to a real. If they do not correspond, an unexpected value may be assigned by the computer, and if a real is assigned to an integer variable, it will be truncated.

---

calculation the number of repetitions must be predetermined. In addition, the program must be changed when different data is to be used. Where punched cards are used for entering data this is not a problem but with microcomputers it means editing the program each time different values are used.

The RESTORE Statement

The **RESTORE** statement which may be used with **READ/DATA** statements directs the computer to go back to the beginning of the data and reread it. The statement must appear on a line by itself.

This is a useful statement when the same data is used in more than one part of the program or in more than one program used one after the other.

LANGUAGE CODING RULE

To reread the constants contained in a DATA statement, use

RESTORE

This statement resets the computer's DATA statement line pointer to the first DATA statement line.
This statement must appear on a line by itself.

Entering Data Using an ASSIGNMENT Statement

The third method of entering data into a program is by an assignment statement in which a value is given [or assigned] to a variable. In Program 1-2, ANSWER.BAS, instead of the INPUT statements we could have written:

```
HN = 348
AGE = 23
```

The program would then go through once and terminate. Obviously this method has very limited flexibility; to run the program with another set of values would require editing the program to enter new assignment statements or using new assignment statements later in the program.

DATA OUTPUT

Information or output can be displayed on the CRT *or* printed on paper [hardcopy]. It is not possible to do both simultaneously in CBASIC without added programming.

If no command is given the information will be displayed on the screen. If the command to use the printer is given, it is essential to couple that command at some later point in the program with the command necessary to restore communications with the CRT.

To Print Hardcopy

To print copy on the printer use the **LPRINTER** statement which will cause the output to be printed instead of being displayed on the screen. Used by itself it will set the print line width to 132 characters.

Again, there is a difference between the compiler and non-compiler versions of CBASIC when using the LPRINTER statement.

Non-compiler versions: To set the line width to any length other than 132 characters, use LPRINTER followed by **WIDTH** and the desired number of characters for the print line. For example:

```
LPRINTER WIDTH 80
```

sets the length of the printed line to 80 characters. An integer value must be used after width; an *integer variable* may be used as in:

```
LPRINTER WIDTH LONG.LINE%
```

SPECIAL PROGRAMMING NOTE

A Reminder to Turn the Printer On: If you are working in an environment where the printer is not on all the time during computer operations, it is a good idea to put a reminder in the program to tell you to turn the printer on. If the printer is not on when an **LPRINTER** statement is encountered, execution will stop and you may not know why, even suspecting a malfunction of the computer. The following **INPUT** statement will avoid this problem.

> **INPUT "Is the printer on? (Yes / No) "; AN$**
> **IF UCASE$ (AN$) = "YES" THEN LPRINTER**

A value must be assigned to the integer variable following WIDTH *before* the LPRINTER statement is used. If the variable is real, it will be rounded to an integer; a string will result in an error.

Compiler versions: The WIDTH parameter may *not* be used with the LPRINTER statement. The width of the printed line is controlled by the specific structure of the PRINT statement. A maximum width of 132 characters is the default width set by the compiler.

After the printed copy has been completed, the computer is instructed to communicate with the CRT instead of the printer. This is done with **CONSOLE**, a single line statement which will return output to the screen.

LANGUAGE CODING RULE

The CONSOLE statement directs the program output to the console screen.

> **CONSOLE**

This statement is used only after an LPRINTER statement in order to return the output to the console screen.

The PRINT Statement

PRINT begins the statement which tells the computer what information you want to print on the printer or display on the CRT.

LANGUAGE CODING RULE

To direct output to the printer and produce hardcopy:

LPRINTER {WIDTH numeric expression }

- **Compiler versions:**
    The WIDTH parameter may *not* be used. The line width is determined by the specific PRINT statement in the program but it may not exceed 132 characters.
- **Non-compiler versions:**
    Without the optional WIDTH portion of the statement, the printer is set to a 132 character print line.
    Printer width may be altered as required during the program. Failure to specify width will result in the computer using the last width statement or the default option of 132 characters if no WIDTH had been defined previously.

With both the compiler and non-compiler versions, after printing has been completed, restore output to the CRT by using:

CONSOLE

PRINT by itself, that is with nothing following in the statement, directs the computer to "print" a blank line. Spacing and readability may not seem very important at this point when you are just learning the essentials of CBASIC but you will find this simple command very helpful when the programs get longer and you want output to be comfortably readable, not only by you but by other users. If you remove the PRINT lines with nothing after the command PRINT from the program ANSWER.BAS and run it again, the difference will be obvious.

PRINT may be followed by any combination of variables and constants, both numeric and string but each must be separated from the next by either a comma [,] or a semicolon [;]. The comma and semicolon control the spacing between successive items to be printed. The following examples illustrate combinations of output information and spacing.

```
1.   PRINT ANSWER
```

In this line from ANSWER.BAS the computer is told to print the last calculated value of the real variable ANSWER. If HN = 342 and AGE = 45 the output will be:

```
34245
```

If the program is run twice the second result will be printed with a blank line separating it from the first output in response to the line **PRINT**.

```
2.   PRINT "The answer is "; ANSWER; "."
```

This statement combines a string constant, the value of the variable, and a second string constant which is a period [.]. The parts are separated by semicolons because we want the output to be a continuous sentence. In this example a *semicolon* [;] used as a separator causes the output to be continued with one blank space after a number and no extra space after a string. The output is:

```
The answer is 34245.
```

```
3.   PRINT "NAME", "ADDRESS", "BALANCE OWED"
```

When the *comma* is used to separate parts of a PRINT statement the parts will be in print areas consisting of 20 characters each. The output is in four print areas for each line or a total of 80 characters. The output for this PRINT statement is

```
NAME                    ADDRESS                 BALANCE OWED
```

If material for a single print area is more than 20 characters, printing will continue into the next column. For example, the statement

```
PRINT "FINS, FUR AND FEATHERS PET SHOP", "222 22ND AVE.","$22.00 OWED"
```

would output

```
FINS, FUR AND FEATHERS PET SHOP         222 22ND AVE.       $22.00 OWED
```

The name goes across the first 20 positions and continues into the second print area; the next string, therefore, starts in the third print area.

With either the comma or semicolon, if the material to be printed extends past the limits of the screen or printer the message will continue on the next line. The screen width is 80 characters which allows for four 20-character areas. Note that during the execution of a program the computer, unlike a text editor, will not keep words whole. If the last column in the above illustration were "$22.00 OWED SINCE LAST MARCH" the line would break, that is, end, after the S in LAST and the continued line would read T MARCH.

LANGUAGE CODING RULE

The **PRINT** statement is used to display copy on the CRT screen or to obtain hard copy using a printer:

PRINT

on a line by itself will "print" a blank line, in other words skip a line.

PRINT <"string constant "> { , or ; " string constant " }

will display or print the string constant enclosed in a pair of quotation marks.

PRINT <variable name> { , or ; variable name }

will display or print the variable or variables following the command.
- If there is more than one variable to be printed:
  and a comma [,] is used between them, CBASIC divides the 80-column output into four print areas of 20 columns each and places one variable in each of the four areas;
  but if a semicolon [;] is used, no spacing is provided between strings but a single space is placed after a numeric variable.
- It is possible to follow the command with any combination of constants and variables.
- A carriage return [*cr*] and a line-feed [*lf*] are automatically printed when the end of a PRINT statement is encountered *unless* there is a comma or semicolon at the end of the line. These continued lines are not terminated until:
  - [a] another PRINT statement that does not end with a comma or semicolon is executed, or
  - [b] the line width is exceeded, or
  - [c] an LPRINTER or CONSOLE statement is encountered, or
  - [d] the program executes a STOP statement.

The TAB Function

TAB is a built-in or intrinsic function which is very useful in positioning output, particularly in printed copy. It performs a function similar to the tab key on a typewriter, sending the cursor or the print head to the indicated position. It is only used in **PRINT** statements.

TAB(30) will position the cursor or print head 30 characters *from the beginning of the line*.

```
PRINT TAB(30); "ADDRESS"
```

will print ADDRESS beginning in the 30th position from the beginning of the line. A semicolon [;] separates the TAB instruction from the material to be printed. A comma instead of a semicolon will be accepted by CBASIC but since a semicolon must be used to separate parts of a longer statement, it is simpler to use uniform separations. In this illustration the computer would first move the cursor to position 30 and then start printing the word, ADDRESS.

TAB may be used as often as needed in a single PRINT statement.

```
PRINT "NAME";TAB(25);"ADDRESS";TAB(50);"AMOUNT OWED";TAB(65);"ACCOUNT NO."
```

would output

```
NAME                    ADDRESS                 AMOUNT OWED    ACCOUNT NO.
```

The expression after TAB should be an integer, an integer variable, or an expression with an integer value. If the value is real it will be rounded to an integer; a string will result in an error. If the expression is more than the line width it will result in an error in non-compiler versions. In compiler versions, there will be an automatic carriage return [cr] and line feed [lf] after every 80 characters on the screen. The following are examples of valid TAB statements.

```
PRINT TAB(K%); X

PRINT TAB(I% + K% * J%); Z
```

PRINT **TAB(90)** is valid in compiler versions only. It will print the next value beginning in position 10 of the next line.

LANGUAGE CODING RULE

To print a value or a string constant at a specific location use:

    TAB <integer value>

The value following TAB must be [a] an integer value, [b] an integer variable, or [c] an integer expression.

CHAPTER 5

An Introduction to
Data Files

Every business keeps records which make up its information system, a collection of data files. The ideal information system provides for rapid and accurate data gathering, recording, processing, storage, and retrieval. In order to design and use computer files, it is necessary to understand some basic computer terms associated with files.

Data files are company records that contain information about similar items of data. There are the payroll file, accounts receivable file, inventory file, personnel file, etc. All the information that refers to a single customer, employee, or product is held in the file as a single entity, which is called a **record**.

A data file consists of a series of records, each containing one or more pieces of information or **fields**. In a personnel record, for example, these fields might include: individual's name, address, social security number, sex, age, present title or position, current salary or pay scale, next of kin, phone number, date of joining the company, previous job history within company, and previous work experience.

In setting up data files, it is important to recognize that records can be either of fixed or variable lengths. Although many computer languages require fixed length fields, this is not required by any version of the CBASIC family.

FILE ORGANIZATION

Records must be arranged in some predetermined way in order to be able to refer to a particular record. With the typical business microcomputer system the file organization can be one of two types, sequential or random.

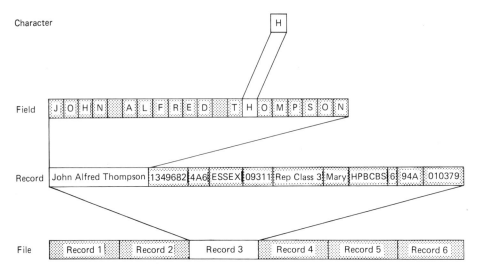

FIGURE 5-1 Composition of a File

A file consists of one or more records. Each record, which is composed of one or more fields, is stored on a disk and terminates with a carriage return [*cr*] and line feed [*lf*]. A field contains an individual data item and usually consists of one or more characters.

Sequential Files

Sequential files, unless they have been sorted [alphabetized or arranged in a numerical sequence], are not stored in any organized way. They are stored on disks in the sequence in which the data is entered. To be of use, they are sorted by some control field or key, for example, item stock number, employee social security number, or customer name. Therefore, they require extensive data manipulation and special programming for sorting and merging.

With the advent of off-line storage devices business records were maintained as sequential files on magnetic tape. A sorted file of the accumulated records to date was called the **master file**. All the current day's data was entered on another tape file and this was known as the **daily file**. After the close of the business day, the daily file was sorted and merged with the master file to create a new master file. The same process was repeated for each business day.

Sequential files, also called **stream** or **serial files**, are still used in some data processing applications, like adding a new amount to a debt to get an outstanding balance, or adding up the orders placed for a particular item. However, they are not efficient when used in an enquiry system, for example to search for a particular customer and show the status of the account.

This is because a sequential file, somewhat like a recording tape on a hi-fi system, must be read starting at the beginning until the desired key [in this illustration the particular customer] is found. Another disadvantage is that it is *not* possible to read and immediately write in the same file. With the advent of data bases, traditional sequential file processing is now used to a very limited extent.

Random Files

Random files are more widely used for most business applications today because it is possible to retrieve a record directly *without* having the computer read the file from the beginning, and it is also possible to search for a specific record, read it, make a modification, and immediately write the revised data on the disk.

There are many forms of random files but they will not be discussed here. The only form of random file available to the programmer with CBASIC is the **relative file.** However, using Digital Research's *"Access Manager"* with the compiler versions it is possible to create and use multi-keyed **indexed sequential files.** In this book our emphasis will be on sequential and relative files.

Finally, it must be noted that unless the lengths of all the records are about equal, the random file will require more disk space than the sequential file. In the illustration of the relative file, **Figure 5-2**, all the space between the end of the data in each record and the cr/lf [carriage return/line feed] is wasted.

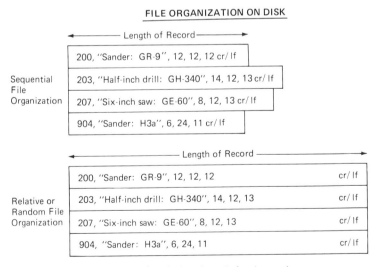

FILE ORGANIZATION ON DISK

Note: cr/lf is the carriage return/line feed at the end of each record.

FIGURE 5-2   File Organization on a Disk

Estimating Record Length

For random files the length of the record must be specified. Each record in a random file must be the same length because the computer uses this information to search for specific records. If the programmer selects a record size that is longer than necessary, there will be wasted space on the disk. But if the selected record length proves to be too short when the program is used, the file can be rewritten with a longer record size and revised field sizes.

For convenience it is customary in computer programming to estimate the maximum length of each field within a record. We will use the following notation in describing the structure of each field:

A for alphabetic data [A through Z]
! for alphanumeric data [letters, numbers, or special symbols],
\# for numerical data [0 through 9], and
. for decimal point.

Using a record in an inventory file, for example, we can define the field structure and size as follows:

ITEM	FIELD STRUCTURE	FIELD SIZE
Product number	A###-##	7
Description	!!!!!!!!!!!!!!!!!!	18
Number on hand	#####	5
Reorder level	####	4
Last purchase price	##.##	5
Special approval code	!!!!!!!!!!!	11

The total number of characters [letters, numbers, spaces, and special symbols] for this record is 50. However, the compiler requires several characters to be *added* as specified in **Table 5-1**, "Special Characters Required for File Construction."

Therefore, to determine the record size of the example just given, we have a total character count of 50 to which we must add:

- 5 characters as field delimiters to separate the six fields
- 6 characters for quotation marks before and after each string for fields one, two, and six
- 2 characters, [cr] carriage return and [lf] line feed, to mark the end of the record

The record length for this inventory file equals 63 characters. A record length of any number of characters may be used, odd or even. For the most

TABLE 5-1   Special Characters Required for File Construction

In determining record size for a random file add:

1. one extra character or byte for a *delimiter* [in this case a comma] after each field except the last one,
2. two extra characters or bytes for quotation marks [" "] one before and one after each field which is defined as a string variable, and
3. two special characters or bytes to indicate the end of the record, namely a carriage return [cr] and line feed [lf].

compact storage of data we would declare this record size as 63; if we wished to allow for future expansion, we would use a larger value.

Although we have designed the fields with fixed lengths, variable length fields may be used *if and only if* the total number of characters does not exceed the specified record length and the program has not been written to limit each field to a particular length. In this example, were it necessary to use 20 characters for the product description in field #2, we would have to reduce another field length by two characters. The total would still be 63 and this input would be acceptable to the computer.

File Maintenance and Buffers

Most of the time file maintenance and the use of buffers is transparent to the user; that is, the user is unaware of these operations since they are controlled by the computer automatically. Some understanding of these operations is necessary, however, in using the **BUFF** portion of the file programming statements.

Most operating systems used with microcomputers perform only one operation at a time for a terminal. Whenever it is necessary to transfer data between the computer's memory and any input or output device, the CPU stops processing for the given terminal. Between transfers data is stored in a portion of memory assigned by the operating system which is known as a **buffer**. Under normal operations CP/M, for example, stores data in a *single sector*, or a 128 byte buffer. The computer waits until the buffer is full or the read/write process has been terminated before transferring data.

The size of the buffer, therefore, determines how often the CPU must transfer data and this affects the speed of program execution. A larger buffer means fewer interruptions which is important when large quantities of data are processed. In all versions of CBASIC the size of the buffer can be modified when using sequential files by using the BUFF portion of the file statement. The BUFF portion of any file statement *cannot* be modified with random files; it is always one.

Naming Files

A filename must conform to specific rules and these vary according to the operating system, whether it be CP/M, MP/M, or PC-DOS. One basic rule common to all operating systems is that the filename contain no more than eight characters, and the filename may be followed by an extension or suffix of up to three characters. The extension is separated from the filename by a period:

filename.extension

When constructing a filename under either CP/M or MP/M, the filename and extension may *not* include any of the following special characters:

< > . , ; : = ? * [ ]

If you are using CP/M version 3 or higher, the following *additional* special characters may *not* be used:

& ! | \ + − /

None of the above special characters are of any advantage in filenames, and some will not produce an error but will not create a file. Although there are some symbols which may be used in filenames, including # and $ used in the following illustrations, it is safer to use only letters and numbers.

When constructing a filename under PC-DOS or MS-DOS, only the following characters may be used in the filename and, if used, the extension:

: all the letters from A through Z,
: all the digits from 0 through 9, and
: the following special characters:

< > ( ) { } # $ % ^ & ! $ ˜ __ − ' \ ¦

No matter which operating system is being used, there are two good programming rules that should be followed.

1. The identifier for the file should have three parts: [a] the filename, [b] a period [.], and [c] an extension. The period and extension are

not required but the extension is very useful when searching through a directory. This is the only place the period may be used in identifying a file.

2. The extension is limited by the operating system to 3 characters. It is good practice to use **FIL** as the extension so that the name is easily recognized as a data file.

The following are samples of acceptable filenames under CP/M and MP/M:

SECURITY.FIL	JOURNAL.FIL	LAW13.FIL
MEDICAL.FIL	{FIRST}.FIL	A.FIL
FUNDS$.FIL	ASIA#3.FIL	205.FIL

The following are samples of acceptable filenames under PC-DOS:

PAY(OLD).FIL	PLANT<2>.FIL	R&D.FIL
#69.FIL	|STOP|.FIL	HIS-HERS.FIL
MONEY$.FIL	HALT!.FIL	C&S-COPY.FIL

FILE STATEMENTS

The compiler and non-compiler versions use the operating system file accessing routines to store and retrieve data in disk files. The language uses a series of statements to perform various file functions.

- **CREATE** originates a new file on a disk. If the filename already exists this statement erases the existing file before creating the new one.
- **OPEN** makes an existing file accessible for processing. If the file does not exist, an error will occur unless an **IF END** statement has been executed.
- **IF END** allows you to transfer control to a particular statement when the end of an active file is reached. Used before an **OPEN** statement, it will prevent a run-time error if the indicated file does not exist.
- **FILE**, available only in *non-compiler versions*, procures an existing file for processing. If the file does not exist, this statement creates one.
- **PRINT #** transfers data from the computer's memory to the disk.
- **READ #** transfers data from the disk to the computer's memory.
- **PRINT USING #** transfers data from the computer's memory to the disk using specific printing options.
- **CLOSE** deactivates a file from further processing. No data can be entered or read from that file until it is reopened with either *FILE* or *OPEN*.

STARTING A NEW FILE: CREATE STATEMENT

A new file, either **sequential** or **random**, is started by using the **CREATE** statement. This tells the computer to add the filename to a disk's directory and whether the file will be accessed randomly or sequentially. If the filename already appears in the directory of the indicated disk, the old file will be erased before the new file is started.

Non-Compiler Versions

For a **random file** the statement could be illustrated by:

```
[1]   CREATE "SECURITY.FIL" RECL 192 AS 1
```

For a **sequential file** the statement could be:

```
[2]   CREATE "B:SECURITY.FIL" AS 2 BUFF 3 RECS 128
```

Parts of the CREATE statement are common to both sequential and random files. For a description of each part of the statement see **Figure 5-3**.

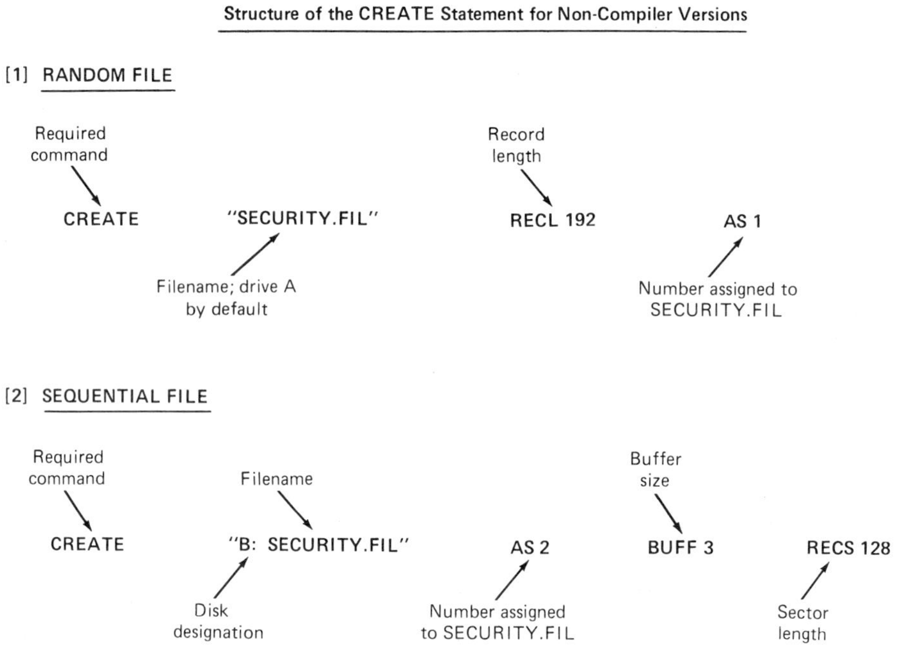

Structure of the CREATE Statement for Non-Compiler Versions

[1] RANDOM FILE

Required command → CREATE   "SECURITY.FIL"   Record length → RECL 192   AS 1
Filename; drive A by default   Number assigned to SECURITY.FIL

[2] SEQUENTIAL FILE

Required command → CREATE   Filename → "B: SECURITY.FIL"   AS 2   Buffer size → BUFF 3   RECS 128
Disk designation   Number assigned to SECURITY.FIL   Sector length

FIGURE 5-3   Structure of the CREATE Statement for Non-Compiler

- **CREATE** is required for *both* types of files.
- If the disk drive is omitted as in [1], the file will automatically go onto the default drive. The disk drive must be specified if it is not the default drive as in [2], **B:SECURITY.FIL**.
- **AS** assigns a number to the file; the file is always referred to by that number in the program. The expression following AS should be an integer between 1 and 20 inclusive or a variable that evaluates to an integer between those limits. A real value will be truncated to an integer; a string will result in an error. CBASIC can operate with more than one file simultaneously but each file must have a different number assigned to it.

For a **random file** the record length *must* be specified. In [1], **RECL 192** specifies a record length of 192 bytes.

For a **sequential file** there is the option of using the **BUFF** and **RECS** parameters, but they must be used together or not at all. The RECS number specifies the size of your disk sector which is usually 128 bytes. The number after BUFF tells the computer how many disk sectors to maintain in buffer storage at one time.

If memory is available the use of more than one sector has the advantage of speeding program execution because reading from and writing to the disk will be less frequent. However, increasing the buffer size has a trade-off. Although a larger buffer would speed operations, it can also create more difficulty if there is a power interrupt. All the data in the buffer would be lost since it has not been written on the disk.

A buffer size of 1, which is a single sector of 128 bytes, would hold 128 characters before disk access would occur. If the buffer was specified as 5, a total of 640 bytes, 640 characters could be held within the buffer before the disk is accessed. Disk access would then occur one-fifth as many times.

The BUFF RECS option is also available for random files but in a limited form which serves no useful purpose. For *random files*, a buffer size of 1 [128 bytes] is required by the compiler. If you designate any larger size a run-time error will occur.

Compiler Versions

For compiler versions the CREATE statement is somewhat different. The optional RECS portion is no longer part of the statement. In its place there is a **MODE** option which is operative *only* under concurrent and multiuser operating systems. The MODE option is explained in Chapter 14.

For a single-user system, the syntax of the CREATE statement is the same as the non-compiler version for a random file but *not* for a sequential file.

For a **random file** the statement could be:

```
CREATE "SECURITY.FIL" RECL 192 AS 1
```

For a **sequential file** the statement could be:

```
CREATE "B:SECURITY.FIL" AS 2 BUFF 3
```

LANGUAGE CODING RULE

The CREATE statement creates a new file on a disk with no information in it.
• The two forms for the *non-compiler* versions are:

For random file:

CREATE <filename> **RECL** <record length> **AS** <file number>

For sequential file:

CREATE <filename> **AS** <record number>
                      [**BUFF** <number of sectors> **RECS** <size>]

• The two forms for the *compiler* versions are:

For random file:

CREATE <filename> **RECL** <record length>
                            AS <file number> [<mode>]

For sequential file:

CREATE <filename> **AS** <record number>
                  [**BUFF** <number of sectors>] [<mode>]

NOTE:

- In the non-compiler version, the RECS option must be used *if* the BUFF option is included when creating a sequential file.
- In the single-user compiler versions, the RECS option is *not* permitted for any type of file.
- In all versions, the BUFF option is omitted if a *random* file is being created; it is automatically set to one.

OPENING AN EXISTING FILE: OPEN STATEMENT

The **OPEN** statement, used to access a file which is already stored on a disk, has exactly the same language structure as the CREATE statement.

To open a *random file*, SECURITY.FIL for example, in all versions except when using the MODE option, the statement would be:

```
OPEN "SECURITY.FIL" RECL 192 AS 1
```

To open a *sequential file*, SECURITY.FIL, the statement would be:

Non-Compiler:

```
OPEN "B:SECURITY.FIL" AS 2 BUFF 3 RECS 128
```

Compiler:

```
OPEN "B:SECURITY.FIL" AS 2 BUFF 3
```

LANGUAGE CODING RULE

The OPEN statement opens an existing file on a designated disk drive for reading, printing, updating, or modification.
• The two forms for the *non-compiler* versions are:

For random file:

    OPEN <filename> **RECL** <record length> **AS** <file number>

For sequential file:

    OPEN <filename> **AS** <record number>
                [**BUFF** <number of sectors> **RECS** <size>]

• The two forms for the *compiler* versions are:

For random file:

    OPEN <filename> **RECL** <record length>
                    AS <file number> [<mode>]

For sequential file:

    OPEN <filename> **AS** <record number>
                [**BUFF** <number of sectors>] [<mode>]

IF END Statement

This statement, which tells the computer where to continue processing when it detects the end of a file, is essential when using files for which you do not know the total number of records. For random files there is a simple programming technique which will make the total number of records readily available and this will be used in the short program at the end of this chapter. With sequential files this statement is required if the whole file is being processed.

For this purpose its use is illustrated by:

```
READ #2; NAME$, STREET.ADDRESS$, ZIP.CODE
IF END #2 THEN 200
```

When the end of the file is detected, execution will continue at line 200.

The IF END statement may be placed before the OPEN statement even if the number has not yet been assigned to the file. If executed before the OPEN statement, it will cause the program to branch to the designated line (usually an error message) if the file does not exist. Without it there would be an error and execution would stop.

The two functions of this statement can be combined by using it *twice* as in the following example.

```
IF END #2 THEN 200
OPEN "SECURITY.FIL" AS 2 BUFF 3 RECS 128
READ #2; NAME$, STREET.ADDRESS$, ZIP.CODE
IF END #2 THEN 350
```

If SECURITY.FIL does not exist, the first line will cause the program to branch to line 200. The third line will send the program to line 350 after the file has been opened, read, and processed, and the end of the file is reached.

If you have not done much programming you may think this emphasis on a non-existent file is excessive, but all it takes is a typographical error in the entry, the wrong disk, or the right disk in the wrong drive.

Any number of IF END statements may be used in the program for a particular file; the last one executed will determine to what line the program branches. It may also be used repeatedly for different files because the number in the statement connects it to the right file. Thus:

```
IF END #3 THEN 100
OPEN "PAYROLL.FIL" AS 3 BUFF 3 RECS 128
```

will cause a branch to line 100 if PAYROLL.FIL does not exist on the disk in the default drive.

LANGUAGE CODING RULE

The IF END statement prevents you from:

- opening a file that does not exist,
- reading past the end of a file,
- trying to create a file when the disk or directory is full, and
- writing to a file when the disk is full.

IF END # <file number> **THEN** <label>

The IF END statement must be on a line by itself.

In the same program:

```
OPEN "ACCOUNTS.FIL" AS 1
READ #1; CUST.NAME$, ACCOUNT.NO
IF END #1 THEN 500
```

will cause a branch to line 500 when ACCOUNTS.FIL has been processed and the end is reached.

Using Variable Names in the CREATE and OPEN Statements

In the illustrations thus far we have used the name of the file in the CREATE and OPEN statements. However, it is frequently more desirable to keep the program flexible and permit it to be used for more than one specific file. This is done by using *variables* for parts of the statements.

For example, instead of the actual filename we can use the variable NOF$ which is defined as a string by an input statement earlier in the program.

```
INPUT "Enter the name of the file ......."; NOF$
....
....
....
OPEN "B:"+ NOF$ RECL 192 AS 1
```

Note the altered position of the quotation marks and the use of + for concatenation.

Similarly RECL, AS, and BUFF may be followed by variables which are evaluated as integers. A real value will be converted to an integer; a string will produce a run-time error. The grammar remains unchanged if a variable is used for any of these three.

STARTING OR OPENING A FILE: FILE STATEMENT

The FILE statement, available only in non-compiler versions, will create a file if none exists *or* open the file if it has already been started. It must be in the form just discussed, with the name of the file first defined by a string variable as shown in the following illustration. The record length, if used, is in parentheses after the variable which defines the name.

```
NAME$ = "SECURITY.FIL"
FILE NAME$(192)
```

These two statements would create SECURITY.FIL, a relative file, on disk A if it does not exist or would open it if it does. No file number is included in the statement. As each file is started or opened it will be assigned the next unused number starting with 1 and going through 20. However, if the program uses more than one file open at the same time it is necessary to keep a record of the file numbers so that they can be referred to later in the program.

For B disk use the concatenation form:

```
FILE "B:" + NAME$
```

The IF END statement cannot be used to detect a file that does not exist because the FILE statement is meant to create one in that case. This means that if the name is entered incorrectly, or the wrong disk is used, or the wrong drive designated, a new file will be opened where none was intended.

LANGUAGE CODING RULE

The FILE statement [available in the non-compiler versions only] opens an existing file *or* if it does not exist, it creates a new file.

FILE <filename> [(record length)] {,<filename>[(record length)]}

The filename *must be a string variable* which has been previously defined and the record length may be a numeric value or an integer variable.

An alternative to the FILE statement for compiler versions is explained in Chapter 10 on advanced file handling.

WRITING TO A FILE: PRINT # STATEMENT

The statement which directs the computer to transfer information from memory to a disk file for permanent storage is either **PRINT #** or **PRINT USING #**. [The PRINT USING # changes the form in which the data will be stored. It is discussed in Chapter 11.] The file must have been activated earlier in the program by a CREATE, OPEN, or FILE statement.

For a *sequential file* the statement is in the form:

```
PRINT #2; 212, "Saber saw"
```

or

```
PRINT #FL.NO%; ITEM.NO%, DESC$
```

The first illustration uses only constants and the second uses only variables, but any combination of constants and variables is permitted.

The first statement would cause the computer to enter, in the next available record of file number 2, the value 212 in the first field and Saber saw in the second field. The computer would follow the same procedure if given the instruction in the second illustration and would use the last values of the variables.

For a *random file* the statement is illustrated by:

```
PRINT #2, 32; 212, "Saber saw"
```

or

```
PRINT #FL.NO%, REC.NO%; ITEM.NO%, DESC$
```

The essential difference in the PRINT # statements for the two types of files is that for random access the *record number*, here 32 or variable REC.NO%, must be included. In a sequential file it cannot be included because there is no way the computer can find a particular record.

Except for this difference, the requirement to specify the record number when using a random file, the grammar is the same.

- String constants must be enclosed in quotation marks.
- The values to be written to the file are separated by commas.
- A semicolon separates the items to be entered from the file number or record number.

LANGUAGE CODING RULE

The PRINT # statement is used to write data to a disk file.

For random files:

PRINT #<file number> , <record number> ; <variable> {, variable}

For sequential files:

PRINT #<file number> ; <variable> {, variable}

- The file number and record number (if used) should be integers or variables which evaluate to integers. Real values will be converted to integers; strings will result in an error.

The IF END statement may be used with PRINT # when writing to a file. In this case, the statement will prevent an error if an attempt is made to write to a file when there is no more disk space available. Part of the record in a sequential file is written on the disk; in a relative file the last record is rewritten when more space is available.

READING FROM A FILE: READ # STATEMENT

The language structure of the **READ #** statement is similar to the form of the PRINT # statement. Constants or variables may be used for the file number and record number but only variable names may follow the semicolon. The following statements illustrate acceptable forms of the READ # statement.

```
READ #6, REC.NO%; ITEM.NO%, DESC$
```

In response to this command the computer would read from random file number 6 the first two fields of the record number indicated by the last value of REC.NO%. These two values would be assigned to the variables ITEM.NO% and DESC$ respectively.

```
READ #FL.NO%; ITEM.NO%, DESC$
```

This command would cause the computer to read the next record in

---

LANGUAGE CODING RULE

The READ # statement is used to read data from a disk file.

For random files:

READ #<file number> , <record number> ; <variable> {, variable}

For sequential files:

READ #<file number> ; <variable> {, variable}

---

sequential file number FL.NO% and assign the values in the two fields to the variables ITEM.NO% and DESC$ respectively.

However:

- If there are more variables listed than there are fields in a record an error will occur when using either a sequential or random file.
- In a sequential file an error will also occur if there are fewer variables than fields in the record.
- Finally, if the value read in the first field to be assigned to ITEM.NO% is real, the value will be truncated; if a string is assigned, an error will occur. The value in the second field to be assigned to DESC$ must be a string.

CLOSING A FILE: CLOSE STATEMENT

A file must be closed when work with it is finished using the statement **CLOSE** followed by the assigned number[s] of the file or files, or a pre-defined integer variable[s], or a combination of both.

```
CLOSE 1,4
```

will close files with the assigned numbers 1 and 4.

```
CLOSE NEW.FIL%
```

will close the file numbered with the *value* of NEW.FIL%.

Any number of files may be closed in one statement provided that the numbers or variables are separated by commas. Closing the file releases the buffer space previously reserved and the numbers assigned to the files, in this illustration, 1 and 4.

Failure to close a file when work with it is finished may ruin it. The CLOSE statement directs the computer to write to the disk any data remaining in the buffer and to update its directory. A statement directing the computer to close a file which is not open will cause an error.

LANGUAGE CODING RULE

The CLOSE statement closes opened files and must be used in conjunction with a FILE, CREATE, or OPEN statement.

CLOSE <file number> {, file number}

There are other commands which first close the file and then execute the command itself. They are **CHAIN**, **END**, and **STOP**. Entering CON-TROL-C [CTRL-C] or encountering a run-time error during execution does *not* close any of the active files.

SPECIAL PROGRAMMING NOTE

In long programs closing and reopening a file periodically during program execution is a valuable safety precaution which can preserve the file in case of inadvertent error or power failure. When using random files, it is safe programming practice to open the file prior to data entry into a record and then close the file immediately after the data and the new index have been written to the disk.

SAMPLE FILE PROGRAMS

We have now covered the basic file statements and are ready to create, add to, and print a file. A few additional statements are needed that have not yet been fully explained but their functions will be apparent if you read them as if they were in English instead of CBASIC. The problem illustrates an inventory file containing:

- The product number,
- Description of the item,

- Number on hand,
- Cost for each item in stock.

Both sequential and random files are shown below. For each, the problem is broken into three parts:

1. Create
2. Add
3. Print

This makes the programs easy to follow although at a more advanced stage they would be combined into one. They are written for non-compiler versions; for compiler versions *omit* RECS from CREATE and OPEN statements and you may declare all variables and avoid the use of $ and %.

Enter and run both the sequential and random file programs using the following data in response to the input requests. Enter a few items using the Create or first program and the remainder using the Add or second program. Note that the file is put on disk B. If you want to use disk A simply *omit* **B:** in the programs.

The data for the file programs which follow is shown in the accompanying list.

PRODUCT NUMBER	DESCRIPTION	NUMBER ON HAND	COST
34G412	Tape reel	200	10.15
35F536	Coverplate	150	1.29
29L381	Switch box	175	1.67
31W129	Work light	128	3.50
33G581	Extension cord	50	9.15
32L606	Outlet	320	1.03

Programming Notes for These Programs

1. This series of programs can be used on any computer but it may be necessary to redefine CLEAR.SCREEN.
2. CBASIC, unlike some other dialects of BASIC, is *not* too fussy about spacing. However, in the CREATE and OPEN statements the spaces left after BUFF, AS, and RECL are required. In addition, when using the name of the file in quotation marks do not leave spaces. To the computer the name "SECURITY.FIL" is not the same as " SECURITY.FIL ". In a string identifier a space is a character.
3. If there are any errors which you correct, remember to recompile the program.

Sequential File Programs

The first program, **Program 5-1**, creates a sequential file SQUINV.FIL on disk B. If you are putting the file on disk A, omit **B:** but remember the quotation marks around the name.

PROGRAM 5-1   **SFILE1.BAS**   [Non-Compiler]

Create a Sequential File, SQUINV.FIL

Copyright 1985, Compulit, Inc.

```
\               Variables: PROD.NO$, PROD.DESC$, ON.HAND%, PROD.COST, AN$
\               Defining CLEAR.SCREEN$ for PC-DOS and MS-DOS
        CLEAR.SCREEN$ = CHR$(27) + "[2J"
\               Create file, SQUINV.FIL, on disk B
        CREATE "B:SQUINV.FIL" AS 1 BUFF 2 RECS 128
10      PRINT CLEAR.SCREEN$
\               Input of data in program
        INPUT "Enter product number.......... "; PROD.NO$    :PRINT
        INPUT "Enter product description...... "; PROD.DESC$  :PRINT
        INPUT "Enter number of units on hand.. "; ON.HAND%    :PRINT
        INPUT "Enter product cost............. "; PROD.COST   :PRINT
\               Write data record to disk
        PRINT #1; PROD.NO$, PROD.DESC$, ON.HAND%, PROD.COST
\               Restart procedure for another entry
        INPUT "Another entry?.....(Y/N)....... "; AN$
        IF UCASE$(AN$) = "Y" THEN 10
\               Close file before terminating program
        CLOSE 1
        END
```

Program 5-2 reopens SQUINV.FIL and permits you to add the items that were not written to the file in the first program. If you are using disk A, remember to change the **OPEN** statement. To keep the program simple there is no provision for an **IF END** statement that goes to an error message. The function of the statement in this program is to branch to the **INPUT** statements when the file has been read to the end. The next item is then recorded as the next record automatically.

PROGRAM 5-2   **SFILE2.BAS**   [Non-Compiler]

Adding Records to Sequential File, SQUINV.FIL

Copyright 1985, Compulit, Inc.

```
\               Define CLEAR.SCREEN$ for PC-DOS and MS-DOS
        CLEAR.SCREEN$ = CHR$(27) + "[2J"
\               Statement to open existing file, SQUINV.FIL, on disk B
        OPEN "B:SQUINV.FIL" AS 1 BUFF 2 RECS 128
\               Read to end of file and permit addition of new data
        IF END #1 THEN 50
10      READ #1;PROD.NO$, PROD.DESC$, ON.HAND%, PROD.COST
        GOTO 10
\               Clear screen and input new data
50      PRINT CLEAR.SCREEN$
        INPUT "Enter product number........... "; PROD.NO$    :PRINT
```

```
      INPUT "Enter product description....... "; PROD.DESC$   :PRINT
      INPUT "Enter number of units on hand... "; ON.HAND%     :PRINT
      INPUT "Enter product cost............. "; PROD.COST     :PRINT
      PRINT #1; PROD.NO$, PROD.DESC$, ON.HAND%,  PROD.COST
\              Procedure to enter another record
      INPUT "Another entry?............(Y/N). "; AN$
      IF UCASE$(AN$) = "Y" THEN 50
\              Close file before terminating program
      CLOSE 1
      END
```

Program 5-3 reopens the file and prints the item list. Again, verify the disk in use for the file. The first line after the PRINT CLEAR.SCREEN$ statement prints the heads in columns because the items are separated by commas. Each column head is a string constant and must be enclosed in quotation marks.

Each record is read and printed in succession. To read the entire file and then print the entire file would require that each record be stored in memory after it is read.

PROGRAM 5-3   SFILE3.BAS   [Non-Compiler]

Read and Print Sequential File, SQUINV.FIL

Copyright 1985, Compulit, Inc.

```
\              Defining CLEAR.SCREEN$ for PC-DOS and MS-DOS
      CLEAR.SCREEN$ = CHR$(27) + "[2J"
      PRINT CLEAR.SCREEN$
\              Print column headings
      PRINT "Product #"," Description","Units on Hand","Cost": PRINT
\              Open file, read and print each record
      OPEN "B:SQUINV.FIL" AS 1 BUFF 2 RECS 128
      IF END #1 THEN 50
10    READ #1; PROD.NO$, PROD.DESC$, ON.HAND%, PROD.COST
      PRINT PROD.NO$, PROD.DESC$, ON.HAND%, PROD.COST
      GOTO 10
\              Close file before terminating program
50    CLOSE 1
      END
```

Relative or Random File Programs

A reasonable record length should be used for random files. There are four fields that must be entered for each record in the problem we are considering:

1. Product number is a string, an alphanumeric field of 6 characters.
2. The longest product description in the data is 14 characters which will be entered as a string.

3. The number on hand is an integer value and its maximum size in this data is 3 characters.
4. The cost of each item is a real value including 4 digits and a decimal point so that its field size is 5 characters.

The total number of field characters is 28, but following the rules given earlier in this chapter we must allow for:

- 3 commas, one between each of the four fields
- 4 quotation marks which enclose the strings in the first and second fields
- 2 special symbols, the carriage return and line feed, which go at the end of the record

Therefore the record size must be at least 35—28 characters for the data and 7 for the record notation required by the file. We should, however, allow for the possibility of longer item descriptions and larger values for the number on hand. We have selected a record length of 50 for the sample programs.

Program 5-4 creates a relative or random file defined by the variable **NOF$**. The first INPUT statement asks for the name of the file and this permits the program to be reused to create a file with a different name. The variable INDEX counts the number of records in the file; it is increased by one in the statement:

```
INDEX = INDEX + 1
```

each time a new item is to be entered. It is stored in the first record by the statement:

```
PRINT #1, 1; INDEX
```

The total number of records in the file is then always available simply by opening the file and reading the first record. One use of this technique will be shown in the second program. Storing the index is not a programming language requirement, but it is valuable when programs become more complex.

SPECIAL PROGRAMMING NOTE

The use of INDEX and its storage in the first record should be part of every random file program. See Programs 5-4 through 5-6 in this chapter for its use.

PROGRAM 5-4   **RFILE1.BAS**   **[Compiler]**

Create Relative File, RELINV.FIL, with INDEX in the First Record

Copyright 1984, 1985, Compulit, Inc.

```
\              Declare variables: string, integer and real
       STRING   AN, CLEAR.SCREEN, NOF, PROD.DESC, PROD.NO
       INTEGER  INDEX, ON.HAND
       REAL     PROD.COST
\              Defining CLEAR.SCREEN for PC-DOS and MS-DOS version 2.0
       CLEAR.SCREEN = CHR$(27) + "[2J"
       PRINT CLEAR.SCREEN
\              Enter file name and open file on disk B
       INPUT "Enter name of file........."; NOF
       CREATE "B:"+ NOF RECL 50 AS 1
\              Initialize INDEX, the record number
       INDEX = 1
\              Clear screen and input data
10     PRINT CLEAR.SCREEN
       INDEX = INDEX + 1
       INPUT "Enter product number.......... "; PROD.NO   : PRINT
       INPUT "Enter product description...... "; PROD.DESC : PRINT
       INPUT "Enter number of units on hand.. "; ON.HAND   : PRINT
       INPUT "Enter product cost ............ "; PROD.COST : PRINT
\              Write data to file; enter number of records in record one
       PRINT #1, INDEX; PROD.NO, PROD.DESC, ON.HAND, PROD.COST
       PRINT #1, 1; INDEX
\              Procedure to enter another set of data
       INPUT "Another entry?... Yes or No? .. "; AN
       IF UCASE$(AN) = "YES" THEN 10
\              Close file before terminating program
       CLOSE 1
       END
```

Program 5-5, the second random file program, reopens the file, reads the index in the first record, and immediately increases INDEX by one. The next item will be written as the next record. Note that the index is written to the file each time an item is added. This is a safety precaution rather than a requirement. If there is an unexpected interruption in processing, the incorrect index would ruin the file.

The only disadvantage of storing the index in the first record is the unused space. However, in complex programs other data can be stored in the same record as will be shown later in the book. There is another method of adding to a relative file, but it is much more complicated and has no advantage.

PROGRAM 5-5   **RFILE2.BAS**   **[Compiler]**

Add to Relative File Using INDEX Stored in First Record

Copyright 1984, 1985, Compulit, Inc.

```
\              Declare variables: string, integer and real
       STRING   AN, CLEAR.SCREEN, NOF, PROD.DESC, PROD.NO
       INTEGER  INDEX, ON.HAND
       REAL     PROD.COST
\              Define CLEAR.SCREEN for PC-DOS and MS-DOS version 2.0
       CLEAR.SCREEN = CHR$(27) + "[2J"
       PRINT CLEAR.SCREEN
```

(continues)

```
\              Input file name and open file on disk B
       INPUT "Enter name of file........."; NOF
       OPEN "B:"+ NOF RECL 50 AS 1
\              Read INDEX, the number of records, stored in record 1
       READ #1, 1; INDEX
\              Clear screen for INPUT of data
10     PRINT CLEAR.SCREEN
\              Increment value of INDEX for next record
       INDEX = INDEX + 1
\              Input of data for next record
       INPUT "Enter product number.......... "; PROD.NO    : PRINT
       INPUT "Enter product description...... "; PROD.DESC  : PRINT
       INPUT "Enter number of units on hand.. "; ON.HAND    : PRINT
       INPUT "Enter product cost............. "; PROD.COST  : PRINT
\              Write data to file and enter INDEX in record 1
       PRINT #1, INDEX; PROD.NO, PROD.DESC, ON.HAND, PROD.COST
       PRINT #1, 1; INDEX
\              Procedure to enter another record
       INPUT "Another entry?... Yes or No? .. "; AN
       IF UCASE$(AN) = "YES" THEN 10
\              Close file before terminating program
       CLOSE 1
       END
```

The third random file program, **Program 5-6**, reopens and prints the file. The method used here does not utilize the stored index because this would require statements that have not yet been covered. Instead, we have used **K** as the variable identifier for the record number and an **IF END** statement to end the reading and printing of the data.

PROGRAM 5-6   RFILE3.BAS   [Compiler]

Print Relative File Using IF END Statement

Copyright 1984, 1985, Compulit, Inc.

```
\              Declare variables: string, integer and real
       STRING    CLEAR.SCREEN, NOF, PROD.DESC, PROD.NO
       INTEGER   INDEX, K, ON.HAND
       REAL      PROD.COST
\              Define CLEAR.SCREEN for PC-DOS and MS-DOS version 2.0
       CLEAR.SCREEN = CHR$(27) + "[2J"
       PRINT CLEAR.SCREEN
\              Input file name; file is on disk B
       INPUT "Enter name of file.............. "; NOF
       PRINT CLEAR.SCREEN
\              Print column headings
       PRINT "Product #", "Description", "Units on Hand", "Cost": PRINT
\              Open file, read and print each record
       IF END #1 THEN 50
       OPEN "B:" + NOF RECL 50 AS 1
\              Reading and printing start with record 2; record 1
\              contains INDEX or total number of records used
       K = 2
10     READ #1, K; PROD.NO, PROD.DESC, ON.HAND, PROD.COST
       PRINT PROD.NO, PROD.DESC, ON.HAND, PROD.COST
       K = K + 1
       GOTO 10
\              Close file before terminating program
50     CLOSE 1
       END
```

The Output

The output shown in **Figure 5-4** is the same for both types of file. This result checks all three programs and should agree with the data table presented earlier. Minor differences such as an incorrect number or letter should be considered entry errors and disregarded. It is unlikely that any major problems will be encountered in these short programs if compile or run-time errors have been corrected.

The appearance of the output can be improved so that, for example, the decimal points line up and zeros are added to complete the cents. This requires the **PRINT USING** statement which is covered in Chapter 11.

ADDITIONAL FILE PROBLEMS

The following two problems require the setting up of random files that will be used with programs developed in the next chapter. Solutions are given at the end of the chapter. If you have difficulty in correcting errors after you have checked the error listings in Appendix D or E, read Chapter 12 for compiling and running a program and the section on debugging in Chapter 13.

Problem 1—Accounts Receivable

Write a program to create and print a random file which contains the following data. The file should be created; data should be entered and

Product #	Description	Units on Hand	Cost
34G412	Tape Reel	200	10.15
35F536	Coverplate	150	1.29
29L381	Switch Box	175	1.67
31W129	Work Light	128	3.5
33G581	Extension Cord	50	9.15
32L606	Outlet	320	1.03

FIGURE 5-4

written to the disk; and the file should be read and printed. Include appropriate column headings.

ACCOUNT NUMBER	CLIENT NAME	AMOUNT OWED
562	Able & Co.	500.00
113	Baker Corp.	400.00
416	Charles Inc.	150.00
126	Davis Co.	200.00
345	Evans Corp.	0.00
256	Francis Ltd.	250.00
492	Georgette	0.00

It is *not* necessary to use the same variable names in this program as in the ones in the next chapter.

There are three variables or fields in each customer record; the first is integer, the second is a string, and the third is real. Names such as NUMBER%, ACCT.NO%, ACTNO%, or even ACCOUNT.NUMBER% may be used for the first variable. The naming of the identifiers is up to you; all the computer looks for is whether the value matches the mode of the variable.

Problem 2—Inventory Decision Analysis

Write a program to set up and print a relative inventory file using the data below. Note that there are five fields; this means that the print statement will have to use the TAB function in order to display each item's information on a single line on the screen. The file should be created, the data entered, the file read and printed, and then closed.

PART NO.	ITEM DESCRIPTION	IN STOCK	REORDER LEVEL	PRICE
152	Quarter-inch drill: MT13	21	24	9
154	Saber saw: MT67	23	12	9
200	Sander: GR-9	12	12	12
203	Half-inch drill: GH-34	14	12	13
207	Six-inch saw: GE-60	8	12	13
901	6-foot ladder: D2	28	24	11
904	Belt sander: H3a	16	24	11
913	Drop cloth 8×12 G3	48	24	4
927	Paint roller set: G23	45	48	4
950	Gutter guard: W14	48	48	2

A Final Note about the Problems

For each of these two problems, one possible solution is shown at the end of the chapter but there are different ways of writing the programs. If you enter the data and get the required printout, you have solved the problem. If not, try debugging your program before looking at the solution at the end of the chapter.

If you have corrected all compiler and run-time errors and still do not get the printout, check the disk directory for the filename. However, even if the filename is in the directory, you cannot be certain that there is anything in the file. You can use the operating system's editor to examine its contents. With other text editors, call the file to see if the data was entered into the file; however, after you have examined the file, using PEACHTEXT 5000, for example, you exit with QUIT and *not* END. End would make the file unusable and other text editors may have a similar requirement. It is also possible to use the debugging program of the operating system to examine the file.

If all else fails, compare your program with the solution.

Solution to File Problems

Program 5-7 is a solution to problem 1 creating a random file including each customer's account number, name, and amount owed.

PROGRAM 5-7   **CUSPROG.BAS**   **[Compiler]**

Solution to Problem 5-1: Create and Print a Relative Customer File

Copyright 1984, 1985, Compulit, Inc.

```
\           Declare variables; initialize INDEX
      STRING   AN, CLEAR.SCREEN, NAME, NOF
      INTEGER  INDEX, K
      REAL     MONEY.OWED
      INDEX = 1
\           Define CLEAR.SCREEN for PC-DOS and MS-DOS version 2.0
      CLEAR.SCREEN = CHR$(27) + "[2J"
\           Clear screen; enter file name and create file on disk B
      PRINT CLEAR.SCREEN
      INPUT "Enter name of file..............."; NOF
      CREATE "B:" + NOF RECL 128 AS 1
\           Increment INDEX, clear screen and enter data
10    INDEX = INDEX + 1
      PRINT CLEAR.SCREEN:    PRINT:    PRINT
      INPUT "Enter account number............"; ACCT.NO%    :PRINT
      INPUT "Enter customer name ............"; NAME        :PRINT
      INPUT "Enter amount owed ............."; MONEY.OWED   :PRINT
\           Print data on disk; enter number of records in record 1
      PRINT #1,INDEX; ACCT.NO%, NAME, MONEY.OWED
      PRINT #1,1; INDEX
\           Restart procedure for another entry
      INPUT "Another entry?..... Yes or No? .."; AN         :PRINT
```
                                                    (continues)

```
        IF UCASE$(AN) = "YES" THEN 10
\                No more entries; clear screen and print column headings
        PRINT CLEAR.SCREEN
        PRINT "Account Number"; TAB(25); "Name"; TAB(45);"Money Owed"
        PRINT
        K = 2
\                Read and print each record beginning with record 2.
20      READ #1,K; ACCT.NO%, NAME, MONEY.OWED
\                When end of file is reached program goes to statement 30
        IF END #1 THEN 30
        PRINT ACCT.NO%; TAB(25); NAME; TAB(47); MONEY.OWED
        K = K + 1
        GOTO 20
\                Close file before ending program
30      CLOSE 1
        END
```

Program 5-8 is one solution to problem 2 requiring the creation of a random file containing inventory data.

PROGRAM 5-8   INVPROG.BAS   [Compiler]

Solution to Problem 5-2: Create and Print Relative Inventory File

Copyright 1985, Compulit, Inc.

```
\                Declaration of variables
        STRING   AN, CLEAR.SCREEN, DESC, NOF
        INTEGER  INDEX, IN.STOCK, K, PART.NO, REORDER.LEVEL
        REAL     PRICE
\                Defining CLEAR.SCREEN for PC-DOS and MS-DOS
        CLEAR.SCREEN = CHR$(27) + "[2J"
        INDEX = 1
\                Clear screen, enter file name and create file on disk B
        PRINT CLEAR.SCREEN
        INPUT "Enter name of file..............."; NOF              :PRINT
        CREATE "B:"+ NOF RECL 128 AS 1
\                Increment index as record number
10      INDEX = INDEX + 1
\                Input data
        INPUT "Enter part number................"; PART.NO      :PRINT
        INPUT "Enter part description .........."; DESC         :PRINT
        INPUT "Enter number in stock............"; IN.STOCK     :PRINT
        INPUT "Enter reorder level............."; REORDER.LEVEL:PRINT
        INPUT "Enter price......................"; PRICE        :PRINT
\                Write record to disk and write INDEX in record 1
        PRINT #1,INDEX; PART.NO, DESC, IN.STOCK, REORDER.LEVEL, PRICE
        PRINT #1,1; INDEX
\                Restart procedure to enter another record
        INPUT "Another entry?.............(Y/N)."; AN           :PRINT
        IF UCASE$(AN) = "Y" THEN 10
\                Clear screen and print column headings
        PRINT CLEAR.SCREEN
        PRINT "Part"; TAB(10); "Item Description"; TAB(40); "In"; TAB(48);\
              "Reorder"
        PRINT "No."; TAB(38); "Stock"; TAB(49);"Level"; TAB(60); "Price"
        PRINT
\                Set counter to record 2 before reading data
    K = 2
\                Read a record K from disk
20      READ #1,K; PART.NO, DESC, IN.STOCK, REORDER.LEVEL, PRICE
\                Send program control to 30 when all data has been read
        IF END #1 THEN 30
\                Display record K on console screen
        PRINT PART.NO; TAB(9); DESC; TAB(38); IN.STOCK; TAB(49);\
              REORDER.LEVEL; TAB(62); PRICE
\                Increment record counter to read next record
        K = K + 1
        GOTO 20
\                Close file before ending program
30      CLOSE 1
        END
```

CHAPTER **6**

Program Logic
Control: Branching

All computers execute programs in a linear sequence proceeding from one statement to the one immediately following *unless* directed by a specific statement to branch elsewhere in the program. Change in the order of processing is produced by one of several **command** or **logic control statements**. By using these statements, we are able to transfer control to another point in the program or repeat the processing of one or more statements. [The repeat commands will be covered in the next chapter.] Control may be transferred to:

- A specific statement anywhere within the program using **GOTO** or **GOSUB**
- Either of two statements depending upon a decision made at the point of transfer using **IF-THEN-ELSE**
- Any of three statements depending upon the sign of a designated variable using the **SGN** function
- Any one of several statements depending on the value of a specific variable or arithmetic expression using **ON-GOTO**

THE UNCONDITIONAL BRANCH: GOTO STATEMENT

The **unconditional branch** or **GOTO** statement directs the program to continue processing at a specific statement number or label. It was used in Program 2-1 in a program to compute straight-line depreciation. It is a simple way to control a repetitive action. Let us return to that portion of the program.

```
10   COST = COST - ANNUAL.DEPRECIATION
     YEAR% = YEAR% + 1
     PRINT YEAR%, ANNUAL.DEPRECIATION, CUMULATIVE.DEPRECIATION, COST
     IF YEAR% = EOP% THEN 30
     GOTO 10
```

The only way in which the program can escape from going back to statement number 10, or "get out of the loop" as it is called in computing, is when the value of YEAR% is equal to the value of EOP%. Then and only then does execution of the program continue at statement number 30.

The statement may be written as two words, **GO TO**, or as one word, **GOTO**. It is always followed by a statement number or label and the program continues to execute at that number or label. If the statement to which the program branched is non-executable, execution begins at the next executable statement. For example:

```
10   REM PROGRAM TO COMPUTE COST
     INPUT "Enter price per unit .......... "; PRICE
     INPUT "Enter number of units sold .... "; UNITS
     COST = PRICE * UNITS
     PRINT "Cost of items sold ........ "; COST
     GOTO 10
```

After the program prints COST it executes the last statement, GOTO 10. Statement 10, however, is a remark, which is non-executable. The program resumes processing at the first input line, requesting the entry of price per unit.

BRANCHING WITH THE IF STATEMENT

Sometimes the programmer wishes to branch to one of two possible procedures or sets of instructions depending on some condition or conditions.

LANGUAGE CODING RULE

The GOTO statement unconditionally transfers execution of the program to the statement identified by a statement number or label. An unconditional branching statement appears as:

GOTO <statement number *or* label>

This conditional branch which instructs the computer to make a simple decision is the **IF statement**.

There are two forms of the IF statement:

    IF ... THEN

In this single alternative decision structure:

- *If the condition is met* the program will:

    1. Branch to a different part of the program and then continue sequential execution

        or

    2. Execute one or more statements before continuing sequential execution of the program.

- *If the condition is not met* the instructions which follow THEN will be ignored and sequential execution will continue at the statement which follows the last part of the THEN sequence. This is an *implied* ELSE procedure.

    IF ... THEN ... ELSE

In this double alternative decision structure:

- *If the condition is met* the program will execute one or more statements following THEN

    or

- *If the condition is not met* the program will execute one or more statements following the ELSE.

The two forms of the **IF** statement can be represented by the flowcharts shown in **Figure 6-1**.

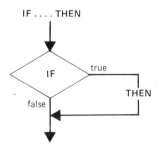
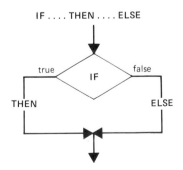

FIGURE 6-1   IF-THEN Flowchart

Using Relational Operators

The portion of the statement following **IF** consists of three parts:

```
<Expression(1)>   <Relational operator>   <Expression(2)>
```

Expression(1) and Expression(2) must both be either numeric or string. The expressions may be any one of the following:

A numeric variable	ACCT.NO%	PRICE
A string variable	NAME$	DATA.FIL$
A numeric constant	1313	99.0
A string literal	"YES"	"QUIT"
An arithmetic expression	HOURS – 40	I% + K%

The two expressions are separated by a **relational** or **logical operator**. In the **IF-THEN** and **IF-THEN-ELSE** statements, only the relational operators shown in Table 6-1, "Relational Operators," may be used.

TABLE 6-1   Relational Operators

RELATIONSHIP	SYMBOL		EXAMPLE
1. Equality	=	EQ	AN$ = "YES"
2. Not equal to	<>	NE	HC% <> 50
3. Less than	<	LT	VALUE < 50.00
4. Less than or equal to	<=	LE	HOURS <= 40
5. Greater than	>	GT	WAGES > 500.00
6. Greater than or equal to	>=	GE	FLG >= SET

NOTE: Either the mathematical symbols or the two-letter mnemonic operators may be used in actual coding.

The IF-THEN Statement

The simpler of the two IF forms is the IF-THEN statement, such as:

```
IF AMOUNT.OWED = 0   THEN 10
```

If the amount owed is equal to zero [indicating that the condition is *true*], the program will go to line label 10. Otherwise the program would proceed to the next statement.

Another illustration of this statement is:

```
IF ACCT.NO% > 999   THEN GOSUB 500
```

LANGUAGE CODING RULE

The IF-THEN statement transfers execution of the program to one of two statements. The single alternative decision structure is:

   IF <expression> **THEN** <statement> or <statement number>

or

   IF <expression> **THEN** <statement> [{ : statement}]

If the account number is greater than 999, the program will go to a subroutine numbered 500. If the account number is less than or equal to 999 the program will continue to the next statement in the program.

A somewhat more complex form of the IF-THEN statement is used when more than *one* instruction is to be executed as in:

```
IF AMOUNT.OWED = O  THEN PRINT NAME$: COUNT% = COUNT% + 1: GOTO 10
```

If the amount owed is equal to zero, the computer is directed to [a] print the name, [b] add one to the count, and [c] then go to statement 10. Note that these individual instructions are separated by *colons* on a *single-line*. If it is not possible to place all the statements on one line, continue the line with a \, but the colons are required before the backslash on each line.

```
IF AMOUNT.OWED > O THEN     \
    PRINT NAME$             :\  REM PRINT THE NAME
    COUNT% = COUNT% + 1     :\  REM ADD 1 TO COUNTER
    SUM = SUM + AMOUNT      :\  REM ADD AMOUNT TO SUM
    PRINT COUNT%, SUM       :\  REM PRINT COUNT AND SUM
    PRINT                       REM SKIP A LINE
```

In a *multi-line IF statement:*

   1. Place a backslash, \, after the THEN to end the line.
   2. Place a colon and a backslash, :\, at the end of each line.
   3. End the last line of instructions *without* any special control symbols.

It is not necessary when using a multi-statement form of IF-THEN to branch to another part of the program. For example in this segment of a program:

```
READ NAME$, AMOUNT.OWED, SALES82, SALES83,SALES84
IF AMOUNT.OWED = 0  THEN PRINT NAME$: COUNT% = COUNT% + 1
YR.TO.DATE.SALES = YR.TO.DATE.SALES + SALES84
```

After the program has executed the READ statement, if the amount owed is equal to zero, it will print the name, add 1 to the count, and go directly to the next statement. If the amount owed is not equal to zero, execution continues with the YR.TO.DATE.SALES statement.

Examples Using the IF-THEN Statement

Here is the first of a series of simple problems illustrating the use of the IF-THEN statement. We will use the company data from problem 1 of Chapter 5 to print a list of companies that owe money and the amount each owes. **Program 6-1** illustrates how this is done using the IF-THEN statement and READ-DATA statements.

PROGRAM 6-1   **IFTHEN.BAS**   **[Non-Compiler]**

Use of IF-THEN Statements

Copyright 1985, Compulit, Inc.

```
\            Defining CLEAR.SCREEN for PC-DOS and MS-DOS
            CLEAR.SCREEN$ = CHR$(27) + "[2J"
            PRINT CLEAR.SCREEN$
\            Input values using READ and DATA statements •
10          READ ACCT.NO%, NAME$, MONEY.OWED
\            Line 99 has trailer to end reading of data
1      IF MONEY.OWED < 0   THEN 99
\            Eliminate printing if no money is owed
2      IF MONEY.OWED = 0   THEN 10
            PRINT ACCT.NO%, NAME$, MONEY.OWED
            GOTO 10
            DATA 562, Able & Co.,    500.00
            DATA 113, Baker Corp.,   400.00
            DATA 416, Charles Inc.,  150.00
            DATA 126, Davis Co.,     200.00
            DATA 345, Evans Corp.,     0.00
            DATA 256, Francis Ltd.,  250.00
            DATA 492, Georgette,       0.00
3           DATA 999, Sign off,     -999.99
99          PRINT: PRINT "Normal termination of program"
            END
```

- *Line 1*   **IF MONEY.OWED < 0 THEN 99** is used to terminate the reading of data by using a *trailer*.
- *Line 2*   **IF MONEY.OWED = 0 THEN 10** instructs the computer to go back and read the next data line: no action is taken because the account does not owe any money.
- *Line 3*   **DATA 999, Sign off, −999.99** is the **trailer** with a negative amount owed so that statement 1 will cause a branch to line label 99 and terminate the program.

In business we generally do not use the READ-DATA form. It is more realistic to create a data file as we did at the end of Chapter 5 and read from it. If you have skipped that exercise, go back and create a file using Program 5-7 with data from problem 1 of Chapter 5. We will use it in several problems.

Program 6-2 prepares the same output, but instead of the READ-DATA statements, it reads the data from a file, CUSDATA.FIL.

PROGRAM 6-2   **IFTHEN2.BAS**   **[Non-Compiler]**

Use of IF-THEN statement; Data Read from CUSDATA.FIL File

Copyright 1985, Compulit, Inc.

```
\              Variables: ACCT.NO%, NAME$, MONEY.OWED, NOF$, REC.NO%
\              Defining CLEAR.SCREEN for PC-DOS and MS-DOS
       CLEAR.SCREEN$ = CHR$(27) + "[2J"
       REC.NO% = 1
       PRINT CLEAR.SCREEN$
       INPUT "Enter name of file..............."; NOF$
       OPEN "B:"+ NOF$ RECL 128 AS 1
       PRINT CLEAR.SCREEN$: PRINT: PRINT
       PRINT "Account Number"; TAB(25); "Name"; TAB(45);"Money Owed"
       PRINT
\              End reading of file
       IF END #1 THEN 20
10     REC.NO% = REC.NO% + 1
       READ #1,REC.NO%; ACCT.NO%, NAME$, MONEY.OWED
\              Skip accounts which do not owe money
       IF MONEY.OWED = 0  THEN 10
       PRINT ACCT.NO%; TAB(20); NAME$; TAB(47); MONEY.OWED
       GOTO 10
20     PRINT
       PRINT "Normal Termination of Program"
       CLOSE 1
       END
```

- The **IF END #1 THEN 20** statement is used to terminate the program by going to statement 20 after the end of the data file has been reached.
- The **IF MONEY.OWED = 0 THEN 10** statement returns the program to read the next record since no money is owed.

We use the variable COUNT% to increment the record number each time the program reads a new record. A more elegant method will be shown in the next chapter, which is devoted to looping.

Try entering this program and running it. Your output should appear as follows:

Account Number	Name	Money Owed
562	Able & Co.	500
113	Baker Corp.	400
416	Charles,Inc.	150
126	Davis Co.	200
256	Francis Ltd.	250

LANGUAGE CODING RULE

The IF-THEN-ELSE statement has a double alternative decision structure which appears as:

IF <expression> **THEN **
    <1st operation statement if true> :\
    [{ 2nd operation statement if true :\   }]
    <last operation statement if true> \   *Note 1*
**ELSE **
    <1st operation statement if false> :\
    [{ 2nd operation statement if false :\   }]
    <last operation statement if false>   *Note 2*

NOTE:

1. The last statement of the list following **THEN** and immediately before the **ELSE** does *not* include a colon; a backslash must be used.
2. The last statement of the list following **ELSE** does *not* end with any special control symbols.

The IF-THEN-ELSE Statement

The more complex version, the **IF-THEN-ELSE** statement, is used where *one of two sets of instructions* is followed depending on whether the condition is true or false.

- If the condition is *true*, then the statements associated with the THEN clause are executed.
- If the condition is not true, that is it is *false*, the statements associated with the ELSE clause are executed.

An Example Using the IF-THEN-ELSE Statement

Again using the customer file, *CUSDATA.FIL*, we illustrate this multiple statement in **Program 6-3**. In this problem, the company has decided to:

1. Charge 1% interest per month on all delinquent accounts of $250.00 or less.
2. Charge 1½% interest per month on any amount over $250.00 in addition to the 1% on the first $250.00.

PROGRAM 6-3   **IFTHEN3.BAS**   **[Non-Compiler]**

Use of IF-THEN-ELSE Statement; Data from CUSDATA.FIL File

Copyright 1985, Compulit, Inc.

```
\                Defining CLEAR.SCREEN for PC-DOS and MS-DOS
             CLEAR.SCREEN$ = CHR$(27) + "[2J"
\                Variables: ACCT.NO%, NAME$, MONEY.OWED, NOF$, REC.NO%
             REC.NO% = 1
             PRINT CLEAR.SCREEN$
             INPUT "Enter name of file..............."; NOF$
             OPEN "B:"+ NOF$ RECL 128 AS 1
             PRINT CLEAR.SCREEN$: PRINT: PRINT
\                Print column headings
             PRINT "Account Number"; TAB(25); "Name"; TAB(40); "Money Owed"; \
                 TAB(55); "Interest"; TAB(65); "New Total Owed"
             PRINT
             IF END #1 THEN 20
10           REC.NO% = REC.NO% + 1
             READ #1,REC.NO%; ACCT.NO%, NAME$, MONEY.OWED
\                Skip account if no money is owed
             IF MONEY.OWED = 0 THEN 10
\                Calculate interest and new amount owed if amount owed is
\                equal to or less than $250.00
             IF MONEY.OWED <= 250.00 THEN \
                 INTEREST = MONEY.OWED * 0.010 : \
                 NEW.TOTAL.OWED = MONEY.OWED + INTEREST \
\                Calculate interest and new amount owed if amount owed is
\                more than $250.00
             ELSE \
                 OVERAGE = MONEY.OWED - 250.00 : \
                 INTEREST = OVERAGE * 0.015 + 2.50 : \
                 NEW.TOTAL.OWED = MONEY.OWED + INTEREST
\                Print data for accounts which owe money
             PRINT ACCT.NO%; TAB(20); NAME$; TAB(42); MONEY.OWED ; \
                 TAB(58); INTEREST; TAB(70); NEW.TOTAL.OWED
             GOTO 10
20           PRINT
             PRINT "Normal Termination of Program"
             CLOSE 1
             END
```

Try this program and compare it with the following output.

Account	Name	Money Owed	Interest	New Total Owed
562	Able & Co.	500	6.25	506.25
113	Baker Corp.	400	4.75	404.75
416	Charles,Inc.	150	1.5	151.5
126	Davis Co.	200	2	202
256	Francis Ltd.	250	2.5	252.5

Normal Termination of Program

Grammar rules must be strictly followed in order to avoid syntax errors. It is good programming practice when using a multi-line format to indent the statements under IF-THEN, place the ELSE on a separate line, and indent the statements under ELSE as shown below:

```
IF MONEY.OWED <= 250.00 THEN \
        INTEREST = MONEY.OWED * 0.01 :\
        NEW.TOTAL.OWED = MONEY.OWED + INTEREST \
ELSE \
        OVERAGE = MONEY.OWED - 250.00 :\
        INTEREST = OVERAGE * 0.015 + 2.50 :\
        NEW.TOTAL.OWED = MONEY.OWED + INTEREST
```

SPECIAL PROGRAMMING NOTE

When you use **IF-THEN** or **IF-THEN-ELSE** you are using a *single* command statement.

- No line number or statement label may be used with any line in a statement list following either THEN or ELSE, although a statement label or line number may appear before the **IF**.
- It is not possible to branch into any portion of the statement; the program can only enter at the first line starting with **IF**.
- No statement may precede the IF statement on the *same* line.
- IF-THEN-ELSE statements may not be nested; that is, an IF may not follow a THEN before the ELSE clause is executed, when using either CBASIC or CBASIC/86. However, this is not a serious drawback since the program problem can often be restated using logical operators. Nested IF statements may be used with the compiler versions by using null or empty statements to force the proper grammar.

USING LOGICAL OPERATORS

In addition to the six relational operators already noted, there are four **logical operators** which may be used to form more complex IF statements. They are: **AND**, **OR**, **XOR**, and **NOT**. The following are examples of these operators:

IF PRICE GT 10.00	**AND**	COUNT% LE 15 **THEN**
IF PRICE EQ 25.00	**OR**	SALES GT 200.00 **THEN**
IF SUM $>= 99.0$	**XOR**	DATE$ = "APRIL 1983" **THEN**
IF FLAG% $<> 3$	**AND NOT**	HOURS > 40 **THEN**

Each logical operator statement, *except* the **NOT** operator, consists of at least five parts:

1. **IF**
2. <relational expression(1)>   PRICE GT 10.00
3. <logical operator>   **AND**, **OR**, **XOR**
4. <relational expression(2)>   COUNT% LE 15
5. **THEN**
6. If the logical operator statement is a double alternative conditional branch, it also includes **ELSE**.

The logical operators will be illustrated individually in problems and programs that follow. Each will use the data from problem 2 of Chapter 5. The data in that file is:

PART NO.	ITEM DESCRIPTION	IN STOCK	REORDER LEVEL	PRICE
152	Quarter-inch drill: MT13	21	24	9
154	Saber saw: MT67	23	12	9
200	Sander: GR-9	12	12	12
203	Half-inch drill: GH-34	14	12	13
207	Six-inch saw: GE-60	8	12	13
901	6-foot ladder: D2	28	24	11
904	Belt sander: H3a	16	24	11
913	Drop cloth 8×12 G3	48	24	4
927	Paint roller set: G23	45	48	4
950	Gutter guard: W14	48	48	2

All items in the data file with numbers below 900 are standard merchandise; those with numbers above 900 are promotional products. In order to clarify the use of logical operators we have classified the product list by inventory/reorder level relationship and price, as shown in **Table 6-2**.

TABLE 6-2   Product List Classified by Inventory/Reorder Level and Price

	PRICE BELOW $10.00	PRICE ABOVE $10.00
In-stock level below Reorder level	152 Quarter-in drill 929 Paint roller set	207 Six-inch saw 904 Belt sander
In-stock level = Reorder level	950 Gutter guard	200 Sander
In-stock level greater than Reorder level	154 Saber saw 913 Drop cloth	203 Half-inch drill 901 6-foot ladder

Using the Logical AND Operator

When we wish to take some action when two or more conditions are true we use the **AND** operator. **Table 6-3**, "The Logical **AND** Operator," illustrates the path the program will take using the **AND** for two conditions.

TABLE 6-3   The Logical AND Operator

RELATIONAL EXPRESSION(1)	RELATIONAL EXPRESSION(2)	PROGRAM GOES TO . . . . THEN	ELSE
True	True	X	
True	False		X
False	True		X
False	False		X

In logical IF statements, the computer evaluates each relational expression to determine whether it is *true* or *false*.

- If we use either the single alternative, **IF-THEN**, or the double alternative, **IF-THEN-ELSE**, the program will go to **THEN** *if and only if both relational expressions are true*.
- If the result of evaluating either of the relational expressions is false, or if they are both false, the program:

  + skips to the first executable statement following the THEN clause if we use the single alternative, IF-THEN; *or*
  + executes the ELSE clause before continuing execution when a double alternative statement is used.

Using the data of the product file we wish to obtain a printout of those products for which: (a) the number of items in stock is greater than the reorder level *and* (b) the price is equal to or greater than $10.00. The logical conditional statement would read:

```
IF IN.STOCK GT REORDER.LEVEL  AND \
    PRICE GE 10.00 THEN \
```

To see how this works, try the following, **Program 6-4**:

PROGRAM 6-4   **IFTHEN4.BAS**   **[Compiler]**

Use of Logical AND Operator in IF Statement; Data from INVDATA.FIL

Copyright 1984, 1985, Compulit, Inc.

```
\             Declare variables
      STRING  CLEAR.SCREEN, NOF, DESC
      REAL    PRICE
      INTEGER ITEM.NO, COUNTER, IN.STOCK, REORDER.LEVEL
\             Define CLEAR.SCREEN for PC-DOS and MS-DOS version 2.0
      CLEAR.SCREEN = CHR$(27) + "[2J"
      COUNTER = 1
      PRINT CLEAR.SCREEN
      INPUT "Enter name of file..............."; NOF
      OPEN "B:"+ NOF RECL 128 AS 1
      PRINT CLEAR.SCREEN
      IF END #1 THEN 20
10    COUNTER = COUNTER + 1
      READ #1,COUNTER; ITEM.NO, DESC, IN.STOCK, REORDER.LEVEL, PRICE
\             Use of logical AND operator with relational operators
      IF IN.STOCK GT REORDER.LEVEL AND \
         PRICE GE 10.00 THEN \
      PRINT ITEM.NO; TAB(8); DESC; TAB(35); IN.STOCK ; \
            TAB(43); REORDER.LEVEL; TAB(52); PRICE
      GOTO 10
20    PRINT
      PRINT "Normal Termination of Program"
      CLOSE 1
      END
```

The output of the program should appear as:

```
203  Half-inch drill: GH-34      14      12      13
901  6-foot ladder: D2           28      24      11

Normal Termination of Program
```

A review of the product data in *Table 6-2* indicates that there are only two items which meet *both* conditions: (1) being overstocked *and* (2) priced above $10.00.

Using the Logical OR Operator

The **OR** operator will cause the program to execute the **THEN** portion of the IF statement when **either** *relational expression is true* or **both** *relational expressions are true*. Only when both relational expressions are *false* will the program proceed to the **ELSE** or the next executable statement. **Table 6-4**, "The Logical **OR** Operator," illustrates the path the program will take when the OR operator is used.

TABLE 6-4   The Logical OR Operator

RELATIONAL EXPRESSION(1)	RELATIONAL EXPRESSION(2)	PROGRAM GOES TO . . . . THEN	ELSE
True	True	X	
True	False	X	
False	True	X	
False	False		X

In this problem we wish to obtain a listing of all products for which:

Either the quantity on hand is equal to or greater than the reorder level, *Or* the item is priced at $10.00 or more.

Replace the two IF lines in Program 6-4 that contain the AND clause with the following two lines and compile and execute the new program.

```
IF IN.STOCK GE REORDER.LEVEL   OR \
    PRICE GE 10.00 THEN \
```

Check the output of your new program containing the OR operator with the following:

```
154   Saber saw: MT67              23    12     9
200   Sander: GR-9                 12    12    12
203   Half-inch drill: GH-34       14    12    13
207   Six-inch saw: GE-60           8    12    13
901   6-foot ladder: D2            28    24    11
904   Belt sander: H3a             16    24    11
913   Drop cloth 8 X 12 G3         48    24     4
950   Gutter guard: W14            48    48     2

Normal Termination of Program
```

The only products not included in this list are those for which the number of items on hand is less than the reorder level *and* which are priced at less than $10.00.

Using the Logical XOR Statement

With this more complex logical operator the program will branch to the:

THEN clause if only **one** of the relational expressions is *true*, or **ELSE** clause if **both** of the expressions are true or if **both** are false.

Table 6-5, "The Logical **XOR** Operator," illustrates the path the program will take when using the **XOR** operator.

TABLE 6-5   The Logical XOR Operator

RELATIONAL EXPRESSION(1)	RELATIONAL EXPRESSION(2)	PROGRAM GOES TO . . . . THEN	ELSE
True	True		X
True	False	X	
False	True	X	
False	False		X

In this example we are interested in determining which items to include in a special sale. In the numbering system used, all items numbered 900 or higher are promotional items which we include frequently in our adds. Using the XOR operator we can obtain a printout of:

All standard items that are overstocked.

All promotional items for which the quantity on hand is less than the reorder level and which we plan to discontinue.

Again we can use Program 6-4 and in place of the two IF lines we substitute the following:

```
IF IN.STOCK GE REORDER.LEVEL   XOR \
   ITEM.NO  GT 900 THEN \
```

If you run this program you will obtain the following output:

```
154   Saber saw: MT67              23    12     9
200   Sander: GR-9                 12    12    12
203   Half-inch drill: GH-34       14    12    13
904   Belt sander: H3a             16    24    11
927   Paint roller set: G23        45    48     4

Normal Termination of Program
```

We now have a list of all standard products where the quantity on hand is equal to or greater than the reorder level and promotional items where the inventory is low.

Using the Logical NOT Operator

This is the only logical operator which may appear next to another logical operator in the IF statement. It can be *excluded* from your programming since the same results can be obtained by writing the IF statement in a different form. It is often used as a direct translation of a condition expressed in English.

For example, a printout of items that are overstocked and *not* priced under $10.00 can be obtained by using the statement:

```
IF  IN.STOCK  GE  REORDER.LEVEL   AND  NOT  \
        PRICE  LT  10.00  THEN  \
```

The same results could be obtained by rewording the IF statement to include items that are overstocked and are priced at or *over* $10.00 as shown below:

```
IF  IN.STOCK  GE  REORDER.LEVEL   AND  \
        PRICE  GE  10.00  THEN  \
```

Use Program 6-4 again but this time first substitute the AND NOT statements, then the AND statement, and compare the results. In both cases you should obtain the same output.

```
200   Sander: GR-9                    12      12      12
203   Half-inch drill: GH-34          14      12      13
901   6-foot ladder: D2               28      24      11
```

There are only three items in the data file for which the quantity on hand is equal to or greater than the reorder level and which are *not* priced below $10.00.

LANGUAGE CODING RULE

The structure of the logical IF statement using **AND**, **OR**, and **XOR**:

IF <1st relational expression><Logical Operator><2nd relational expression>**THEN **

<statement> *or* <line number> *or* <statement> [: {statement}]

NOTE: The same grammar rules apply as for the double alternative decision structure noted earlier in the rule for IF-THEN-ELSE if there are multiple statements after THEN and/or multiple statements after **ELSE**.

Using Multiple Logical Operators

Several logical operators may be used within a single IF statement. In Program 6-4 earlier in this section we obtained a printout of products for which the number of items in stock is greater than the reorder level *and* the price of the item is equal to or greater than $10.00. If, in addition, the list is to include only the promotional items, those with numbers 900 or higher, we would write the statement as:

```
IF IN.STOCK GT REORDER.LEVEL  AND \
    PRICE GE 10.00   AND \
    ITEM.NO GE 900   THEN \
```

Additional illustrations of both the relational and logical IF statements will be found in succeeding chapters, particularly in sort and merge techniques, the design of input screens and the design of data output.

BUSINESS PROBLEMS USING IF STATEMENTS

Two programs are included to illustrate business situations in which more advanced versions of relational and logical operators are used.

The first is a modification of Program 6-3 in which we computed interest charges for some accounts at 1% and for other accounts at 1½%. In addition to the printout providing a listing of all the accounts, the money originally owed, the interest and the new balance, we can also compute:

- The total number of accounts paying 1% interest and the total amount of money they owe
- The total number of accounts paying 1½% interest and the total amount of money they owe
- The grand total outstanding

Before you look at the solution, **Program 6-5**, try to write it on your own. Remember, the best way to learn how to program is by writing programs.

PROGRAM 6-5   **IFTHEN5.BAS**   **[Compiler]**

Use of Logical OR Operator in IF Statement; Data from CUSDATA.FIL

Copyright 1985, Compulit, Inc.

```
\             Declaration of variables
    INTEGER  ACCT.NO, COUNTER, TALLY1, TALLY2
    STRING   CLEAR.SCREEN, NAME, NOF
    REAL     INTEREST, MONEY.OWED, NEW.TOTAL.OWED, OUTSTANDING
    REAL     OUTSTANDING1, OUTSTANDING2, OVERAGE
\             Defining CLEAR.SCREEN for PC-DOS and MS-DOS
    CLEAR.SCREEN = CHR$(27) + "[2J"
\             Initialization of varaibles
```

(continues)

```
         COUNTER = 1:   TALLY1 = 0:    TALLY2 = 0
         OUTSTANDING = 0:  OUSTANDING1 = 0:  OUTSTANDING2 = 0
         PRINT CLEAR.SCREEN
         INPUT "Enter name of file..............."; NOF
         OPEN "B:"+ NOF RECL 128 AS 1
         PRINT CLEAR.SCREEN
\               Print column headings
         PRINT "Account Number"; TAB(25);"Name"; TAB(40);"Money Owed"; \
             TAB(55);"Interest"; TAB(65);"New Total Owed"
         PRINT
         IF END #1 THEN 20
10       COUNTER = COUNTER + 1
         READ #1,COUNTER; ACCT.NO, NAME, MONEY.OWED
\               Determine if money is owed
         IF MONEY.OWED = 0 THEN \
             PRINT ACCT.NO, TAB(20);NAME; TAB(42);MONEY.OWED: GOTO 10
\               Compute interest and accumulate new amount owed when
\               money owed is less than or equal to $250.00
         IF MONEY.OWED <= 250.00 THEN \
             INTEREST = MONEY.OWED * 0.01 : \
             NEW.TOTAL.OWED = MONEY.OWED + INTEREST : \
             TALLY1 = TALLY1 + 1 : \
             OUTSTANDING1 = OUTSTANDING1 + NEW.TOTAL.OWED \
\               Compute interest and accumulate new amount owed when
\               money owed is more than $250.00
         ELSE \
             OVERAGE = MONEY.OWED - 250.00 : \
             INTEREST = OVERAGE * 0.015 + 2.50 : \
             NEW.TOTAL.OWED = MONEY.OWED + INTEREST : \
             TALLY2 = TALLEY2% + 1 : \
             OUTSTANDING2 = OUTSTANDING2 + NEW.TOTAL.OWED \
             PRINT ACCT.NO; TAB(20); NAME; TAB(42); MONEY.OWED ; \
                 TAB(58); INTEREST; TAB(70); NEW.TOTAL.OWED
         GOTO 10
20       CLOSE 1:   PRINT:    PRINT
\               Print final summary data
         PRINT "1%   Interest:  "; TALLY1; "Customer(s) owe "; OUTSTANDING1
         PRINT "1.5% Interest:  "; TALLY2; "Customer(s) owe "; OUTSTANDING2
         OUTSTANDING = OUTSTANDING1 + OUTSTANDING2
         PRINT " Total owed                      "; OUTSTANDING
         PRINT: PRINT
         PRINT "Normal Termination of Program"
         END
```

The output for the preceding program is:

```
Account      Name         Money Owed    Interest     New Total Owed


  562      Able & Co.        500          6.25          506.25

  113      Baker Corp.       400          4.75          404.75

  416      Charles,Inc.      150          1.5           151.5

  126      Davis Co.         200          2             202

  345      Evans Corp.        0

  256      Francis Ltd.      250          2.5           252.5

  492      Georgette          0


  1%    Interest: 3 Customer(s) owe    606

  1.5% Interest: 2 Customer(s) owe    911

        Total owed                   1517


Normal Termination of Program
```

The second program, **Program 6-6**, shows the use of a multiple series of
logical IF statements to illustrate a more complex problem faced by a

business concern. In this illustration, the firm decided to increase the interest charged on outstanding accounts but because of existing agreements with old customers, the new rate would apply only to newer customers.

In this program, old customers [those with account numbers below 300] would pay:

- no charges if the amount owed was $250.00 or less
- only 1% on any amount over $250.00

New customers [those with account numbers 300 or greater] would now have to pay:

- 1% on amounts of $250.00 or less
- 1% on the first $250.00 and 1.5% on any amounts in excess of $250.00

PROGRAM 6-6   **IFTHEN6.BAS**   **[Compiler]**

Use of Multiple IF-THEN Statements; Data from CUSDATA.FIL File

Copyright 1985, Compulit, Inc.

```
\               Declaration of variables
        INTEGER ACCT.NO, COUNTER
        REAL    INTEREST, MONEY.OWED, NEW.TOTAL.OWED
        STRING  NAME, NOF, CLEAR.SCREEN
\               Defining CLEAR.SCREEN for PC-DOS and MS-DOS
        CLEAR.SCREEN = CHR$(27) + "[2J"
        COUNTER = 1
        PRINT CLEAR.SCREEN
        INPUT "Enter name of file..............."; NOF
        OPEN "B:"+ NOF RECL 128 AS 1
        PRINT CLEAR.SCREEN
\               Print column headings
        PRINT "Account Number"; TAB(25);"Name"; TAB(40);"Money Owed"; \
            TAB(55);"Interest"; TAB(65);"New Total Owed"
        PRINT
\               IF statement to end file processing
        IF END #1 THEN 20
\               Start reading with second record
10      COUNTER = COUNTER + 1
        READ #1,COUNTER; ACCT.NO, NAME, MONEY.OWED
\               Separate accounts if no money is owed
        IF MONEY.OWED = 0 THEN \
            PRINT ACCT.NO; TAB(20);NAME; TAB(42);"    0": GOTO 10
\               Separate old and new accounts
        IF ACCT.NO > 300 THEN 15
\               Calculate interest on old accounts by amount owed
        IF MONEY.OWED <= 250 THEN\
            INTEREST = 0\
        ELSE\
            INTEREST = (MONEY.OWED - 250) * .01
        GOTO 18
\               Calculate interest on new accounts by amount owed
15      IF MONEY.OWED <= 250 THEN\
            INTEREST = MONEY.OWED * .01\
        ELSE\
            INTEREST = (MONEY.OWED - 250) * .015 + 2.50
18      NEW.TOTAL.OWED = MONEY.OWED + INTEREST
        PRINT ACCT.NO; TAB(20); NAME; TAB(42); MONEY.OWED ; \
            TAB(58); INTEREST; TAB(70); NEW.TOTAL.OWED
        GOTO 10
20      CLOSE 1:  PRINT:   PRINT
        PRINT "Normal Termination of Program"
        END
```

If you run this program you should obtain the following output:

Account	Name	Money Owed	Interest	New Total Owed
562	Able & Co.	500	6.25	506.25
113	Baker Corp.	400	1.5	401.5
416	Charles,Inc.	150	1.5	151.5
126	Davis Co.	200	0	200
345	Evans Corp.	0		
256	Francis Ltd.	250	0	250
492	Georgette	0		

```
Normal Termination of Program
```

BRANCHING ON THE SIGN OF A VALUE: THE SGN FUNCTION

Another way of branching in a program is by using the built-in function, **SGN**. This function returns a single numeric value representing the sign of a numeric constant, variable or expression. For example, for the variable X:

- -1 will be returned if X is negative
- 0 will be returned if X is zero
- $+1$ will be returned if X is positive

This branching technique can be used in two different ways. First in its simpler form, it can be used in combination with or within an IF statement as illustrated by the following:

```
TRUE% = SGN(BALANCE)
IF TRUE% = 0 OR TRUE% = 1 THEN 562
```

The program would first determine the sign of BALANCE, setting the value of TRUE% to −1 if the balance is negative, 0 if balance equals zero, and +1 if the balance is positive. Then the IF statement would transfer control of the program to statement label 562 if the balance is zero or positive, and continue sequential execution if BALANCE is negative.

```
IF SGN(BALANCE) = -1 THEN 50
```

would cause the program to branch to label 50 if balance is negative.

```
IF SGN(ON.HAND - REORDER.LEVEL) = 1 THEN 76
```

would direct the program to label 76 for all items for which the number of units on hand is greater than the reorder level. If the number of items on hand is equal to or less than the reorder level, the program would continue with the next statement.

LANGUAGE CODING RULE

The SGN function may be used in two ways:

<integer variable> = **SGN**(<constant> *or* <variable> *or* <arithmetic expression>)

or

IF SGN(<variable> *or* <arithmetic expression>**) THEN** <statement label>

GOSUB may be used with the statement label, as shown:

IF SGN(<arithmetic variable> = <-1, 0, *or* 1> **THEN GOSUB** <statement label>)

A Three-Way Branch

The second way to use the SGN function, and often more effective, is the three-way branch. Remember the results of the SGN function are -1, 0, and $+1$, and we can convert these to positive values by adding 2 so that the results would be:

$$-1 + 2 = 1 \qquad \text{if the value tested is negative}$$
$$0 + 2 = 2 \qquad \text{if the result is zero}$$
$$+1 + 2 = 3 \qquad \text{if the value is positive}$$

By using this modification, we can direct the program to any of three branches with the following statement:

```
ON SGN(BALANCE) + 2   GOTO 100, 200, 300
```

so that the program would branch to statement label 100 if the balance is negative, to label 200 if balance is zero, and to label 300 if the balance is positive. The structure of the ON-GOTO statement is explained next.

MULTIPLE BRANCHING: THE ON-GOTO STATEMENT

Earlier we noted that the IF statement permitted branching to one or two paths and the SGN function could be used to branch to two or three paths.

The **ON-GOTO** statement permits branching to as many statement labels as we wish. One example was just shown when using the SGN function, where three branches were used.

Another example is based on classifying the products used earlier in this chapter, Table 6-2, by including a lead code with the data that:

- Identifies standard merchandise priced below $10.00
- Identifies standard merchandise priced at $10.00 or more
- Identifies promotional items priced below $10.00
- Identifies promotional items priced at $10.00 or more

```
ON LEAD.CODE% GOTO 50, 80, 120, 170
```

would result in the program branching to one of four locations depending on the variable, LEAD.CODE%.

There is a matching between the variable, LEAD.CODE% in this case, with each of the labels after the GOTO:

VALUE OF LEAD.CODE%	SENDS PROGRAM TO ASSOCIATED LABEL
1	50
2	80
3	120
4	170

All items in category 1 are processed starting at statement label 50, those in 2 at label 80, items in 3 at label 120, and items in 4 at label 170.

If the value of the variable is zero or greater than the number of labels after GOTO, a run-time error will occur. There is no restriction on the labels which may be associated with any value of the variable. For example, in the earlier illustration under the SGN function with a three-way branch:

```
ON SGN(BALANCE) + 2  GOTO 100, 200, 300
```

In this case, the labels associated with the expression, SGN(BALANCE) + 2 are:

VALUE OF SGN(BALANCE) + 2	SENDS PROGRAM TO ASSOCIATED LABEL
1	100
2	200
3	300

We might decide to take the *same* action if the balance is zero or positive. We would write this statement as:

```
ON SGN(BALANCE) + 2  GOTO 100, 200, 200
```

LANGUAGE CODING RULE

The ON statement transfers the execution of the program to one of several statement numbers or labels. There are two forms.

ON <numeric expression> **GOTO** <statement label> {,<statement label>}

or

ON <numeric expression> **GOSUB** <statement label> {,<statement label>}

- The numeric expression determines the branch to which program execution is transferred. A string expression will cause an error.
- Execution speed is greater if the numeric expression is in integer form.
- If the numeric expression is evaluated at less than one or greater than the number of labels, a run-time error will occur in the non-compiler versions. In compiler versions, the results are unpredictable.
- There is no limit to the number of labels allowed in the statement.

Joining Programs with a Menu

The **ON-GOTO** statement is an integral part of any program which includes discrete sets of operations, such as the joining of three of the programs presented in Chapter 5. There are three programs for a relative file:

- Program 5-4 to create the file
- Program 5-5 to add to an existing file
- Program 5-6 to display the disk file on the screen

We can combine all three programs into one and select any one part by using the ON-GOTO statement.

The construction of this program is segmented in order to illustrate various programming techniques. There are six segments.

1. Initialization takes care of the basic housekeeping requirements.
2. Menu provides the user with a choice of options.
3. Create portion is used to start a new file.
4. Open section permits the opening and adding to an existing file.
5. Print section displays the disk file on the screen.
6. Close terminates the program and returns the user to the system.

Segments 1 and 2 will be left until later because they are new material. Instead we will start with segment 3.

Segment 3: Creating a New File

Segment 3 is a modification of Program 5-4 that was used to create a new data file.

```
\                    Routine to CREATE a file
100      PRINT CLEAR.SCREEN$
         CREATE "B:"+ NOF$ RECL 50 AS 1
         INDEX% = 1
150      PRINT CLEAR.SCREEN$
\                Start data records in record number 2
         INDEX% = INDEX% + 1
         INPUT "Enter product number.......... "; PROD.NO$  : PRINT
         INPUT "Enter product description...... "; PROD.DESC$: PRINT
         INPUT "Enter number of units on hand.. "; ON.HAND%  : PRINT
         INPUT "Enter product cost ............ "; PROD.COST : PRINT
\              Print data to file and INDEX in record number 1
         PRINT #1,INDEX%; PROD.NO$, PROD.DESC$, ON.HAND%, PROD.COST
         PRINT #1,1; INDEX%
         INPUT "Another entry?........(Y/N).... "; AN$
         IF UCASE$(AN$) = "Y" THEN 150
\              Close file before return to MENU
         CLOSE 1
         GOTO 26
```

After PRINT CLEAR.SCREEN$ we have used all the program from the original CREATE statement to the conclusion of the program, but left out the END statement. We have introduced labels 100 and 150 which are needed later by other segments of the program.

Segment 4: Adding to an Existing File

Only part of Program 5-5, which was used to add to an existing file, is used as segment 4; it has been modified by leaving out the input portion of the original program. Once the file has been opened, the procedure to add new data is the same as that used when the file was created. Therefore, instead of including unnecessary duplicated statements, we transfer control of the program with the last statement to label 150, which is in the preceding segment.

```
\                    Routine to ADD TO the file
200      PRINT CLEAR.SCREEN$
\              Branch to error routine if file name does not exist
         IF END #1 THEN 390
         OPEN "B:"+ NOF$ RECL 50 AS 1
         READ #1,1; INDEX%
\              Use same code for data entry as in CREATE routine
         GOTO 150
```

There is one additional modification, the second line, which protects the user of the program if an attempt is made to open a non-existent file. The user is informed of the mistake and is given the chance to correct the error without having the program terminate with an error message on the screen. The following statements perform this function:

```
\                   Error routine for incorrect file name
390     PRINT "File by that name does NOT exist.":  PRINT
        INPUT "Press any letter to continue."; KEY$
        GOTO 26
```

[See Special Programming Note on page 23 for an explanation of how to keep copy on the screen; also see page 250]

Segment 5: Displaying the File's Contents

Most of the original Program 5-6 is used to display the output of the file. In each of the two segments so far we have closed the file prior to any transfer to another segment of the program.

```
\                   Routine to DISPLAY the file
300     PRINT CLEAR.SCREEN$
\                   Print column headings
        PRINT "Product #", "Description", "Units on Hand", "Cost": PRINT
        IF END #1 THEN 390
        OPEN "B:"+ NOF$ RECL 50 AS 1
        K% = 2
\                   Read record number K%
350     READ #1,K%; PROD.NO$, PROD.DESC$, ON.HAND%, PROD.COST
\                   Terminate file reading
        IF END #1 THEN 380
\                   Display record number K%
        PRINT PROD.NO$, PROD.DESC$, ON.HAND%, PROD.COST
        K% = K% + 1
        GOTO 350
380     PRINT: PRINT: PRINT
\                   Hold display on screen
        INPUT "Press any letter and RETURN to continue."; KEY$
\                   Close file before return to MENU
        CLOSE 1
        GOTO 26
```

Segment 6: Termination of the Program

The last segment of the program is good programming practice so that the user knows the program is finished completely without a hang-up.

```
400     PRINT CLEAR.SCREEN$
        PRINT "Program terminated."
        END
```

All the preceding segments were based on programs which had been used before. The initialization of variables and the MENU are now added.

Segment 1: Initialization of the Program

This program does not require much initialization. Aside from the REM statements, only defining the clear screen command, CLEAR.SCREEN$, which is machine dependent, is included.

```
\                     Defining CLEAR.SCREEN for PC-DOS and MS-DOS
            CLEAR.SCREEN$ = CHR$(27) + "[2J"
   26       PRINT CLEAR.SCREEN$:   PRINT:   PRINT
```

Segment 2: The Menu and Control of the Program

A critical part of the entire program is contained in this section. A menu is created to permit the user to select any of the three procedures. There are several human-factor programming techniques used.

- A means of exiting from the program is included as the first choice in the menu.
- A warning message about creating a new file with the same name as an existing file is printed on the screen.
- After the user has indicated a choice, the statement immediately following the input of that choice, MC%, verifies whether the choice is within the limits set by the program, that is, if the value entered is between 1 and 4. If the value is outside these limits, the program automatically clears the screen and reprints the menu.

```
\                   Display MENU
            PRINT "What do you want to do?":          PRINT
            PRINT "  [1]  Exit from program":         PRINT
            PRINT "  [2]  Create a NEW file":         PRINT
            PRINT "  [3]  Add to an existing file":   PRINT
            PRINT "  [4]  Print a file.":             PRINT
\                   Warning to prevent destruction of an existing file
            PRINT:   PRINT:  PRINT "NOTE:"
            PRINT "* Warning: If you create a new file and a file by that name
exists,               you will destroy the existing file.":   PRINT:   PRINT
\                   Choice of routine
            INPUT "  Enter the appropriate number:   "; MC%
\                   Return to MENU if choice is out of bounds
            IF MC% < 1 OR MC% > 4 THEN 26
\                   Skip file name entry if choice is program termination
            IF MC% = 1 THEN 50
            PRINT CLEAR.SCREEN$
            INPUT "Enter name of file........";NOF$
\                   Branch to chosen routine
   50       ON MC% GOTO 400, 100, 200, 300
```

The ON-GOTO statement directs the transfer of control based on the value entered for MC%. If MC% = 1 the program transfers to label 400; if MC% = 2 the transfer is to label 100. With MC% equal to 3 or 4, program control is transferred to labels 200 and 300, respectively.

The first IF statement after the entry of MC% verifies that the user entered a value between 1 and 4. The second IF statement permits skipping the entry of the filename since the program is being terminated. The extra spacing in the warning line was included so that the copy is aligned when displayed on the screen.

The Complete Program

Joining the six segments produces a single program, **Program 6-7**, which could be used as a prototype for creating, adding to, or displaying any random file.

PROGRAM 6-7   MENUPRO.BAS   [Non-Compiler]

Create, Add to, or Display a Relative File

Copyright 1985, Compulit, Inc.

```
\                Defining CLEAR.SCREEN for PC-DOS and MS-DOS
          CLEAR.SCREEN$ = CHR$(27) + "[2J"
26        PRINT CLEAR.SCREEN$:    PRINT:    PRINT
\                Display MENU
          PRINT "What do you want to do?":            PRINT
          PRINT " [1]  Exit from program":            PRINT
          PRINT " [2]  Create a NEW file":            PRINT
          PRINT " [3]  Add to an existing file":      PRINT
          PRINT " [4]  Print a file.":                PRINT
\                Warning to prevent destruction of an existing file
          PRINT:    PRINT:   PRINT "NOTE:"
          PRINT "* Warning: If you create a new file and a file by that name
exists,           you will destroy the existing file.":  PRINT:    PRINT
\                Choice of routine
          INPUT "  Enter the appropriate number:  "; MC%
\                Return to MENU if choice is out of bounds
          IF MC% < 1 OR MC% > 4 THEN 26
\                Skip file name entry if choice is program termination
          IF MC% = 1 THEN 50
          PRINT CLEAR.SCREEN$
          INPUT "Enter name of file........."; NOF$
\                Branch to chosen routine
50        ON MC% GOTO 400, 100, 200, 300
\                Routine to CREATE a file
100       PRINT CLEAR.SCREEN$
          CREATE "B:"+ NOF$ RECL 50 AS 1
          INDEX% = 1
150       PRINT CLEAR.SCREEN$
\                Start data records in record number 2
          INDEX% = INDEX% + 1
          INPUT "Enter product number.......... "; PROD.NO$  : PRINT
          INPUT "Enter product description...... "; PROD.DESC$: PRINT
          INPUT "Enter number of units on hand.. "; ON.HAND%  : PRINT
          INPUT "Enter product cost ............ "; PROD.COST : PRINT
\                Print data to file and INDEX in record number 1
          PRINT #1,INDEX%; PROD.NO$, PROD.DESC$, ON.HAND%, PROD.COST
          PRINT #1,1; INDEX%
          INPUT "Another entry?........(Y/N).... "; AN$
          IF UCASE$(AN$) = "Y" THEN 150
\                Close file before return to MENU
          CLOSE 1
          GOTO 26
\                Routine to ADD TO the file
200       PRINT CLEAR.SCREEN$
\                Branch to error routine if file name does not exist
          IF END #1 THEN 390
          OPEN "B:"+ NOF$ RECL 50 AS 1
          READ #1,1; INDEX%
\                Use same code for data entry as in CREATE routine
          GOTO 150
\                Routine to DISPLAY the file
300       PRINT CLEAR.SCREEN$
\                Print column headings
          PRINT "Product #", "Description", "Units on Hand", "Cost": PRINT

          IF END #1 THEN 390
          OPEN "B:"+ NOF$ RECL 50 AS 1
          K% = 2
\                Read record number K%
350       READ #1,K%; PROD.NO$, PROD.DESC$, ON.HAND%, PROD.COST
\                Terminate file reading
          IF END #1 THEN 380
\                Display record number K%
          PRINT PROD.NO$, PROD.DESC$, ON.HAND%, PROD.COST
          K% = K% + 1
          GOTO 350
```

(continues)

```
380       PRINT: PRINT: PRINT
\                   Hold display on screen
          INPUT "Press any letter and RETURN to continue."; KEY$
\                   Close file before return to MENU
          CLOSE 1
          GOTO 26
\                   Error routine for incorrect file name
390       PRINT "File by that name does NOT exist.":   PRINT
          INPUT "Press any letter to continue."; KEY$
          GOTO 26
400       PRINT CLEAR.SCREEN$
          PRINT "Program terminated."
          END
```

CHAPTER 7

Program Logic Control:
Repetitive Operations

In many business and technical programs we encounter a set of statements that have to be executed repeatedly, a process commonly called **looping**. We have encountered looping in several programs used earlier in this book by combining the IF statement with a GOTO statement. We noted that this was an elementary way of executing a repetitive action. A more powerful, computer-efficient, and useful set of statements is available, namely:

- **FOR-NEXT**, which is usually used when the number of repetitions is known before the execution of the statements is begun, and
- **WHILE-WEND**, which is generally used when the number of repetitions is not known.

REPETITIVE ACTION—THE FOR-NEXT STATEMENTS

The **FOR-NEXT** statements are used for both processing and counting. The FOR statement precedes the instruction or set of instructions to be repeated, and the NEXT statement appears after the final statement in that set as shown in **Figure 7-1**. Technically the FOR and NEXT are two statements but they must always be used together.

The Structure of the FOR-NEXT Statements

We used the FOR-NEXT statements [lines 9 through 11] in Program 1-1 in which we computed interest at a given rate for a specific number of compounding periods per year.

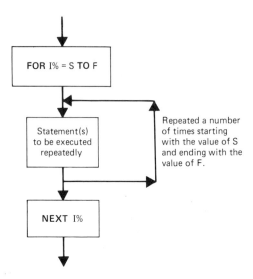

FIGURE 7-1   FOR-NEXT Flowchart

```
FOR K% = 1 TO PERIODS%
          AMOUNT = AMOUNT + AMOUNT * PERIOD.RATE
NEXT
```

There are six key elements in the FOR statement:

- The statement begins with **FOR**.
- The K% is the *Index* for the loop and is used by the computer to count the number of times the statements enclosed in the loop are executed.
- The equal sign, =, is part of the necessary grammar.
- The 1 is the *initial value* of K% when it starts the loop.
- **TO** is also part of the grammar.
- PERIODS% is the *final value* of the loop index.

Samples of a Simple Loop

Before we explore specific business applications of FOR-NEXT statements, let's try a few simple programs

The first program, **Program 7-1**, calculates the sum of the first 100 integers.

PROGRAM 7-1   **LOOP.BAS**   **[Non-Compiler]**

Simple FOR-NEXT Loop; Sum of Integers between 1 and 100

Copyright 1984, 1985, Compulit, Inc.

```
\          SUM% = 0
           FOR I% = 1 TO 100
                  SUM% = SUM% + I%
           NEXT
           PRINT "Sum ="; SUM%
           END
```

To understand how the loop process works, let us follow the sequence of computer operations for several of the iterations using the FOR-NEXT loop, remembering that we initialized SUM% as zero.

```
Line 1:                    FOR I% = 1 TO 100
Line 2:                        SUM% = SUM% + I%
Line 3:                    NEXT
```

To do this we look at storage areas within the computer that are set aside for I% and SUM%.

	Value in Storage	
	I%	SUM%
1. When the computer comes to line 1, it sets the value of I% to 1.	1	0
2. At line 2, it adds the value of I% [1] to the value stored in SUM% [0].	1	1
3. At line 3, 1% is increased to 2 and the program loops back to line 1 where the computer checks to see if the value of I% has not exceeded the upper limit, 100.	2	1
4. Since I% is less than 100, the program continues to line 2 and adds the value of I% [2] to that of SUM% [1] and stores the new total in SUM%.	2	3
5. Again at line 3, I% is increased and the program returns to line 1.	3	3
6. Since I% is less than 100, the program goes to line 2 and adds the value of I%[3] to SUM%[3] and stores the new total.	3	6

The above procedure is repeated until the value of I% *exceeds* 100 so that during the last loop, we would have:

	Value in Storage	
	I%	SUM%
1. At line 1 the value of I% would be 100 and SUM% would be 4950.	100	4950
2. At line 2, I% is added to SUM% and stored.	100	5050
3. I% is incremented by one at line 3 and returns to line 1. Since I% is now greater than 100, control of the program proceeds to the line after NEXT.	101	5050

SPECIAL PROGRAMMING NOTE

When we have the same variable on both sides of an equal sign in an arithmetic statement, such as SUM% = SUM% + I%, it is recommended that the variable be initialized, as in SUM% = 0, at the beginning of the program. In this way, if we return to accumulate another sum, the value stored for SUM% is replaced by zero.

Try entering and executing the program. The line *Sum = 5050* should appear on the CRT as output.

The second program, **Program 7-2**, is similar to the first, except that we want to obtain the sum of all the *odd* values between 1 and 100. To do this we use the **STEP** portion of the FOR-NEXT statement. In programming form this appears as:

```
FOR I% = 1 TO 100 STEP 2
```

However, STEP and the value following it are **not** *used when the value is 1*.

PROGRAM 7-2   **LOOP2.BAS**   **[Non-Compiler]**

Simple FOR-NEXT Loop; Sum of Odd Integers between 1 and 100

Copyright 1984, 1985, Compulit, Inc.

```
          SUM% = 0
\              Use STEP 2 to skip even integers
          FOR M% = 1 TO 100 STEP 2
               SUM% = SUM% + M%
          NEXT
          PRINT "Sum of the odd values ="; SUM%
          END
```

In this program, the value of the index, M%, starts with 1; the next time it goes through the loop it has been incremented to 3 by the STEP 2 portion of the statement. The value of M% increases to 5, 7, 9, etc., until its value reaches 101. At that point since M% is greater than 100, the program does *not* go through the loop but control passes to the statement immediately following NEXT, the PRINT statement. Try this program and you will find that the answer equals 2500.

The FOR-NEXT statement does *not* have to begin with a 1 after the equal sign. The third program, **Program 7-3**, is another variation of the FOR-NEXT statement and is used to compute the sum of all the *even* values between 1 and 100. Since we want only the even values, we do not start the loop with 1 but rather with 2.

PROGRAM 7-3   **LOOP3.BAS**   **[Non-Compiler]**

Simple FOR-NEXT Loop Which Does Not Begin with 1

Copyright 1984, 1985, Compulit, Inc.

```
\            Loop begins with 2 and adds only even integers to 100
               SUM% = 0
         FOR INDEX% = 2 TO 100 STEP 2
               SUM% = SUM% + INDEX%
         NEXT
         PRINT "Sum of the even values ="; SUM%
         END
```

In this program INDEX% starts with the value of 2 and is incremented by 2 during each successive loop. When you try this program you will find that the sum of the even values equals 2550.

Summary of the FOR-NEXT Statement

From the three simple programs used thus far, it is evident that when using the FOR-NEXT statement:

- *The index* is a user-selected variable name, such as I%, M%, K%, INDEX%, etc. Although it may be any numeric variable, it is good programming form to use an integer variable because the program executes faster.
- *The initial value* is user-determined and may be any value.
- *The final value* is likewise user-determined.
- *The increment* or the value after STEP may range from 1 to any value. As noted earlier, if the increment is 1, it is not necessary to include "STEP 1" in the statement.

The increment may be a negative value but in that case the initial value must be greater than the final value. The following illustrates some of the statements just used and an alternative form using a negative step.

STATEMENT USED	ALTERNATIVE FORM
FOR I% = 1 TO 100	FOR I% = 100 TO 1 STEP -1
FOR M% = 1 TO 100 STEP 2	FOR M% = 99 TO 1 STEP -2
FOR INDEX% = 2 TO 100 STEP 2	FOR INDEX% = 100 TO 2 STEP -2

In these cases there is no need to use the negative step value, but there are programming situations in which the negative step is used because the program will execute faster.

Where the STEP variable is computed within a program, it should be tested to make certain that it does not have the value of zero. Should the program encounter a STEP of zero, it will hang the system by going into an endless loop.

Another problem in using the FOR-NEXT statement is encountered by those who use a colon [:] to write multiple statements on a single line. Placing a NEXT statement on the same line as an IF may allow a premature ending of the loop. The statements:

```
FOR K% = 4 TO 20
IF K% = 10 THEN PRINT K%: PRINT: NEXT
```

will not work properly. Instead it should be written as:

```
FOR K% = 4 TO 20
IF K% = 10 THEN PRINT K%: PRINT
NEXT
```

A Simple FOR-NEXT Loop

One application of the FOR-NEXT statement can be illustrated in the computation of depreciation by the double-declining-balance method. The algorithm is simply:

- The annual depreciation for any year, except the last one, is equal to twice the book value (cost less accumulated depreciation) of the item divided by the number of useful years of the asset.
- The last year's depreciation is equal to the cost less the sum of all the prior years' depreciation.

We compute the annual depreciation for all the years except the last one by using a FOR-NEXT loop, where [a] we calculate the annual depreciation, [b] determine the cumulative depreciation, and [c] print the individual year's depreciation.

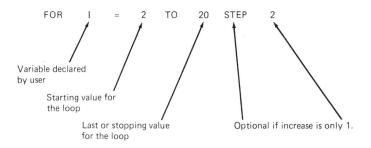

FIGURE 7-2   FOR-NEXT Language Structure

LANGUAGE CODING RULE

The FOR statement controls the execution of a FOR-NEXT loop and the NEXT statement indicates the end of the loop.

FOR <index variable> = <numeric expression> **TO** <numeric expression> [**STEP** <numeric expression>]

program statements within the loop

NEXT [index variable]

- The numeric expressions following the equal sign may be constants or variables.
- The index variable and the numeric expressions following the equal sign should be matched, that is, all real or all integer; otherwise, unnecessary code is generated and program execution is slowed. This is especially true for the index variable and the numeric expression following STEP; unless they are matched types a compiler error will occur.
- If the increment is 1, the STEP part should *not* be used because it slows the execution of the program.
- An integer value used for control may not exceed 32,766; a larger value causes an endless loop.
- The statements within a FOR-NEXT loop are *always executed at least once* no matter what the initial and ending values are.

```
FOR I% = 1 TO YEARS% - 1
        ANNUAL.DEPRECIATION = (2 * (COST - CUM.DEP)) / YEARS%
        CUM.DEP = CUM.DEP + ANNUAL.DEPRECIATION
        PRINT ANNUAL.DEPRECIATION
NEXT
```

A more efficient program would use an array in which the value of the annual depreciation is stored, and the output is printed as a unit instead of calculating and printing for each year. The program can also be expanded to print the book value of the asset as well. **Program 7-4** illustrates the use of two loops, one for computation and the other for counting, and an array to store the annual values.

PROGRAM 7-4   **LOOP4.BAS**   **[Compiler]**

Depreciation Using Two Loops and Array

Copyright 1984, 1985, Compulit, Inc.

```
\              Declaration of variables
       INTEGER YEARS, I
       REAL    ANNUAL.DEPRECIATION, CUM.DEP, COST
       STRING  CLEAR.SCREEN, AN
\              Defining CLEAR.SCREEN for PC-DOS and MS-DOS version 2.0
10     CLEAR.SCREEN = CHR$(27) + "[2J"
\              Dimension array to store annual depreciation
       DIM ANNUAL.DEPRECIATION(30)
       CUM.DEP = 0
\              Enter original values
       PRINT CLEAR.SCREEN
       INPUT "Original cost of equipment ............  "; COST:  PRINT
       INPUT "Enter total useful life of equipment ... "; YEARS
\              Compute annual depreciation for all years except last
       FOR I = 1 TO YEARS - 1
               ANNUAL.DEPRECIATION(I) = (2 * (COST - CUM.DEP)) / YEARS
               CUM.DEP = CUM.DEP + ANNUAL.DEPRECIATION(I)
       NEXT
\              Compute last year's depreciation
       ANNUAL.DEPRECIATION(YEARS) = COST - CUM.DEP
\              Display output
       PRINT CLEAR.SCREEN
       FOR I = 1 TO YEARS
               PRINT "Year "; I, ANNUAL.DEPRECIATION(I)
       NEXT
       INPUT "Another computation? ... [YES/NO] ....  "; AN
       IF UCASE$(AN) = "YES" THEN 10
       PRINT: PRINT "Normal termination of program"
       END
```

To test this program we assume we have purchased a microcomputer for $3,000.00 and determine that it has a five-year useful life. The two input values would be 3000 and 5. The output of the annual depreciation for the five years would be 1200, 720, 432, 259.20, and 388.80.

A Double FOR-NEXT Loop

In some business applications it is useful to use one or more FOR-NEXT loops within another, technically known as *nesting*. Any nested loop must be completely contained *within* another. **Figure 7-3** illustrates legal and illegal nested loops.

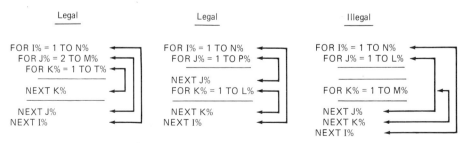

FIGURE 7-3   Legal and Illegal Nested FOR-NEXT Loops

Program 7-5 is an example of a double-nested loop which can be used to display unit sales by quarter. Input statements are used for data entry, but the program is easily modified to use data stored in a disk file. The program is designed to accept up to 25 products, and the unit sales by quarter are stored in a table form.

PROGRAM 7-5   TWOLOOP.BAS   [Non-Compiler]

Illustration of Nested FOR-NEXT Loops

Copyright 1985, Compulit, Inc.

```
        DIM UNITS%(25,4), PRODUCT$(25)
\               Defining CLEAR.SCREEN for PC-DOS and MS-DOS
        CLEAR.SCREEN$ = CHR$(27) + "[2J"
\               Counter for number of products
        CTR% = 0
        PRINT CLEAR.SCREEN$
\               Loop to enter up to 25 product names
        FOR I% = 1 TO 25
\               Direction to end loop for less than 25 products
                PRINT "Enter END for product name to terminate program"
                PRINT:   PRINT
                INPUT "Enter product name .......... "; PRODUCT$(I%)
                IF UCASE$(PRODUCT$(I%)) = "END" THEN 20
\               Loop to enter quarterly sales for each product
                FOR J% = 1 TO 4
                        PRINT
                        PRINT "Enter sales for quarter"; J%
                        INPUT "Number of units ...... "; UNITS%(I%,J%)
                NEXT
\               Increase counter
                CTR% = CTR% + 1
                PRINT CLEAR.SCREEN$
        NEXT
20      PRINT CLEAR.SCREEN$
        PRINT TAB(28); "Unit Sales by Quarter"
        PRINT:   PRINT: PRINT
\               Counter used for outer limit of loop
        FOR I% = 1 TO CTR%
\               Provide variable TAB for display of quarterly sales
                SPACE% = 25
                PRINT PRODUCT$(I%);
                FOR J% = 1 TO 4
                        PRINT TAB(SPACE%); UNITS%(I%,J%);
                        SPACE% = SPACE% + 15
                NEXT
                PRINT: PRINT
        NEXT
        PRINT:   PRINT:   PRINT "Normal termination of program"
        END
```

Naturally, the output would depend upon the data entered. Here, however, is a sample output of the program, without the termination of program line.

```
Unit Sales by Quarter

Switch box              300        850       600        250

Light switch            750        950       900        850
```

```
Duplex outlet          250      750      800      450

In-line switch         200      300      250      500
```

A Modified Menu Program

In Chapter 5 we introduced a series of individual programs to create, add to and print relative files. In Chapter 6 we combined these programs into one with a menu to illustrate the ON-GOTO statement. That program, *Program 6-7*, did not use the *INDEX* stored in the first record in the print section. This can be done using a FOR-NEXT loop and will make the program more efficient as shown in **Program 7-6**. The program is designed for use with the CBASIC Compiler for either 8-bit or 16-bit microcomputers. Note the use of procedure labels in place of the conventional number labels making the program much easier to follow and understand.

This is a **boilerplate program**; that is, the program is structured so that it can be modified easily for any data you wish to use. Furthermore, additional procedures can be included, such as sorting and searching, when they are explained in later chapters.

PROGRAM 7-6   **MENUPRO1.BAS**   [Compiler]

Create, Add to, or Display a Relative File

Copyright 1984, 1985, Compulit, Inc.

```
          STRING   CLEAR.SCREEN, NOF, AN, PROD.NO, PROD.DESC
          INTEGER  I, K, MC, INDEX, ON.HAND
          REAL     PROD.COST
\                  Defining CLEAR.SCREEN for PC-DOS and MS-DOS
          CLEAR.SCREEN = CHR$(27) + "[2J"
MENU:             \ ....... Program Menu
          PRINT CLEAR.SCREEN:    PRINT:    PRINT
          PRINT "What do you want to do?":          PRINT
          PRINT " [1]  Exit from program":          PRINT
          PRINT " [2]  Create a NEW file":          PRINT
          PRINT " [3]  Add to an existing file":    PRINT
          PRINT " [4]  Print a file.":              PRINT
          PRINT:   PRINT:   PRINT "NOTE:"
          PRINT "* Warning: If you create a new file and a file by that name
exists,            you will destroy the existing file.":  PRINT:   PRINT
          INPUT "  Enter the appropriate number:  "; MC
          IF MC < 1 OR MC > 4 THEN GOTO MENU
          IF MC = 1 THEN GOTO PICK
          PRINT CLEAR.SCREEN
          INPUT "Enter name of file........."; NOF
PICK:             \ ....... Branch statement
          ON MC GOTO QUIT.PROGRAM, NEW.FILE, ADD.FILE, PRINT.FILE
NEW.FILE:         \ ....... Procedure to create a new file
          PRINT CLEAR.SCREEN
          CREATE "A:" + NOF RECL 50 AS 1
          INDEX = 1
INPUT.OF.DATA:  \ ....... Data entry routine
          PRINT CLEAR.SCREEN
          INDEX = INDEX + 1
          INPUT "Enter product number.......... "; PROD.NO   : PRINT
          INPUT "Enter product description...... "; PROD.DESC : PRINT
          INPUT "Enter number of units on hand.. "; ON.HAND   : PRINT
```

```
          INPUT "Enter product cost ............ "; PROD.COST : PRINT
          PRINT #1,INDEX; PROD.NO, PROD.DESC, ON.HAND, PROD.COST
          PRINT #1,1; INDEX
          INPUT "Another entry?.. Yes or No? ... "; AN
          IF UCASE$(AN) = "YES" THEN GOTO INPUT.OF.DATA
          CLOSE 1
          GOTO MENU
ADD.FILE:       \ ....... Procedure to add to an existing file
          PRINT CLEAR.SCREEN
          IF END #1 THEN ERROR.ROUTINE
          OPEN "A:" + NOF RECL 50 AS 1
          READ #1,1; INDEX
          GOTO INPUT.OF.DATA
PRINT.FILE:     \ ....... Procedure to print hardcopy of file
          PRINT CLEAR.SCREEN
          LPRINTER
          PRINT "Product #", "Description", "Units on Hand", "Cost": PRINT
          IF END #1 THEN ERROR.ROUTINE
          OPEN "A:" + NOF RECL 50 AS 1
          READ #1, 1; INDEX
          FOR K = 2 TO INDEX
                READ #1,K; PROD.NO, PROD.DESC, ON.HAND, PROD.COST
                PRINT PROD.NO, PROD.DESC, ON.HAND, PROD.COST
          NEXT
          CONSOLE
          CLOSE 1
          GOTO MENU
ERROR.ROUTINE:  \ ....... Recovery routine if wrong file name is used
          PRINT "File by that name does NOT exist.":  PRINT
          INPUT "Press any letter to continue."; KEY$
          GOTO MENU
QUIT.PROGRAM:   \ ....... Termination of program
          PRINT CLEAR.SCREEN
          PRINT "Program terminated."
          END
```

WHILE-WEND STATEMENTS

If the number of repetitions is known before the loop is begun, the FOR-NEXT statements are the appropriate construct to use. Otherwise, the WHILE-WEND statements should be used.

The major difference between these two pairs of statements is in the way the computer evaluates them:

- In the FOR-NEXT set, the computer determines whether or not the loop has been exceeded only *after* the index has been incremented and control has returned to the FOR statement.
- With the WHILE statement, the evaluation is performed *prior* to execution of the WHILE statement.

Like the FOR-NEXT statements, the WHILE statement is always used in conjunction with the WEND statement. Just as we must have a NEXT statement to match each FOR statement, we must have a WEND statement to match each WHILE statement.

A Simple WHILE-WEND Test Program

Although the WHILE-WEND statements have many applications, some programmers encounter difficulty in using them because the expression is a

Boolean or logical operator type. A simple program, **Program 7-7**, shows the basic structure of the WHILE statement.

PROGRAM 7-7   **WHILE.BAS**   [Non-Compiler]

Simple WHILE-WEND Program

Copyright 1984, 1985, Compulit, Inc.

```
\             Defining CLEAR.SCREEN$ for PC-DOS and MS-DOS
       CLEAR.SCREEN$ = CHR$(27) + "[2J"
10     PRINT CLEAR.SCREEN$
       INPUT "Enter the value of I% ....... "; I%
       PRINT: PRINT
\             I% decreases after each print; printing continues until I% = 0
       WHILE I%
             PRINT I%
             I% = I% - 1
       WEND
       INPUT "Another test?  YES or NO    "; ANS$
       IF UCASE$(AN$) = "YES" THEN 10
       END
```

In this program, the I% following the WHILE is the logical expression. As long as I% does *not* equal zero [false to the computer], the statements between the WHILE and WEND are executed. In order to terminate the

---

LANGUAGE CODING RULE

The **WHILE** statement controls the execution of the loop and the **WEND** statement is used to indicate the end of the loop.

WHILE <logical expression>

program statements within the loop

WEND

- All the statements between the WHILE and WEND are executed until the value of the logical expression is logical false or zero.
- If the logical expression is zero initially, the statements within the WHILE-WEND loop will *not* be executed at all. [This is not true for the FOR-NEXT loop which is always executed at least one time.]
- The logical expression should be in integer form; this reduces execution time.
- If a real expression is used, it will be rounded to an integer taking extra time. A string expression will result in an error.
- Like the FOR-NEXT statements, the WHILE-WEND statements may be nested.

program, we have used the statement I% = I% − 1, which reduces the value of I% so that it eventually reaches zero. Try this program by entering different values for I%.

If I% is entered as 0 [zero], then no values of I% are printed and the program only prints the line, "Another test? YES or NO." If a negative number is entered for I%, we have a runaway program and it will be necessary to reboot the system. Therefore, when using the WHILE statement the programmer must:

- Be certain that the data for the logical expression does *not* include a negative value, or
- Include a test statement immediately before the WHILE statement to provide for an escape from the loop, such as:

```
IF I% < 0 THEN 10
```

A Short Business Application of WHILE-WEND

Program 7-8 is a modification of Program 6-2 where we listed those accounts which owed money. In this program using the WHILE statement, we have introduced an interest charge of 1% for the month on money owed. [Several statement labels are used for reference in the program which follows but are *not* required; only statement label 99 is necessary.]

PROGRAM 7-8   **WHILE1.BAS**   **[Compiler]**

WHILE-WEND with Data Statements

Copyright 1984, 1985, Compulit, Inc.

```
\              Declaration of variables
        REAL   AMOUNT.OWED, OLD.AMOUNT, CHARGE, AMOUNT.DUE
        STRING CLEAR.SCREEN, NAME
\              Defining CLEAR.SCREEN for PC-DOS and MS-DOS
        CLEAR.SCREEN = CHR$(27) + "[2J"
        PRINT CLEAR.SCREEN
100     AMOUNT.OWED = 1
        WHILE AMOUNT.OWED
            READ NAME, AMOUNT.OWED
110         IF NAME = "END" THEN 99
            OLD.AMOUNT = AMOUNT.OWED
120         CHARGE = 0.0: AMOUNT.DUE = 0
            CHARGE = AMOUNT.OWED * 0.01
            AMOUNT.DUE = AMOUNT.OWED + CHARGE
            PRINT NAME, OLD.AMOUNT, CHARGE, AMOUNT.DUE
130         AMOUNT.OWED = 1
        WEND
99      PRINT
        DATA "Don Mills", 212.50
        DATA "Robin Zemble", 0
        DATA "Judy Barta", 299.95
        DATA "Bob Shook", 150.00
        DATA "Rebecca Highland", 0
        DATA "END", 0
        END
```

In order to invoke the WHILE statement we set AMOUNT.OWED to 1 immediately before entering the loop in statement 100. We have used a *trailer* and statement 110 to terminate the reading of data. It is necessary to reinitialize CHARGE and AMOUNT.DUE to zero in statement 120 each time the program goes through the loop. Finally, statement 130 is used to force the WHILE loop to continue after an account that owes no money has been encountered. Unlike the output for Program 6-2, this output would include the names of all accounts including those who do not owe any money.

WHILE-WEND for Screen Control

Another use for the WHILE statement is to hold copy on the screen until the reader strikes a key. The following can be introduced in any part of a program where you wish to maintain the screen display.

```
PRINT "PRESS ANY KEY TO CONTINUE"
WHILE NOT CONSTAT%
WEND
```

There are several disadvantages in using this set of three statements and you can test it for yourself with **Program 7-9**. When you have tested as many keys as you want, reboot to end execution.

PROGRAM 7-9 **WHILE2.BAS** [Compiler]

WHILE-WEND to Hold Copy on Screen

Copyright 1984, 1985, Compulit, Inc.

```
\              Declaration of variables
        STRING AN, CLEAR.SCREEN
\              Defining CLEAR.SCREEN for PC-DOS and MS-DOS
        CLEAR.SCREEN = CHR$(27) + "[2J"
10      PRINT CLEAR.SCREEN
        PRINT "Let's try this!"
        PRINT: PRINT
        PRINT "Press any key to continue"
        WHILE NOT CONSTAT%
        WEND
        PRINT:  PRINT "You pressed it":  PRINT
        PRINT "If key pressed is echoed, use backsapce to delete"
        PRINT: PRINT
        INPUT "Continue? ... Yes or No? .... "; AN
        IF UCASE$(AN) = "YES" THEN 10
        END
```

The user is told to press "any key," but depending upon the keyboard, certain keys create problems. On the Columbia Data Products' MPC and IBM's PC, for example, pressing the *scroll-lock* or *control* keys, or *page up*, *page down*, or 5 on the keypad will not produce a response. When using a Hazeltine 1500 terminal, striking the *right arrow* key causes the program to enter an infinite loop. Even worse, if the user accidently was pressing the *control* key and struck the letter *C* [CTRL-C], the system would reboot.

In the *Special Programming Note* on page 53, we indicated the use of INPUT LINE to hold copy on the screen. Two other methods are explained in the following note.

WHILE-WEND in Place of GOTO

Some programmers avoid using a GOTO statement to branch back to an earlier part of a program. Instead they use the WHILE-WEND statements. **Program 7-10** shows the use of WHILE-WEND in place of the GOTO statement in a program to compute the declining-balance method of depreciation. The control is achieved by the use of the following statements:

SPECIAL PROGRAMMING NOTE

There are two other ways to *hold copy on the screen* in addition to the use of INPUT LINE.

First, there is a single *dummy* INPUT statement, which can be inserted as needed:

INPUT "Press any letter to continue ...."; PL$

Any string variable, not otherwise used by the program, can be used as the *dummy* input. We selected PL$ to stand for answer. With this statement the user is directed to use a *letter* rather than any *key*. This technique sometimes creates a problem with inexperienced users who fail to press the *return* key after striking the letter.

The second method is somewhat longer, but it is safer and more certain, especially in programs which will be used by individuals with varying microcomputer experience. Only the *space bar* is accepted as input. To do this, it is necessary, in the initial phase of a program, to include the statement which identifies the *space bar* to the computer:

SPACE.BAR$ = CHR$(32)

This is standard ASCII code with 8-bit and 16-bit microcomputers. Within the program, as often as required, the following two statements are used:

9901 PRINT "Press SPACE BAR to continue"
        IF CHR$(CONCHAR%) <> SPACE.BAR$ THEN 9901

The statement label, 9901, must be changed each time this hold technique is used in the same program

---

| REPEAT = 1 | Sets value of repeat so that program will enter WHILE loop. |
| WHILE REPEAT | Initial WHILE statement with control. |

. . . program statements are located here . . .

REPEAT = 0	Sets value of REPEAT to permit exit from loop at WEND.
INPUT "Another computation..	Holds screen to await for user reply.
IF UCASE$(AN) = "YES" THEN REPEAT = 1	If user wishes another run and enters YES, the value of REPEAT is set to 1 so the WHILE-WEND will continue in the loop.
WEND	Program passes through WEND statement and ends when REPEAT = 0.

PROGRAM 7-10   **WHILE3.BAS**   **[Compiler]**

Use of WHILE-WEND to Replace a GOTO

Copyright 1985, Compulit, Inc.

```
\           Declaration of variables
        INTEGER YEARS, I, REPEAT
        REAL    ANNUAL.DEP, CUM.DEP, COST, PERCENT, NEW.COST
        STRING  CLEAR.SCREEN, AN
\           Defining CLEAR.SCREEN for PC-DOS and MS-DOS
        CLEAR.SCREEN = CHR$(27) + "[2J"
        REPEAT = 1
        CUM.DEP = 0.0
\           Start of WHILE-WEND loop
        WHILE REPEAT
        PRINT CLEAR.SCREEN
        INPUT "Enter the cost of the item ...... "; COST
        INPUT "Enter the expected life in years . "; YEARS
        PRINT CLEAR.SCREEN
        PRINT TAB(15);"Annual"; TAB(31);"Cumulative"; TAB(51); "Book Value"
        PRINT "Year"; TAB(12);"Depreciation"; TAB(30);"Depreciation"; \
              TAB(49);"(End of Year)"
        PRINT TAB(52);COST
        PERCENT = 2 * (1.0 / YEARS)
        FOR I = 1 TO YEARS
              ANNUAL.DEP = COST * PERCENT
              CUM.DEP    = CUM.DEP + ANNUAL.DEP
              NEW.COST   = COST - ANNUAL.DEP
              PRINT TAB(3);I; TAB(15);ANNUAL.DEP; TAB(33);CUM.DEP; \
                    TAB(52);NEW.COST
              COST       = NEW.COST
```

```
NEXT
REPEAT = Ø:  PRINT
INPUT "Additional data to run?  Yes or No?   "; AN
IF UCASE$(AN) = "YES" THEN REPEAT = 1
WEND
PRINT "Normal termination of program"
END
```

Additional illustrations of the WHILE-WEND statements will be used in later chapters, such as sorting and advanced file handling, as well as in others.

CHAPTER **8**

Functions, Subroutines, and String Manipulation

In this chapter we will cover several programming techniques which can simplify and shorten your programming efforts, including:

- Built-in functions
- User-defined functions
- Functions for string manipulation
- ASCII control and systems functions
- Subroutines

BUILT-IN FUNCTIONS

A **function** is a program that performs a computation or operation that returns a *single* value as a result. We have already encountered the use of several **built-in functions** in previous chapters. A built-in function is part of the language, incorporated in the compiler, similar to the INPUT and PRINT statements. Earlier in this volume we used several built-in functions, such as:

- **TAB** in the PRINT statement; TAB moves the cursor on the screen or the printhead on the printer to a specific column.
- **INT** which returns the integer portion of a real number as a real value compared with the function **INT%** which returns the integer portion of a real number as an integer.
- **UCASE$** which converts lower case letters in a string to upper case.
- **SGN** in a branching statement; SGN returns an integer value which represents the sign of a number. If the value is negative, -1 is returned; 0 if the value is zero; and $+1$ if the value is positive.

Most built-in functions, aside from those which manipulate strings and are covered later in this chapter, are used in mathematical and scientific programming. **Table 8-1** contains a list of these built-in functions and their use.

TABLE 8-1   Built-in Functions

FUNCTION	OPERATION PERFORMED	EXAMPLE
ABS	Returns the absolute value of a number.	X = ABS(TEMP)
ATN	Produces the arctangent of a number.	Y = ATN(RAD)
COS	Returns the cosine of a number.	Z = COS(ANGLE)
EXP	Returns the constant *e* raised to an exponent.	A = EXP(LTYEARS)
FLOAT	Converts an integer to a real number.	D = FLOAT(N%)
INT	Returns integer portion of a real number as a real number.	H = INT(HOURS)
INT%	Returns integer portion of a real number as an integer.	I% = INT%(HOURS)
LOG	Produces the natural logarithm of a number.	B = LOG(SUMX)
MOD	Used in modular arithmetic to return the remainder from an integer division.	J = MOD(K%, M%)
RND	Generates and returns a random number.	C = RND(X)
SGN	Determines the sign of a value.	IF SGN(TEMP) THEN
SIN	Produces the sine of a number.	E = SIN(ANGLE)
SQR	Returns the square root of a value.	SD = SQR(VARIANCE)
TAN	Produces the tangent of a number.	R = TAN(ANGLE)

Note: To convert a *natural* logarithm to a *common* logarithm, multiply the natural logarithm by 0.4342944819; for example:

$$COM.LOG.N = LOG(N) * 0.4342944819$$

USER-DEFINED FUNCTIONS

Often you can save time in programming when you have a repetitive operation by creating your own function. You may do this *if only one value is* produced by the operation. With CBASIC, you may use either single-line or multiple-line functions. The **DEF** statement, used to define a function you create, must come before the function is used in the program.

Single-Line User-Defined Functions

Let us take a simple, single-line function for a company that prepares a variety of products which it wishes to mark in both ounces and grams. To convert ounces to grams we multiply the number of ounces by 28.35. Thus we can define this function in the statement:

```
DEF FNMETRIC.WGT = OUNCES * 28.35
```

[**FN** must start the name of the function in non-compiler versions; it is optional in compiler versions.]

Program 8-1 illustrates the use of this function.

PROGRAM 8-1   **DEFINE.BAS**   **[Non-Compiler]**

Single-Line User-Defined Function

Copyright 1985, Compulit, Inc.

```
    \           Defining CLEAR.SCREEN for PC-DOS and MS-DOS
            CLEAR.SCREEN$ = CHR$(27) + "[2J"
    \           Define the function
            DEF FN.METRIC.WGT (NEW.WEIGHT) = OUNCES * 28.35
    10  PRINT CLEAR.SCREEN$
        INPUT "Enter weight in ounces .... "; OUNCES
    \           Use the defined function
        GRAMS = FN.METRIC.WGT (NEW.WEIGHT)
        PRINT "The product weighs "; OUNCES; "ounces."
        PRINT "The product weighs "; GRAMS; "grams."
        PRINT: INPUT "Any additional entries?  Yes or No? "; ANS$
        IF UCASE$(ANS$) = "YES" THEN 10
        PRINT "Normal termination of the program"
        END
```

This program illustrates an application of a user-defined function. It could have been written without the definition line; the second line below statement 10 would then be:

```
GRAMS = OUNCES * 28.35
```

Another single-line function is used to determine the greater of two values. Note the difference in preparing the function definition since there are now two values which are used as input into the function. Try entering **Program 8-2** and testing the algorithm.

PROGRAM 8-2   **DEFINE2.BAS**   **[Non-Compiler]**

Defined Function Determines the Larger of Two Values

Copyright 1985, Compulit, Inc.

```
\              Defining CLEAR.SCREEN for PC-DOS and MS-DOS
          CLEAR.SCREEN$ = CHR$(27) + "[2J"
\              Define the function
          DEF FN.LARGER (X, Y) = ( X + Y + ABS ( X - Y )) / 2
10        PRINT CLEAR.SCREEN$
          INPUT "Enter the first value ....... "; FV
          INPUT "Enter the second value ...... "; SV
\              Use the function
          GV = FN.LARGER (FV,SV)
          PRINT
          PRINT "The first value entered was ....... "; FV
          PRINT "The second value entered was ...... "; SV
          PRINT "The greater of the two values is .. "; GV
          PRINT: INPUT "Another test?  Yes or No?    "; ANS$
          IF UCASE$(ANS) = "YES" THEN 10
          PRINT "Normal termination of program"
          END
```

As illustrated in Program 8-2 it is not necessary to use the same variable names in the definition of the function and in the statement using the function. In defining the function we used X and Y but in obtaining GV, we used FV and SV. However, the identifiers in the definition must be the same mode as the identifiers in the program statement.

SPECIAL PROGRAMMING NOTE

With user-defined functions, it is possible to use different variable names within the function from those used in the program. However:

- The same number of parameters must appear in the function and the program.
- The parameters must be listed in the same sequence.
- The parameters must be matched in mode—real for real, integer for integer.

Multiple Single-Line User-Defined Functions

Several single-line functions may be used in one program, and the same function may be used more than once. In this illustration we have a company that [a] offers a 15% discount on each item that sells for $75.00 or more and [b] adds an 8% sales tax to the adjusted list price. **Program 8-3** is an example of the use of more than one user-defined function within a single program, and the use of a function more than once.

PROGRAM 8-3   **DEFINE3.BAS**   **[Non-Compiler]**

Use of More Than One User-Defined Function

Copyright 1985, Compulit, Inc.

```
\               Defining CLEAR.SCREEN for PC-DOS and MS-DOS
        CLEAR.SCREEN$ = CHR$(27) + "[2J"
\               Function to compute tax
        DEF FN.TAX (LIST.PRICE) = LIST.PRICE * 1.08
\               Function to round value to nearest cent
        DEF FN.ROUND (DISCOUNT) = INT(DISCOUNT * 100 + 0.5) / 100
10      PRINT CLEAR.SCREEN$
        INPUT "Enter list price of item ....... "; LIST.PRICE
        PRINT: PRINT:
        DISCOUNT = 0
        PRINT "List price of item is ......... "; LIST.PRICE
\               Calculate discount
        IF LIST.PRICE >= 75 THEN \
                DISCOUNT = LIST.PRICE * 0.15:\
                LIST.PRICE = LIST.PRICE * 0.85
\               Calculate and round selling price; round discount
        SELLING.PRICE = FN.TAX (LIST.PRICE)
        SELLING.PRICE = FN.ROUND (SELLING.PRICE)
        DISCOUNT = FN.ROUND(DISCOUNT)
        PRINT "Discount on item is ........... "; DISCOUNT
        PRINT "Selling price of item is ...... "; SELLING.PRICE
        PRINT: PRINT
        INPUT "Wish to check another item?  Yes or No?  "; ANS$
        IF UCASE$(ANS$) = "YES" THEN 10
        PRINT: PRINT "Normal termination of program"
        END
```

LANGUAGE CODING RULE

A single-line user-defined function is defined by the **DEF** statement.

DEF <function name> [(formal parameters)] = <expression>

- The function definition must appear in the program before the function is used in the program
- The data type used in the expression must correspond to the data type used in the function name.
- For non-compiler versions, the function name must begin with FN.

Multiple-Line User-Defined Functions

There are times when more than one line is needed to define a user-defined function. The basic principles are the same as for a single-line function with two modifications:

- First, a RETURN statement must appear at least once within the function, although any number of RETURN statements may be used within the function, and
- Second, the FEND statement must appear as the last line of the user definition.

SPECIAL PROGRAMMING NOTE

When using single-line and/or multiple-line user-defined functions, it is good programming practice to place the definition[s] as early in the program as possible. Also, set off each function with a REM statement preceding it.

Program 8-4 is an example of a multiple-line user-defined function. The function computes overtime pay as part of a payroll program.

PROGRAM 8-4   **FUNCTION.BAS**   **[Compiler]**

Multi-Line Defined Function

Copyright 1984, 1985, Compulit, Inc.

```
\              Declaration of variables
        REAL    HOURS, OVER.PAY, OVER.TIME, PAY, RATE, REGULAR.PAY
        STRING CLEAR.SCREEN, AN
\              Defining CLEAR.SCREEN for CP/M 86
        CLEAR.SCREEN = CHR$(27) + CHR$(69)
\              Define function to calculate and print wage payment
        DEF FNOT (HOURS)
            OVER.TIME = HOURS - 40
            REGULAR.PAY = 40 * RATE
            OVER.PAY = OVER.TIME * 1.5 * RATE
            PAY = REGULAR.PAY + OVER.PAY
            PRINT "Regular pay ...... "; REGULAR.PAY
            PRINT "Overtime pay ..... "; OVER.PAY
            PRINT "Total pay ........ "; PAY:  PRINT
            RETURN
        FEND
10      PRINT CLEAR.SCREEN
        PAY = 0.0
        INPUT "Rate of pay ..... "; RATE
        INPUT "Hours of work ... "; HOURS
\              Use function if there is overtime
        IF HOURS > 40 THEN\
            PAY = FNOT (HOURS) \
        ELSE \
            PAY = HOURS * RATE: \
            PRINT: PRINT "Hours .... "; HOURS: \
                   PRINT "Rate ..... "; RATE: \
                   PRINT "Pay ...... "; PAY
        PRINT:  INPUT "Continue?  Yes or No? .... "; AN
        IF UCASE$(AN) = "YES" THEN 10
        PRINT "Normal termination of program"
        END
```

LANGUAGE CODING RULE

A multiple-line user-defined function is defined by the **DEF** statement.

> **DEF** <function name> [(formal parameters)] \
>   [CBASIC statements]
> _____-
>
> _____-
>
> _____-
>
>   **RETURN**
> **FEND**

- The **DEF** statement starts the definition and the **FEND** statement terminates the function.
- Common statements may not be used.
- A **GOTO** statement that references a line outside of the function is illegal.
- A **DIM** statement allocates a new array on each execution of the function and the data from the previous execution is destroyed.

THE CALL STATEMENT

There is another way to execute a multiple-line user-defined function when using the compiler versions of CBASIC Compiler. The **CALL** statement may be used instead. This statement is used *entirely differently* in the non-compiler version and will be covered later. The definition of the multiple-line function must follow the same rules as noted earlier and as demonstrated in Program 8-4.

LANGUAGE CODING RULE

The CALL statement when used with the CBASIC Compiler transfers control of the program to a multiple-line function.

> **CALL** <function name> [formal parameters]

In Program 8-4, the program executed the multi-line function with the statement:

```
PAY = FNOT (HOURS)
```

In **Program 8-5** we not only show the use of the CALL statement but also illustrate another approach to writing programming code. The same problem is used but we have created a multiple-line function which determines pay under normal and overtime conditions. This shortens the main program and makes the function usable in many different programs.

If the defined functions are kept in a library, any function can then be included in a program using a text editor. An alternative method [*available only with the compiler versions*] is to incorporate the functions in the CBASIC library. The required function[s] will then be included in the program by the link editor.

PROGRAM 8-5   **FNCALL.BAS**   **[Compiler]**

CALL Statement with Defined Function

Copyright 1984, 1985, Compulit, Inc.

```
\              Declaration of variables
        REAL    HOURS, OVER.PAY, OVER.TIME, PAY, RATE, REGULAR.PAY
        STRING AN, CLEAR.SCREEN
\              Defining CLEAR.SCREEN for CP/M 86
        CLEAR.SCREEN = CHR$(27) + CHR$(69)
\              Definition of multi-line function
        DEF FNPAY (HOURS)
            PAY = 0.0
            IF HOURS > 40 THEN \
                OVER.TIME = HOURS - 40: \
                REGULAR.PAY = 40 * RATE: \
                OVER.PAY = OVER.TIME * 1.5 * RATE: \
                PAY = REGULAR.PAY + OVER.PAY: \
                PRINT "Regular pay ...... "; REGULAR.PAY: \
                PRINT "Overtime pay ..... "; OVER.PAY: \
                PRINT "Total pay ........ "; PAY:  PRINT: \
                RETURN \
            ELSE \
                PAY = HOURS * RATE: \
                PRINT: PRINT "Hours .... "; HOURS: \
                    PRINT "Rate ..... "; RATE:  \
                    PRINT "Pay ...... "; PAY: \
                RETURN
        FEND
\              Main program using CALL statement and defined function
10      PRINT CLEAR.SCREEN
        INPUT "Rate of pay ..... "; RATE
        INPUT "Hours of work ... "; HOURS
        CALL FNPAY (HOURS)
        PRINT: INPUT "Continue?  Yes or No? .... "; AN
        IF UCASE$(AN) = "YES" THEN 10
        PRINT "Normal termination of program"
        END
```

We changed the name and structure of the function in this illustration. Also note that the RETURN statement may be used more than once within the definition of a multiple-line function.

In the non-compiler version, the **CALL** statement is used to link a machine-language subroutine to the program.

```
LANGUAGE CODING RULE

The CALL statement in the non-compiler versions joins a machine-
language subroutine to the CBASIC program.

    CALL <numeric expression>

    • The numeric expression is the address of the machine-language
      subroutine.
```

STRING MANIPULATION

A number of built-in functions are available to enable the programmer to
process individual characters or manipulate strings. One of the arithmetic
operators can also be used to manipulate strings. These techniques are the
basis for solving many practical business problems such as alphabetizing,
numeric sorting, searching, and data file merging.

Concatenation

We start with the simplest of string manipulations, that is, joining strings.
This is done with the *addition* arithmetic operator [+], the only one which
may be used with strings.

For example, if we have the following strings:

```
BLANK$ = " "
FIRST.NAME$ = "Rebecca"
MIDDLE.NAME$ = "Frances"
LAST.NAME$ = "Highland"
```

The following concatenation statement:

```
FULL.NAME$ = FIRST.NAME$ + BLANK$ + MIDDLE.NAME$ + BLANK$ + LAST.NAME$
```

would result in:

Rebecca Frances Highland

Determining the Length of a String

When you are using a specific length record with relative files or you are designing screen inputs or output [covered in Chapter 11], you may wish to determine the length of a string so that the copy does not overflow its allotted space. To do this we use the **LEN** function. Another important use of this function is in sorting strings [Chapter 9].

The built-in LEN function returns an integer value equal to the number of characters in the string including letters, numbers, symbols, and blanks.

LANGUAGE CODING RULE

The LEN function returns the length of a string as an integer.

<integer variable> = **LEN** (<string expression>)

• If you evaluate a null string, the integer value will be equal to zero.

For example, for the string expression

```
SLEEP$ = "WINKIN, BLINKIN, & NOD, INC,"
```

the statement I% = LEN(SLEEP$) will return I% =28.

Program 8-6 illustrates a simple use of the LEN function.

PROGRAM 8-6   **LENGTH.BAS**   **[Non-Compiler]**

Test of the LEN Function

Copyright 1985, Compulit, Inc.

```
\            Defining CLEAR.SCREEN for PC-DOS and MS-DOS
         CLEAR.SCREEN$ = CHR$(27) + "[2J"
10       PRINT CLEAR.SCREEN$
         PRINT "A string is any combination of letters, symbols and spaces"
         PRINT: INPUT "Enter a string: ";LINE COPY$
\            Use of LEN function
         NUMBER% = LEN (COPY$)
         PRINT: PRINT "The string length is "; NUMBER%; " characters."
         PRINT: INPUT "Wish to try again?  Yes or No?  "; AN$
         IF UCASE$(AN$) = "YES" THEN 10
         END
```

Selecting Parts of a String

There are three built-in string functions which permit you to select any character or characters that are part of a string. Their grammar structure is similar.

LEFT$	returns the leftmost characters,
RIGHT$	returns the rightmost characters, and
MID$	permits the isolation of any character or characters.

LANGUAGE CODING RULE

The LEFT$ function returns a string composed of a specific number of characters starting at the left side of the string.

\<string identifier\> = **LEFT$** (\<string expression\>, \<numeric value\>)

- The string identifer is the name of the string containing the characters you wish to separate.
- The string expression is the string you wish to "decompose."
- The numeric value specifies the number of characters you wish to return. It must be positive; a negative numeric value will result in an error. If the numeric value is greater than the length of the string expression, the entire string will be returned.

LANGUAGE CODING RULE

The RIGHT$ function is similar to the LEFT$ but returns a string composed of a specific number of characters from the right side of the string.

\<string identifier\> = **RIGHT$** (\<string expression\>, \<numeric value\>)

- The string identifer is the name of the string containing the characters you wish to separate.
- The string expression is the string you wish to "decompose."
- The numeric value specifies the number of characters you wish to return. It must be positive; a negative numeric value will result in an error. If the numeric value is greater than the length of the string expression, the entire string will be returned.

LANGUAGE CODING RULE

The MID$ function returns a segment of a string.

\<string identifier\> = **MID$** (\<string expression\>,\<number 1\>,\<number 2\>)

- The *string identifier* is the name of the string you wish to create.
- *Number 1* is an integer value specifying the first character of the original string you wish to return. If this value is greater than the length of the string, a null string is returned.
- *Number 2* is an integer value that specifies the total number of characters you wish to return.

For example, for the string expression:

```
STR$ = "Built-in functions are a programming aid"
```

BEGIN$ = LEFT$ (STR$,6)	will return	Built-
FINISH$ = RIGHT$ (STR$,5)	will return	g aid
PART$ = MID$ (STR$,7,2)	will return	in

If the string being evaluated by the LEFT$, RIGHT$, or MID$ function is a blank or **null string**, a run-time error will occur. If you are uncertain about the contents of a string, it is best to test the string with the LEN function before using the LEFT$, RIGHT$, or MID$ functions. If the LEN function results in zero, these other functions cannot be used. The following is a simple test procedure:

```
M% = LEN (STRING.EXPRESSION$)
IF M% = 0 THEN 13;
----use of LEFT$, RIGHT$, or MID$ function----
--------------------------------------------------
13----continuation of program----
```

Program 8-7 will familiarize you with the use of these three functions. It is written in the compiler version. If you use a non-compiler version, eliminate the two lines defining the strings and integers and end each string variable name with a $ and each integer variable name with a % sign.

PROGRAM 8-7   **L-R-M.BAS**   [Compiler]

Test of LEFT, RIGHT, MID Functions

Copyright 1984, 1985, Compulit, Inc.

```
\               Declaration of variables
        STRING  COPY, LCOPY, RCOPY, CCOPY, AN, CLEAR.SCREEN
        INTEGER N, SN, SL
\               Defining CLEAR.SCREEN for PC-DOS and MS-DOS
        CLEAR.SCREEN = CHR$(27) + "[2J"
10      PRINT CLEAR.SCREEN
        PRINT "                TEST OF LEFT, RIGHT AND MID FUNCTIONS": PRINT
        PRINT "A string is any set of letters, symbols and spaces."
        INPUT "Enter a string: "; COPY:  PRINT
        INPUT "How many letters do you want to take off? "; N
        LCOPY = LEFT$  (COPY, N)
        RCOPY = RIGHT$ (COPY, N):     PRINT
        PRINT "The LEFT function produced: "; LCOPY:  PRINT
        PRINT "The RIGHT function produced: "; RCOPY:  PRINT
        PRINT "We will now test the MID function."
        INPUT "At what character (from the left) do you wish to start? "; SN
        INPUT "How many characters do you want in the final string?   "; SL
        CCOPY = MID$ (COPY, SN, SL):  PRINT
        PRINT "The MID function produced:   "; CCOPY:  PRINT
        INPUT "Want to try again?  Yes or No? "; AN
        IF UCASE$(AN) = "YES" THEN 10
        PRINT:  PRINT "Normal termination of program"
        END
```

You can test Program 8-7 by entering the string:

```
This is a test of string manipulation
```

In response to the first question about the number of letters you wish, enter *4*.

- The LEFT$ function should result in a string *This*.
- The RIGHT$ function will produce a string *tion*.

In the test of the MID$ function, enter the value *11* as the first value and *4* as the second value.

- The result would be the word *test*.

Converting Numbers to Strings and Strings to Numbers

There are times in programming when it is convenient to change numbers to strings and/or numeric strings to numbers. This is particularly true if you wish to store account number, names, addresses, and zip codes in a table or matrix, which has a string identifier. Later, you may wish to sort by account number or zip code and use a numeric sort. There are two built-in functions:

STR$ which converts a numeric value to a string, and
VAL   which converts a numeric string to a real value.

LANGUAGE CODING RULE

STR$ converts a numeric value to a string.

<string variable> = **STR$** (<numeric variable or expression>)

When using the STR$ function, if the numeric variable is an integer, it will be automatically changed to real as it is converted into a string.

LANGUAGE CODING RULE

VAL converts a numeric string to a real numeric value.

<real variable> = **VAL** (<digit string expression>)

When we convert a digit string to a numeric value using the VAL function, the string is processed from left to right until either the end of the string is reached or a non-digit character is encountered. A sign may precede the first numeric value. For example:

STATEMENT	DIGIT STRING A$	RESULT
X = VAL (A$)	1313.26	1313.26
Y = VAL (A$)	562 Croydon	562
Z = VAL (A$)	+1126	+1126
H = VAL (A$)	11-11-84	11

The VAL function will return zero [0] if either the string is null [that is, blank] or the string starts with an alphabetic character.

STATEMENT	DIGIT STRING A$	RESULT
A = VAL (A$)	"" [null string or blank]	0
B = VAL (A$)	H42617	0

Finding a Character Pattern in a String

The MATCH function searches a string for a single or series of characters that matches the user-defined string. It can be used, for example, to search for a specific zip code in a mailing list or a company name in a list of customers.

This function returns the position of the first occurence in the string being searched that matches the user-defined string. The user-defined string may contain any series of specific letters and/or digits or symbols. The string may also contain a wild card matching characters that represent different classes of characters. For example, the symbol # represents any digit. If the user-defined string were 10.##, any value between 10.00 and 10.99 would be considered a match

---

LANGUAGE CODING RULE

MATCH returns the position of the first occurrence of a specified character pattern in a string.

<integer variable> = **MATCH**
        (<pattern string, string expression, numeric expression>)

- The pattern string may contain any single or series of letters and/or digits, or any of the following specially defined symbols.

  # to represent any single digit
  ! represents any single upper case or lower case letter
  ? is used to indicate any character

- The string expression is the string which will be searched. The numeric expression is an integer value specifying the position in the string expression at which to begin the search.
- If either the string expression or the pattern string is a null string, or there is no match, the value returned is 0 [zero].
- To search for any of the special characters which may be used in the pattern string, use a backslash [\] before that character; any symbol appearing after the backslash is a literal.

Program 8-8 can be used to illustrate many applications of the MATCH function by varying the parameters. All three parameters of the function statement—the pattern string, the string expression, and numeric expression—are entered by the user.

PROGRAM 8-8   **FIND.BAS**   **[Non-Compiler]**

Illustration of MATCH Function

Copyright 1985, Compulit, Inc.

```
\              Defining CLEAR.SCREEN for PC-DOS and MS-DOS
        CLEAR.SCREEN$ = CHR$(27) + "[2J"
10      PRINT CLEAR.SCREEN$
        INPUT "Enter the Pattern String  "; LINE PS$:     PRINT
        INPUT "Enter the String          "; LINE COPY$:   PRINT
        INPUT "Enter starting position    "; SP%:          PRINT
\              Use of MATCH function
        I% = MATCH (PS$, COPY$, SP%)
        PRINT I%: PRINT
        INPUT "Try again?  Yes or No?     "; AN$
        IF UCASE$(AN$) = "YES" THEN 10
        END
```

The following are samples of input into the program and the resulting position value indicated:

	INPUT		OUTPUT
PATTERN STRING	STRING EXPRESSION	NUMERIC EXPRESSION	VALUE
the	Now is the time for all	1	8
the	NOW IS THE TIME FOR ALL	1	0
#	26 November 1977	1	1
#	26 November 1977	3	13
###	26 November 1977	1	13
!	26Rebecca	1	3
ti?	repetition	1	5
?	How are you? Fine.	1	1
\?	How are you? Fine.	1	12

Translating Lower Case to Upper Case

To convert a lower case string to upper case, use the UCASE$ function. This does not change the original string. We have used this function throughout the book as part of the restart procedure within a program, making it possible for the user to enter *yes*, *Yes*, *YEs* or any other combination of upper case and lower case letters which the computer converts into all capitals in the statement:

```
IF UCASE$ (AN$) = "YES" THEN 10
```

LANGUAGE CODING RULE

The UCASE$ function is used to convert lower case characters into upper case or capital letters.

<string variable> = **UCASE$ (**<string expression>**)**

ASCII CODE AND ITS CONTROL FUNCTIONS

ASCII stands for the American Standard Code for Information Interchange. It is a standard binary code that has been adopted to represent alphanumeric and special characters used by the computer. The code length that is most commonly used for the internal representation of a character contains 8 bits per character. This is true for alphanumeric characters and symbols, as well as the control and graphics characters used by microcomputers.

With an 8-bit binary code consisting of 1's and 0's, we have created 256 distinct characters. **Table 8-2** contains several examples of characters and their ASCII codes [in binary] with their decimal and hexadecimal equivalents.

TABLE 8-2   Characters and Their ASCII Codes

| | ASCII | | |
CHARACTER	BINARY	DECIMAL	HEXADECIMAL
A	01000001	065	41
S	01010011	083	53
a	01100001	097	61
7	00110111	055	37
+	00101011	043	2B
]	01011101	093	5D

For a complete table of ASCII binary, decimal, and hexadecimal codes, see Appendix C.

Several built-in functions utilizing the ASCII code will be covered here. Other ASCII-oriented built-in functions will be covered in appropriate sections later. The functions explained here include:

ASC	which returns the ASCII decimal code for the first character of a string.
CHR$	which returns a character for a single ASCII decimal value.
CONCHAR%	which reads a character from the keyboard and returns the decimal ASCII representation of that character as well as displaying the character on the screen.
INKEY	which is similar to the CONCHAR% function but does *not* display the character on the console screen.

The ASC Function

A simple program, **Program 8-9**, will enable you to see how the **ASC** function works. Try it to become familiar with the returned code since it provides you with a better understanding of character control and will assist you in using other related functions.

PROGRAM 8-9   **ASCII.BAS**   **[Non-Compiler]**

Use of ASC Function

Copyright 1985, Compulit, Inc.

```
\              Defining CLEAR.SCREEN for PC-DOS and MS-DOS
        CLEAR.SCREEN = CHR$(27) + "[2J"
10      PRINT CLEAR.SCREEN
        INPUT "Type a single letter, number or symbol  "; A$
\              Use of ASC function
        ASCIIVAL%  = ASC(A$)
        PRINT "Character entered from keyboard ....  "; A$
        PRINT "ASCII value of that character ......  "; ASCIIVAL%
        PRINT: INPUT "Want to try another?  Yes or No?     "; AN$
        IF UCASE$(AN$) = "YES" THEN 10
        END
```

LANGUAGE CODING RULE

The ASC function converts the first character of a string into a decimal value.

<integer variable> = **ASC** (<string expression>)

• The string expression must contain at least one character; an execution error occurs if a null string is encountered.

The ASC function has many uses, one of which is to produce a discrete numerical identifier for alphanumeric lists such as customer names and addresses. These numerical identifiers help in speeding searches and sorts. **Program 8-10** is a demonstration program of the technique for creating discrete identifiers.

To simplify presentation and limit execution time, only the first five characters are transformed. To be used in a real-time environment, a more complex program is required. Because the ASC function results in an error when a blank is encountered, a test of the character to be converted should be incorporated into a comprehensive program. Also it would be necessary to include, for example, the street name and zip code, to assure the creation of discrete identifiers.

PROGRAM 8-10 **DISCRETE.BAS** **[Compiler]**

Create Discrete Numeric Identifiers for Alphanumeric Code

Copyright 1984, 1985, Compulit, Inc.

```
\               Declare variables
        INTEGER CODE, I
        REAL    IDENTIFIER, K, KODE
        STRING  AN, CLEAR.SCREEN, NAME
\               Define CLEAR.SCREEN for CP/M 86
        CLEAR.SCREEN = CHR$(27) + CHR$(69)
        DIM CODE(5), KODE(5)
10      IDENTIFIER = 0
        PRINT CLEAR.SCREEN
        INPUT "Enter name ....... "; NAME
\               Transform first five characters to ASCII code
        FOR I = 1 TO 5
                CODE(I) = ASC (MID$ (NAME, I, 1))
        NEXT
\               Transformation for five-letter code
        K = 10000
        FOR I = 1 TO 5
                KODE(I) = FLOAT (CODE(I)) * K
                K = K / 10
        NEXT
\               Create identifier for name
        FOR I = 1 TO 5
                IDENTIFIER = IDENTIFIER + KODE(I)
        NEXT
\               Display name and identifier
        PRINT: PRINT: PRINT
        PRINT "Name entered ....... "; NAME: PRINT
        PRINT "Identfier for name ..... "; IDENTIFIER
        PRINT: PRINT: PRINT
        INPUT "Another name for identifying?  Yes or No?  "; AN
        IF UCASE$(AN) = "YES" THEN 10
        PRINT "Normal termination of program"
        END
```

Run this program to see how the discrete codes are computed. If you enter the name *Highland*, the computer determines the ASCII decimal code for each of the first five letters:

H   72
i   105

g   103
h   104
l   108

The program multiplies each of these values as if they were decimal values to transform them, as follows:

72	×	10,000	=	720,000
105	×	1,000	=	105,000
103	×	100	=	10,300
104	×	10	=	1,040
108	×	1	=	108

The sum of these transformed values is equal to 836448. We can compare this with other names as shown below:

NAME	NUMERIC IDENTIFIER
Highland	836448
Johnson	862615
Shreve	946528
Chapman	784929

The CHR$ Function

The **CHR$** function returns a single character string which is represented by an ASCII decimal value. It is used for various control functions. We used it earlier to define the clear screen function for use with different terminals and monitors. For example, when using MS-DOS with a Princeton Graphics System color monitor, we defined clear screen as:

```
CLEAR.SCREEN = CHR$(27) + "[2J"
```

With a Princeton Graphics Systems color monitor and a 16-bit Columbia Data Products MPC-1600 microcomputer operating under CP/M86 we defined it as:

```
CLEAR.SCREEN = CHR$(27) + CHR$(69)
```

The string CLEAR.SCREEN is translated by these statements into *key* terminology. The clear screen is achieved by striking the *control* key together with the letter *F* for the 8-bit system. For the 16-bit configuration, clear is accomplished by striking the *escape* key together with the letter *E*.

LANGUAGE CODING RULE

The CHR$ function is used to return a single ASCII character string that has a specified ASCII decimal value.

<alphabetic variable> = **CHR$ (**<numeric expression>**)**

- If the numeric expression is real, the function converts the value into an integer.

Here is a short, simple program, **Program 8-11**, to help you test the CHR$ function.

PROGRAM 8-11   **CHR.BAS**   **[Non-Compiler]**

Test of CHR$ Function

Copyright 1985, Compulit, Inc.

```
\          Defining CLEAR.SCREEN for PC-DOS and MS-DOS
          CLEAR.SCREEN$ = CHR$(27) + "[2J"
10        PRINT CLEAR.SCREEN$
          PRINT "This is a test of the CHR$ function": PRINT
          PRINT "The ASCII values range from 000 to 255."
          PRINT "The ASCII character will be displayed for any "
          PRINT "of the values in this range.  However, if "
          PRINT "255 is entered the ASCII character is "
          PRINT "a blank 'FF' and it will be necessary to"
          PRINT "press the return key to continue."
          PRINT: PRINT
          INPUT "Enter ASCII decimal value of character .... "; X
\               Use of CHR$ function
          A$ = CHR$(X)
          PRINT: PRINT: PRINT "Character is: "; A$
          PRINT: INPUT "Another try?  Yes or No?  "; AN$
          IF UCASE$(AN$) = "YES" THEN 10
          END
```

If you try this program and enter 7 when asked for a decimal value of a character, the microcomputer's "bell" will sound. Enter 82 and the letter R will be printed. If you enter 32, which is the decimal ASCII value for a space, nothing will be printed.

Copying a String a Specified Number of Times

The **STRING$** function, available in the compiler version, is used to replicate a string a given number of times. It reduces memory fragmentation when large strings have to be constructed and executes significantly faster than concatenation.

It is a specialized function used by advanced programmers. One application, for example, is creating test data for a file to test a program. Another example is the design of an input screen to simplify data entry. **Program 8-12** illustrates a simple application of this function.

PROGRAM 8-12   **STRING.BAS**   **[Compiler]**

Test of STRING$ to Repeat a String

Copyright 1984, 1985, Compulit, Inc.

```
STRING   ST, A
INPUT "Enter a string "; ST
PRINT
PRINT "String printed 5 times:"
PRINT
A = STRING$ (5, ST)
PRINT
PRINT A
PRINT
PRINT "Same string printed 20 times:"
PRINT
A = STRING$ (20, ST)
PRINT A
PRINT
PRINT "Normal termination of program"
END
```

This program produces two sets of output. The user is requested to enter a string, for example: [blank] HJH

The first output would be the string printed five times:

HJH HJH HJH HJH HJH

This would be followed by the string printed 20 times and the program would then be terminated.

LANGUAGE CODING RULE

The STRING$ function produces a string that consists of a single string repeated a specified number of times.

<string variable> = **STRING$**(<integer variable>,<string expression>**)**

The integer variable specifies the number of times the string expression should be copied. The string expression can be a string variable or a string constant.

Another application of the STRING$ function is contained in **Program 8-13** in which both a string expression and then an ASCII code is entered as part of the program.

PROGRAM 8-13   **STRING2.BAS**   **[Compiler]**

Use of STRING$ with Variable Parameters

Copyright 1984, 1985, Compulit, Inc.

```
\               Declaration of variables
        INTEGER N, K
        STRING  H, A, AN
\               Input of number of times to repeat and string
10      INPUT "Enter number of times to copy string "; N
        PRINT
        INPUT "Enter string: "; H
        A =  STRING$ (N, H)
        PRINT A
        PRINT
        INPUT "Enter number of times to copy string "; N
        PRINT
\               Enter decimal ASCII code
        INPUT "Enter a single ASCII value:  "; K
\               Convert decimal ASCII value to character
        H = CHR$ (K)
        A =  STRING$ (N, H)
        PRINT A
        INPUT "Again?  "; AN
        IF UCASE$ (AN) = "YES" THEN 10
        PRINT "Normal termination of program"
        END
```

The first part of this program is similar to the previous one except that you can control the number of times the string will be repeated. For the second test, if you have graphics and use a monitor, enter 1840 as the number of times to repeat the string. Try different tests using such ASCII code values as: 001, 002, 176. Refer to the ASCII code table in the appendix for other choices. The 1840 value entered will fill the screen with the ASCII character. If you are writing a program and want to have the bell ring for an extended time, enter different values for the number of times you want to copy the string [N in Program 8-13] and enter the ASCII code 007 [K in the program].

The CONCHAR% Function

When the **CONCHAR%** function is used, the program will halt and wait for a single character input from the keyboard. The character will be displayed on the screen and you can set a variable equal to the ASCII decimal value of that character. This function can also be used with the CHR$ function in various program control situations.

LANGUAGE CODING RULE

The CONCHAR% function halts a program to read a single character from the keyboard, displays that character on the console screen, and returns the ASCII decimal value of that character.

<integer variable> = **CONCHAR%**

- If the ASCII decimal value is less than 33, no character will be displayed. However, some earlier versions of the compiler echo the control characters.

Program 8-14 demonstrates the use of this function. In addition to the normal response of displaying the input character on the console screen, the program also prints the ASCII decimal value of the character, and the character itself using the CHR$ function.

PROGRAM 8-14   **CONCHAR.BAS**   **[Non-Compiler]**

Test of CONCHAR% Function

Copyright 1985, Compulit, Inc.

```
\             Defining CLEAR.SCREEN for PC-DOS and MS-DOS
         CLEAR.SCREEN$ = CHR$(27) + "[2J"
10       PRINT CLEAR.SCREEN$
         PRINT "Press any key"
\             Use of CONCHAR% function
         RESPONSE% = CONCHAR%
         PRINT
\             Display result
         PRINT RESPONSE%, CHR$(RESPONSE%)
         PRINT: INPUT "Another try?  Yes or No?    "; AN$
         IF UCASE$(AN$) = "YES" THEN 10
         PRINT "Normal termination of program"
         END
```

When testing this program, if you press the letter *H*, the letter will be displayed on one line and on the line immediately after will be 72, the ASCII decimal value of the letter, and H, the letter itself. Similarly, if you enter !, the character will be printed as well as 33, the ASCII decimal value of an exclamation point. There is a *warning*, however, when using an IBM PC or a microcomputer with a keyboard with a *PrtSc* key. Do not press this key as an input character since it will print the entire screen; if the printer is not on, the program will hang.

LANGUAGE CODING RULE

The INKEY function is similar to the CONCHAR% function *but* it does not display the character entered on the console screen. It is not available for non-compiler versions of CBASIC.

<integer variable> = **INKEY**

- This function is very useful for entry of password or any other data you do not wish to display on the screen.

The INKEY Function for the Compiler Versions

The **INKEY** function, available only in CBASIC compiler, is similar to the CONCHAR% function *except* that it does not display the character on the console screen. It too halts the program during execution until a key is struck. This function will accept any character including control characters. Because this function does not echo the keys pressed on the console screen, it is useful in entering a password for access or program control.

Program 8-15 shows the operation of the INKEY function. You are requested to enter a six-character password. Notice that when you enter the characters of the password, they do *not* appear on the console screen. The PRINT statement in the program to display the entered password is there only to show you that the computer has accepted the input.

When testing this program, try using control keys as well; that is, press the *control* key and a letter at the same time. For example, hold the control key down and press the letters *A* through *F*.

PROGRAM 8-15   **NON-ECHO.BAS**   **[Compiler]**

Demonstration of INKEY function

Copyright 1984, 1985, Compulit, Inc.

```
        STRING   CLEAR.SCREEN, AN, PW
        INTEGER  I
\               Declare CLEARN.SCREEN for PC-DOS and MS-DOS
        CLEAR.SCREEN = CHR$(27) + "[2J"
10      PRINT CLEAR.SCREEN
        PW = ""
        PRINT "Enter your password - use 6 letters.":  PRINT: PRINT
        FOR I = 1 TO 6
                PW = PW + CHR$ (INKEY)
        NEXT
        PRINT:  PRINT "Your password is: "; PW
        PRINT:  INPUT "Another try?  YES or NO? "; AN
        IF UCASE$(AN) = "YES" THEN 10
        PRINT "Normal termination of program"
        END
```

DESIGN AND USE OF SUBROUTINES

A **subroutine** is a sequenced set of statements that performs a specific computation; it may be used at one or more points in a computer program. Subroutines may also be used to create your own library, storing them as individual units on a disk, and then transferring those that are needed into a program by using a text editor. This eliminates the need for reentry of the short program or subroutine.

In business data processing, there are a number of procedures [subroutines] which can be used in many different programs. For example, you can create a library of subroutines to:

- Find the sum and/or average of a set of values
- Center copy on the console screen
- Determine the number of days between two dates
- Sort a list of names and addresses
- Compute the present value of an annuity
- Compute different types of depreciation
- Encode and decode data
- Compute trend lines

In the technical and scientific fields, there are also many uses for subroutines, including those that:

- Perform integration using Simpson's rule or the trapezoidal method
- Compute analysis of variance
- Solve equations with complex variables
- Perform matrix operations
- Generate various statistical distributions

Any subroutine within the program is "called" by a **GOSUB** statement. The subroutine starts with a label line and ends with the **RETURN** statement. Execution of the program returns to the line immediately after the GOSUB line in the program, generally known as the **main program**. This operation is shown in **Figure 8-1**.

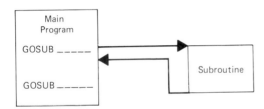

FIGURE 8-1   Relationship of Subroutine to Main Program

LANGUAGE CODING RULE

The GOSUB statement in a program executes the subroutine identified with the label.

GOSUB <label>

- The GOSUB may be written as one word or two, GO SUB.

- The label is numeric in the non-compiler version of CBASIC and may be either numeric or alphabetic in the CBASIC Compiler versions.

Subroutine to Center Copy on Console Screen

Program 8-16 is an example of a main program containing a subroutine which centers the input copy on the console screen. The subroutine may be used with any other program in which you wish to center copy on the screen. Note the use of the LEN function to prevent the program from hanging if you enter more than 80 characters, the maximum width of the screen.

PROGRAM 8-16   **CENTER.BAS**   **[Compiler]**

Subroutine to Center Copy on Screen

Copyright 1984, 1985, Compulit, Inc.

```
\            Declare variables
        INTEGER DIF, H, L
        STRING  AN, BLANK, CLEAR.SCREEN, COPY, HEAD, TITLE
\            Define CLEAR.SCREEN for PC-DOS and MS-DOS version 2.0
        CLEAR.SCREEN = CHR$(27) + "[2J"
10      PRINT CLEAR.SCREEN
        INPUT "Enter copy:  "; COPY
\            Test for 80 character screen
        IF LEN (COPY) <= 80 THEN 20
        PRINT: PRINT "Copy may not exceed 80 characters."
        PRINT
        PRINT "To try again press any key"
\            Hold copy on screen
        H = CONCHAR% : PRINT: GOTO 10
20      GOSUB CENTER.COPY
        PRINT: PRINT: PRINT
        GOTO 99
CENTER.COPY:    \ Routine to center copy on screen
        BLANK = " "
        HEAD  = ""
        L    = LEN (COPY)
        DIF = INT% ((80 - L)/2)
\            Determine number of blank spaces before copy starts
```

```
WHILE DIF
        HEAD = HEAD + BLANK
        DIF = DIF - 1
WEND
\            Start printing with the blank spaces before copy
    TITLE = HEAD + COPY
    PRINT: PRINT: PRINT
    PRINT TITLE
    RETURN
\            End of subroutine
99  INPUT "Want to try again?  Yes or No?   "; AN
    IF UCASE$(AN) = "YES" THEN 10
    PRINT "Normal termination of program"
    END
```

This program has been written for use with CBASIC Compiler. To use with non-compiler versions, substitute a numeric label for CENTER.COPY, delete the declaration statements, and use the appropriate $ and % symbols with the variable names.

A Data Analysis Subroutine

Program 8-17 illustrates the use of a data analysis subroutine. In situations where you are working with a series of values, it provides some of the basic statistical information. The demonstration program is written for use with only 20 values, but the subroutine may be used with any number of values determined by the main program by changing the dimension statement.

PROGRAM 8-17   STAT.BAS   [Compiler]

Statistical Subroutine: Sum, Mean, Maximum, Minimum, Standard Deviation

Copyright 1985, Compulit, Inc.

```
\            Declaration of variables
    INTEGER I, N
    REAL    MAXIMUM, MEAN, MINIMUM, STANDARD.DEVIATION, SUMX, SUMX2, X
    STRING  AN, CLEAR.SCREEN, SPACE.BAR
\            Defining CLEAR.SCREEN for PC-DOS and MS-DOS
    CLEAR.SCREEN = CHR$(27) + "[2J"
\            Define space bar
    SPACE.BAR = CHR$(32)
10  PRINT CLEAR.SCREEN
\            Establish storage for 20 values
    DIM X(20)
    PRINT "You may enter up to 20 values to test this program.": PRINT
    INPUT "How many values will you enter?     "; N
\            Check for more than 20 values
    IF N <= 20 THEN 20
    PRINT "Number of values must not exceed 20."
\            Hold message on screen
    PRINT "Press any key to continue"
    I = CONCHAR%
    GOTO 10
\            Enter data values
20  FOR I = 1 TO N
        PRINT CLEAR.SCREEN: PRINT: PRINT: PRINT
        PRINT "Enter value #"; I
        INPUT X(I)
    NEXT
\            Program goes to subroutine to perform statistical analysis
```

(continues)

```
              GOSUB 1000
\                     Subroutine returns here
              PRINT CLEAR.SCREEN
              INPUT "Want to try this again?  Yes or No?  "; AN
              IF UCASE$(AN) = "YES" THEN 10
              PRINT "Normal termination of program"
              GOTO 9999
\                     Statistical subroutine
\                     Initialize sums and maximum and minimum
1000      SUMX = 0
              SUMX2 = 0
              MAXIMUM = -1.00E-64
              MINIMUM =  9.99E62
\                     Calculate sums and determine maximum and minimum
              FOR I = 1 TO N
                      SUMX  = SUMX  + X(I)
                      SUMX2 = SUMX2 + X(I) * X(I)
                      IF X(I) > MAXIMUM THEN\
                              MAXIMUM = X(I)
                      IF X(I) < MINIMUM THEN\
                              MINIMUM = X(I)
              NEXT I
\                     Calculate mean and standard deviation
              MEAN = SUMX / N
              STANDARD.DEVIATION = SQR( (SUMX2 / N) - MEAN * MEAN)
\                     Display all results
              PRINT CLEAR.SCREEN
              PRINT "You have entered "; N; " values.": PRINT
              PRINT "The sum of the series is .................. ";SUMX: PRINT
              PRINT "The average [mean] value of the series is . ";MEAN: PRINT
              PRINT "The maximum value of the series is ........ ";MAXIMUM: PRINT
              PRINT "The minimum value of the series is ........ ";MINIMUM: PRINT
              PRINT "The standard deviation of the series is ... ";STANDARD.DEVIATION
1010      PRINT: PRINT: PRINT "                    Press Space Bar to continue"
\                     Hold copy on screen
              IF CHR$(CONCHAR%) <> SPACE.BAR THEN 1010
              RETURN
9999      END
```

Suggested Sources for Subroutine

There are several books on the market which are devoted solely to subroutines. Although the subroutines are not written in CBASIC, they can easily be converted to CBASIC.

John P. Grillo and J. D. Robertson: *Subroutine Sandwich*. New York: John Wiley & Sons, 1983.
John P. Grillo and J. D. Robertson: *More Subroutine Sandwich*. New York: John Wiley & Sons, 1983.
F. R. Ruckdeschel: *Basic Scientific Subroutines*. Peterborough, NH: Byte/McGraw-Hill, 1981.

CHAPTER 9

Sorting: Techniques and Programming

Sorting is the process of arranging items in order. It is an essential part of many business operations. Arranging items in order is undertaken to prepare printouts in a sequence more meaningful for the reader, merge master files with daily records, save mailing cost by preparing mail by zip code packets, aid in search of files, and numerous other applications, not only in business but also in scientific processing of data and even in the operation of a computer's operating system.

In business we sort records based on a specific field. We can arrange data alphabetically, numerically, or by a particular attribute such as sales area, product line, or account activity. In the early days of computing with the use of sequential files on magnetic tape, sort operations sometimes accounted for more than half of all the computer processing time. Over the years, the techniques of sorting have become highly sophisticated, and there are a number of technical books devoted solely to this topic.

Sort techniques and programs have colorful names: **bubble sort, shaker sort, quick sort, shell sort, heap sort, tree sort**, to mention just a few. Sorting techniques traditionally are classified into internal methods and external methods; the former perform all sorting within the computer memory, while the latter use disk space for temporary storage during the sort. In this chapter we will consider only some elementary internal sorts.

THE BUBBLE SORT

The **bubble sort** is the easiest to understand and the easiest to explain. It is called a bubble sort because the lower or smaller values "float up." It is, however, a slow method with certain limitations, as will be shown later in a comparison of sorting methods.

In this section we will present several versions of the bubble sort, first in order to explain how it works, and second, to show different programming techniques to do the same job. We start by using the simplest sort written in the simplest fashion, one using a series of IF statements.

How the Bubble Sort Works

The bubble sort in **Program 9-1** exchanges individual elements or values that are stored in the computer side by side by using the relational operator, <= [less than or equal to]. For simplicity, we will use a numeric sort with only five values: 5, 7, 11, 8, and 2.

PROGRAM 9-1   **BUBBLE.BAS**   **[Non-Compiler]**
Bubble Sort with Numeric Data

Copyright 1985, Compulit, Inc.

```
\               Defining CLEAR.SCREEN for PC-DOS and MS-DOS
        CLEAR.SCREEN$ = CHR$(27) + "[2J"
        PRINT CLEAR.SCREEN$
        DIM X(10)
        FOR I% = 1 TO 5
               READ X(I%)
        NEXT
\               I% = 6 at the end of loop; decrease by 1 in next statement
        N% = I% - 1
\               Start of sort; M% controls progression through values
\               J% controls number of times through values
        J% = N%
10      J% = J% - 1:  M% = 0
20      M% = M% + 1
\               Comparison of consecutive values
        IF X(M%) <= X(M%+1) THEN 30
\               Switch values if out of sequence
        SAVE = X(M%):  X(M%) = X(M%+1):  X(M%+1) = SAVE
30      IF J% > M% THEN 20
\               Restart comparison procedure
        IF J% > 1  THEN 10
\               End of sort; start of printout
        FOR M% = 1 TO 5
               PRINT X(M%)
        NEXT
        DATA 5, 7, 11, 8, 2
        END
```

The data is read into the computer and stored as a list or an array X(I%) as shown in **Figure 9-1**.

Positional value within the array	1	2	3	4	5
Values:	5	7	11	8	2

FIGURE 9-1   Bubble Sort—Starting Array

[A]. Let's follow the sort through the first M% loop, while J% = 4.

Program Statements	*Explanation*
`10 J% = J% - 1:   M% = 0`	1. We start with J% = 4 and M% = 0.
`20 M% = M% + 1`	2. M% is set to 1.
`   IF  X(M%) <= X(M%+1)  THEN  30`	3. X(1) is compared with X(2), that is, 5 <= 7. Since 5 is less than 7, the program proceeds to statement 30.
`30 IF  J% > M%  THEN  20`	4. Since J% = 4 is greater than M% = 1, the program goes to statement 20.

[B]. The program is now ready to go through the loop the second time.

`20 M% = M% + 1`	1. M% is increased to 2; J% is still = 4.
`   IF  X(M%) <= X(M%+1)  THEN  30`	2. X(2) is compared with X(3), or 7 <= 11. Since 7 is less than 11, again the program proceeds to statement 30.
`30 IF  J% > M%  THEN  20`	3. Since 4 is greater than 2, execution goes back to statement 20.

[C]. The program now goes through the loop the third time.

`20 M% = M% + 1`	1. M% is increased to 3.
`   IF  X(M%) <= X(M%+1)  THEN  30`	2. X(3) is compared with X(4), or 11 <= 4.

`   SAVE = X(M%)`
`   X(M%) = X(M%+1)`
`   X(M%+1) = SAVE`
	3. Since 11 is greater than 4, the two values are interchanged in this three-line routine.

```
30 IF J% > M% THEN 20
```
4. Since 4 is greater than 3, execution is again at line 20.

[D]. We now enter the final loop of pass 1.

```
20 M% = M% + 1
```
1. M% now has the value of 4.

```
   IF X(M%) <= X(M%+1) THEN 30
```
2. X(4) or 11 is compared with X(5) or 2.

```
   SAVE = X(M%)
   X(M%) = X(M%+1)
   X(M%+1) = SAVE
```
3. Since 11 is greater than 2, another interchange takes place in these three statements.

```
30 IF JX > MX THEN 20
```
4. Now J% and M% both equal 4 so the program continues to the next statement.

```
   IF JX > 1 THEN 10
```
5. Since J% = 4 and is greater than 1, the program returns to statement 10.

We have just completed pass 1 of the sort and the array would appear in computer memory as shown in **Figure 9-2**. Note that the largest value is last in the array and need no longer be included in the comparisons. Therefore J% which controls the number of comparisons is reduced by one.

[**E**]. We are now ready to start pass 2 of the sort loop with J% =3.

```
10 J% = J% - 1: M% = 0
```
1. J% now is 3 and M% is set to 0.

```
20 M% = M% + 1
   IF X(M%) <= X(M%+1) THEN 30
```
2. M% again is set to 1.

3. X(1) is compared with X(2), 5 with 7. Since

Positional value within the array	1	2	3	4	5
Values:	5	7	8	2	11

FIGURE 9-2   Bubble Sort—End of Pass 1

	5 is less than 7, the program goes to statement 30.
`30 IF J% > M% THEN 20`	4. 3 is greater then 1, and the program goes to statement 20.

[F]. The second loop of phase 2 is now begun:

`20 M% = M% + 1`	1. M% is set to 2.
`   IF X(M%) <= X(M%+1) THEN 30`	2. X(2) compared with X(3) or 7 with 8. Since 7 is less than 8, the program skips to statement 30.
`30 IF J% > M% THEN 20`	3. 3 is greater than 2; execution continues at statement 20.

[G]. The third or final loop of pass 2 is begun.

`20 M% = M% + 1`	1. M% is now set to 3.
`   IF X(M%) <= X(M%+1) THEN 30`	2. X(3) compared with X(4) or 8 and 2.
`   SAVE = X(M%)`	3. Since 8 is greater than 2, the values are interchanged in this procedure.
`   X(M%) = X(M%+1)`	
`   X(M%+1) = SAVE`	
`30 IF J% > M% THEN 20`	4. Now J% and M% are equal to 3 and program proceeds to next statement.
`   IF J% > 1   THEN 10`	5. Since J% is 3, program goes to 10.

At the end of pass 2, the values have been rearranged in the array so that they would be stored in computer memory as shown in **Figure 9-3**.

Positional value within the array	1	2	3	4	5
Values:	5	7	2	8	11

FIGURE 9-3   Bubble Sort—End of Pass 2

Note that during pass 1, the program made four loops through the sort array and moved the largest value to the bottom. During pass 2 the program went through the loop only three times since the largest value was already in last place. By the end of pass 2 the next smaller number is in next-to-the-last position in the array. As we continue, the program will make one less loop during each pass.

When we have completed pass 3 the data within the array is stored as shown in **Figure 9-4**.

Positional value within the array	1	2	3	4	5
Values:	5	2	7	8	11

FIGURE 9-4   Bubble Sort—End of Pass 3

The completely sorted array is shown in **Figure 9-5**.

Positional value within the array	1	2	3	4	5
Values:	2	5	7	8	11

FIGURE 9-5   Bubble Sort—Final Array

Using a FOR-NEXT Loop Bubble Sort

The same algorithm that has been used in the preceding program can be written using nested FOR-NEXT loops as shown in **Program 9-2**, written for compiler versions. The sort procedure contains the same number of statements, takes somewhat less time to execute, and, to an experienced programmer, it is more compact. In this program we saved the original data in an array $X(I\%)$ and placed the sorted data in an array $Y(I\%)$ and included both in the printout.

PROGRAM 9-2   **LOOP5.BAS**   **[Compiler]**

Bubble Sort with FOR-NEXT Loop

Copyright 1985, Compulit, Inc.

```
\               Declaration of variables
        INTEGER I, J, N, SAVE, X, Y
        STRING  CLEAR.SCREEN
\               Defining CLEAR.SCREEN for PC-DOS and MS-DOS
        CLEAR.SCREEN = CHR$(27) + "[2J"
\               Save storage for original array and sorted array
        DIM X(5), Y(5)
        FOR I = 1 TO 5
                READ X(I)
                Y(I) = X(I)
        NEXT
        N = I
\               Start of bubble sort
100     FOR I = 1 TO N-2
                FOR J = I+1 TO N-1
                        IF Y(I) > Y(J) THEN \
                        SAVE = Y(I): Y(I) = Y(J): Y(J) = SAVE
        NEXT J
        NEXT I
\               Printout of original and sorted arrays
        PRINT CLEAR.SCREEN
        FOR I = 1 TO 5
                PRINT X(I), Y(I)
        NEXT
        DATA 12, 8, 5, 5, 9
        END
```

Using a FLAG to Terminate Needless Iterations

If you examine the DATA statement in the preceding program you will note that most of the values are in almost-sorted order. The bubble sort program that has been used would, however, continue the comparisons even after the data is completely sorted. The iterations or loops continue as long as J% is greater than 1 in Program 9-1 or until the index is satisfied in Program 9-2. The sorting time can be reduced when the data is mostly sorted by introducing a **FLAG**.

The FLAG statement is used to indicate whether or not an exchange of values has taken place during a single pass. If none has taken place, the sort is terminated and the output is begun. **Program 9-3** is an example of a bubble sort with a flag. Although it too is a bubble sort, the specific algorithm is different from those used in the previous two programs.

PROGRAM 9-3   **FLAG.BAS**   **[Non-Compiler]**

Bubble Sort with Flag Using Double FOR-NEXT Loop

Copyright 1985, Compulit, Inc.

```
\               Defining CLEAR.SCREEN$ for MS-DOS and PC-DOS
        CLEAR.SCREEN$ = CHR$(27) + "[2J"
        PRINT CLEAR.SCREEN$
```

(continues)

```
        DIM X(5)
        FOR I% = 0 TO 4
              INPUT "Enter value ....   "; X(I%)
        NEXT
        N% = I%
\             Start of sort routine with flag
        FOR I% = 0 TO N%-1
           FLAG% = 0
           FOR J% = 0 TO N%-I%-2
                IF X(J%+1) < X(J%) THEN \
\                    Set FLAG% to 1 if values have been switched
                  SAVE = X(J%): X(J%) = X(J%+1): X(J%+1) = SAVE: FLAG% = 1
           NEXT
\             End sort if no switch has been made
           IF FLAG% = 0 THEN 10
        NEXT
\             Display sorted data
10      PRINT: PRINT
        FOR M% = 0 TO 4
           PRINT X(M%)
        NEXT
        PRINT: PRINT "Normal termination of program."
        END
```

We have included this sort routine as a subroutine, which can be added to any program for a numeric sort. To use the subroutine, the variable X has to be dimensioned in the main program and the statement **GOSUB 200** included within the main program where the sort is required.

```
\    SUBROUTINE: BUBBLE SORT WITH FLAG
200 FOR I% = 1 TO N%-1
      FLAG% = 0
      FOR J% = 1 TO N%-I%-2
           IF X(J%+1) < X(J%) THEN \
           SAVE = X(J%): X(J%) = X(J%+1): X(J%+1) = SAVE: FLAG% = 1
      NEXT J%
      IF FLAG% = 0 THEN RETURN
    NEXT I%
    RETURN
```

A WHILE-WEND Bubble Sort

Another variation of the bubble sort uses the WHILE-WEND statements as shown in **Program 9-4**. Instead of the DATA statements used in the earlier programs in this chapter, we have used the INPUT statement so that you can try this program with any data you wish using up to 50 numeric values. SIGNAL% is set to 1 just prior to the WHILE statement so that the program proceeds through the loop.

PROGRAM 9-4   **WWSORT.BAS**   **[Compiler]**

Bubble Sort with WHILE-WEND Statements

Copyright 1985, Compulit, Inc.

```
\                Ddeclaration of variables
         INTEGER I, J, M, N, SIGNAL
         REAL    SAVE, X
         STRING  CLEAR.SCREEN
\                Defining CLEAR.SCREEN for PC-DOS and MS-DOS
         CLEAR.SCREEN = CHR$(27) + "[2J"
         DIM X(50)
\                Input of data
         FOR I = 1 TO 50
         PRINT CLEAR.SCREEN
                 PRINT "Enter 99999 to terminate entry": PRINT: PRINT
                 INPUT "Enter value ....... "; X(I)
                 IF X(I) = 99999 THEN 5
         NEXT
5        N = I - 1
         J = N
         SIGNAL = 1
\                Start of WHILE-WEND sort routine
         WHILE SIGNAL
10           J = J - 1
             IF J = 0 THEN 40
             M = 0:   SIGNAL = 0
20           M = M + 1
             IF X(M) <= X(M+1) THEN 30
                 SAVE = X(M): X(M) = X(M+1): X(M+1) = SAVE: SIGNAL = 1
30           IF J > M THEN 20
             GOTO 10
         WEND
\                End of sort routine - start printout
40       FOR M = 1 TO N
                 PRINT X(M)
         NEXT
         END
```

A COMPARISON OF SORTS

The sort algorithms are a subject in themselves and many books have been written solely about sort routines. Each type takes different times to execute, and the time of execution is also data-dependent.

The **bubble sort** interchanges two values as soon as it finds they are in reverse order. It is simple to program and is fast if there is a small number of values. How small small is depends upon the authority used, and ranges from as low as 15 to as high as 50 values. It works quickly with a large number of values *if* most of them are already in sequence.

The **shell sort** is more complicated in its operation, programming, and explanation. It is considerably faster than the bubble sort once the list of items or values exceeds 50. However, if the list is "more or less" sorted before the sort is begun, the bubble sort with a flag is often faster than the shell sort.

The **quick sort** is one of the faster internal sorts and works well with long lists of items or values. It compares poorly with the simple bubble sort with flag, however, when used with any list which is already partially sorted. In some ways, it is similar to the bubble sort without a flag in that it must complete all its sorting loops whether or not the list or array is already sorted.

An analysis of sorting times under different conditions will help you understand the need for the proper selection of a sort procedure. In **Table 9-1** we have used a basic time unit of 1, the time needed to sort 500 values that are in sequence into an ordered array with a bubble sort including a flag. Also we compare the various types of sorts under three conditions:

- If the data is already sorted *prior to* using the sort routine
- If the data is arranged as we would find them in no particular order as in normal, everyday operations
- If the data was sorted in reverse or inverted order, such as high to low, or names from Z to A

TABLE 9-1   Comparison of Sorting Times by Different Sort Methods for 500 Numeric Values

TYPE OF SORT	SORTED OR ORDERED ARRAY	RANDOMLY DISTRIBUTED	INVERSE ORDER
Bubble sort			
without flag	270	540	840
with flag	1	500	740
Shell sort	14	44	63
Quick sort	8	18	10

Base time [one time unit] was time needed to sort a set of 500 numeric values that were in numerical sequence into an ordered array using a bubble sort with flag.

A SHELL SORT PROGRAM

Since most business operations require considerable sorting, we have included a **shell sort** which can be used in place of the bubble sort. **Program 9-5** is a sample of a modified shell sort. Again we provided for data input so that you can compare the bubble sort with the shell sort for various sequences of numeric data.

PROGRAM 9-5   **SHELL.BAS**   [Compiler]

Modified Shell Sort

Copyright 1985, Compulit, Inc.

```
\               Declaration of variables
        INTEGER I, J, K, L, M, N, T
        REAL    SAVE, X
        STRING  CLEAR.SCREEN
\               Defining CLEAR.SCREEN for PC-DOS and MS-DOS
        CLEAR.SCREEN = CHR$(27) + "[2J"
        DIM X(100)
\               Input of data
        FOR I = 1 TO 100
        PRINT CLEAR.SCREEN
        PRINT "Enter 99999 to terminate data input": PRINT: PRINT
        PRINT "You are inputting value "; I: PRINT: PRINT
        INPUT "Enter value ....... "; X(I)
        IF X(I) = 99999 THEN 6
        NEXT
6       N = I - 1
\               Start of sort routine
        M = N
10      M = INT (M/2)
        IF M = 0 THEN 50
           K = N - M:   J = 1
20         I = J
30         L = I + M
        IF X(I) <= X(L) THEN 40
           SAVE = X(I): X(I) = X(L): X(L) = SAVE: I = I - M
        IF I >= 1 THEN 30
40         J = J + 1
        IF J <= K THEN 20
        GOTO 10
\               End of sort routine - start of printout
50      PRINT CLEAR.SCREEN
        FOR T = 1 TO N
           PRINT X(T)
        NEXT
        END
```

A QUICK SORT PROGRAM FOR FAST SORTING

An even faster sorting procedure for a large series of values, especially if their number is in excess of 100, is the **quick sort** algorithm. It is exceedingly complex to explain and is more difficult for the average programmer to code. **Program 9-6** contains a quick sort in subroutine form. It starts with label 1000 and ends with the statement, GOTO 1100. It can be taken as a unit and added to any program where a sort is required.

PROGRAM 9-6   **QUICK.BAS**   [Compiler]

Quick Sort for Numeric Data Using a Subroutine

Copyright 1985, Compulit, Inc.

```
\               Declaration of variables
        INTEGER STACK, I, N, K, T, SP, IN, VTS, VBS, PTS, PBS
        REAL X, XZ
```

(continues)

```
        STRING CLEAR.SCREEN, AN
\                Defining CLEAR.SCREEN for PC-DOS and MS-DOS
        CLEAR.SCREEN = CHR$(27) + "[2J"
5       DIM X(100), STACK(100)
        FOR I = 1 TO 100
        PRINT CLEAR.SCREEN
        PRINT "Enter 99999 to terminate input": PRINT: PRINT
        PRINT "You are inputting value "; I: PRINT: PRINT
        INPUT "Enter value ....... "; X(I)
        IF X(I) = 99999 THEN 10
        NEXT
10      N = I - 1
        PRINT CLEAR.SCREEN
        FOR K = 1 TO N
                PRINT X(K),
        NEXT
        PRINT: PRINT
        GOSUB 1000
        FOR T = 1 TO N
                PRINT X(T)
        NEXT
        PRINT: INPUT "Another run?  Yes or No?  "; AN
        IF UCASE$(AN) = "YES" THEN 5
        GOTO 2000
\                Quick sort subroutine
1000    IN = 0:   SP = 0:   IN = IN + 1
        STACK(SP+1) = 1:   STACK(SP+2) = N
1100    IF IN = 0 THEN RETURN
        IN = IN - 1:   SP = 2 * IN:   VTS =STACK(SP+1)
        VBS =STACK(SP+2):   XZ = X (VTS):   PTS = VTS:   PBS = VBS + 1
1200    PBS  = PBS - 1
        IF PBS  = PTS THEN 1400
        IF XZ <= X(PBS) THEN 1200
        X(PTS) = X(PBS)
1300    PTS  = PTS  + 1
        IF PBS = PTS  THEN 1400
        IF XZ >= X(PTS) THEN 1300
        X(PBS) = X(PTS): GOTO 1200
1400    X(PTS) = XZ
        IF VBS - PTS >= 2 THEN\
            SP = 2 * IN:   STACK(SP +1) = PTS  +1:\
            STACK(SP+2) = VBS : IN = IN + 1
        IF PBS - VTS >= 2 THEN\
            SP = 2 * IN:   STACK(SP +1) = VTS:\
            STACK(SP+2) = PBS - 1: IN = IN + 1
        GOTO 1100
        RETURN
2000    PRINT: PRINT "Normal termination of program"
        END
```

SORTING ALPHABETIC OR STRING DATA

Thus far we have presented various sort algorithms usable with numeric data. Now we turn to alphabetizing a list of string values. The basic method is the same as used for numeric data but with one addition. All the strings must be the *same length* because in CBASIC a shorter string will precede a longer string regardless of the spelling. For example, Uri will come before Annabelle unless we make the two strings the same length. This is done by adding a **filler** and then truncating all the strings to the same length for the sort procedure.

In **Program 9-7** we have used the simple IF-loop bubble sort. The filler used is FILL$, a set of 15 blanks. It is defined at the start of the program as:

```
FILL$ = "                     "
```

This FILL$ is added to each string by concatenation and the total is truncated to 15 characters by the LEFT$ command. This was done since none of the original strings exceeded 15 characters. The concatenation and truncation are done with one line of code:

```
ST$(K%) = LEFT$(X$ + FILL$, 15)
```

The number of blanks and the point at which the total is truncated are optional but the filler must be long enough to take care of the shortest string. For example, if the filler is 10 blanks and the total is truncated at 15 characters, Uri will contain only 13 characters and still be shorter than, and come before, Annabelle.

In addition, the length of each name must be stored in an array so that after sorting, the names can be printed without the added blank spaces. In a simple list, such as we are using here, the blanks would make no difference but when we print in columns or other forms the blanks could distort the results. The number of characters in each name is stored in the array LG%(K%) by a FOR-NEXT loop with the statement:

```
LG%(K%) = LEN(X$)
```

The statement to print the name with only the original characters is:

```
PRINT LEFT$(ST$(K%), LG%(K%))
```

where ST$ is the string and LG% is the length of the original string.

PROGRAM 9-7   STRINGST.BAS   [Non-Compiler]
Bubble Sort for Alphabetic Data

Copyright 1985, Compulit, Inc.

```
\                   Provide storage for 20 values and the lengths of 20 values
         DIM ST$(20), LG%(20)
\                   15 blank spaces to be added to each length of each value
         FILL$ = "               "
         FOR K% = 1 TO 10
             READ X$
\                Add blanks to string and truncate at 15 characters
             ST$(K%) = LEFT$(X$ + FILL$, 15)
\                Store original length of string
             LG%(K%) = LEN(X$)
         NEXT
         DATA ZELDA, ANNABELLE, BOB, FRANK, GINA, XAVIER, ROBERTA, KATE
         DATA JAMES, URI
\                Start of sort routine
         J% = 10
20       J% = J% - 1
         FLAG% = 0
         M% = 0
30       M% = M% + 1
         IF ST$(M%) <= ST$(M%+1) THEN 40
\                Switch string and length
         SAV$ = ST$(M%): ST$(M%) = ST$(M% + 1): ST$(M% + 1) = SAV$
         SAV% = LG%(M%): LG%(M%) = LG%(M% + 1): LG%(M% + 1) = SAV%
\                Set FLAG% to 1 if switch has been made
                                                    (continues)
```

```
            FLAG% = 1
40          IF J% > M% THEN 30
            IF J% > 1 AND FLAG% <> 0 THEN 20
\                Start printout of sorted data
            FOR K% = 1 TO 10
            PRINT LEFT$(ST$(K%), LG%(K%))
            NEXT
            END
```

The string data, entered with READ-DATA statements in the program, is output in alphabetical order.

ANNABELLE
BOB
FRANK
GINA
JAMES
KATE
ROBERTA
URI
XAVIER
ZELDA

A Quick Sort Subroutine for Alphabetic Data

Both the shell sort and quicksort algorithms become more complex in CBASIC when used with string data. Because of the *fill* it is necessary to store the original length of the string along with the string itself as was done in Program 9-7. In **Program 9-8** we have used three subroutines consecutively to produce a string sort; all are required in any string quicksort.

1. Subroutine 500 determines the length of the original string, adds the fill [a series of blanks], converts the numeric string length to a string variable, and stores the original string, fill, and length as a string. For example, if we use Rebecca Highland:

   - The routine determines its length, LON%, as 16.
   - It adds the fill and creates a string 33 characters long, the original 16 characters followed by 17 blanks.
   - It converts the length, LON%, to a string and adds it to the 33 characters, producing a string 35 characters long. The result is shown below with "b" used for a blank space.

   ```
   REBECCA HIGHLANDbbbbbbbbbbbbbbbbb16
   ```

2. Subroutine 1000 is the quick sort routine used earlier but modified to handle a string instead of a numeric value.
3. Subroutine 1500 strips off the two rightmost characters to determine the length of the original string, and then proceeds to remove the excess fill and restore the original string.

In the program we have used the INPUT LINE command to make it possible to enter a comma [,] as part of the alphabetic input.

```
INPUT "Enter string ............. "; LINE X$(I%)
```

PROGRAM 9-8   **QUICK2.BAS**   **[Compiler]**

Quick Sort for Alphabetic Data

Copyright 1985, Compulit, Inc.

```
\                    Declaration of variables
          STRING CLEAR.SCREEN, X, XZ, FILLER, BLANK, LD, FD, LON
          INTEGER STACK, I, IN, J, K, N, T, SP
          INTEGER FDD, LDD, VTS, VBS, PTS, PBS, LONN
\                    Defining CLEAR.SCREEN for PC-DOS and MS-DOS
          CLEAR.SCREEN = CHR$(27) + "[2J"
          DIM X(100), STACK(100)
          FILLER = "                                    "
          BLANK = " "
          FOR I = 1 TO 100
          PRINT CLEAR.SCREEN
          PRINT "Enter  END  to terminate input": PRINT: PRINT
          PRINT "You are inputting string      "; I: PRINT: PRINT
          INPUT "Enter string ............... "; LINE X(I)
          IF UCASE$(X(I)) = "END" THEN 10
          NEXT
10        N = I - 1
          PRINT CLEAR.SCREEN
          FOR K = 1 TO N
                PRINT X(K),
          NEXT
          PRINT: PRINT
          GOSUB 500
          GOSUB 1000
          GOSUB 1500
          FOR T = 1 TO N
                PRINT X(T)
          NEXT
          GOTO 1313
\                    Subroutine to determine length of string and fill
500       FOR J = 1 TO N
                LONN = LEN(X(J))
                IF LONN < 10 THEN \
                    LON = BLANK + STR$(LONN) \
                ELSE \
                    LON = STR$(LONN)
                X(J) = LEFT$(X(J) + FILLER, 33)
                X(J) = X(J) + LON
          NEXT
          RETURN
\                Quicksort subroutine
1000      IN = 0:    SP = 0:    IN = IN + 1
          STACK(SP+1) = 1:   STACK(SP+2) = N
1100      IF IN = 0 THEN RETURN
          IN = IN - 1:    SP = 2 * IN:    VTS =STACK(SP+1)
          VBS  = STACK(SP+2):    XZ = X(VTS):   PTS = VTS:   PBS = VBS + 1
1200      PBS  = PBS - 1
          IF PBS  = PTS THEN 1400
          IF XZ <= X(PBS) THEN 1200
          X(PTS) = X(PBS)
1300      PTS  = PTS  + 1
          IFF PBS = PTS   THEN 1400
          IF XZ >= X(PTS) THEN 1300
          X(PBS) = X(PTS): GOTO 1200
1400      X(PTS) = XZ
          IF VBS - PTS >= 2 THEN\
                SP = 2 * IN:    STACK(SP + 1) = PTS + 1:\
                STACK(SP+2) = VBS : IN = IN + 1
          IF PBS - VTS >= 2 THEN\
                SP = 2 * IN:    STACK(SP +1) = VTS:\
                STACK(SP+2) = PBS - 1: IN = IN + 1
```

(continues)

```
          GOTO 1100
\                 Subroutine to restore original size of string
1500      FOR J = 1 TO N
              LD = RIGHT$(X(J),1)
              FD = MID$(X(J),34,1)
              IF FD = BLANK THEN \
                  FDD = 0 \
              ELSE \
                  FDD = ASC(FD) - 48
              LDD = ASC(LD) - 48
              LONN = 10 * FDD + LDD
              X(J) = LEFT$(X(J), LONN)
          NEXT
          RETURN
1313      PRINT: PRINT "Normal termination of program"
          END
```

SUGGESTED READING ON SORTING TECHNIQUES

Because sorting of data is often encountered in business operations and because sorting of large files takes so much computer time, we have included several references for experienced readers interested in developing their own sort programs.

Alfred Aho, John Hopcroft, and Jeffrey Ullman: *The Design and Analysis of Computer Algorithms*. Reading MA: Addison-Wesley Publishing Co., 1975. [Chapter 3] Intermediate level book with algorithms in Pascal.

Sara Baase: *Computer Algorithms: Introduction to Design and Analysis*. Reading MA: Addison-Wesley Publishing Company, 1978. [Chapter 2] Intermediate level volume with algorithms in English with mathematical notation.

Taylor L. Booth and Yi-Tzuu Chien: *Computing: Fundamentals and Applications*. Santa Barbara CA: Hamilton Publishing Company, 1974. [Chapter 9] Introductory volume with algorithms shown in flowchart form.

Olle Dopping: *Computers and Data Processing*. Copenhagen, Denmark: Studentlitteratur Lund Akademisk Forlag, 1970. [Chapter 17] Introductory level volume with descriptive explanations.

V. A. Dyck, J. D. Lawson, and J. A. Smith: *Introduction to Computing*. Reston VA: Reston Publishing Company, Inc., 1979. [Chapter 12] Introductory level volume with algorithms in Pidgin Algol and programs in Fortran.

Ivan Flores: *Computing Sorting*. Englewood Cliffs NJ: Prentice-Hall, Inc., 1969. Intermediate volume with special mathematical notation for the sort algorithms.

Donald Knuth: *The Art of Computer Programming* [Volume 3]. Reading MA: Addison-Wesley Publishing Co., 1973. Advanced volume and basic source in this field.

Lydia Kronsjo: *Algorithms: Their Complexity and Efficiency*. New York NY: John Wiley & Sons, 1979. Intermediate level with algorithms in mathematical notation.

Harold Lorin: *Sorting and Sort Systems*. Reading MA: Addison-Wesley Publishing Co., 1975. Advanced volume with Pidgin Algol algorithms; an excellent reference.

CHAPTER 10

Advanced Data
File Handling

Business data is kept in files and all the following illustrations will use files to show sorting, merging, and modifying data in a practical situation. Sequential and relative files are treated separately because the methods which apply to one are either not applicable or not efficient for the other.

It must be emphasized that the programs used in this chapter to illustrate file manipulation have been written so that they are easy to understand and adapt but are not the most sophisticated or efficient. This applies particularly to the search and sort techniques for which there is an extensive literature available for reference.

SEQUENTIAL FILES

Sorting Sequential Files

Using Program 5-1 as a model, set up a master file of customers and a daily file using the data later in this section. [Make a copy of Program 5-1, SFILE1.BAS, and change the filename, the names of the variables, and the PRINT # statement.] Although the zip code is an integer, define it as a string. If it is defined as an integer, it will be outside the limits for integers for some zip codes. If it is defined as a real value, the lead zero which is used in some zip codes will not be printed. In addition, if all the variables are strings, we will be able to use string arrays in the sort and merge programs.

These files will be used to illustrate one way in which sequential files are handled in a business situation. Each day the **daily file** of new customers is sorted and merged with the sorted **master file** which is the accumulated list of customers.

For the master file use:

Compute-All	190 School St.	Elmont NY	11003
Tried & True	500 Legal St.	Princeton NJ	08540
Organic Foods	1200 Health St.	Plantation TX	77363
Silver & Gold	100 Jewel St.	Americus KS	66835
Compute-All	2000 Brayne St.	Five Points CA	93624
Brown and Greene	55 Rainbow Ave.	Princeton NJ	08540
Ven-tel Inc.	299 Walsh St.	Santa Clara CA	95051

For the daily file use:

Tried & True	122 Law St.	Five Points CA	93624
Brown and Greene	55 Rainbow Ave.	Princeton NJ	08540
Furry Friends Inc.	33 Pet Lane	Edgewater FL	32032
Flower Shop	444 Carnation Ave.	St. Paul MN	55105

Before the daily file can be combined, or merged, with the master file both files have to be sorted by customer name.

First, the data from the unsorted file is read into a two-dimensional array by the following statements.

Each record is read using an array identifier for the four fields.

```
READ #1; F$(1), F$(2), F$(3), F$(4)
```

The four fields then are placed in one row of the two-dimensional array.

1. The name is concatenated with FILL$ and truncated; this new string is placed in the first position of each row and will be used in sorting. The length of the name is stored in LG%(K%).

```
SRT$(JJ%,1) = LEFT$(F$(1) + FILL$, 20)
LG%(JJ%) = LEN(F$(1))
```

2. The remaining three fields are positioned in the second, third, and fourth columns of the array.

```
FOR K% = 2 TO 4
    SRT$(JJ% , K%) = F$(K%)
NEXT K%
```

The second step is to sort the array. The use of the two-dimensional array makes it possible to code the "save and switch" procedure for all the variables in three lines using a FOR-NEXT loop. Without the array, the four variables would each require three lines of code for the same instructions. The array LG%(M%) requires separate code because it is an integer variable.

```
FOR K% = 1 TO 4
    SAV$(K%) = SRT$ (M%, K%)
    SRT$(M%, K%) = SRT$(M%+1, K%)
    SRT$(M%+1, K%) = SAV$(K%)
NEXT
SAV% = LG%(M%)
LG%(M%) = LG%(M% + 1)
LG%(M% + 1) = SAV%
```

The third step is to write the data to a new file; this is also simplified by using the array.

```
FOR K% = 1 TO JJ%
    PRINT #2; LEFT$(SRT$(K%,1),LG%(K%)),SRT$(K%,2),SRT$(K%,3),SRT$(K%,4)
NEXT
```

Program 10-1 is the complete program to sort by the first field and write the results to a new file. The sort used is the simple bubble sort with flag and an IF-THEN loop. The nested FOR-NEXT loops require the number of records in the file to be known. In sequential files a counter can be included or a WHILE-WEND loop can be used in place of the FOR-NEXT. The file names are entered in response to INPUT statements.

PROGRAM 10-1   **SEQUSRT.BAS**   **[Non-Compiler]**

Read Sequential File and Sort by Alphabetic First Field

Copyright 1985, Compulit, Inc.

```
\               Blank spaces to be added to string data
        FILL$ = "                    "
\               Arrays to read values and store lengths of strings;
\               matrix to store and switch records
        DIM SRT$(50, 4), F$(4), SAV$(4), LG%(50)
        INPUT "Enter the name of the file.........";NOF$
        INPUT "Enter the name of the sorted file...";NOF1$
\               Open existing file and create file for sorted data
        OPEN NOF$ AS 1
        CREATE NOF1$ AS 2
        JJ% = 0
\               Read four fields of a record into an array
10      READ #1; F$(1), F$(2), F$(3), F$(4)
        IF END #1 THEN 15
        JJ% = JJ% + 1
\               Add FILL$ to first field, truncate at 20 characters, store in
\               first column of matrix
        SRT$(JJ%,1) = LEFT$(F$(1) + FILL$, 20)
\               Store original length
        LG%(JJ%) = LEN(F$(1))
\               Store remaining fields in matrix
                            (continues)
```

```
        FOR K% = 2 TO 4
            SRT$(JJ% , K%) = F$(K%)
        NEXT
        GOTO 10
\               Sort routine with FLAG% starts here
15      J% = JJ%
20      J% = J% - 1
        FLAG% = 0
        M% = 0
30      M% = M% + 1
        IF SRT$(M%,1) <= SRT$(M%+1, 1) THEN 40
        FOR K% = 1 TO 4
            SAV$(K%) = SRT$ (M%, K%): SRT$(M%, K%) = SRT$(M% + 1, K%)
            SRT$(M% + 1, K%) = SAV$(K%)
        NEXT
        SAV% = LG%(M%): LG%(M%) = LG%(M% + 1): LG%(M% + 1) = SAV%
        FLAG% = 1
40      IF J% > M% THEN 30
        IF J% > 1 AND FLAG% <> 0 THEN 20
\               Sorted data written to a new file
        FOR K% = 1 TO JJ%
            PRINT #2; LEFT$(SRT$(K%,1),LG%(K%)),SRT$(K%,2),SRT$(K%,3),SRT$(K%,4)
        NEXT
        CLOSE 1,2
        END
```

The sorted file is displayed using **Program 10-2**. To print hardcopy insert an LPRINTER statement before label 10 and a **CONSOLE** statement before label 20. Again the array is used to make the program more efficient.

PROGRAM 10-2   SEQUPRNT.BAS   [Non-Compiler]

Print Sorted Sequential File Using an Array

Copyright 1985, Compulit, Inc.

```
        DIM F$(4)
        INPUT "Enter name of file.......";NOF$
        OPEN NOF$ AS 1
        IF END #1 THEN 20
\               Read four fields into array
10      READ #1; F$(1), F$(2), F$(3), F$(4)
\               Print four fields from array
        FOR K% = 1 TO 4
            PRINT F$(K%),
        NEXT
        PRINT
        GOTO 10
20      END
```

When the master and daily files have been sorted and printed the outputs are:

For the master file:

Brown and Greene	55 Rainbow Ave.	Princeton NJ	08540
Compute-All	190 School St.	Elmont NY	11003
Compute-All	20.900 Brayne St.	Five Points CA	93624
Organic Foods	120.90 Health St.	Plantation TX	77363
Silver & Gold	100 Jewel St.	Americus KS	66835
Tried & True	500 Legal St.	Princeton NJ	08540
Ven-tel Inc.	299 Walsh St.	Santa Clara CA	95051

For the daily file:

Brown and Greene	55 Rainbow Ave.	Princeton NJ	08540
Flower Shop	444 Carnation Ave.	St. Paul MN	55105
Furry Friends Inc.	33 Pet Lane	Edgewater FL	32032
Tried & True	122 Law St.	Five Points CA	93624

Sorting by Zip Code

To sort a file by zip code is simpler because there are the same number of characters in every zip code. The fill and truncation procedure is, therefore, not necessary, although the zip code has been defined as a string. The comparison statements are rewritten to compare the zip codes instead of the names.

Program 10-3 arranges the records in order of zip code. If used for the master file, the first two records in the sorted file will be the two customers in Princeton NJ with zip code 08540. A mailing list sorted by zip code could save postage costs.

PROGRAM 10-3   **SEQUSRT2.BAS**   **[Non-Compiler]**

Sort a Sequential File by Fourth Field

Copyright 1985, Compulit, Inc.

```
\              Two arrays to store four fields; matrix to store all records
        DIM SRT$(50, 4), F$(4), SAV$(4)
        INPUT "Enter the name of the file.........";NOF$
        INPUT "Enter the name of the sorted file...";NOF1$
\              Open existing file; create file for sorted records
        OPEN NOF$ AS 1
        CREATE NOF1$ AS 2
        JJ% = 0
\              Read four fields of each record into an array
10      READ #1; F$(1), F$(2), F$(3), F$(4)
        IF END #1 THEN 15
        JJ% = JJ% + 1
\              Store four fields as one row of the matrix
        FOR K% = 1 TO 4
            SRT$(JJ% , K%) = F$(K%)
        NEXT
        GOTO 10
\              Sort routine with flag starts here
15      J% = JJ%
20      J% = J% - 1
        FLAG% = 0
        M% = 0
30      M% = M% + 1
        IF SRT$(M%,4) <= SRT$(M%+1, 4) THEN 40
\              Loop to switch rows of matrix
        FOR K% = 1 TO 4
            SAV$(K%) = SRT$ (M%, K%): SRT$(M%, K%) = SRT$(M% + 1, K%)
            SRT$(M%+1, K%) = SAV$(K%)
        NEXT
        FLAG% = 1
```

                (continues)

```
40       IF J% > M% THEN 30
         IF J% > 1 AND FLAG% <> 0 THEN 20
\                Sorted matrix is written to a new file
         FOR K% = 1 TO JJ%
           PRINT #2; SRT$(K%, 1),SRT$(K%,2),SRT$(K%,3),SRT$(K%,4)
         NEXT
\              Close original and sorted files
         CLOSE 1,2
         END
```

Merging Sorted Sequential Files

The final step is to merge the two files into a new third file. The new file should not contain duplicate customers. Therefore, the program must eliminate one entry for Brown and Greene which appears in both lists. Compute-All which is listed twice in the master file is not a duplicate because the addresses are not the same.

The program first compares two names, one from each file; if they are the same it compares the addresses. If both the names and addresses are the same, only one is written to the merged file. If the names are the same but the addresses are different, both records are included in the merged file. Although we are using strings, the fill and truncation are not needed for this comparison where the decision is only "same" or "different."

Program 10-4 will merge the sorted master and daily files into a new third file. The file names are entered in response to INPUT statements.

PROGRAM 10-4   **MERGE.BAS**   **[Non-Compiler]**

Merge Two Sorted Sequential Files

Copyright 1985, Compulit, Inc.

```
\              Enter three file names
         INPUT "Enter name of master file...."; NOF1$
         INPUT "Enter name of daily file....."; NOF2$
         INPUT "Name of merged file.........."; NOF3$
\              Open two sorted files; create new file for merged data
         OPEN NOF1$ AS 1
         OPEN NOF2$ AS 2
         CREATE NOF3$ AS 3
\              Provide blanks to add to string data for matching
         FILL$ = "                                        "
10       IF END #1 THEN 40
\            Read a name from each sorted file
         READ #1; NAME1$, ST.AD1$, CI.ST1$, ZIP1$
20       IF END #2 THEN 50
         READ #2; NAME2$, ST.AD2$, CI.ST2$, ZIP2$
\            Compare names
32       IF NAME1$ <> NAME2$   THEN 35
\            If names and addresses are the same, print one record
\            to new file. Read next value in both files
         IF ST.AD1$ = ST.AD2$   THEN\
             PRINT #3; NAME2$, ST.AD2$, CI.ST2$, ZIP2$:\
             GOTO 10\
\            If names match but addresses do not, print both records to
\            new file
           ELSE\
             PRINT #3; NAME1$, ST.AD1$, CI.ST1$, ZIP1$:\
             PRINT #3; NAME2$, ST.AD2$, CI.ST2$, ZIP2$:\
             GOTO 10
\            If names are different, add FILL$ to both and truncate
35       XNAME1$ = LEFT$(NAME1$ + FILL$, 40)
```

```
           XNAME2$ = LEFT$(NAME2$ + FILL$, 40)
  \                Compare names, print in correct order to new file,
  \                read next records
           IF XNAME1$ > XNAME2$  THEN\
                   PRINT #3; NAME2$, ST.AD2$, CI.ST2$, ZIP2$:\
                   GOTO 20\
                ELSE\
                   PRINT #3; NAME1$, ST.AD1$, CI.ST1$, ZIP1$:\
                   READ #1;  NAME1$, ST.AD1$, CI.ST1$, ZIP1$:\
                   XNAME1$ = LEFT$( NAME1$ + FILL$, 40):\
                   GOTO 32
  \                If one file is finished, read and print the other to end
  40       IF END #2 THEN 60
  45       READ #2; NAME2$, ST.AD2$, CI.ST2$, ZIP2$
           PRINT #3; NAME2$, ST.AD2$, CI.ST2$, ZIP2$
           GOTO 45
  50       PRINT #3; NAME1$, ST.AD1$, CI.ST1$, ZIP1$
           IF END #1 THEN 60
  55       READ #1; NAME1$, ST.AD1$, CI.ST1$, ZIP1$
           PRINT #3; NAME1$, ST.AD1$, CI.ST1$, ZIP1$
           GOTO 55
  \                Close all files
  60       CLOSE 1,2,3
           PRINT "NORMAL TERMINATION"
           END
```

The new merged master file can be displayed or printed using Program 10-2. The output is:

Brown and Greene	55 Rainbow Ave.	Princeton NJ	08540
Compute-All	190 School St.	Elmont NY	11003
Compute-All	2000 Brayne St.	Five Points CA	93624
Flower Shop	444 Carnation Ave.	St. Paul MN	55105
Furry Friends Inc.	33 Pet Lane	Edgewater FL	32032
Organic Foods	1200 Health St.	Plantation TX	77363
Silver & Gold	100 Jewel St.	Americus KS	66835
Tried & True	500 Legal St.	Princeton NJ	08540
Tried & True	122 Law St.	Five Points CA	93624
Ven-tel Inc.	299 Walsh St.	Santa Clara CA	95051

The list is correctly sorted, the duplicate name is printed only once, and Tried & True is included twice because it was in both lists but with different addresses.

Searching for a Record in a Sorted Sequential File

Program 10-5 will search the file for a record and display it. The method used is the simplest to understand and explain but not the most efficient. Although the file is already sorted, this fact is used only to a limited extent. Each record is read and matched against the required name and displayed if a match is found. Because there are duplicate names in the list, the read, match, and display continue until a new name is read. The file is then closed without additional records being read and the program terminates. Note the use of FLAG% to branch to different parts of the program when [1] the required record has been found and a duplicate may exist and, [2] when the name has not yet been found.

An IF END statement precedes the OPEN statement to give the user the option of entering a corrected filename. If the file is read to the end but the name is not found, the file is closed, the user is notified and given the opportunity of searching again without restarting the program.

PROGRAM 10-5   **SEQUSUR.BAS**   **[Non-Compiler]**

Search Sorted Sequential File by First Field

Copyright 1985, Compulit, Inc.

```
\               Defining CLEAR.SCREEN for PC-DOS and MS-DOS
        CLEAR.SCREEN$ = CHR$(27) + "[2J"
        SPACE$ = CHR$(32)
        PRINT CLEAR.SCREEN$
5       INPUT "Enter name of file for search  "; NOF$:   PRINT
        IF END #1 THEN 30
8       OPEN NOF$ AS 1
\               Flag changes to 1 when the name is found and displayed
        FLAG% = 0
        INPUT "Enter customer name for search  "; XNAME$:    PRINT
12      READ #1; NAME$, ST.AD$, CI.ST$, ZIP$
        IF END #1 THEN 20
\               Compare record name with name for search
        IF UCASE$(NAME$) <> UCASE$(XNAME$) AND FLAG% = 0 THEN 12
\               If names are different but match was found, end reading
        IF UCASE$(NAME$) <> UCASE$(XNAME$) AND FLAG% = 1 THEN 40
\               If names are the same, display record and read next record
\               File may contain record with same name but different address
        PRINT NAME$, ST.AD$, CI.ST$, ZIP$:   PRINT:   PRINT
15      PRINT "Press SPACE BAR to continue "; SPACE$
        IF CHR$(CONCHAR%) <> SPACE$ THEN 15
        FLAG% = 1:    GOTO 12
\               Note end of file but name not found
20      INPUT "Customer name not found. Try again?  (Y/N).. "; ANS
        IF UCASE$(AN$) = "Y" THEN CLOSE 1:    GOTO 8
        GOTO 40
\               Recovery routine for file that does not exist
30      INPUT "File does not exist. Try another name?..(Y/N). "; ANS
        IF UCASE$(AN$) <> "Y" THEN 45
        GOTO 5
40      CLOSE 1
45      PRINT "Normal termination of program"
        END
```

Changing or Deleting a Record

Changing a record in a sequential file requires that every record be read and written to a new file, in changed or unchanged form. Therefore, all changes and deletions should be done as part of the daily update, a complex programming problem beyond the scope of this book. However, **Program 10-6** shows the basic procedure of searching for and changing a record.

Each record is read, matched against the required name and address [to take care of duplicate names], and either written to the new file or displayed as the record to be changed. After the changes have been made and checked, the record is written to the new file. The program then reads the old file and writes to the new file without matching until the end of file is reached.

If the filename is entered incorrectly the user is notified and can then reenter the name. However, if the customer name is incorrect and is not found the user is notified but must restart the program. A new, duplicate file has been created under a new name and should be erased.

PROGRAM 10-6   **SEQALTER.BAS**   **[Non-Compiler]**

Alter a Record in a Sequential File

Copyright 1985, Compulit, Inc.

```
\           Defining CLEAR.SCREEN for PC-DOS and MS-DOS
           CLEAR.SCREEN$ = CHR$(27) + "[2J"
\           FLAG% will indicate change in record
           FLAG% = 0:   SPACE$ = CHR$(32)
           PRINT CLEAR.SCREEN$
           INPUT "Enter name of new file.. "; NOF1$:     PRINT
\           Create new file to rewrite current file and changed record
           CREATE NOF1$ AS 2
5          INPUT "Enter name of current file.. "; NOF$:   PRINT
           IF END #1 THEN 30
           OPEN NOF$ AS 1
10         INPUT "Enter customer name in record to be changed... ";XNAME$:  PRINT
           INPUT "Enter street address in record to be changed.. ";XST.AD$: PRINT
12         READ #1; NAME$, ST.AD$, CI.ST$, ZIP$
           IF END #1 THEN 40
\           If record was found, read and rewrite file to end
           IF FLAG% = 1 THEN PRINT #2; NAME$, ST.AD$, CI.ST$, ZIP$:  GOTO 12
\           If not the record to be changed, write it to new file
           IF UCASE$(NAME$)<>UCASE$(XNAME$) OR UCASE$(ST.AD$)<>UCASE$(XST.AD$)\
              THEN PRINT #2; NAME$, ST.AD$, CI.ST$, ZIP$:  GOTO 12
           PRINT CLEAR.SCREEN$
           PRINT "This is the record to be altered.":    PRINT
\           Display record when match is found
           PRINT NAME$, ST.AD$, CI.ST$, ZIP$:   PRINT
13         PRINT "Press SPACE BAR to continue."; SPACE$
           IF CHR$(CONCHAR%) <> SPACE$ THEN 13
\           Enter correct data
14         INPUT "Enter correct name........... "; NAME$:      PRINT
           INPUT "Enter correct street address... "; ST.AD$:    PRINT
           INPUT "Enter correct city and state... "; CI.ST$:    PRINT
           INPUT "Enter correct zip code......... "; ZIP$:      PRINT
\           Check new data
           PRINT NAME$, ST.AD$, CI.ST$, ZIP$:                 PRINT
           INPUT "Are the entries correct now?...(Y/N) "; ANS$:  PRINT
\           Reenter data if not correct
           IF UCASE$(ANS$) <> "Y" THEN 14
\           Write correct record to new file; change FLAG% to 1
           PRINT #2; NAME$, ST.AD$, CI.ST$, ZIP$
           FLAG% = 1:  GOTO 12
\           Error routine for file that does not exist
30         INPUT "File does not exist. Try again?..(Y/N)"; ANS$:   PRINT
           IF UCASE$(ANS$) <> "Y" THEN 45
           GOTO 5
40         IF FLAG% = 1 THEN 42
\           Note that file was read completely but name was not found
           PRINT "Name not found; restart program to try again."
41         PRINT "Press SPACE BAR to continue."; SPACE$
           IF CHR$(CONCHAR%) <> SPACE$ THEN 41
\           Close both files
42         CLOSE 1,2
45         PRINT: PRINT "Normal termination"
           END
```

Deleting a Record

Program 10-6 can be used with a few changes to delete rather than to alter a record in a sequential file. In **Program 10-7** the file is searched until the required record is found. When it is, the PRINT # statement is skipped, FLAG% is reset, and the remainder of the file is read and written to the new file without any further matching.

PROGRAM 10-7   **SEQDELET.BAS**   **[Non-Compiler]**

Delete a Record in a Sequential File

Copyright 1985, Compulit, Inc.

```
\           Defining CLEAR.SCREEN for PC-DOS and MS-DOS
      CLEAR.SCREEN$ = CHR$(27) + "[2J"
\           FLAG% will indicate that record has been deleted
      FLAG% = 0:    SPACE$ = CHR$(32)
      PRINT CLEAR.SCREEN$
      INPUT "Enter name of new file.. "; NOF1$:    PRINT
\           Create file for rewritten records
      CREATE NOF1$ AS 2
5     INPUT "Enter name of current file.. "; NOF$:   PRINT
      IF END #1 THEN 30
      OPEN NOF$ AS 1
10    INPUT "Enter customer name in record to be deleted...   ";XNAME$:  PRINT
      INPUT "Enter street address in record to be deleted..  ";XST.AD$: PRINT
12    READ #1; NAME$, ST.AD$, CI.ST$, ZIP$
      IF END #1 THEN 40
\           If record to be deleted was found, continue reading and
\           writing to new file
      IF FLAG% = 1 THEN PRINT #2; NAME$, ST.AD$, CI.ST$, ZIP$:  GOTO 12
\           Compare name and address with record to be deleted
\           If different, write record to new file and continue reading
      IF UCASE$(NAME$)<>UCASE$(XNAME$) OR UCASE$(ST.AD$)<>UCASE$(XST.AD$)\
           THEN PRINT #2; NAME$, ST.AD$, CI.ST$, ZIP$:   GOTO 12
\           When match if found, change FLAG% to 1; continue reading
      FLAG% = 1:    GOTO 12
\           Error routine for file that does not exist
30    INPUT "File does not exist. Try again?..(Y/N)"; AN$:    PRINT
      IF UCASE$(AN$) <> "Y" THEN 45
      GOTO 5
\           If record was found and file has been rewritten, end execution
40    IF FLAG% = 1 THEN 42
\           Note that name was not found
      PRINT "Name not found; restart program to try again."
41    PRINT "Press SPACE BAR to continue."; SPACE$
      IF CHR$(CONCHAR%) <> SPACE$ THEN 41
\           Close both files
42    CLOSE 1,2
45    PRINT: PRINT "Normal termination"
      END
```

In both the alter and delete programs a new, updated file has been created under a new name. In practice, the new file becomes the master and should have the name of the old file. For example, the payroll file should have a set name. Therefore, the program should delete the old master and rename the new file with the established name. A printout of the old file should be kept since it will be deleted. The addition of two lines in the program [the first and third lines below] deletes the old file and changes the name of the new file. Beginning with label 42 the program would read:

```
42          DELETE 1
            CLOSE 2
            CHANGE% = RENAME (NOF$,NOF1$)
45          PRINT: PRINT "Normal termination"
            END
```

The **DELETE** statement removes the file [NOF$] from the disk directory. It must be used before the file is closed and a CLOSE 1 statement is no longer necessary.

LANGUAGE CODING RULE

The **DELETE** statement deactivates a file from processing, removes its name from the disk's directory, reallocates the buffer space that the file used, and any IF END statement assigned to the file number has no further effect.

DELETE <file number> {, <file number>}

The **RENAME** statement permits the programmer to change the name of any disk file during program execution. The name change can be verified by using the following:

```
CHANGE.NAME% = RENAME (NEW.FILE, OLD.FILE)
PRINT CHANGE.NAME%
```

If the name has been changed, the value of CHANGE.NAME% would be equal to -1 but a zero would be printed if the name was not changed. However, if the new name assigned in the statement already exists in the disk's directory, an execution error will occur. Furthermore, the RENAME statement may be used only after the file has been closed.

LANGUAGE CODING RULE

The **RENAME** statement is used to change a file's name during the execution of a program.

<integer variable> = **RENAME** (<new filename>, <old filename>**)**

• The file must be closed *before* this statement is used.

RELATIVE FILES

Adding New Names to the Master File

Set up the relative master file using a program similar to Program 5-4 and the same data as we used in the sequential file earlier in this chapter on page 182. Change the record length to 75; also change the variable names in the declaration statements, the INPUT statements, and PRINT # statement. The new customers will be added each day to the master file; duplicates will be eliminated and a separate file of new customers will be created each day.

Duplicates are eliminated by the following FOR-NEXT loop. The loop begins with K% = 2 because the first record is used to store the index, or number of records in the file.

```
FOR K% = 2 TO INDEX1%
        READ #1,K%; NAME1$, ST.AD1$
        IF NAME1$ <> NAME$ THEN 20
        IF ST.AD1$ <> ST.AD$ THEN 20
            PRINT "Duplicate name. Press space bar for next entry."
                IF CHR$(CONCHAR%) = SPACE$ THEN 10
20      NEXT
```

If the name and address are not duplicates then the customer data is written to both the master and new daily files in two PRINT # statements.

The data in the daily file is added to the master file to create an updated master by using **Program 10-8**.

PROGRAM 10-8   **RELADD.BAS**   **[Non-Compiler]**

Add to Relative File and Start New File for Additions

Copyright 1985, Compulit, Inc.

```
\              Defining CLEAR.SCREEN for PC-DOS and MS-DOS
        CLEAR.SCREEN$ = CHR$(27) + "[2J"
        PRINT CLEAR.SCREEN$
        INPUT "Enter name of master file.......... ";NOF$
        INPUT "Enter name of file for additions.... ";NOF1$
\              Open master file and read index
        OPEN NOF$ RECL 75 AS 1
        READ #1,1; INDEX1%
\              CREATE file for new names
        CREATE NOF1$ RECL 75 AS 2
        INDEX2% = 1
10      INPUT "Enter customer name........ ";NAME$
        INPUT "Enter street address........ ";ST.AD$
\              Read file beginning with second record to search for duplicate
        FOR K% = 2 TO INDEX1%
                READ #1, K%; NAME1$, ST.AD1$, CI.ST1$, ZIP1$
                IF NAME1$ <> NAME$ THEN 20
                IF ST.AD1$ <> ST.AD$ THEN 20
                    PRINT
                    PRINT "Duplicate name. Press any letter to continue."
                H% = INKEY
                    PRINT
                INPUT "Another entry?...Y or N.."; AN$
                IF UCASE$(AN$) = "Y" THEN 10
                GOTO 25
```

```
20        NEXT
\                      If loop is completed without finding a duplicate
\                      enter remaining data
          INPUT "Enter city and state........ ";CI.ST$
          INPUT "Enter zip code.............. ";ZIP$
\                      Increase index in both files
          INDEX1% = INDEX1% + 1
          INDEX2% = INDEX2% + 1
\                      Write new data to both files
          PRINT #1,INDEX1%; NAME$, ST.AD$, CI.ST$, ZIP$
          PRINT #2,INDEX2%; NAME$, ST.AD$, CI.ST$, ZIP$
\                      Write new index to both files
          PRINT #1,1; INDEX1%
          PRINT #2,1; INDEX2%
          PRINT CLEAR.SCREEN$
\                      Provide for additional new names
          INPUT "Another addition?...Enter Y or N.. ";AN$
          IF UCASE$(AN$) = "Y" THEN 10
\                      Close both files
25        CLOSE 1, 2
          END
```

Sorting a Relative File with Pointers

A relative file can be sorted in the same way as a sequential file but this would not use an important advantage of the relative file, that any record can be accessed by record number without reading the file from the beginning. We will illustrate a different sorting procedure in which there is no actual switching of records. Instead, a number will be assigned to each record which will indicate to the computer the order in which the records are to be printed.

The first step is to store the names and record numbers in two arrays by a FOR-NEXT loop. The name is again filled and truncated. The three other fields need not be read or stored because there will be no actual or physical movement of records.

```
FOR K% = 2 TO INDEX%
        READ #1, K%; NAME$
        ST$(K%-1) = LEFT$(NAME$ + FILL$, 35)
        R%(K%-1) = K%
NEXT
```

The two arrays are then sorted by the "save and switch" technique we have been using. To keep the illustration simple, we will use a series of five names rather than the actual file data.

ARRAYS BEFORE SORT		ARRAYS AFTER SORT	
ST$(K$−1) (Name)	R%(K%−1) (Record #)	ST$(K%−1) (Name)	R%(K%−1) (Record #)
Uri	2	Anna	4
Barbara	3	Barbara	3
Anna	4	Frank	5
Frank	5	Uri	2
Zelda	6	Zelda	6

The next step is to add a number, called a **pointer**, to each record. The pointer will tell the computer the order in which the records are to be printed. The number of the first record, which is 4 in this illustration, is assigned to an integer identifier by the statement:

```
START% = R%(1)
```

The value of START% is stored with the index in the first record.

```
PRINT #1,1; INDEX%, START%
```

Each of the records is then assigned a pointer which tells the computer which record is to be printed next. This is done with the following FOR-NEXT loop. Note that this time the entire record must be read because the pointer, P%, will be added as a new field at the end of the record.

```
START% = R%(1)
PRINT #1,1; INDEX%, START%
FOR J% = 1 TO (INDEX% -1)
        READ #1, R%(J%); NAME$, ST.AD$, CI.ST$, ZIP$
        P% = R%(J% + 1)
        PRINT #1, R%(J%); NAME$, ST.AD$, CI.ST$, ZIP$, P%
NEXT
```

The illustration with five names would have the following pointers.

RECORD #	NAME	POINTER (P%)
2	Uri	6
3	Barbara	5
4	Anna	3
5	Frank	2
6	Zelda	

The printing begins with record START%, in this case, #4. When the record is read the value of the pointer is recorded, in this case 3. This tells the computer to read and print record #3 next. When record 3 is read, the pointer says the next record is #5. This procedure continues until the last record is read and printed and the loop is completed. Note that the last record does not need a pointer because nothing is read or printed after it.

The statements to begin the printing of the sorted file and the READ and PRINT loop are shown in the following.

```
READ #1, START%; NAME$, ST.AD$, CI.ST$, ZIP$, P%
PRINT NAME$, ST.AD$, CI.ST$, ZIP$
FOR J% = 1 TO (INDEX% - 2)
        K% = P%
        READ #1, K%; NAME$, ST.AD$, CI.ST$, ZIP$, P%
        PRINT NAME$, ST.AD$, CI.ST$, ZIP$
NEXT
```

Program 10-9 is the complete program to sort and print a relative file using pointers.

PROGRAM 10-9   RELSORT.BAS   [Non-Compiler]

Sort Relative File Using Pointers and Nested Loops

Copyright 1985, Compulit, Inc.

```
\               Defining CLEAR.SCREEN for PC-DOS and MS-DOS
        CLEAR.SCREEN$ = CHR$(27) + "[2J"
        PRINT CLEAR.SCREEN$
        INPUT "Enter name of file to be sorted....... "; NOF$:    PRINT
        INPUT "Enter Today's Date."; LINE TODAYS.DATE$
\               Open file and read INDEX%
        OPEN NOF$ RECL 75 AS 1
        READ #1,1; INDEX%
\               Provide arrays and blank spaces needed in sort routine
        DIM ST$(20), R%(20)
        FILL$ = "                              "
        FLAG% = 0
\               Read name in each record. Add FILL$, truncate at 35 characters
\               and store in ST$ array.  Store record number in R% array
        FOR K% = 2 TO INDEX%
            READ #1, K%; NAME$
            ST$(K%-1) = LEFT$(NAME$ + FILL$, 35)
            R%(K%-1) = K%
        NEXT
\               Sort routine starts here
        N% = INDEX% -1
        FOR I% = 1 TO N% -1
        FLAG% = 0
            FOR J% = 1 TO N% - I%
                IF UCASE$(ST$(J% + 1)) < UCASE$(ST$(J% )) THEN\
                SAV$ = ST$(J%): ST$(J%) = ST$(J% + 1): ST$(J% + 1) = SAV$:\
                SAV% = R%(J%): R%(J%) = R%(J% + 1): R%(J% + 1) = SAV%:\
                FLAG% = 1
            NEXT
            IF FLAG% = 0 THEN 40
        NEXT
\               Placing pointers starts here
40      START% = R%(1)
        PRINT #1,1; INDEX%, START%
        FOR J% = 1 TO (INDEX% -1)
            READ #1, R%(J%); NAME$, ST.AD$, CI.ST$, ZIP$
            P% = R%(J% + 1)
            PRINT #1, R%(J%); NAME$, ST.AD$, CI.ST$, ZIP$, P%
        NEXT
        INPUT "Do you want to display the sorted file?...(Y/N).. ";ANS
        IF UCASE$(ANS) <> "Y" THEN 50
\               Display of sorted file starts here
        PRINT CLEAR.SCREEN$
\               Print date and column heads
        PRINT "Today's date is.."; TODAYS.DATE$: PRINT: PRINT
        PRINT "NAME", "STREET ADDRESS", "CITY AND STATE", "ZIP"
```

(continues)

```
        PRINT
\               Print first record in sorted file using START%
        READ #1, START%; NAME$, ST.AD$, CI.ST$, ZIP$, P%
        PRINT NAME$, ST.AD$, CI.ST$, ZIP$
\               Print remaining records in sorted file using pointers
        FOR J% = 1 TO (INDEX% - 2)
                K% = P%
                READ #1, K%; NAME$, ST.AD$, CI.ST$, ZIP$, P%
                PRINT NAME$, ST.AD$, CI.ST$, ZIP$
        NEXT
50      CLOSE 1
        END
```

A Menu Program for a Relative File

Program 10-10 will combine all the routines necessary to create and add to a relative file, alter or delete a record, sort using pointers, and finally print the sorted file. The choice of routines is provided by a menu.

The following essential safeguards have been included.

- A warning statement is printed with the menu to prevent the destruction of a file which has already been created.
- After work with each routine is completed, the file is closed and reopened if additional work is to be done.
- When a choice is made by number, as in the ON-GOTO statement, the next statement returns execution to the menu or a reentry line if the number entered is outside the limits of choice.

The program is broken into sections with comments for each, but if you remove all discussion and run the sections one after the other, you will have a working program. To try the program use the data in Chapter 5, page 81; the variable identifiers will not need to be changed.

Section 1 includes the *definitions* needed to clear the screen and hold copy on the screen, and the *subroutines*. The first subroutine opens the file and reads the index or indicates that the filename is incorrect. The second subroutine holds data on the screen. The subroutines are placed at the beginning of the program because the computer, during program execution, begins its search for the subroutine at the beginning.

```
\               Defining CLEAR.SCREEN for PC-DOS and MS-DOS
        CLEAR.SCREEN$ = CHR$(27) + "[2J"
        SPACE$ = CHR$(32)
\               Bypass the subroutines
        GOTO 25
\               Subroutine to check file name, open file and read INDEX%
800     PRINT CLEAR.SCREEN$
        IF END #1 THEN 810
        OPEN "B:"+ NOF$ RECL 50 AS 1
        READ #1, 1; INDEX%
        GOTO 820
\               If file name does not exist, program ends
810     PRINT "File by that name does not exist"
        GOSUB 900: STOP
820     RETURN
\               Subroutine to hold data on screen
900     PRINT: PRINT "Press SPACE BAR to continue."
        IF CHR$(CONCHAR%) <> SPACE$ THEN 900
        RETURN
```

Section 2 requests the name of the file, displays the menu, and branches execution to the routine chosen. If the number entered as a choice is not listed in the menu the program returns to the menu to give the user another opportunity to choose a routine.

```
\                    Enter file name and date
25        PRINT CLEAR.SCREEN$
          INPUT "Enter name of file.... "; NOF$
          INPUT "Enter today's date";LINE TODAYS.DATE$
26        PRINT CLEAR.SCREEN$:
\                    Display menu
          PRINT "What do you want to do?":            PRINT
          PRINT "  [1]  Exit from program":           PRINT
          PRINT "  [2]  Create a NEW file":           PRINT
          PRINT "  [3]  Add to an existing file":     PRINT
          PRINT "  [4]  Search by product number":    PRINT
          PRINT "  [5]  Change part of a record ":    PRINT
          PRINT "  [6]  Delete a record ":            PRINT
          PRINT "  [7]  Sort and print the file":     PRINT
          PRINT:  PRINT "NOTE:"
\                    Warning not to destroy an existing file
          PRINT "Warning: If you create a new file and a file by that name exists,
you will destroy the existing file.":  PRINT
\                    Enter menu choice by number
          INPUT "  Enter the appropriate number:  "; MC%
\                    Return to menu if choice is out of bounds
          IF MC% < 1 OR MC% > 7 THEN 26
50        ON MC% GOTO 700, 100, 200, 300, 400, 500, 600
```

Section 3 creates the file on the disk in drive B, starts the index at 1, and goes to the INPUT section which is also the routine used to add records to the file. After the data has been entered and written to the file the user is given the option of continuing entry or returning to menu. The file is closed before execution returns to menu.

```
\                    Routine to create a file and initialize INDEX%
100       PRINT CLEAR.SCREEN$
          CREATE "B:"+ NOF$ RECL 50 AS 1
          INDEX% = 1
\                    Increase INDEX% and enter data
150       PRINT CLEAR.SCREEN$
          INDEX% = INDEX% + 1
          INPUT "Enter product number.......... "; PROD.NO$   : PRINT
          INPUT "Enter product description...... "; PROD.DESC$: PRINT
          INPUT "Enter number of units on hand.. "; ON.HAND%  : PRINT
          INPUT "Enter product cost ............ "; PROD.COST : PRINT
          PRINT #1,INDEX%; PROD.NO$, PROD.DESC$, ON.HAND%, PROD.COST
          PRINT #1,1; INDEX%
          INPUT "Another entry?........(Y/N).... "; ANS$
          IF UCASE$(ANS$) = "Y" THEN 150
          CLOSE 1
          GOTO 26
```

Section 4 is the routine to add to an existing file. Execution begins with the subroutine that opens the file and then goes back to line 150 to increase the index, INPUT the data, and close the file. This arrangement avoids the need to repeat the entire INPUT section which was also used when the file is created. An alternate method would be a subroutine for the input of data.

```
\               Routine to add to file; open file, then use data entry
\               procedure from create routine
200     GOSUB 800
        GOTO 150
```

Section 5 searches for a particular product number and displays the record when it is found. If the entire file is read and the record is not found the user is notified and given the option of reentering the product number and searching again. This section of the program only displays the indicated record, but the search procedure is the basis of many kinds of file manipulation and is used in the next two routines.

```
\               Routine to search by product number
300     GOSUB 800
310     INPUT "Enter product number for search... ";XPROD.NO$
\               Read file from second to last record
        FOR K% = 2 TO INDEX%
                READ #1,K%; PROD.NO$, PROD.DESC$, ON.HAND%, PROD.COST
\               Compare each product number with the one entered for search
                IF PROD.NO$ <> XPROD.NO$ THEN 320
                PRINT PROD.NO$, PROD.DESC$, ON.HAND%, PROD.COST
                PRINT
\               Hold data on screen
                GOSUB 900
                CLOSE 1: GOTO 26
320     NEXT
\               Note that loop has been completed without finding number
        INPUT "Product number not found. Try again?...(Y/N).."; ANS$: PRINT
        IF UCASE$(ANS$) <> "Y" THEN CLOSE 1: GOTO 26
        GOTO 310
```

Section 6, the routine to change part of a record, displays the record to be changed and gives the user the opportunity of reentering the product number if it was incorrectly entered. There are then two choices for change, the number of units on hand or the product cost. For this particular file these were the only two fields that would need to be altered, but the same method could be extended to all the fields of the record in a different kind of file.

When the record has been altered, it is again displayed for the user to check and if correct it is written to the file. The file is then closed and the program returns to menu.

```
\               Routine to change part of a record
400     GOSUB 800
410     INPUT "Enter product number in record to be changed. ";XPROD.NO$:PRINT
\               Read file from second to last record
        FOR K% = 2 TO INDEX%
                READ #1,K%; PROD.NO$, PROD.DESC$, ON.HAND%, PROD.COST
\               Compare each product number with number entered for search
                IF PROD.NO$ = XPROD.NO$ THEN 415
        NEXT
\               Note that loop has been completed but product is not found
        INPUT "Product number not found. Try again?...(Y/N).."; ANS$: PRINT
        IF UCASE$(ANS$) <> "Y" THEN CLOSE 1: GOTO 26
415     PRINT PROD.NO$, PROD.DESC$, ON.HAND%, PROD.COST:      PRINT
\               Check if correct record has been found
        INPUT "Is this the record to be changed?..(Y/N) ";ANS$:  PRINT
        IF UCASE$(ANS$) <> "Y" THEN 410
\               Choose field to be changed
420     PRINT "Which do you want to change?":  PRINT
```

(continues)

```
        PRINT "(1) Number of units on hand" :  PRINT
        PRINT "(2) Product cost"             :  PRINT
        INPUT "Enter your choice by number.......  "; NO%:      PRINT
\               Return to choice if number is out of bounds
        IF NO% < 1 OR NO% > 2 THEN 420
\               Branch to chosen number
        IF NO% = 2 THEN 430
        INPUT "Enter correct number of units on hand... ";ON.HAND%:  PRINT
        GOTO 440
430     INPUT "Enter correct product cost............. ";PROD.COST: PRINT
440     INPUT "Another change in this record?..(Y/N)... ";ANS:      PRINT
        IF UCASE$(ANS) = "Y" THEN 420
        PRINT PROD.NO$, PROD.DESC$, ON.HAND%, PROD.COST:           PRINT
        INPUT "Is entry correct now?.......(Y/N)...... ";ANS
        IF UCASE$(ANS) <>"Y" THEN 420
        PRINT #1,K%; PROD.NO$, PROD.DESC$, ON.HAND%, PROD.COST
        CLOSE 1: GOTO 26
```

Section 7, used to delete a record, again searches by product number and checks whether the correct record has been found. If it is not the correct record the program goes back to the input of the product number; if it is the correct product the program changes the product number to "DELETED" and changes all the other fields to blank or zero. The user is then given the option of deleting another record without returning to the menu. This option can also be added to the routine to change a record [Section 6]. If the product number entered in response to the input statement is not found the user is notified and given the option of reentering the number.

```
\               Routine to delete a record
500     GOSUB 800
510     INPUT"Enter number of product to be deleted..  ";XPROD.NO$: PRINT
\               Read file from second to last record
        FOR K% = 2 TO INDEX%
                READ #1,K%; PROD.NO$, PROD.DESC$
\               Compare each product number with number entered for search
                IF PROD.NO$ <> XPROD.NO$ THEN 520
                PRINT PROD.NO$, PROD.DESC$:                  PRINT
\               Check if correct record has been found
                INPUT "Is this the correct product?..(Y/N)   ";ANS
                IF UCASE$(ANS) <> "Y" THEN 510
\               Change all fields in deleted record
                PROD.NO$ = "DELETED": PROD.DESC$ = " "
                ON.HAND% = 0: PROD.COST = 0
\               Print changed record to file
                PRINT #1,K%; PROD.NO$, PROD.DESC$, ON.HAND%, PROD.COST
                GOTO 530
520     NEXT
\               Note that loop was completed without finding product number
        INPUT "Product number not found. Try again?..(Y/N)..."; ANS
        IF ANS <> "Y" THEN CLOSE 1: GOTO 26
        GOTO 510
\               Note that record has been deleted
530     PRINT "Product number ";XPROD.NO$;" has been deleted.":  PRINT
        INPUT " Another deletion? .. (Y/N)   ";ANS
        IF UCASE$(ANS) <> "Y" THEN CLOSE 1: GOTO 26
        GOTO 510
```

Section 8 sorts by the first field, the product number, and prints the sorted file. The product number in this file is a uniform six-character string and filling and truncating are not necessary. A bubble sort with nested loops and a flag is used here, but the more sophisticated and rapid methods described in Chapter 9 may be substituted.

The printing of the file follows the sorting automatically because there is no reason to sort a relative file unless it is to be printed. A caution to the user to be sure the printer is on is included. There is no option to display rather than print; a display would require the addition of a counter to stop and hold the display on the screen after each group of approximately 10 records is on the screen. For test purposes to display a short file, place REM before the LPRINTER and CONSOLE statements.

```
\               Routine to sort by product number and print file
600     GOSUB 800
\               Sort routine starts here
        DIM PRNO$(20), R%(20)
        FOR K% = 2 TO INDEX%
                READ #1,K%; PROD.NO$
                PRNO$(K%-1) = PROD.NO$
                R%(K%-1) = K%
        NEXT
        N% = INDEX% - 1
        FOR I% = 1 TO N%-1
                FLAG% = 0
                FOR J% = 1 TO N%-I%
                        IF PRNO$(J% + 1) < PRNO$(J%) THEN\
                        SAV$ - PRNO$(J%):  PRNO$(J%) = PRNO$(J% + 1):\
                        PRNO$(J% + 1) = SAV$:\
                        SAV% = R%(J%): R%(J%) = R%(J% + 1): R%(J% + 1) = SAV%:\
                        FLAG% = 1
                NEXT
                IF FLAG% = 0 THEN 610
        NEXT
\               Place pointers in records for printing sorted file
610     START% = R%(1)
        FOR J% = 1 TO (INDEX% - 1)
                READ #1, R%(J%); PROD.NO$, PROD.DESC$, ON.HAND%, PROD.COST
                P% = R%(J% + 1)
                PRINT #1, R%(J%); PROD.NO$, PROD.DESC$, ON.HAND%, PROD.COST, P%
        NEXT
\               Printing of file starts here; check if printer is on
        PRINT "Be sure the printer is on."
        PRINT:  GOSUB 900
\               Engage printer and print
        LPRINTER WIDTH 80
        PRINT "Today's date is "; TODAYS.DATE$:  PRINT: PRINT
        PRINT "Product #", "Description", "Units on Hand", "Cost": PRINT
        READ #1, START%; PROD.NO$, PROD.DESC$, ON.HAND%, PROD.COST, P%
        PRINT PROD.NO$, PROD.DESC$, ON.HAND%, PROD.COST
        FOR J% = 1 TO (INDEX% - 2)
                K% = P%
                READ #1, K%; PROD.NO$, PROD.DESC$, ON.HAND%, PROD.COST, P%
                PRINT PROD.NO$, PROD.DESC$, ON.HAND%, PROD.COST
        NEXT
\               Disengage printer and return to console screen
        CONSOLE
        CLOSE 1: GOTO 26
```

Section 9 simply notifies the user that execution of the program has terminated and a system prompt will follow.

```
700     PRINT CLEAR.SCREEN$
        PRINT "Program terminated."
        END
```

An additional section to allow a new record to be substituted for a deleted record would avoid the waste of disk space. A simple method of doing this is to add a routine to open the file, search for product number DELETED, input the new data and write it to the file, close the file, and return to menu. The new routine would be added to the menu and the ON-GOTO, and the line following ON-GOTO would be changed to include the number of the new routine.

Other changes could make the program with this new option more compact.

- The print statement could be directed to skip DELETED and just print the numbers of such records at the end of the printout. The search for DELETED is then avoided. As a safety measure the record should be displayed before the new data is entered and written to the record.
- The lines to input the data and write to the file should be a subroutine since the same five lines would be used in three routines.

All the sections without the additions are combined in **Program 10-10** written for non-compiler versions of CBASIC. A compiler version of this program, named MENUPRO3.BAS, can be found on the supplementary disk that can be ordered for this book.

PROGRAM 10-10   **MENUPRO2.BAS**   **[Non-Compiler]**

Menu Program to Process a Relative File

Copyright 1985, Compulit, Inc.

```
\              Defining CLEAR.SCREEN for PC-DOS and MS-DOS
        CLEAR.SCREEN$ = CHR$(27) + "[2J"
        SPACE$ = CHR$(32)
\              Bypass the subroutines
        GOTO 25
\              Subroutine to check file name, open file and read INDEX%
800     PRINT CLEAR.SCREEN$
        IF END #1 THEN 810
        OPEN "B:"+ NOF$ RECL 50 AS 1
        READ #1, 1; INDEX%
        GOTO 820
\              If file name does not exist, program ends
810     PRINT "File by that name does not exist"
        GOSUB 900: STOP
820     RETURN
\              Subroutine to hold data on screen
900     PRINT: PRINT "Press SPACE BAR to continue."
        IF CHR$(CONCHAR%) <> SPACE$ THEN 900
        RETURN
\              Enter file name and date
25      PRINT CLEAR.SCREEN$
        INPUT "Enter name of file.... "; NOF$
        INPUT "Enter today's date";LINE TODAYS.DATE$
26      PRINT CLEAR.SCREEN$:
\              Display menu
        PRINT "What do you want to do?":          PRINT
        PRINT "  [1]  Exit from program":          PRINT
        PRINT "  [2]  Create a NEW file":          PRINT
        PRINT "  [3]  Add to an existing file":    PRINT
        PRINT "  [4]  Search by product number":   PRINT
        PRINT "  [5]  Change part of a record ":   PRINT
        PRINT "  [6]  Delete a record ":           PRINT
        PRINT "  [7]  Sort and print the file":    PRINT
```

(continues)

```
          PRINT:   PRINT "NOTE:"
\                  Warning not to destroy an existing file
          PRINT "Warning: If you create a new file and a file by that name exists,
you will destroy the existing file.":  PRINT
\                  Enter menu choice by number
          INPUT "   Enter the appropriate number:  "; MC%
\                  Return to menu if choice is out of bounds
          IF MC% < 1 OR MC% > 7 THEN 26
50        ON MC% GOTO 700, 100, 200, 300, 400, 500, 600
\                  Routine to create a file and initialize INDEX%
100       PRINT CLEAR.SCREEN$
          CREATE "B:"+ NOF$ RECL 50 AS 1
          INDEX% = 1
\                  Increase INDEX% and enter data
150       PRINT CLEAR.SCREEN$
          INDEX% = INDEX% + 1
          INPUT "Enter product number.......... "; PROD.NO$   : PRINT
          INPUT "Enter product description...... "; PROD.DESC$: PRINT
          INPUT "Enter number of units on hand.. "; ON.HAND%  : PRINT
          INPUT "Enter product cost ........... "; PROD.COST : PRINT
          PRINT #1,INDEX%; PROD.NO$, PROD.DESC$, ON.HAND%, PROD.COST
          PRINT #1,1; INDEX%
          INPUT "Another entry?........(Y/N).... "; AN$
          IF UCASE$(AN$) = "Y" THEN 150
          CLOSE 1
          GOTO 26
\                      Routine to add to file; open file, then use data entry
\                      procedure from create routine
200       GOSUB 800
          GOTO 150
\                  Routine to search by product number
300       GOSUB 800
310       INPUT "Enter product number for search... ";XPROD.NO$
\                  Read file from second to last record
          FOR K% = 2 TO INDEX%
               READ #1,K%; PROD.NO$, PROD.DESC$, ON.HAND%, PROD.COST
\                  Compare each product number with the one entered for search
               IF PROD.NO$ <> XPROD.NO$ THEN 320
               PRINT PROD.NO$, PROD.DESC$, ON.HAND%, PROD.COST
               PRINT
\                  Hold data on screen
               GOSUB 900
               CLOSE 1: GOTO 26
320       NEXT
\                  Note that loop has been completed without finding number
          INPUT "Product number not found. Try again?...(Y/N).."; AN$: PRINT
          IF UCASE$(AN$) <> "Y" THEN CLOSE 1: GOTO 26
          GOTO 310
\                  Routine to change part of a record
400       GOSUB 800
410       INPUT "Enter product number in record to be changed. ";XPROD.NO$:PRINT
\                  Read file from second to last record
          FOR K% = 2 TO INDEX%
               READ #1,K%; PROD.NO$, PROD.DESC$, ON.HAND%, PROD.COST
\                  Compare each product number with number entered for search
               IF PROD.NO$ = XPROD.NO$ THEN 415
          NEXT
\                  Note that loop has been completed but product is not found
          INPUT "Product number not found. Try again?...(Y/N).."; AN$: PRINT
          IF UCASE$(AN$) <> "Y" THEN CLOSE 1: GOTO 26
415       PRINT PROD.NO$, PROD.DESC$, ON.HAND%, PROD.COST:          PRINT
\                  Check if correct record has been found
          INPUT "Is this the record to be changed?..(Y/N) ";AN$:  PRINT
          IF UCASE$(AN$) <> "Y" THEN 410
\                  Choose field to be changed
420       PRINT "Which do you want to change?":  PRINT
          PRINT "(1) Number of units on hand" :  PRINT
          PRINT "(2) Product cost"            :  PRINT
          INPUT "Enter your choice by number....... "; NO%:       PRINT
\                  Return to choice if number is out of bounds
          IF NO% < 1 OR NO% > 2 THEN 420
\                  Branch to chosen number
          IF NO% = 2 THEN 430
          INPUT "Enter correct number of units on hand... ";ON.HAND%:  PRINT
          GOTO 440
```

```
430        INPUT "Enter correct product cost.............. ";PROD.COST: PRINT
440        INPUT "Another change in this record?..(Y/N)... ";ANS:        PRINT
           IF UCASE$(AN$) = "Y" THEN 420
           PRINT PROD.NO$, PROD.DESC$, ON.HAND%, PROD.COST:              PRINT
           INPUT "Is entry correct now?.......(Y/N)...... ";ANS
           IF UCASE$(AN$) <>"Y" THEN 420
           PRINT #1,K%; PROD.NO$, PROD.DESC$, ON.HAND%, PROD.COST
           CLOSE 1: GOTO 26
\                  Routine to delete a record
500        GOSUB 800
510        INPUT"Enter number of product to be deleted..  ";XPROD.NO$: PRINT
\                  Read file from second to last record
           FOR K% = 2 TO INDEX%
                   READ #1,K%; PROD.NO$, PROD.DESC$
\                  Compare each product number with number entered for search
                   IF PROD.NO$ <> XPROD.NO$ THEN 520
                   PRINT PROD.NO$, PROD.DESC$:                           PRINT
\                  Check if correct record has been found
                   INPUT "Is this the correct product?..(Y/N)   ";ANS
                   IF UCASE$(AN$) <> "Y" THEN 510
\                  Change all fields in deleted record
                   PROD.NO$ = "DELETED": PROD.DESC$ = " "
                   ON.HAND% = 0: PROD.COST = 0
\                  Print changed record to file
                   PRINT #1,K%; PROD.NO$, PROD.DESC$, ON.HAND%, PROD.COST
                   GOTO 530
520        NEXT
\                  Note that loop was completed without finding product number
           INPUT "Product number not found. Try again?..(Y/N).."; ANS
           IF AN$ <> "Y" THEN CLOSE 1: GOTO 26
           GOTO 510
\                  Note that record has been deleted
530        PRINT "Product number ";XPROD.NO$;" has been deleted.":  PRINT
           INPUT " Another deletion? .. (Y/N)   ";ANS
           IF UCASE$(AN$) <> "Y" THEN CLOSE 1: GOTO 26
           GOTO 510
\                  Routine to sort by product number and print file
600        GOSUB 800
\                  Sort routine starts here
           DIM PRNO$(20), R%(20)
           FOR K% = 2 TO INDEX%
                   READ #1,K%; PROD.NO$
                   PRNO$(K%-1) = PROD.NO$
                   R%(K%-1) = K%
           NEXT
           N% = INDEX% - 1
           FOR I% = 1 TO N%-1
                   FLAG% = 0
                   FOR J% = 1 TO N%-I%
                           IF PRNO$(J% + 1) < PRNO$(J%) THEN\
                           SAV$ = PRNO$(J%):  PRNO$(J%) = PRNO$(J% + 1):\
                           PRNO$(J% + 1) = SAV$:\
                           SAV$ = R%(J%): R%(J%) = R%(J% + 1): R%(J% + 1) = SAV%:\
                           FLAG% = 1
                   NEXT
                   IF FLAG% = 0 THEN 610
           NEXT
\                  Place pointers in records for printing sorted file
610        START% = R%(1)
           FOR J% = 1 TO (INDEX% - 1)
                   READ #1, R%(J%); PROD.NO$, PROD.DESC$, ON.HAND%, PROD.COST
                   P% = R%(J% + 1)
                   PRINT #1, R%(J%); PROD.NO$, PROD.DESC$, ON.HAND%, PROD.COST, P%
           NEXT
\                  Printing of file starts here; check if printer is on
           PRINT "Be sure the printer is on."
           PRINT:  GOSUB 900
\                  Engage printer and print
           LPRINTER WIDTH 80
           PRINT "Today's date is "; TODAYS.DATE$:  PRINT: PRINT
           PRINT "Product #", "Description", "Units on Hand", "Cost": PRINT
           READ #1, START%; PROD.NO$, PROD.DESC$, ON.HAND%, PROD.COST, P%
           PRINT PROD.NO$, PROD.DESC$, ON.HAND%, PROD.COST
           FOR J% = 1 TO (INDEX% - 2)
                   K% = P%
                   READ #1, K%; PROD.NO$, PROD.DESC$, ON.HAND%, PROD.COST, P%
                   PRINT PROD.NO$, PROD.DESC$, ON.HAND%, PROD.COST
```

(continues)

```
            NEXT
    \                  Disengage printer and return to console screen
            CONSOLE
            CLOSE 1: GOTO 26
    700     PRINT CLEAR.SCREEN$
            PRINT "Program terminated."
            END
```

TO CHANGE A DISK DURING EXECUTION

The **INITIALIZE** statement permits the user to change disks during program execution without returning to the operating system. This is particularly useful when working with very long files or with a program that manipulates different files kept on different disks, for example, customer names by section of the country. In a program with a menu the ability to change disks could be included as one of the options.

All files must be closed and the disks must be changed *before* the INITIALIZE statement is executed.

In the non-compiler version the statement is simply INITIALIZE; it will reset all disks in use. With the compiler versions in a multi-user system an optional tail may be included specifying which disks are to be initialized. Reading from right to left, the tail starts with B [for binary] and the next digits represent drives A through P. A one [1] directs the computer to initialize that disk; a zero [0] means no change.

INITIALIZE 11B	resets drives A and B
INITIALIZE 101B	resets drives A and C but not B
INITIALIZE 1010B	resets drives B and D but not A and C

The following program segment illustrates a procedure which could be included as part of a menu program. It is assumed, as we have consistently recommended, that the files have been closed before the program returns to MENU for a new choice of options.

```
REM Routine to Change a disk during program execution
    PRINT "Change to required disk":            PRINT
    INPUT "Press any letter to continue.";H$:   PRINT
    INITIALIZE
    INPUT "Enter name of new file"; NOF1$:       PRINT
    INPUT "Enter record length..."; REC.LGTH%:  PRINT
    INPUT "Enter file number....."; FILE.NO%:   PRINT
    OPEN "B:"+ NOF1$ RECL REC.LGTH% AS FILE.NO%
    GOTO 26
```

In practice, both the record length and the file number would be entered in response to INPUT statements in the main program and the disk changing routine would return to that point. Only the first three statements and a GOTO would be needed in the illustration above. This would also avoid the need to return to MENU with a file open as we have done here. [Line 26 is the menu in Program 10-10.]

LANGUAGE CODING RULE

The INITIALIZE statement permits the changing of disks or other removable storage media during the execution of a program.

INITIALIZE   for the non-compiler version

or

INITIALIZE [numeric expression]   for the compiler version

- All files must be closed and the storage media changed *before* the INITIALIZE statement is executed.
- With the compiler version, specific drives can be designated by entering a series of binary values as the numeric expression. A drive is reset with a binary 1 and unchanged with a 0. Drives A through P are assigned from right to left; for example,

INITIALIZE 1110B

resets drives B, C, and D. The statement without any binary tail would reset all drives.

DETERMINING FILE SIZE

The **SIZE** function returns the size, in kilobytes [1024 bytes], of a specified file or files. The file size in bytes is divided by 1024 and any decimal remainder will be rounded up to the next higher integer. The filenames must be strings, ending in $, or enclosed in quotation marks, or with a compiler version declared as a string. The form is:

K% = SIZE (file specification)

Variations in the file specifications are:

K% = SIZE (CUSPRO$ + TEST$)	returns the total size of both files
K% = SIZE ("*.FIL")	returns the combined size of all .FIL files
K% = SIZE ("B:*.*")	returns the total size for all files on drive B

Determining Available Disk Space

The SIZE function may also be used to determine how much space is available on a disk during the execution of a program. For example, we wish to create a new file, NEW.FIL, which would be about 40% greater than an existing file, OLD.FIL. To determine if enough space is available on the disk for the enlarged file, we would first have to know how many blocks the disk contains.

> If you are using PC-DOS version 1.1, there are 8 sectors [a sector equals 512 bytes] per track and 40 tracks per side. There are two sectors per block. With a double-sided disk there are 320 blocks on the disk.
>
> Under PC-DOS version 2.0 or higher, or MS-DOS 2.11, there are 9 sectors per track with 40 tracks per side. The number of blocks on a double-sided disk is 360.
>
> With JFORMAT [Tall Tree Systems of Palo Alto CA], there are 10 sectors per track. With a double-sided disk, there are 400 blocks on the disk.

If we are using the MS-DOS 2.11 operating system with OLD.FILE on disk A, and wish to place NEW.FIL on disk B, we could use the following procedure:

```
\    Declaration of variables
     INTEGER NEW.FILE.SIZE, FREE.SPACE, HOLD
     - - - - - - - - - - -

     - - - - - - - - - - -
\    Determine the size of the new file in number of blocks
     NEW.FILE.SIZE = 1.40 * SIZE ("OLD.FIL")
\    Calculate the amount of space available in blocks
     FREE.SPACE = 360 - SIZE ("B:*.*")
\    Test if there is enough space
     IF FREE.SPACE > NEW.FILE.SIZE THEN 100
     PRINT "Insufficient space to start NEW.FIL"
     PRINT "Replace disk in drive B"
     PRINT "Press any letter after you have replaced the disk"
     HOLD = INKEY
     INITIALIZE 10B
\    If there is sufficient space, program branches to this point
100 OPEN "B:NEW.FIL" RECL 128 AS 3
```

With some versions of CBASIC it is *not* possible to use the SIZE function directly in a PRINT statement. For example:

```
PRINT "The size of the Phone List file is "; SIZE (PHONELIST.FIL)
```

will *not* print the size of the file. To do so first obtain the numeric value of the size function and then print that variable:

```
IFILE.SIZE% = SIZE (PHONELIST.FIL)
PRINT "The size of the Phone List file is "; IFILE.SIZE%
```

LANGUAGE CODING RULE

The SIZE function checks a specified disk and returns the number of kilobyte blocks [1024 bytes] in a specified file or files.

<integer variable> = **SIZE** (<file specification>)

- The file specification must be a string variable or a string constant. The integer variable returned is the file size in kilobyte blocks; any fractional part increases the value returned to the next higher integer. This is *not* true for executable files, namely, .COM, .CMD, and .EXE files.
- The following are examples of the SIZE statement.

STATEMENT	RETURNS FILE SIZE OF
H% = SIZE("*.COM")	All the .COM files on default disk
H% = SIZE(FILE$)	Previously defined string variable, FILE$
H% = SIZE("C:*.*")	All files on disk C

THE COMPILER-VERSION ALTERNATIVE FOR THE FILE STATEMENT

As noted earlier in Chapter 5 the non-compiler FILE statement does not exist in the compiler versions. However, by using the SIZE function we can develop the compiler version alternative. This function enables us to create or open a file as the FILE statement does in the non-compiler versions. The basic procedure is contained in three statements:

```
IF SIZE (NOF$) = 0 \
        THEN CREATE NOF$ RECL 128 AS 1 :\
        ELSE OPEN NOF$ RECL 128 AS 1
```

The first statement determines if there is a file NOF$ on the disk. If none is encountered, SIZE (NOF$) is evaluated as zero by the computer and execution would be transferred to the THEN statement, which would *create* a new file. If a file already exists by that name on the disk, SIZE (NOF$) is evaluated by the computer as greater than zero and execution is transferred to the ELSE clause and the file is *opened*.

The dangers of using the FILE statement, noted earlier in Chapter 5, also apply to the use of this technique. However, some error-detecting controls can be written into the program. **Program 10-11** is an example of the use of the SIZE function together with user controls.

The program contains two subroutines for error detection. After the user has entered the name of the file, the program responds in either of two ways:

- If a new file is to be created, the user is informed and is permitted to correct the filename entry by pressing the ESCAPE key.
- If an old file is to be opened, again the user is informed. If there is any error, pressing the ESCAPE key will permit the user to restart the program.

This demonstration program also includes the printing of the file after the last data has been entered. The program has been written in the PC-DOS version and must be linked with PCSCRN.L86 after it has been compiled. If you use any other versions of the language, remove the statement, %INCLUDE PCSCRN.DEF, define CLEAR.SCREEN in ASCII format for your terminal or monitor, and replace the CALL CLS statements with PRINT CLEAR.SCREEN statements.

PROGRAM 10-11	**SIZEFN.BAS**	**[Compiler]**

Use of SIZE Function in Place of FILE Statement

Copyright 1985, Compulit, Inc.

```
\              Declaration of variables
      STRING NOF, COPY, AN, CLEAR.SCREEN, SPACE.BAR, ESCAPE.KEY
      INTEGER I, INDEX
%INCLUDE PCSCRN.DEF
\              With the CP/M CBASIC Compiler version remove the %INCLUDE
\              statement and substitute: CLEAR.SCREEN = CHR$(27) + CHR$(69).
\              Replace each CALL CLS with PRINT CLEAR.SCREEN
      SPACE.BAR = CHR$(32)
      ESCAPE.KEY = CHR$(27)
      GOTO 10
\              Error-detection procedure when creating a new file
1000          CALL CLS
      PRINT "You are CREATING a NEW file named "; NOF: PRINT
      PRINT "If you have made an error, press ESCAPE key."
1001          PRINT: PRINT "To continue, press SPACE BAR."
      IF CHR$(CONCHAR%) = ESCAPE.KEY THEN 10
      IF CHR$(CONCHAR%) <> SPACE.BAR THEN 1001
      RETURN
\              Error-dectection procedure when opening an existing file
```

```
2000            CALL CLS
                PRINT "You are OPENING a file named "; NOF: PRINT
                PRINT "If you have made an error, press ESCAPE key."
2002            PRINT: PRINT "To continue, press SPACE BAR."
                IF CHR$(CONCHAR%) = ESCAPE.KEY THEN 10
                IF CHR$(CONCHAR%) <> SPACE.BAR THEN 2002
                RETURN
10      CALL CLS
        INPUT "Enter name of file    "; NOF
\               Create a file if NOF does not exist; open the file if it exists
        IF SIZE (NOF) = 0 \
                THEN GOSUB 1000 :\
                        CREATE NOF RECL 128 AS 1 :\
                        INDEX = 1:\
                        GOTO 20 \
                ELSE GOSUB 2000 :\
                        OPEN NOF RECL 128 AS 1 :\
                        READ #1,1; INDEX
\               Procedure to enter test data in the file
20      CALL CLS
        INDEX = INDEX + 1
        INPUT "Enter your copy:  "; COPY
        PRINT #1,INDEX; COPY: PRINT: PRINT
        PRINT #1,1; INDEX
        INPUT "Another entry? Yes or No?    "; AN
        IF UCASE$(AN) = "YES" THEN 20
        CLOSE 1
\               Reopen file and display test data
30      OPEN NOF RECL 128 AS 1
        READ #1,1; INDEX
        CALL CLS
        FOR I = 2 TO INDEX
                READ #1,I; COPY
                PRINT COPY
        NEXT
        PRINT: PRINT "Normal termination of program"
        CLOSE 1
        END
```

If you run this program, the first screen will appear as:

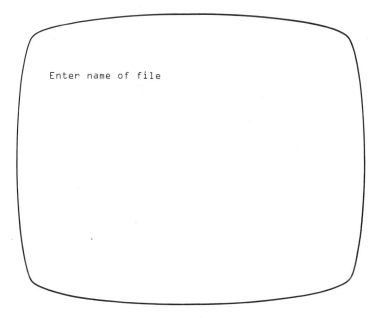

Enter name of file

FIGURE 10-1   Filename Screen of Program 10-11

After you have entered the filename, for example, DOCUMENT. FIL, and *if* the filename does not appear in the disk's directory, the next screen will appear as:

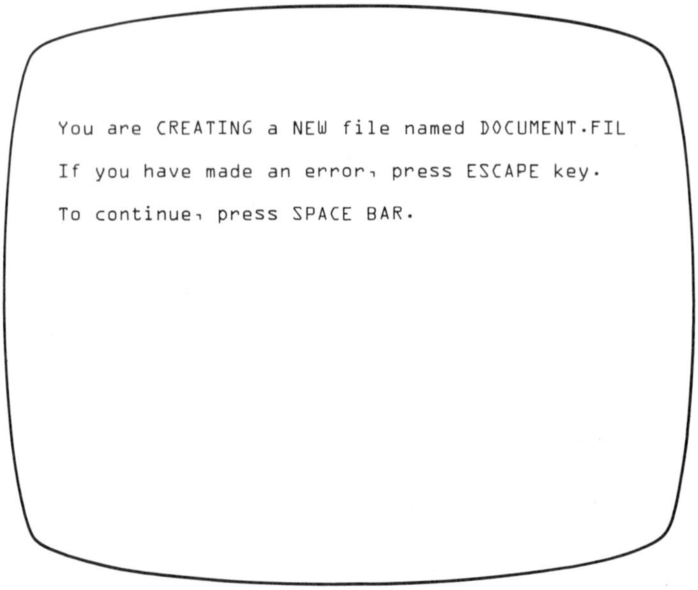

```
You are CREATING a NEW file named DOCUMENT.FIL

If you have made an error, press ESCAPE key.

To continue, press SPACE BAR.
```

FIGURE 10-2   CREATE Screen of Program 10-11

If after you have entered the filename, DOCUMENT. FIL, and the file exists on the disk, the screen you would see after the initial screen will be:

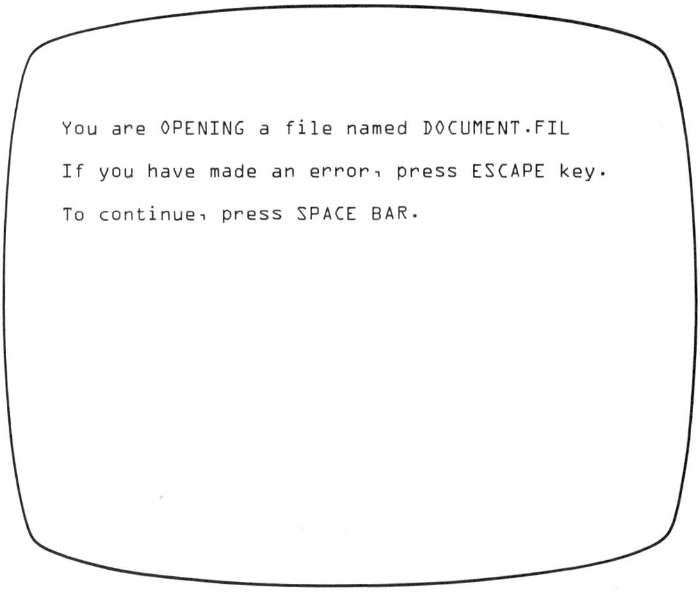

```
You are OPENING a file named DOCUMENT.FIL

If you have made an error, press ESCAPE key.

To continue, press SPACE BAR.
```

FIGURE 10-3   OPEN Screen of Program 10-11

Using these error-detection procedures will reduce the risk of opening a new file instead of updating an existing file. If the user planned to open a new file, the routine would provide added confirmation of the procedure. However, both these routines are operator-dependent; all they do is *reduce* the possibility of error, they cannot prevent it.

USING FIXED LENGTH FIELDS IN A RECORD

Some programmers turning from COBOL and other high-level languages used on mainframes are more comfortable using fixed rather than variable length fields. Although it is not necessary to follow this procedure with CBASIC, there are times when it is helpful. When working with long records and large files, fixed fields provide assurance that there is sufficient space for all fields within a record.

Consider the construction of a personnel file for a company with regional offices and some 500 employees in which each individual's record would contain:

FIELD NAME	TYPE	FIELD SIZE [NUMBER OF CHARACTERS]
NAME	String	24
STREET.ADDRESS	String	22
CITY.STATE	String	20
ZIP.CODE	Numeric	5
BRANCH.OFFICE	String	14
DEPARTMENT	String	18
OFFICE.PHONE	Numeric	4
TITLE	String	20
EMPLOYEE.NO	String	12
MESSAGE.CENTER	Numeric	5
SUPERVISOR.NAME	String	22
HOME.PHONE	String	12
NEXT.OF.KIN	String	22
PHONE.OF.KIN	String	12
MEDICAL.PLAN	String	14
DENTAL.PLAN	String	14
PENSION.PLAN	String	14
DATE.OF.EMPLOYMENT	String	10

In a CBASIC file, each field is separated from the next by a comma and each string is enclosed within quotation marks. Of the 18 fields in this example, 15 fields are strings and 3 are numeric. This would require, in addition to the two end-of-record characters, 17 commas to separate the fields and 30 quotation marks to enclose the strings.

Each record would contain 279 bytes: 230 bytes for the data, 47 bytes for the file definition, and 2 bytes for end-of-record indicators. With 500 employees the 47 file characters would result in the use of 23,500 bytes for overhead or some 16.8% of each record.

There are two problems associated with the building of this file. The first is the need for a data entry guide to make certain that no field exceeds its predetermined length. The second is the extra disk space required by the commas and quotation marks. In this illustration we will use CBASIC Compiler with the understanding that all variables have been declared at the beginning of the program.

Controlling the Field Size

The first problem of restricting field size can be solved by using the LEN function and a prompt if the field size is exceeded. [Another method will be shown later in Chapter 11.]

When the prompt for each field is entered, the field size can be noted:

```
PRINT "Name may not exceed 24 characters."
INPUT "Enter name :"; NAME
```

Once the entry has been made, the size of NAME is determined by using the LEN function:

```
20  FIELD.LENGTH = LEN (NAME)
```

A test is made to determine if the length of the entry is within the set limit. In the case of NAME we have set the field size to 24 characters. If the entry is too long, a prompt guide is displayed for the reentry of the field:

```
IF FIELD.LENGTH <= 24 THEN 50
PRINT:  PRINT "Name may not be greater than 24 characters; reenter."
PROMPT.GUIDE = STRING$ (24, "_"):   PRINT
PRINT ""; PROMPT.GUIDE
INPUT ""; NAME
GOTO 20
50  --------------
```

The PRINT " "; used in the fourth line prints a null string before printing the prompt guide. A null prompt string is used in the sixth line for inputting the corrected name so that the cursor is aligned with the prompt guide and no question mark is printed as would occur if the prompt string was not used.

SPECIAL PROGRAMMING NOTE

When an INPUT statement is used without a **prompt string**, the computer responds with a question mark and awaits an input. To suppress the ?-prompt, use a **null string**, " ", as a dummy prompt string, for example:

INPUT " "; VALUE

The length of a numeric variable can be determined by changing it to a string:

```
FIELD.LENGTH = LEN (STR$(ZIP.CODE))
```

where ZIP.CODE is a numeric value.

Program 10-12 illustrates part of this file program in order to show the use of the various functions and the prompt guide.

PROGRAM 10-12   **FIXED.BAS**   [Compiler]

Fixed Field Lengths with Test for Length and Entry Guide

Copyright 1985, Compulit, Inc.

```
\              Declaration of variables
        STRING AN, NAME, PROMPT.GUIDE, CLEAR.SCREEN
        INTEGER FIELD.LENGTH
        REAL ZIP.CODE
\              Defining CLEAR.SCREEN for PC-DOS and MS-DOS
        CLEAR.SCREEN = CHR$(27) + "[2J"
\              State permitted length for name
10      PRINT CLEAR.SCREEN
        PRINT "Name may not exceed 24 characters."
        INPUT "Enter name :"; NAME
\              Check on length of name
20      FIELD.LENGTH = LEN (NAME)
        IF FIELD.LENGTH <= 24 THEN 50
\              Instruction and guide to reenter name
        PRINT:  PRINT "Name may not have more than 24 characters; reenter."
        PROMPT.GUIDE = " " + STRING$ (24, "_"):   PRINT
        PRINT ""; PROMPT.GUIDE
        INPUT ""; NAME
        GOTO 20
50      PRINT
\              State permitted length for zip code
        PRINT "Zip code may not exceed 5 digits."
        INPUT "Enter zip code: "; ZIP.CODE
\              Convert zip code to string and check length
60      FIELD.LENGTH = LEN (STR$(ZIP.CODE))
        IF FIELD.LENGTH <= 5 THEN 100
        PRINT
\              Instruction on zip code length and guide for entry
        PRINT "Zip code may not be greater than 5 digits; reenter."
```

(continues)

```
        PROMPT.GUIDE = " " + STRING$ (5, "_"):    PRINT
        PRINT ""; PROMPT.GUIDE
        INPUT ""; ZIP.CODE
        GOTO 60
100     PRINT
        PRINT NAME, ZIP.CODE:    PRINT
        INPUT "Another test?  Yes or No? ... "; AN
        PRINT
        IF UCASE$(AN) = "YES" THEN 10
        PRINT "Normal termination of program."
        END
```

The STRING$ function cannot be used with the non-compiler version, but the same result can be achieved using a different programming technique. A FOR . . . NEXT loop replaces the function; the outer limit of the FOR statement determines the length of the prompt guide:

```
PRINT "  ";
FOR I% = 1 TO 5
        PRINT "_";
NEXT
PRINT
INPUT ""; ZIP.CODE
GOTO 60
```

How to Compress a Data File

The second problem in dealing with a large number of fields within a record, especially in very long files, is the overhead in disk space required for the delimiters. The excess commas and quotation marks can be reduced by converting the entire record to a single string. But there is a trade-off. To save disk space we require extra programming and execution time; the saving in disk space should be evaluated in comparison with the loss in programming and execution time.

In this example, we can combine the various fields by concatenation. In the illustration of the personnel file, this would be written as:

```
EMPLOYEE.DATA = NAME + STREET.ADDRESS + CITY.STATE
```

The next field, ZIP.CODE, cannot be added as it now stands. Any numeric value must be converted to string format *before* it is concatenated. The field, ZIP.CODE, a five-digit numeric value, is converted to a string by:

```
CODE.ZIP  = STR$ (ZIP.CODE)
```

where CODE.ZIP is declared as a string and ZIP.CODE declared as a real value. It is then possible to concatenate all the fields into a single string, EMPLOYEE.DATA, and save 45 bytes per record.

The fields must be separated when reading the data back from a disk. Each record would be read as a single string, EMPLOYEE.DATA, and would be segmented by using the MID$ function. The first eight fields are:

VARIABLE	EXPRESSION TO OBTAIN VARIABLE	
NAME	NAME =	MID$ (EMPLOYEE.DATA,1,24)
STREET.ADDRESS	STREET.ADDRESS =	MID$ (EMPLOYEE.DATA, 25,22)
CITY.STATE	CITY.STATE =	MID$ (EMPLOYEE.DATA,47,20)
ZIP.CODE	ZIP.CODE =	VAL(MID$ (EMPLOYEE.DATA,67,5))
BRANCH.OFFICE	BRANCH.OFFICE =	MID$ (EMPLOYEE.DATA,72,14)
DEPARTMENT	DEPARTMENT =	MID$ (EMPLOYEE.DATA,86,18))
OFFICE.PHONE	OFFICE.PHONE = INT(VAL(MID$(EMPLOYEE.DATA,102,4)))	
TITLE	TITLE =	MID$ (EMPLOYEE.DATA,106,20)

In this illustration, the digit string for OFFICE.PHONE is first changed to a real number by using the VAL function and then converted to an integer by the INT function. If the file is to be sorted by office phone number, this conversion to integer should be used because an integer will execute faster. However, if the file is used solely for data search, it is more convenient to create all variables as strings; this reduces program complexity both in data compression and in data separation.

CHAPTER 11

The Design of
Input and Output

The design of the input and output segments of a program involves an understanding of two fundamental components, the computer and the user who is either entering the data or reading the output. The design of the console screen for input influences the ease of data entry and the rate of entry errors. The design of console screen and printer output has a direct impact on the readability of the information. The design of both is complex and is replete with psychological and physiological principles. In this chapter only some of the highlights of design will be covered, including such topics as:

- applications of the PRINT USING statement with numeric data, strings, and data files,
- cursor control for both input and output,
- use of console screen and printer layout forms, and
- techniques for holding copy on the screen.

PRINT USING FOR NUMERIC DATA

We have already printed out numeric data which was understandable but not in a form acceptable for a report. We could understand, for example, that if the data concerned money then 19.5 was the same as $19.50 but certainly we would not use 19.5 in a hardcopy printout. Or, we may have been able to space the columns properly by using TAB statements but then the decimal points did not line up.

The PRINT USING statement permits considerable flexibility in determining the form of numeric data output and is very important in business programming where the desired final form of output is frequently different from the form of the calculated results.

The **PRINT USING** statement has two parts, the **format string** which defines the forms to be used and the **list of variables** which are to be printed using the forms.

LANGUAGE CODING RULE

Specific formats for output data can be specified with the PRINT USING statement.

PRINT USING <format string>; expression {, expression}

- The format string is the model for the output and may contain numeric and/or string data fields as well as literal data. Null strings may not be used as a format string.
- The different format strings that may be used with this statement are shown in Table 11-1 on page 225.

Positioning the Dollar Sign and Decimal Point

We will start with a form which will print *one variable*. In a problem where COST = 19.5, using the statement:

```
PRINT USING "$$##,##"; COST
```

would result in the output: **$19.50**.

- The two leading **$$** place a "floating" dollar sign immediately before the most significant digit.
- The # symbol stands for a numeric digit. This statement tells the computer that COST will have no more than two digits before the decimal point and that there should be two digits after the decimal point, using zeros instead of blanks where necessary. Values will be *rounded* to two decimal places.
- The number will be right justified within the field. Therefore, if the same statement is used for a series of values, one under the other, the decimal points will line up.

An illustration is a program which calculates the discount on a series of items and prints the results in a column. For three items the discounts are:

29.625, 1.32, and .59. The following PRINT USING statement is executed each time a new discount is calculated and printed.

```
PRINT USING "$$##.##"; DISCOUNT
```

The output is:

```
$29.63
 $1.32
 $0.59
```

1. The first discount has been rounded.
2. The $ "floats" leaving no space before the first digit.
3. The third discount has a zero before the decimal point because it is less than one [1].

One Form with More Than One Variable

One form can be used to print more than one variable in the same form. The variables are matched against the form and if there are more variables than forms the same form is used again.
   Where COST1 = 19.5, COST2 = 29.568, and COST3 = .27 the statement:

```
PRINT USING "$$##.##"; COST1, COST2, COST3
```

will result in the following output:

```
$19.50 $29.57   $0.27
```

Exponential Format

Exponential format in a PRINT USING statement is indicated by an upward arrow, ˆ , immediately following the last character of the form string. More than one upward arrow may be used but the output will not change. The following statements:

```
X = 1678.246: Y = -1678.246
PRINT USING "##.##ˆ    "; X, Y
```

will output:

```
16.78E 02   -1.68E 03
```

Note that:

- the string form [##.##] allows for two digits before the decimal point. If the number is *negative,* one # will be used for the minus sign and there will be one digit before the decimal point. The exponent is 03 instead of 02 as it is for the positive value.
- The values are rounded.

For X = 0.2478 and Y = −0.2478 the same PRINT USING statement will output

```
24.78E-02   -2.48E-01
```

Determining Field Width

The maximum number of characters allocated for the printing of a numeric variable is the number of symbols the form contains, including # signs, $ signs, asterisks, decimal point, commas, and trailing minus sign. Although each # sign in the field indicates a space allocated for a digit, a space will be used for a lead minus sign or a comma if necessary. Therefore, it is good practice to provide for these characters if either a negative number or a large number may be encountered. Illustrations are shown in the following sections, "Printing Numbers with Commas" and "Provision for Negative Numbers." *For exponential format allow four characters for the exponent.*

Spaces between Values

In the PRINT USING statement the commas between the variables *do not* cause the values to be printed in 20-character print areas as they do in the PRINT statement. A semicolon may be used between variables in the same way the comma is used; it makes no difference.

No provision was made for spaces between printed values in the PRINT USING just illustrated [using one form with more than one variable]. The space between the first two values is a blank left because there are two $ signs in the form and only one is printed. There are two spaces between the second and third values because, in addition to the space for the $ sign, there was provision for two digits before the decimal point and the value has only one. Again we will use COST1 = 19.5, COST2 = 29.568, and COST3 = .27.

If the lead $ signs are omitted the PRINT USING statement is:

```
PRINT USING "##.##"; COST1, COST2, COST3
```

There is no space between values provided for in the statement and the output is:

```
19.5029.57 0.27
```

Additional spacing between the values can be added in the form string. A blank space within the quotation marks will be part of the output. If the last PRINT USING statement is rewritten as:

```
PRINT USING "$$##.##      "; COST1, COST2, COST3
```

the output would be:

```
$19.50      $29.57      $0.27
```

Printing Numbers with Commas

A comma [,] inserted anywhere in the PRINT USING form string will cause numeric data to be printed with commas between groups of three digits as numbers are commonly written. Although only one comma anywhere in the form string is required, each comma used is counted in the field width and as many as will be printed should be included in the form.

For example, PRINT USING "#### ,###.###" will print a maximum of seven digits before the decimal point. One of the # signs will be used for a comma. To print up to eight digits before the decimal point, insert a second comma in the form string.

```
PRINT USING "##,###,###.###"
```

Asterisks to Fill Blanks

Asterisks [*] can be used to fill in blanks in numeric printouts for values which have fewer digits than allowed for in the form. Two lead asterisks in the form string will fill in all unused positions in the number and thus prevent fraudulent alteration by the addition of digits in financial data. The statements:

```
PAYMENT = 29.568
PRINT USING "***,###.##"; PAYMENT
```

will output

```
*****29.57
```

The double $ and double * cannot be used together, but the $ can be used as a literal character and will be printed.

```
PRINT USING "$***,###.##"; COST
```

will output

```
$*****29.57
```

Provision for Negative Values

Negative values will be printed with a **floating** minus sign [−] immediately in front of the most significant digit but the sign should be allowed for with an additional # in the form string. The minus sign will then be printed only if the value is negative. However, if the form for the value is defined with a floating dollar sign the $ will not be printed if the value is negative.

For BALANCE = −68.56 the statement

```
PRINT USING "$$###.##"; BALANCE
```

will output

```
-68.56
```

The minus sign is included but *not* the $.

The $ can also be printed with negative numbers by including it in the form as a literal character but then it does not float. Unless asterisks are also included, there will be empty spaces between the dollar and minus sign if the value to be printed has fewer digits than provided for in the form string.

For BALANCE = −3.45, the statement:

```
PRINT USING "$###.##"; BALANCE
```

will output

```
$  -3.45
```

```
PRINT USING "$*****#.##"; BALANCE
```

will output

```
$***-3.45
```

The minus sign can be printed at the right-hand side of the value by including it in the form.

For BALANCE = −68.56 , the statement:

```
PRINT USING "$$##.##-"; BALANCE
```

will output

$68.56-

PRINT USING with TAB

The TAB statement can be used with a long PRINT USING instruction as an alternate method of leaving required spacing between printed values instead of counting spaces within the form string.

For A1 = 19 and A2 = 231.219 , the statements:

```
PRINT USING "##.##"; A1;
PRINT TAB(10);
PRINT USING "$$###.##"; A2
```

would result in:

19.00 $231.22

- The semicolons [;] at the end of the first and second lines are used *to continue the printing on one line*.
- The PRINT USING and PRINT TAB statements may not be combined on one line although generally these statements do not have to be on a line by themselves.

Combining Multiple Forms and Variables

The form string may include more than one instruction and the list of variables will be printed in these different forms. For the values:

```
PRICE = 1.98      NO.SOLD = 220       TOTAL.SALE = 43.560

PRINT USING "$$##.##      ###       ***,###.##";PRICE, NO.SOLD, TOTAL.SALE
```

will output:

$1.98   220   *****43.56

Multiple Uses for One Form String

If the same form string is to be used in different parts of a program it will save time to first define the form as a string constant. The two statements:

```
FORM$ = "$$##,##    ###     ***,###,##"
PRINT USING FORM$; PRICE, NO,SOLD, TOTAL SALE
```

will result in the same output as the single PRINT USING statement and FORM$ can be used again in another part of the program.

Error Message: Using More Digits Than Allowed

If NO.SOLD in the above illustration had been entered incorrectly as 2220, instead of as 220, with one digit more than allowed for in the form, the output would appear as:

```
% 2220
```

The % indicates that the value has more digits than the form and the value is output as it was entered or calculated in the program. However, the error message [%] appears only when there is no lead character in the form. If either PRICE or TOTAL.SALE has too many digits the % error message does not appear and the value is printed completely as far as space allows.

For PRICE entered as 198 and TOTAL.SALE entered as 44355.56 the statement:

```
PRINT USING "$$##,##,,,,***,###,##"; PRICE, TOTAL,SALE
```

would output:

```
$198,00    *44,355,56
```

In addition to the fact the the values do not follow the form in the PRINT USING statement, the numbers would have run into each other if sufficient space had not been included in the form string.

PRINT USING WITH STRINGS

When programming PRINT USING with strings, three special characters used in the form string determine how many characters will be printed for the string variable.

- An exclamation point [!] limits the output to the first character of the string, a useful technique when an initial is to printed instead of a name.
- An ampersand [&] is used for a variable length string field.
- A pair of slashes [/ /] is used to designate a string field with a fixed length. The length of the field is equal to the number of characters

inserted between the slashes *plus 2*. Although any characters may be inserted between the slashes, it will make counting simpler if a mnemonic method is used. For example, the character could be a period with every fifth position a 5. The form /....5....5....5../ has 19 places. The variable is left-justified within the field and blanks are added at the right side if the variable has fewer characters than the form allows.

As an illustration we will print the name *Benjamin Charles Donner* in different ways. The name will be separated into three variables because the parts follow different forms. The periods in the form string are treated as literal characters and will be printed.

The statement common to all the following illustrations is:

```
NAME1$ = Benjamin: NAME2$ = Charles:   NAME3$= Donner
```

STATEMENT	OUTPUT
PRINT USING"!. !. &"; NAME1$, NAME2$, NAME3$	B. C. Donner
PRINT USING"& !. &"; NAME1$, NAME2$, NAME3$	Benjamin C. Donner
PRINT USING"/./ !. &"; NAME1$, NAME2$, NAME3$	Ben C. Donner

Escape Character

The special characters used as part of a form string, such as #, /, &, can be printed as **literals** by preceding them with a backslash [\], called the escape character. The backslash indicates that the next consecutive character is to be treated as literal data and not used as a printing instruction.

For example:

1. To print a number symbol [#] before account number 578 the PRINT USING statement would be:

```
PRINT USING "\####"; ACCT.NO%
```

and the result would be

```
#578
```

2. For NAME1$= TOM and NAME2$= MARY the statement

```
PRINT USING "& \& & \!";NAME1$,NAME2$
```

will result in the output:

```
TOM & MARY !
```

The ampersand [&] and exclamation point [!] are printed as literals because each is preceded by a backslash [\].

The escape character [\] may not be the last character in the form string.

With some CBASIC compilers the use of the literal, %, may cause problems; for example:

```
PRINT USING "###\%"; PERCENT
```

may cause the trunction of output. If you encounter this with your compiler, you may use the % only in a PRINT statement.

TABLE 11-1   Special Characters in Format Strings

CHARACTER	MEANING
!	Single-character string field
#	Digit position in numeric field
&	Variable length string field
/	Fixed length string field delimiter
**	Asterisk fill in numeric field
$$	Float a $ in numeric field
.	Decimal point position in numeric field
−	Leading or trailing sign in numeric field
^	Exponential position in numeric field
,	Place a comma every third digit before decimal point
\	Escape character

PRINT USING WITH NUMBERS AND STRINGS

Since business reports and other printouts frequently combine numeric and string data, the first illustration will format and print a part number, a description, and price. The description will be limited to a fixed field of 17 characters, the part number will have a lead #, and the price will have a lead $. The statements are:

```
PART.NO% = 375: DESC$ = "Adjustable chair": PRICE = 59.95
PRINT USING "\####   /....5....5....5/   $$##.##"; PART.NO%, DESC$, PRICE
```

The output will be:

```
#375  Adjustable chair   $59.95
```

Program 11-1 uses similar data but a literal expression is the first part of the format string. In addition, the description is printed as a variable length string.

PROGRAM 11-1   **PRNTUSE.BAS**   **[Non-Compiler]**
PRINT USING Statement with Numbers, Strings, and Literals

Copyright 1985, Compulit, Inc.

```
10      READ COMP.NO%, DESC$, PRICE
        IF COMP.NO% = 0 THEN 50
        PRINT USING "COMPONENT PART \####    &    $$##.##";\
           COMP.NO%, DESC$, PRICE
        GOTO 10
        DATA 375, Adjustable-back chair, 59.95
        DATA 298, Metal desk, 89.25
        DATA 520, Rolling typewriter table, 29.75
        DATA 0," ", 0
50      END
```

The output is:

```
COMPONENT PART #375   Adjustable-back chair    $59.95

COMPONENT PART #298   Metal desk    $89.25

COMPONENT PART #520   Rolling typewriter table   $29.75
```

- The description lines up in a column because a string is left-justified within its field.
- The last variable, PRICE, is not in column form because the description was printed as a variable length field with three spaces allowed after it. To print PRICE in a column, the description must be a fixed length field as in the following statement in which 24 spaces are allocated for it.

```
PRINT USING"Component Part\####    /....5....5....5....5../      $$##.##";\
   COMP.NO%, DESC$, PRICE
```

With the same program and this PRINT USING statement the output is:

```
      Component Part #375   Adjustable-back chair     $59.95
      Component Part #298   Metal desk                $89.25
      Component Part #520   Rolling typewriter table  $29.75
```

Using More Variables Than Forms

If the list of variables is longer than the number of forms, the computer will go back to the beginning of the form list. Therefore, if there are more variables than forms, the additional ones should be matched against the form string *in order*. If the next variable to be printed is real and the next form is integer, the real value will be rounded to an integer.

As an illustration use COST = 39.95 as an additional variable in the last PRINT USING statement. We have also changed the description to "Adjustable chair" and allowed for spaces before the added variable. The statement is:

```
PRINT USING "\####   /....5....5....5/   $$##,##      "; PART,NO%, DESC$,\
         PRICE, COST
```

The output is now:

```
#375    Adjustable chair    $59,95    # 40
```

The value of COST, 39.95, has been printed according to the first form, \####, which indicates a lead # and up to a three-digit integer, although the variable identifier and the value are real.

If the next variable is a string and the next form is numeric, the numeric form will be treated as literal data and printed. For a second illustration we use STATUS$ = OVERSTOCKED as the fourth variable instead of COST. The PRINT USING statement now produces:

```
#375    Adjustable chair    $59,95    ####    OVERSTOCKED
```

The first part of the form string [####] was printed as literal characters and the second part [/....5....5....5/] was used as the pattern for OVERSTOCKED.

PRINT USING STATEMENTS WITH DATA FILES

Program 11-2 creates a sequential file, enters two records, closes and reopens the file, and prints it out with a PRINT USING statement.

The variables are an item number, description, dimensions, and price. Each set of dimensions is entered as two integer variables, S1% and S2%.

PROGRAM 11-2   PRNTUSE2.BAS   [Non-Compiler]

PRINT USING Statement; Data Read from Sequential File

Copyright 1985, Compulit, Inc.

```
    \              Create test file
           CREATE "PROD.FIL" AS 1
    10     READ PROD.NO%, ITEM$, S1%, S2%, PRICE
           IF PROD.NO% = 0 THEN 50
           PRINT #1;PROD.NO%, ITEM$, S1%,S2%, PRICE
           GOTO 10
           DATA 197, INDEX FORMS (5M),  3,  5, 10.95
           DATA 228, RING BINDER, 8, 11, 15.95
           DATA 0,0,0,0,0
    50     CLOSE 1
    \              Open test file, read and print data
           OPEN "PROD.FIL" AS 1
           IF END #1 THEN 100
    60     READ #1;PROD.NO%, ITEM$, S1%, S2%, PRICE
           PRINT USING "\####      /....5....5....5/    #\""X ##\""
$$##.##";PROD.NO%, ITEM$, S1%, S2%, PRICE
           GOTO 60
    100    END
```

The output is:

```
#197      INDEX FORMS (5M)              3"X  5"    $10.95
#228      RING BINDER                   8"X 11"    $15.95
```

Several points should be noted.

- The string variable, ITEM$, is defined as having a fixed length of 17 characters. If the field is of variable length, the data will not line up in columns.
- The form #\" "X ##\" " is used to print the quotation marks used here for inches. This complex form is required because the data is stored in, and retrieved from, a file. If the data is simply read from a DATA statement or entered as part of an INPUT statement, the entire dimension can be treated as one string variable.

Figure 11-1 shows the structure of this statement; the exact statement is contained in the program.

Printing # and $ Only with First Item

Program 11-3 is a modification of Program 11-2; it will print a lead # and a lead $ only in the first line. The clear screen command, column headings, and a third item have been added.

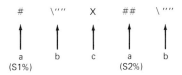

FIGURE 11-1   Structure of a PRINT USING Statement

(a)   The dimensions are broken into two integer variables, S1% and S2%. For example, 3"x5" is read in as 3, 5. S1% is defined as having one digit, S2% as having two.

(b)   The quotation marks are printed by using \" ", the escape character and two adjacent quotation marks.

(c)   The X [for "by" as in 3"X 5"] is inserted as a literal character in the PRINT USING form string. A space is left after the X to make the printout more readable.

PROGRAM 11-3   **PRNTUSE3.BAS**   **[Compiler]**

PRINT USING Statement; Data from File, First Line Different

Copyright 1985, Compulit, Inc.

```
\              Declaration of variables
        INTEGER PROD.NO, S1, S2
        REAL    PRICE
        STRING  CLEAR.SCREEN, ITEM
\              Defining CLEAR.SCREEN for PC-DOS and MS-DOS
        CLEAR.SCREEN = CHR$(27) + "[2J"
        PRINT CLEAR.SCREEN
\              Create file with test data
        CREATE "PROD.FIL" AS 1
10      READ PROD.NO, ITEM, S1, S2, PRICE
        IF PROD.NO = 0 THEN 50
        PRINT #1;PROD.NO, ITEM, S1,S2, PRICE
        GOTO 10
        DATA 197, INDEX FORMS (5M),  3,  5, 10.95
        DATA 228, RING BINDER, 8, 11, 15.95
        DATA 389, ENVELOPES (GROSS), 6, 9, 29.45
        DATA 0,0,0,0,0
50      CLOSE 1
\              Print column headings
        PRINT "PROD.NO";TAB(13);"DESCRIPTION";TAB(34);"SIZE";TAB(45);"PRICE"
        PRINT
\              Open file, read and print first record with # and $ signs
        OPEN "PROD.FIL" AS 1
        IF END #1 THEN 100
        READ #1;PROD.NO, ITEM, S1, S2, PRICE
        PRINT USING "\####      /....5....5....5/    #\"" X ##\""
$$##.##";PROD.NO, ITEM, S1, S2, PRICE
\              Read and print remaining records without # and $ signs
60      READ #1;PROD.NO, ITEM, S1, S2, PRICE
        PRINT USING " ###      /....5....5....5/    #\"" X ##\""
##.##";PROD.NO, ITEM, S1, S2, PRICE
        GOTO 60
100     END
```

The output is:

```
PROD.NO        DESCRIPTION        SIZE          PRICE

#197           INDEX FORMS (5M)   3" X  5"    $10.95
 228           RING BINDER        8" X 11"     15.95
 389           ENVELOPES (GROSS)  6" X  9"     29.45
```

The program now:

Prints the headings before reopening the file
Reads and prints the first item using the first PRINT USING statement
Reads and prints the remaining items using the second PRINT USING
    statement

PRINT USING # and READ # LINE Statements

The data going into a file on the disk can be formatted by a PRINT USING #
statement which has the same rules for the form string as the PRINT USING
statement. The data is then placed in the file as a single line and must be read
from the file with a **READ # LINE** statement.

PRINT USING # is similar to PRINT USING except for the inclusion
of the file number and, for a relative file, the record number. However,
when the data is read from the file with a READ # LINE statement a new
string variable [INFO$] is introduced. The value of this variable is the en-
tire record which will be read from the disk and printed in the form in which
it was put into the file.

The following statements show the combination of PRINT USING #
and READ # LINE.

```
READ NO%, COST, DESC$
DATA 220, 4.445, 6" HAND SAW
PRINT USING "###      $$###.##   /....5..../";#1,1; NO%, COST, DESC$
-------
-------
-------
READ #1, 1;LINE INFO$
PRINT INFO$
```

The output is:

```
220    $4.45   6" HAND SAW
```

The output follows the form in the PRINT USING # statement. The
real value for cost has been rounded and printed with a lead $.

```
LANGUAGE CODING RULE

The PRINT USING # statement can be used to write to files.

    PRINT USING <format string>; # <file number>
                [, record number]; <expression> {, expression>}
```

```
LANGUAGE CODING RULE

The READ # LINE statement reads one complete record from a file and
assigns the information to a single string variable.

    READ # <file number> [, record number]; LINE <string variable>

• The READ # LINE statement may be used with either sequential or
  random files.
```

SCREEN AND CURSOR CONTROLS

Screen controls [boldface copy, large size type, blinking, etc.] and cursor movement controls can be included in a CBASIC program. Some 15 control functions are part of the PC-DOS and MS-DOS compiler versions of the language; they are invoked with a CALL statement. You can also implement additional functions by creating your own function statements using ANSI.SYS, part of the PC-DOS and MS-DOS operating systems, versions 2.0 or higher, which allows application programs to utilize hardware-dependent features of the operating system.

Similarly, under CP/M for both non-compiler and compiler versions, you can create these functions using various **escape codes** which are incorporated in the operating system. They are called escape codes since many functions start with the escape key [ESC] or CHR$(27) in ANSI code. In each case, invoking of the ESC key informs the computer that the string that follows will do something to control the console screen.

In this section, we will discuss three different groups of screen and cursor controls:

1. The 15 functions that are built into CBASIC compiler for PC-DOS and also work with MS-DOS for compatible computers.

2. The MS-DOS ANSI escape sequences.
3. The CP/M escape sequences for non-compiler and compiler versions.

BUILT-IN COMPILER FUNCTIONS

These functions are part of the CBASIC Compiler version for the IBM PC and many of the compatibles. They require a special procedure using two subsets of the compiler disk, **PCSCRN.DEF** and **PCSCRN.L86**.

How to Invoke the Cursor Control Library

1. To incorporate cursor control into a program using PC-DOS, you need two programs provided by Digital Research, PCSCRN.DEF and PCSCRN.L86, on the compiler disk.
2. A %INCLUDE directive must be used at the beginning of the source program as shown in Program 11-4.
3. After the source program has been compiled without errors, it is linked by using the following statement immediately after the system prompt, **A>**:

```
LINK86 PROGRAM.NAME, PCSCRN.L86
```

Clear Screen

Up to this point, we have used an ASCII-defined string, **CLEAR.SCREEN**, to clear the console screen during program execution. As noted previously, this command is operating system and hardware dependent. The built-in function, **CALL CLS**, can be used to replace the PRINT CLEAR.SCREEN as shown in **Program 11-4**, a modification of Program 8-6 that was used to illustrate the LEN function.

PROGRAM 11-4   **CLSC.BAS**   **[Compiler]**

Use of CALL CLS Function to Clear Screen

Copyright 1985, Compulit, Inc.

```
   \          Declaration of variables
          INTEGER NUMBER
          STRING COPY, AN
          %INCLUDE PCSCRN.DEF
   10     CALL CLS
```

```
PRINT "A string is any combination of letters, symbols and spaces"
PRINT:   INPUT "Enter a string: "; LINE COPY
NUMBER = LEN (COPY)
PRINT:   PRINT "The string length is "; NUMBER; " characters."
PRINT: PRINT
INPUT "Wish to try again?  Yes or No?   "; AN
IF UCASE$(AN) = "YES" THEN 10
END
```

LANGUAGE CODING RULE

The CLS function is used to clear the entire screen when using CBASIC Compiler.

CALL CLS

- This function clears the screen and returns the cursor to the **home position** or upper left-hand corner.

Selecting Video Mode

Three video modes—**normal**, **blinking**, and **reverse**—are available to the user with the function, **PRTSTR**, which requires *two* parameters in the form shown in the accompanying language guide.

LANGUAGE CODING RULE

The **PRTSTR** function is used to display copy in normal, blinking or video mode.

CALL PRTSTR (" <string> ", <integer value>)

- The integer can be *one* of three values which determines the video mode in which the string will appear:

VIDEO MODE	INTEGER VALUE
Normal	7
Blinking	135
Reverse	112

Program 11-5 demonstrates the use of this function for displaying all three modes on the console screen.

PROGRAM 11-5   **MODE.BAS**   **[Compiler]**

Use of PRTSTR Function

Copyright 1985, Compulit, Inc.

```
\              Declaration of variable
        INTEGER H
        STRING  AN
        %INCLUDE PCSCRN.DEF
10      CALL CLS
        PRINT: PRINT
\              Integer controls mode: 7 is normal; 112 is reverse
\              135 is blinking
        CALL PRTSTR("This is normal display",7)
        PRINT: PRINT
        CALL PRTSTR("This is reverse video ",112)
        PRINT: PRINT
        CALL PRTSTR("This is blinking mode ",135)
        PRINT: PRINT: PRINT "Press any key to continue."
        H = INKEY
        INPUT "Want to continue?  Yes or No?     "; AN
        IF UCASE$(AN) = "YES" THEN 10
        END
```

Blinking or reverse modes can also be obtained by using either of two specific functions in the cursor control series, PCSCRN.DEF. For the blinking mode use

    CALL   PRTBLNK (" <string> ")

For the reverse mode use

    CALL   PRTREV (" <string> ")"

When any of these three functions is used in a source program, an end of line is *not* automatically included by the function, or by pressing the return key at the end of the function statement. It is, therefore, necessary to include a PRINT statement after the function call to terminate the line.

Positioning the Cursor

There are six functions for controlling the position of the cursor. The console screen is divided into 24 rows and 80 columns; when using any of the cursor control functions, you must remember that Digital Research has designated the rows from **0** [zero] through **23** and the columns from **0** [zero] through **79**.

You may encounter some difficulty with the cursor control functions because of this difference. In all the examples given here and in the following chapters we use the normal screen convention in explaining the position of the cursor. We will refer to the cursor, for example, in row 10 and column 10, but in programming we will adjust for the zero position included in the compiler's functions by using 9 for the tenth row or column.

CURSOR MOVEMENT	FUNCTION TO USE
Move cursor up one line or row	UPCUR
Move cursor down one line or row	DWNCUR
Move cursor one column to the right	CUR.RT
Move cursor one column to the left	CUR.LT
Position cursor to a specified position	SETCUR
Move cursor to row 0 and column 0	HOME

CALL HOME moves the cursor to the upper left corner of the console screen or to row 0 and column 0.

LANGUAGE CODING RULE

HOME is used to move the cursor to the upper left corner of the screen.

CALL HOME

LANGUAGE CODING RULE

To move the cursor one row up or down, or one row to the right or left, **CALL** the appropriate function.

CALL UPCUR *or* **CALL DWNCUR**
CALL CUR.RT *or* **CALL CUR.LT**

- If you move the cursor off the screen in any direction, confusing results can occur.

Program 11-6 is a test of the simple cursor controls. FOR-NEXT loops have been used to provide for multiple line movement of the cursor. The program first positions the cursor 10 rows from the top and 10 columns from the left. The second cursor position is 20 rows down and 12 columns in. To keep copy on the screen between the tests, we have used the INKEY function; press any letter to continue.

PROGRAM 11-6 **CURSOR.BAS** **[Compiler]**

Test of Simple Cursor Controls

Copyright 1985, Compulit, Inc.

```
\            Declaration of variables
       INTEGER I, H
       %INCLUDE PCSCRN.DEF
       CALL CLS
       PRINT "This is a test of cursor positions.":  PRINT
       PRINT "To continue program at any point, press any letter."
       H = INKEY
       CALL CLS
\            Test of screen operation and home
       PRINT "123456789012345678901234567890"
       FOR I = 2 TO 22
              PRINT I
       NEXT
\            Test of cursor to print in 10, 10
       PRINT "Cursor is 10 rows down and 10 columns from the left."
       CALL SETCUR (0,0)
       FOR I = 1 TO 9
              CALL DWNCUR
              CALL CUR.RT
       NEXT
       H = INKEY
\            Next test 10 lines down and 2 right
       CALL SETCUR (9,9)
       PRINT "Cursor is in 20th row and 12th column."
       FOR I = 1 TO 9
              CALL DWNCUR
       NEXT
       FOR I = 1 TO 11
              CALL CUR.RT
       NEXT
       H = INKEY
       CALL CLS
       END
```

The easier way to position the cursor in any specific position is by calling the SETCUR function as shown in **Program 11-7**. The first test places the cursor in the top row [row 0] and column 30. The program's second test permits you to enter the row and column as part of the program prior to positioning the cursor. The INKEY function is used within the program to maintain copy on the screen; press any letter to continue.

LANGUAGE CODING RULE

SETCUR is used to position the cursor in a specific row and column.

CALL SETCUR (<row>, <column> **)**

· Both the row and column designators must be in integer form.

PROGRAM 11-7   **SETCURFN.BAS**   **[Compiler]**

Use of SETCUR Function to Position Cursor

Copyright 1985, Compulit, Inc.

```
\              Declaration of variables
        INTEGER COLUMN, H, ROW
        STRING  AN
        %INCLUDE PCSCRN.DEF
10      CALL CLS
\              Test of SETCUR function
        PRINT "THIS IS A TEST OF POSITION"
        PRINT: PRINT
        PRINT "Cursor is at top of the screen and 30 columns from the left."
        PRINT "Press any letter to continue."
        CALL SETCUR (0,29)
        H = INKEY
\              Test of positioning by input
        CALL CLS
        INPUT "Enter row for cursor ... 0 through 23: "; ROW
        INPUT "Enter column .......... 0 through 79: "; COLUMN
        PRINT
        PRINT "Cursor at row "; ROW; "and column "; COLUMN
        CALL SETCUR (23, 0)
        PRINT "Press any letter to continue"
        CALL SETCUR (ROW, COLUMN)
        H = INKEY
        CALL CLS
        INPUT "Want to try again?  Yes or No?     "; AN
        IF UCASE$(AN) = "YES" THEN 10
        END
```

To Determine Position of the Cursor

There are two ways to obtain the position of the cursor. One is the built-in function, **POS**, and the other is a cursor function, **GETPOS**. These can be used in programming for control of layout.

The GETPOS cursor function has a form similar to the SETCUR function which positions the cursor. It returns a single integer value that represents the current row and column position of the cursor. The integer can be decoded to obtain the specific row and column, as shown in the accompanying language coding and in **Program 11-8**.

PROGRAM 11-8   **CURPOS.BAS**   **[Compiler]**

Use of GETPOS Function to Determine Cursor Position

Copyright 1985, Compulit, Inc.

```
\              Declaration of variables
        INTEGER COLUMN, ROW, C, H, R, X
        STRING  AN
        %INCLUDE PCSCRN.DEF
10      CALL CLS
```

(continues)

```
\               Test of cursor to print in row and column
         PRINT "To continue the program at any point "
         PRINT "press any letter": PRINT: PRINT
         INPUT "Enter row number .... Ø through 23    :"; ROW
         INPUT "Enter column number . Ø through 79    :"; COLUMN
         PRINT
         PRINT "Cursor has been set at Row"; ROW; " and at Column "; COLUMN
         CALL SETCUR (ROW, COLUMN)
         H = INKEY
\               Test of GETPOS
         X = GETPOS
         R = X/256
         C = X - R * 256
         CALL SETCUR (2Ø,Ø)
         PRINT "The GETPOS function computed the cursor position at"
         PRINT "row = "; R; " and column = "; C
         H = INKEY
         CALL CLS
         PRINT: INPUT "Want to try again?  Yes or No?     "; AN
         IF UCASE$(AN) = "YES" THEN 1Ø
         END
```

LANGUAGE CODING RULE

The GETPOS function returns the current row and column position of the cursor.

    <integer variable> = **GETPOS**

- Although only a single variable is obtained, you can compute the row and column by using the following two statements:

ROW% = <integer value obtained> / 256
COLUMN% = <integer value obtained> - ROW% * 256

The POS function provides the column positional value of the next character to be printed on the console or printer. It is different from the GETPOS function in that it only obtains the column position but it can be used for both the console screen and printer hardcopy.

LANGUAGE CODING RULE

The **POS** function returns the next column position to be printed or displayed.

    <integer variable> = **POS**

- This function returns inaccurate values if a control character or backspace character has been used in the line it evaluates.

The Other Cursor Functions

Three other cursor functions are available, which are convenient in special applications. Their language structure is identical in that each follows a CALL statement *without* any parameters.

FUNCTION	OPERATION	USE
ERAEOL	Deletes any text that follows the cursor [to the right] on the same line; the cursor remains in its original position.	CALL ERAEOL
ERAEOS	Deletes all copy from the next line through the end of the screen. Copy on the same line as the cursor is *not* deleted and the cursor remains in its original position.	CALL ERAEOS
ADDLINE	Inserts a new line and moves all copy on the console screen down one line. The line the cursor is on remains blank.	CALL ADDLINE

MS-DOS ANSI ESCAPE SEQUENCES

With the addition of more elaborate hardware designs, particularly the graphics additions, it has become more difficult for applications programs to utilize hardware-dependent features and maintain compatibility between systems. Both PC-DOS and MS-DOS operating systems, version 2.0 and higher, include an ANSI.SYS segment to provide an ANSI terminal standard description with the operating system.

To utilize these escape sequences you must add two files to the disk containing the CBASIC compiler and the disk which will contain the final executable program.

- First, transfer **ANSI.SYS** from the operating system disk to both the disk containing the compiler and the executable program.
- Second, create a **CONFIG.SYS** file on the two disks [you can use a text editor to do this] or if a CONFIG.SYS file already exists, add the following:

```
DEVICE = \ANSI.SYS
```

When you boot the compiler disk, it will read the CONFIG.SYS file automatically and load the ANSI.SYS file into memory.

Creating Screen/Cursor Controls

The CHR$(27) is the ANSI code for ESC [escape].

- The following statement will **clear the screen** using the ANSI escape sequence under MS-DOS:

```
PRINT CHR$(27) + "[2J"
```

- To **return cursor to the home position** in the upper left-hand corner of the screen [row 0 and column 0], the ANSI escape sequence would be:

```
PRINT CHR$(27) + "[H"
```

Since all the escape functions begin with the ESC key followed by a [, we can simplify our coding by defining the ESC and [as a string, for example:

```
E$ = CHR$(27) + "["
```

In fact, we can declare each of these functions at the beginning of a program so that we do not need to type specialized code each time we wish to use a specific function.

```
E$ = CHR$(27) + "["
CLEAR.SCREEN$  = E$ + "2J"
HOME$          = E$ + "H"
BOLD$          = E$ + "1m"
BACKGROUND$    = E$ + "4m"
BLINK$         = E$ + "5m"
REVERSE$       = E$ + "7m"
RESTORE$       = E$ + "0m"
SCREEN40$      = E$ + "11"    [one followed by a lower case L]
SCREEN80$      = E$ + "31'    [three followed by a lower case L]
```

The SCREEN40$ sets the screen for 40 character width when using color. If you use a black-and-white monitor, use a 0 [zero] in place of the 1 [one]. The command for an 80-character screen width is a 2 for black-and-white and a 3 for color. Medium and high resolution screens are also available for use with graphics.

The grammar is very critical in preparing these function definitions. No extra spaces may be included within the strings. For example, in clearing the screen the string used is "2J" and may *not* be " 2J" or "2 J". Also both upper case and lower case letters are specified and may not be interchanged.

For example to print a 40-character screen, the string used is "1l", a 1 followed by a lower case L.

The function definitions may be written in somewhat different forms. To position the cursor at a specific row and column, the ESC character is used in each but the string may be written in the forms shown:

```
CHR$(27) + "[18;40H"
CHR$(27) + "[" + "18;40H"
CHR$(27) + "[" + "18" + ";" + "40" + "H"
CHR$(27) + "[" +  R$  + ";" +  C$  + "H"
```

where 18 is the row and 40 is the column. In the fourth form shown above, the R$ is a variable for the row and the C$ is the variable for the column.

Program 11-9 contains a number of ANSI escape sequences usable under MS-DOS. There are a number of others you can create and use; refer to your operating system manual for additional details.

PROGRAM 11-9   **MSSCREEN.BAS**   **[Compiler]**

Demonstration of MS-DOS Escape Sequences

Copyright 1985, Compulit, Inc.

```
\             Escape routines work with PC-DOS and MS-DOS
\
\             Initialization of control variables
\
   STRING   POSITION.CURSOR, CLEAR.SCREEN, BOLD, LEAD
   STRING   BACKGROUND, BLINK, REVERSE, RESTORE.SCREEN, AN, BELL
   STRING   COLOR.SCREEN, SCREEN40C, SCREEN80C, BW.SCREEN
   STRING   SCREEN40BW, SCREEN80BW, ROW, COLUMN, OFFSET
   STRING   CUR.UP, CUR.DOWN, CUR.RIGHT, CUR.LEFT
   INTEGER  H
   BELL = CHR$(07)
   LEAD = CHR$(27)+ "["
   CLEAR.SCREEN = LEAD + "2J"
\
\             With a monochromatic console screen, BACKGROUND will produce
\             underlined characters; with a color monitor, output will
\             appear in the background color on black.
   BACKGROUND =   LEAD + "4m"
   BOLD       =   LEAD + "1m"
   BLINK      =   LEAD + "5m"
   REVERSE    =   LEAD + "7m"
   RESTORE.SCREEN   =   LEAD + "0m"
\
\             In the COLOR.SCREEN declaration 37 sets the foregound
\             color and 44 sets the blackground color.  See the MS-DOS
\             manual for full foreground/background codes.
   COLOR.SCREEN = LEAD + "37;44m"
   BW.SCREEN    = LEAD + "37;40m"
   SCREEN40C    = LEAD + "11"
   SCREEN80C    = LEAD + "31"
   SCREEN40BW   = LEAD + "01"
   SCREEN80BW   = LEAD + "21"
\
\             Beginnning of the program
10 PRINT CLEAR.SCREEN
   PRINT BOLD; "Bold face copy"
   PRINT RESTORE.SCREEN: PRINT
   PRINT BLINK; "Blinking copy"
```

(continues)

```
        PRINT RESTORE.SCREEN: PRINT
        PRINT BACKGROUND; "Underscore copy"
        PRINT RESTORE.SCREEN: PRINT
        PRINT REVERSE; "This copy is in reverse"
        PRINT RESTORE.SCREEN: PRINT
\               Ring bell before printing next line
        PRINT BELL
\               Position cursor for row 22 and column 0
        POSITION.CURSOR = LEAD + "22;0H"
        PRINT POSITION.CURSOR;  "Press any letter to continue"
        H  = INKEY
\               Character size test -- black and white
        PRINT CLEAR.SCREEN
        PRINT BW.SCREEN
        PRINT "This displays two size characters in black-and-white"
        PRINT
        PRINT POSITION.CURSOR;  "Press any letter to continue"
        H  = INKEY
        PRINT SCREEN40BW; "This is a 40-character screen"
        PRINT POSITION.CURSOR; "Press any letter to continue"
        H  = INKEY
        PRINT SCREEN80BW; "This is an 80-character screen"
        PRINT POSITION.CURSOR; "Press any letter to continue"
        H  = INKEY
\               Character size test -- for color monitors
        PRINT COLOR.SCREEN
        PRINT CLEAR.SCREEN
        PRINT "This displays two size characters for color monitor"
        PRINT POSITION.CURSOR; "Press any letter to continue"
        H  = INKEY
        PRINT COLOR.SCREEN
        PRINT CLEAR.SCREEN
        PRINT SCREEN40C; "This is a 40-character screen"
        PRINT POSITION.CURSOR; "Press any letter to continue"
        H  = INKEY
        PRINT SCREEN80C; "This is an 80-character screen"
        PRINT POSITION.CURSOR; "Press any letter to continue"
        H  = INKEY
\               Cursor positioning test
        PRINT BW.SCREEN
        PRINT CLEAR.SCREEN
        PRINT "This is a demonstration of cursor positioning":  PRINT
        PRINT "First enter row between 0 and 23"
        PRINT "Second, enter column between 0 and 79"
        PRINT "Finally, you will be able to move the cursor:"
        PRINT "[a] to the right            [b] down"
        PRINT "[c] to the left             [d] up"
        PRINT "by a given number of space; enter this value but for"
        PRINT "this test enter a value between 1 and 5":  PRINT: PRINT
        INPUT "Enter row     [0 TO 23] .......... "; ROW
        INPUT "Enter column [0 to 79] .......... "; COLUMN
        INPUT "Enter offset value between 1 and 5 "; OFFSET
        PRINT CLEAR.SCREEN
        POSITION.CURSOR = LEAD + "23;0H"
        PRINT POSITION.CURSOR; "Press any letter to continue"
\               These are cursor control statements
        POSITION.CURSOR = LEAD + ROW + ";" + COLUMN + "H"
        CUR.UP    = LEAD + OFFSET + "A"
        CUR.DOWN  = LEAD + OFFSET + "B"
        CUR.RIGHT = LEAD + OFFSET + "C"
        CUR.LEFT  = LEAD + OFFSET + "D"
        PRINT POSITION.CURSOR;
        H = INKEY
        PRINT CUR.RIGHT;
        H = INKEY
        PRINT CUR.DOWN;
        H = INKEY
        PRINT CUR.LEFT;
        H = INKEY
        PRINT CUR.UP;
        H = INKEY
        PRINT CLEAR.SCREEN
        INPUT "Again? Yes or No? "; AN
        IF UCASE$(AN) = "YES" THEN 10
        PRINT "Normal termination of program"
        END
```

The PRINT statements used with the MS-DOS escape functions should end with a semicolon [;]. This is done to keep the cursor in the set position since many systems return the cursor to column 0 of the next row after a PRINT escape-sequence statement.

CP/M ESCAPE SEQUENCES FOR SCREEN CONTROL

The CP/M escape sequences are similar to those used with MS-DOS and PC-DOS. These are shown in **Table 11-2** and can be incorporated into a

---

TABLE 11-2   CP/M Escape Code Sequence
Each of the following *must* be preceded by ESC, that is CHR$(27), plus the character indicated in string form, that is, within quotation marks. Some of the CP/M86 **escape codes** and their functions include:

ESCAPE CODE	FUNCTION
a	Sets console mode
b	Sets foreground color
c	Sets background color
p	Enter reverse video
q	Exit from reverse video
r	Enter high intensity mode
u	Exit from high intensity
s	Enter blinking mode
t	Exit from blinking mode
j	Saves cursor position
k	Restores cursor position
A	Moves cursor up one row
B	Moves cursor down one row
C	Moves cursor one column to right
D	Moves cursor one column to left
E	Clears screen and home cursor
H	Returns cursor home [does not clear screen]
K	Erases to end of the line
Y	Positions cursor

Escape codes a, b, c, and Y must be followed by selection characters. For example, ESC + "a3" calls for an 80-column color screen; ESC + "b6" would set foreground color to yellow; and ESC + "c1" would set background color to blue.
See the CP/M operating system manual for additional information.

CBASIC program which will work under either the non-compiler or compiler versions with CP/M80 and CP/M86. Some variations may be encountered because of the differences between terminals and monitors; check
your hardware manual and the CP/M operating system's manual.

CONSOLE SCREEN AND PRINTER LAYOUT FORMS AND DESIGN

Two types of layout forms are available to aid in the design of the console
screen and hardcopy.

> The layout of the console screen is important for both data entry
> and data display. The console screen of a terminal or monitor
> consists of 24 rows from top to bottom and 80 columns from left to
> right. Row 25 is *not* used for normal output but can be used for
> special messages, such as those found with text editors.

> The layout of hardcopy helps in making the printed copy more
> readable. Printer layout forms generally are available showing 66
> lines and 132 columns.

Screen Layout Forms

Many programmers find it convenient to use a *CONSOLE SCREEN DIS-
PLAY DESIGN FORM*, **Figure 11-2**, for planning both input and output
screens and *PRINTER LAYOUT FORM*, **Figure 11-3**, for planning hardcopy output.

It may take extra time to use a layout form at first but the results are
worth it. There are several ways to translate the layout form into positioned
copy on the screen or printed page. These include the use of:

- TAB to indicate the column in which to begin printing
- PRINT by itself to skip a line or row
- PRINT USING statements
- Cursor control functions

Design of an Input Screen

A well-designed screen makes the input of data easier and faster and with
fewer errors; when used for the display of information, the well-designed
screen makes it easier to read and/or find specific information. Assume that
an entry clerk is required to enter several fields, such as name, address, city,
state, and zip code. Generally, the size of each field has been set by the

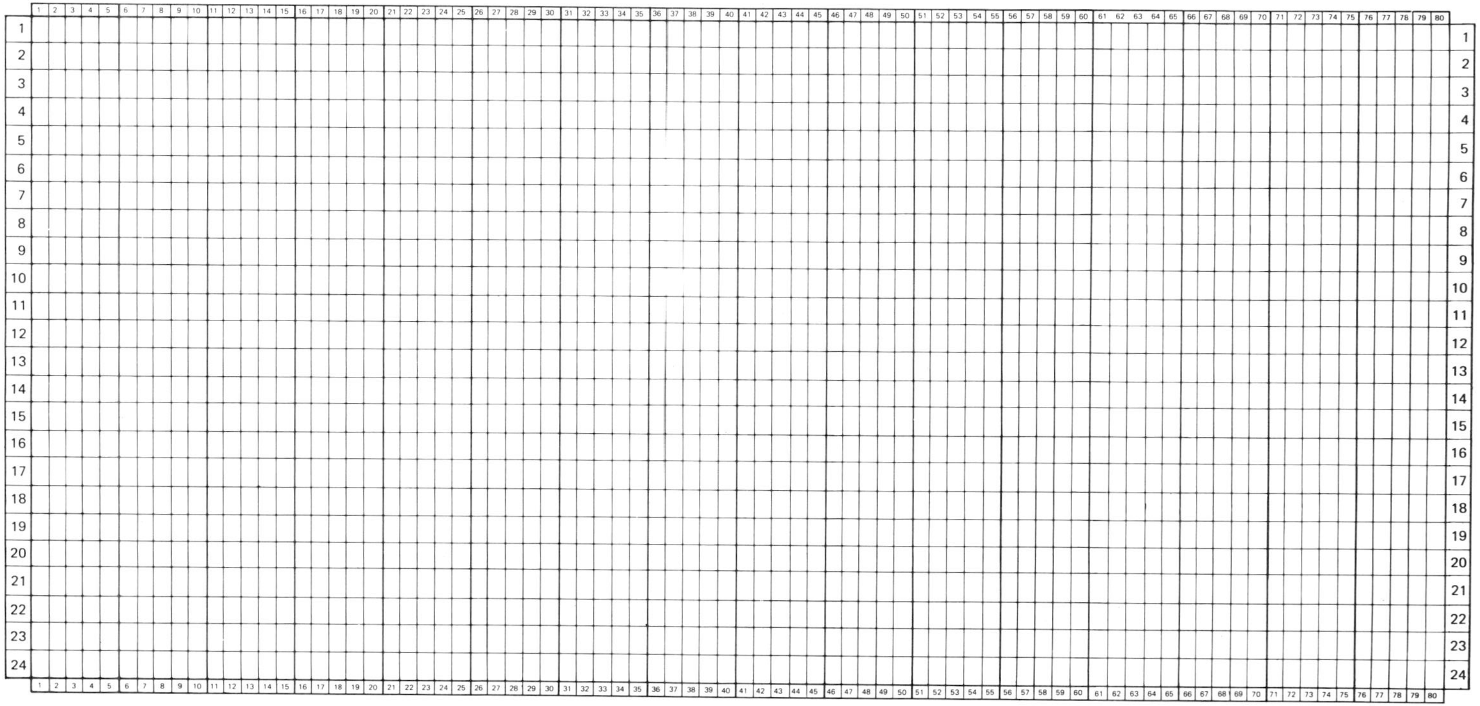

FIGURE 11-2 Console Screen Display Design Form

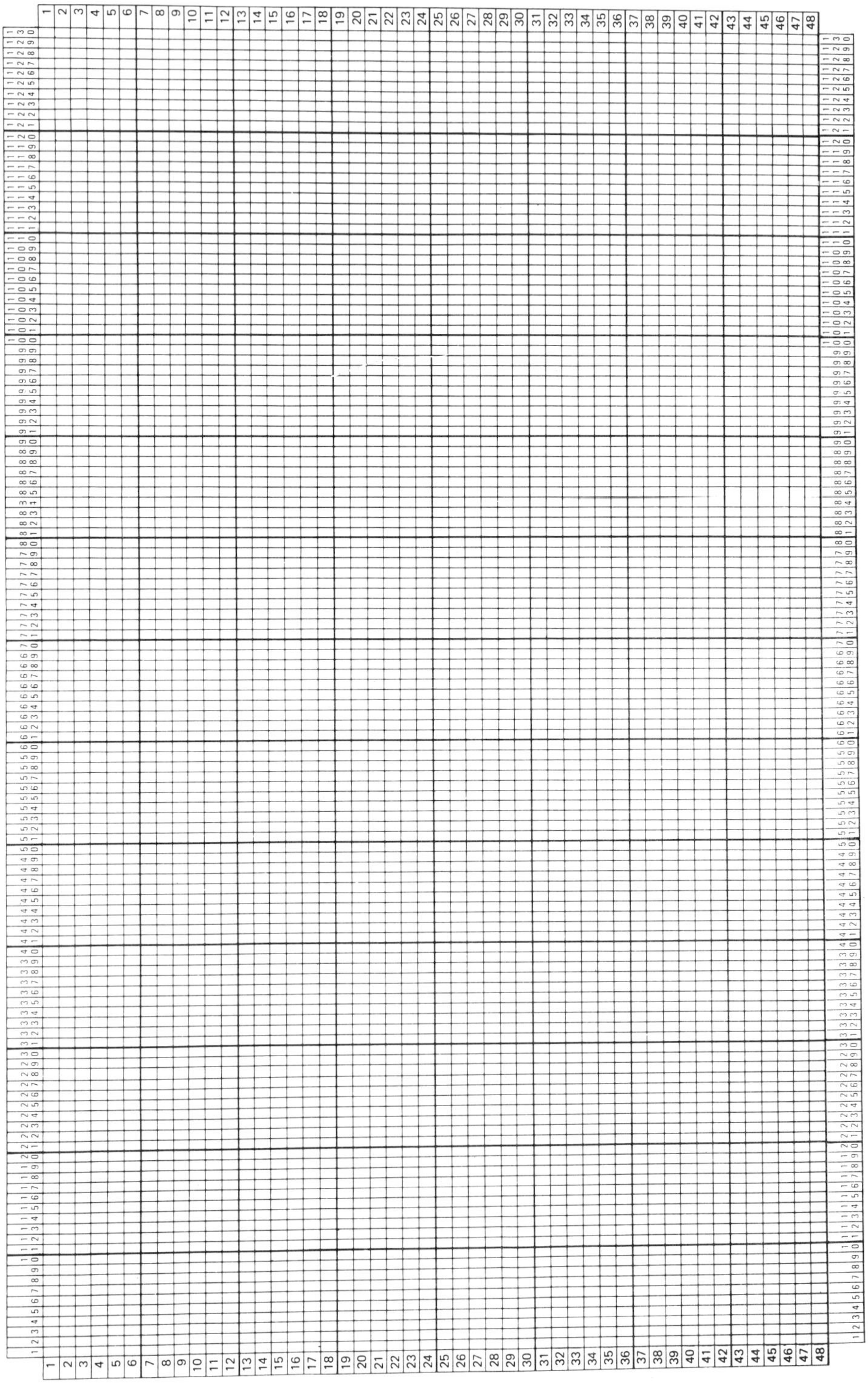

FIGURE 11-3 Printer Layout Form

programmer so that it is necessary to limit the number of characters for each field, as in preparing mailing labels.

The following illustration is one example of how the input screen can be designed using the cursor extensions discussed earlier in this chapter. The console screen contains all the information that will be requested of the data entry clerk and the size of each field is shown by a series of periods. After the screen is displayed, the program automatically sets the cursor at the line for data entry.

Program 11-10 illustrates this technique and is written in CBASIC Compiler form. In this program, used to create a mailing list file, we have set the length of each field as follows:

Name	25 characters
Address	25 characters
City	15 characters
State	2 characters
Zip code	5 characters

These lengths were established to fit the label size that will be used and permit the use of a 90-character record size for storage on a disk. At the start of the program the screen display is as shown in **Figure 11-4**.

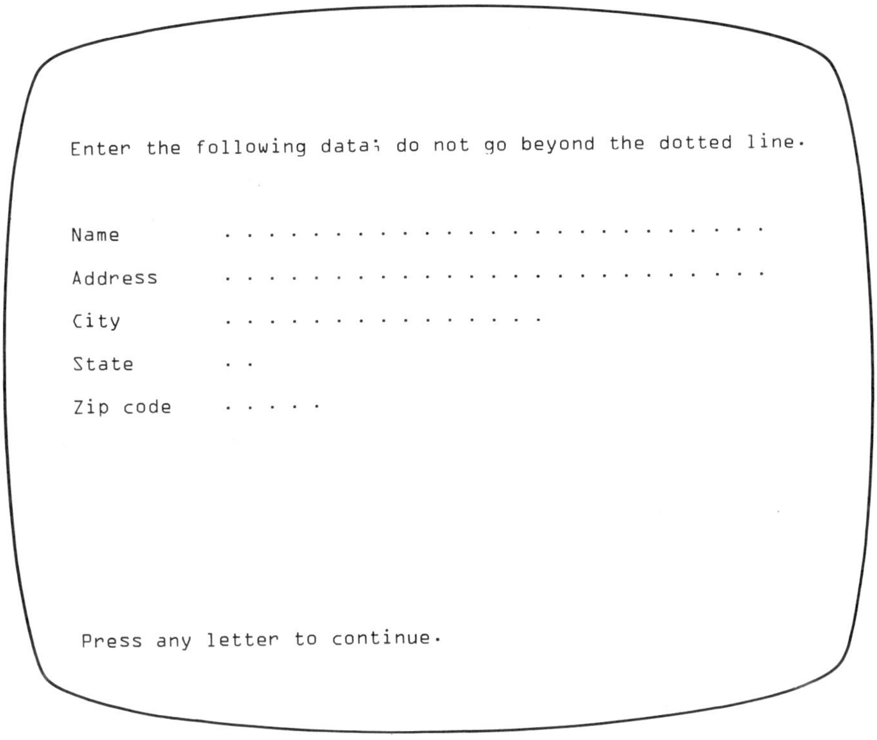

```
Enter the following data; do not go beyond the dotted line.


Name          . . . . . . . . . . . . . . . . . . . . . . . . .

Address       . . . . . . . . . . . . . . . . . . . . . . . . .

City          . . . . . . . . . . . . . . . .

State         . .

Zip code      . . . . .




Press any letter to continue.
```

FIGURE 11-4 Fixed-Field Layout Design

Once the entry clerk presses a letter to continue, a routine in the program erases the instruction line at the bottom. This procedure uses some of the cursor control functions, namely:

```
CALL SETCUR (23,0):  CALL ERAEOL
```

The SETCUR function repositions the cursor at the beginning of the final instruction line, "Press any letter to continue." The ERAEOL function erases everything in row 23 through the end of the line.

With the instruction line removed the cursor is positioned at the first character for entry of name. We have eliminated the question mark that normally appears following an INPUT statement by using a null prompt string. For example, to obtain the input for the first entry, the statement used is INPUT " "; NAME.

A LEN statement is used after each entry to determine if the number of characters entered did not exceed the field size. If the number of characters entered is greater than that allowed, an error message appears on the console screen and the clerk is requested to reenter the data. This is accomplished by using a common subroutine for all entries and a test procedure with each entry. This test procedure for entry of the NAME, which has a maximum field length of 25 characters, follows:

```
20          CALL SETCUR(02,12): INPUT ""; NAME
            TEST = LEN(NAME)
            IF TEST > 25 THEN \
                    GOSUB INPUT.ERROR :\
                    CALL SETCUR (02,13):  CALL ERAEOL  :\
                    CALL SETCUR (02,13)  :\
                    CALL PRTSTR (".......................",7)  :\
                    GOTO 20
```

The INPUT.ERROR subroutine which is used if the field length is exceeded is called by the test following each entry of data. The subroutine is:

```
INPUT.ERROR:       \ Routine if data entered exceeds data length
        PRINT BELL
        CALL SETCUR(21,0)
        PRINT "Data entry exceeds prompt guide:  REENTER data"
        CALL SETCUR(23,0)
        PRINT "                Press any letter to continue"
        H = INKEY
        CALL SETCUR(20,0):       CALL ERAEOS
        RETURN
```

Test this program to see the effect on screen layout and data entry. The program uses many of the cursor functions described earlier and can be modified to meet various data input needs.

PROGRAM 11-10   INPUTSCN.BAS   [Compiler]

Use of Predefined Input Screen as Guide for Input

Copyright 1985, Compulit, Inc.

```
\               Declaration of variables
        STRING   NAME, ADDRESS, CITY, STATE, ZIP.CODE, AN, BELL
        INTEGER  TEST, H
        BELL     = CHR$(07)
        %INCLUDE PCSCRN.DEF
        GOTO 10
INPUT.ERROR:     \ Routine if data entered exceeds data length
        PRINT BELL
        CALL SETCUR(21,0)
        PRINT "Data entry is too long; it exceeds prompt guide:  REENTER data"
        CALL SETCUR(23,0)
        PRINT "               Press any letter to continue"
        H = INKEY
        CALL SETCUR(20,0):       CALL ERAEOS
        RETURN
\               Start of main program
10      CALL CLS
\               Instructions to the data entry clerk
        PRINT "Enter the following data; do not go beyond dotted line.": PRINT
\               Set strings in reverse video and periods in normal video
        CALL PRTSTR("Name",112)
        CALL PRTSTR("       .....................",7)
        PRINT: PRINT: PRINT
        CALL PRTSTR("Address",112)
        CALL PRTSTR("       .....................",7)
        PRINT: PRINT: PRINT
        CALL PRTSTR("City",112)
        CALL PRTSTR("       ...............",7)
        PRINT: PRINT: PRINT
        CALL PRTSTR("State",112)
        CALL PRTSTR("       ..",7)
        PRINT: PRINT: PRINT
        CALL PRTSTR("Zip Code",112)
        CALL PRTSTR("       .....",7)
\               Instruction to entry clerk to continue
        CALL SETCUR (23,0)
        PRINT "Press any letter to continue."
        H = INKEY
\               Removal of instruction line at bottom of screen
        CALL SETCUR (23,0):  CALL ERAEOL
\               Move cursor to obtain input for each item; use of null string\
[""] after INPUT eliminates question mark
\               Input of data, length verification and error routines
20      CALL SETCUR(02,12): INPUT ""; LINE NAME
        TEST = LEN(NAME)
        IF TEST > 25 THEN \
                GOSUB INPUT.ERROR :\
                CALL SETCUR (02,13):  CALL ERAEOL :\
                CALL SETCUR (02,13) :\
                CALL PRTSTR ("....................",7) :\
                GOTO 20
30      CALL SETCUR(05,12): INPUT ""; LINE ADDRESS
        TEST = LEN(ADDRESS)
        IF TEST > 25 THEN \
                GOSUB INPUT.ERROR :\
                CALL SETCUR (05,13):  CALL ERAEOL :\
                CALL SETCUR (05,13) :\
                CALL PRTSTR ("....................",7) :\
                GOTO 30
```

(continues)

```
40        CALL SETCUR(08,12): INPUT "";LINE CITY
          TEST = LEN(CITY)
          IF TEST > 15 THEN \
                GOSUB INPUT.ERROR :\
                CALL SETCUR (08,13):  CALL ERAEOL :\
                CALL SETCUR (08,13) :\
                CALL PRTSTR ("..............",7) :\
                GOTO 40
50        CALL SETCUR(11,12): INPUT ""; STATE
          TEST = LEN(STATE)
          IF TEST > 2 THEN \
                GOSUB INPUT.ERROR :\
                CALL SETCUR (11,13):  CALL ERAEOL :\
                CALL SETCUR (11,13) :\
                CALL PRTSTR ("..",7) :\
                GOTO 50
60        CALL SETCUR(14,12): INPUT ""; ZIP.CODE
          TEST = LEN(ZIP.CODE)
          IF TEST > 5 THEN \
                GOSUB INPUT.ERROR :\
                CALL SETCUR (14,13):  CALL ERAEOL :\
                CALL SETCUR (14,13) :\
                CALL PRTSTR (".....",7) :\
                GOTO 60
\                 Printout of data on new screen
          CALL CLS
          PRINT: PRINT: PRINT
          PRINT "---------------------------"
          PRINT "|  "; NAME; TAB(30); "|"
          PRINT "|  "; ADDRESS; TAB(30); "|"
          PRINT "|  "; CITY; ", "; STATE; "  "; ZIP.CODE; TAB(30); "|"
          PRINT "---------------------------"
          PRINT: PRINT
          INPUT "Try again?  Yes or No?      "; AN
          IF UCASE$(AN) = "YES" THEN 10
          PRINT "Normal termination of program."
          END
```

HOLDING COPY ON THE SCREEN

Thus far we have included several techniques for holding copy on the screen which we should like to review and evaluate. Each method works but some are more foolproof than others. With some the user can abort the program in responding incorrectly to the prompt. Inadvertently pressing the control key [CTRL] when the user decides to press the letter C will cause the program to abort, and there are other such combinations that will cause difficulties.

The following is an analysis of seven techniques which can be used to keep copy on the console screen:

INPUT statement
INPUT-LINE statement
INKEY function
CONCHAR% function
WHILE-WEND statements
Use of CHR$ and CONCHAR% with SPACE.BAR$
Use of CHR$ and CONCHAR% during FOR-NEXT loop

The INPUT Statement

One method used is the INPUT statement which automatically halts operations as the computer awaits an input. To hold copy on the screen, this statement is included with a dummy variable:

```
INPUT "Press any letter and Return key to continue ... "; H$
```

The H$ is a dummy variable and is ignored by the program, except that it is necessary to enter some letter and press return to continue execution. The danger with this command is that if the user has a finger on the control key [CTRL] and selects the letter C, the program is aborted and there is a return to the system.

The INPUT-LINE Statement

In Chapter 4 the INPUT-LINE statement for copy control was illustrated as:

```
INPUT "Press the Return Key to continue"; LINE H$
```

H$ is a dummy variable. Any letter pressed will be echoed on the screen. This statement has the same weakness as the INPUT statement; pressing CONTROL-C will cause the program to abort.

The INKEY and CONCHAR% Functions

Both these functions, described earlier in Chapter 8, can be used to hold copy on the screen. The difference between them is that the CONCHAR% function will echo or display the key struck, while the INKEY function does not. Their programming form is:

```
I% = INKEY
J% = CONCHAR%
```

In both cases, the I% and J% [or any integer variable you wish to assign] are dummy variables that are not used within the program. If either of these statements is used, include a PRINT line *immediately before* it in the form:

```
PRINT "Press any letter to continue."
```

The advantage of either method over the INPUT and INPUT-LINE statements is that any control character as well as any letter is accepted; there is no damage to the program and execution continues.

The WHILE-WEND Statements

In Chapter 7, the WHILE-WEND statements were used to hold copy on the console screen:

```
PRINT "Press any Key to continue."
WHILE NOT CONSTAT%
WEND
```

Again there is a problem. An inexperienced user may press certain keys that will not respond to this command. For example, pressing any of the function keys on an IBM-PC or Columbia Data Products MPC will not remove the copy from the console screen and permit the program to continue execution. With some terminals, such as a Hazeltine 1500, striking the *right arrow* key causes the program to enter an infinite loop. Pressing the *space bar* or striking any letter or number will work.

CONCHAR% = SPACE$ Technique

Several human engineering studies in the use of microcomputers and terminals have shown that it is more efficient to direct the user to press a specific key rather than *any* key. The return key is a specific key but it is marked *Enter* on some computer keyboards or designated by a backwards arrow [←] on others. An easily found key is the *space bar*, and the authors prefer this method to the others.

To use this technique, first define the *space bar* or *space* in ASCII code at the start of the program as:

```
SPACE.BAR$ = CHR$(32)
```

This definition of the space bar is virtually universal in microcomputers and is not machine dependent. To hold the copy on the screen use the following form:

```
1313      PRINT "Press Space Bar to continue."
          IF CHR$(CONCHAR%) <> SPACE.BAR$ THEN 1313
```

The PRINT statement should have a line label or a statement number. Unless the user presses the space bar, the print message will be repeated. This is a directed user response and no other key or control character will permit the program to continue execution.

LANGUAGE CODING RULE

The CONSTAT% function returns the console ready status as a logical value.

<integer variable> = **CONSTAT%**

- The console ready status indicates that a character has been entered at the console keyboard but has not yet been read by the program. The value is -1 or a logical true if the console is ready; the value is 0 or a logical false if the console is not ready.

Use of a Dummy FOR-NEXT Loop

Copy can be held on the screen for a given period of time and then have it automatically proceed to the next screen *without* any response by the user. The length of time that the copy is held on the screen depends upon the time value you have included in the program.

This is done by using a dummy FOR-NEXT loop at the appropriate place in the program. **Program 11-11** is an example of the use of this dummy loop. For illustration purposes, you can test various values to determine screen timing. Most computer systems will perform about 500 loops in one second. The time you hold the copy on the screen depends on the amount of copy to be read. A typical user will take about one minute to read the 24 lines of a single screen.

PROGRAM 11-11   **PAUSE.BAS**   [Compiler]

Program to Hold Copy on Screen for Variable Time

Copyright 1985, Compulit, Inc.

```
\              Declaration of variables
       REAL   M, N
       STRING CLEAR.SCREEN, AN
\              Defining CLEAR.SCREEN for PC-DOS and MS-DOS
       CLEAR.SCREEN = CHR$(27) + "[2J"
10     PRINT CLEAR.SCREEN
       INPUT "Enter the delay time in seconds ....... "; N
\              About 500 loops will be performed with certain CPU chips
\              per second; test your CPU processor with a stop watch
       M = N * 500
       FOR I = 1 TO M
       NEXT
       PRINT "This line will appear"; N; " second(s) later.": PRINT
       INPUT "Try again?  Yes or No?  "; AN
       IF UCASE$(AN) = "YES" THEN 10
       END
```

STARTING A NEW PAGE WHEN PRINTING

When printing hardcopy there are times when you may wish to start a new page. This can be done with all versions of CBASIC by using the CHR$ function. First define the new page using the decimal ASCII code:

```
NEW.PAGE = CHR$(12)
```

NEW.PAGE must be declared as a *string* or written as NEW.PAGE$. This statement may be placed anywhere *before* you include the LPRINTER statement for the first time; a recommended position is in the initialization section near the beginning of the program.

To start a new page include the following statement at the point in the program where a new page is desired:

```
PRINT NEW.PAGE
```

This forces a form feed on the printer and the copy is now ready to print on the very first line of the page. If you wish to leave some blank space at the top of the page, use the PRINT statement to produce the blank lines. For example, if you wish to go to a new page, skip five blank lines, and start printing on line six, you can write:

```
STRING NEW.PAGE
NEW.PAGE = CHR$(12)
```

Program goes here

```
PRINT NEW.PAGE
FOR I% = 1 TO 5
    PRINT
NEXT I%
```

PRINTING TIME AND DATE

Both the current date and current time can be displayed on the console screen or printed on hardcopy in the PC-DOS and MS-DOS compiler versions of CBASIC. They are obtained by using two built-in functions, DATE$ and TIME$. **Program 11-12** can be used to try these two functions.

PROGRAM 11-12   **DAYTYM.BAS**   **[Compiler]**

Use of DATE$ and TIME$ Functions

Copyright 1985, Compulit, Inc.

```
\               Declaration of variables
        STRING CURRENT.DATE, CURRENT.TIME, AN, CLEAR.SCREEN
\               Defining CLEAR.SCREEN for PC-DOS and MS-DOS
        CLEAR.SCREEN = CHR$(27) + "[2J"
10      PRINT CLEAR.SCREEN
\               Call DATE$ and TIME$ functions
        CURRENT.DATE = DATE$
        CURRENT.TIME = TIME$
\               Output of date and time
        PRINT "Date is ........ "; CURRENT.DATE
        PRINT
        PRINT "Time is ........ "; CURRENT.TIME
        PRINT
        INPUT "To check again enter YES  "; AN
        IF UCASE$(AN) = "YES" THEN 10
        PRINT "Normal termination of program. "
        END
```

In this program the STRING identifier statement is used to define variable names. However, DATE$ and TIME$ are function names and *must* be retained in their exact form. The output from this program naturally depends upon when you run it. You can test it better if you enter YES for the INPUT to check again and see the elapsed time.

The output of Program 11-12 for both the date and the time is six-character strings which are understandable only if you know the output format of the functions. Seeing 850402 on the screen or printout would be confusing to the typical user. Instead, Program 11-12 can be modified so that the output is in more readable form as shown in **Program 11-13**.

LANGUAGE CODING RULE

The DATE$ function is used to obtain the current date during the execution of a program so that it may be printed on the console screen or printout.

<string variable> = **DATE$**

• This function returns a six character string in the form YYMMDD. YY is the last two digits of the year; MM is a two-digit designation of the month; and DD is one of 31 digit combinations indicating the date.

LANGUAGE CODING RULE

The TIME$ function is used to obtain the current time during the execution of a program so that it may be printed on the console screen or printout.

<string variable> = **TIME$**

- This function returns a six-character string in the form HHMMSS. HH is the hour on the basis of a 24-hour clock; MM is minutes; and SS is seconds.

PROGRAM 11-13   **DAYTYM1.BAS**   [Compiler]

Output of Date and Time in Readable Format

Copyright 1985, Compulit, Inc.

```
\            Declaration of variables
        STRING CURRENT.DATE, CURRENT.TIME, AN, CLEAR.SCREEN
        STRING YR, MO, DAY, HR, MIN, SEC, SPACE
        SPACE = "/"
\            Defining CLEAR.SCREEN for PC-DOS and MS-DOS
        CLEAR.SCREEN = CHR$(27) + "[2J"
10      PRINT CLEAR.SCREEN
\            Call DATE$ and TIME$ functions
        CURRENT.DATE = DATE$
        CURRENT.TIME = TIME$
\            Change date to readable format with slashes
        YR = MID$ (CURRENT.DATE,1,2)
        MO = MID$ (CURRENT.DATE,3,2)
        DAY= MID$ (CURRENT.DATE,5,2)
        CURRENT.DATE = "DATE = " + MO + SPACE + DAY + SPACE + YR
\            Change time to readable format with slashes
        HR = MID$ (CURRENT.TIME,1,2)
        MIN= MID$ (CURRENT.TIME,3,2)
        SEC= MID$ (CURRENT.TIME,5,2)
        CURRENT.TIME = "TIME = " + HR + SPACE + MIN + SPACE + SEC
\            Printout of date and time
        PRINT "Date is ........ "; CURRENT.DATE
        PRINT
        PRINT "Time is ........ "; CURRENT.TIME
        PRINT
        INPUT "To check again enter YES  "; AN
        IF UCASE$(AN) = "YES" THEN 10
        PRINT "Normal termination of program. "
        END
```

The output from this program would appear as:

```
Date is.........04/02/85

Time is.........13/48/13
```

This program can be further expanded so that April is printed instead of 04. The time is given as 13 hours, 48 minutes, and 13 seconds; another extension is the conversion of a 24-hour day clock to a 12-hour day clock.

The time function is particularly useful in testing the execution of portions of a program or a total program. Both functions can be added as two fields to every record in a data file so that you have a record of the date and time a specific entry was made. Or you may wish to store the DATE$ function in the first record of a relative file to indicate the last date the file was opened.

CHAPTER 12

Compiling and Running a Program

In Chapter 1 we introduced the minimum essentials necessary to compile and run a program. In this chapter we will examine this process in more detail and explain the different options available to the user at this stage of program development. There is one major section for the CBASIC Compiler versions and another section for the non-compiler versions of CBASIC.

A **compiler**, one of a class of programs technically known as **translators**, accepts a **source code** program and codes it into another language as an **object code** program. Depending upon the type of compiler, this translation can be carried to different levels of completeness:

- To assembly code, a set of mnemonic instructions and symbolic address references
- To machine code, in binary or hexadecimal form
- To execution

The source code in this instance is in one of the versions of CBASIC. The object code depends upon whether we are using the compiler or non-compiler versions.

With the non-compiler versions of CBASIC, an **interpreter**, one form of compiler, is used to translate the source code program into an intermediate form. The interpreter is not an efficient compiler, but it does produce object code more quickly than the compiler version. It is therefore possible for the user to test the grammar of the program and make modifications rapidly.

On the other hand, the compiler versions of CBASIC take longer for the translation but they generate a more efficient, compact object program which can be executed more rapidly. The compiler translates the source program into machine code modules. It is then necessary to use a **link editor**, which unites the machine code modules with routines from an indexed library into an executable program for subsequent loading into memory and execution.

USING THE COMPILER VERSION OF CBASIC

The compiler versions of CBASIC consist of an executable file and three overlays, portions of the compiler which are read sequentially from a disk into memory and then executed. These programs must all be on the default drive although the source program may be on any logical drive. The executable program, for example, is designated as:

- CB80.COM for an 8-bit microcomputer
- CB86.CMD for a 16-bit microcomputer under CP/M or MP/M
- CB86.EXE for a 16-bit microcomputer under PC-DOS or MS-DOS

The overlay files are identified as CB80.OV1, CB80.OV2, and CB80.OV3 for the 8-bit version, and CB86.OR1, CB86.OR2, and CB86.OR3 for the 16-bit versions.

How to Compile a Program

The first step in compiling a CBASIC program when using a compiler version is to enter CB86, CB80, or the command module name and the filename without the BAS file extension after the system prompt, followed by a carriage return:

```
A:   CB86 <filename>   <CR>
```

or

```
A>   CB80 <filename>   <CR>
```

The compiler translates the source code program into a relocatable object file. During this phase of compilation, the compiler generates three temporary work files:

CB86	CB80
filename.$PA	PA.TMP
filename.$QC	QCODE.TMP
filename.$DA	DATA.TMP

```
---------------------------------------------------
CB86 CBASIC Compiler                    Version 1.0
Serial No. 000-000-00013    All rights reserved
Copyright (c) 1982,1983  Digital Research, Inc.
---------------------------------------------------
    1:   0000h        REM  PROGRAM 1-2      ANSWER.BAS
    2:   0000h        INPUT "ENTER YOUR HOUSE NUMBER.........."; HN
    3:   001ah        PRINT
    4:   001dh        INPUT "ENTER YOUR AGE IN YEARS.........."; AGE
    5:   002eh        PRINT
    6:   0031h        ANSWER = (2* HN + 5)* 50 + AGE + 365 - 615
    7:   006dh        PRINT ANSWER
    8:   0076h        PRINT
    9:   0079h        PRINT "HOUSE NUMBER IS ON THE LEFT; AGE IS ON THE RIGHT."
   10:   0082h        END
end of compilation
no errors detected
code area size:     130        0082h
data area size:     148        0094h
common area size:   0          0000h
symbol table space remaining: 41116
```

FIGURE 12-1   Compiler Output of ANSWER.BAS [Program 1-2]

If the compilation is successful, that is, there are no grammar errors, the compiler automatically erases these files. If the compilation is not successful the files are listed in the disk directory. Once the errors are corrected and the program is recompiled, the compiler automatically erases these files from the disk.

Certain phases of the compilation process are combined into a module called a pass. There are three passes during the entire compilation process and these appear on the console screen unless the display is suppressed. Using Program 1-2 as an illustration, the output on the screen would appear as shown in **Figure 12-1**.

In the listing each line of the program, including the comment lines, is numbered. In line 12 the 001dh is the relative address for the relocatable code for the source program line: INPUT "ENTER YOUR AGE IN YEARS.........."; AGE. The total number of compile-time errors appears after the line, "end of compilation." If there are none, it will say so.

Following the listing of the error count is data indicating the size of storage areas required by the program. This is shown in decimal and hexadecimal form. In this case the 130 and 148 indicate the number of bytes required for the program coding and the data storage areas, respectively. Since no COMMON statement is used, the value is 0 for the third storage area.

To complete the compilation process, the compiler generates a relocatable object file; it has the file name with an .OBJ or .REL file extension for CB86 and CB80 respectively. However, if any errors are found, no .OBJ or REL file is created.

Compiler Errors

There are three different types of errors that may be reported by the compiler:

1. File-system and memory-space errors include such mistakes as invalid command lines, read errors, and out-of-memory conditions. There are 10 errors of this type and they are listed in Appendix D.
2. The most common errors are compile or syntax errors and include invalid characters, improper data type specifications, and missing delimiters.
3. These are internal failures and are exceedingly rare. If they should occur, communicate with the Digital Research Technical Support Center.

The programmer will generally encounter type-2 errors, those involving improper entry or incorrect syntax. When one of these errors occurs, a caret [^] is printed together with an error number in the listing of the program to note that a specific type of error has been encountered. Here are several examples of what might occur during the compilation of Program 1-2.

- If line 14 in the program had been incorrectly entered—*HN$* in place of *HN*—the error message would appear as:

```
6:   0031h          ANSWER = (2* HN$ + 5)* 50 + AGE + 365 - 615
                               ^ 27
```

The caret points to the string variable; error message 27 in Appendix D is:

27   Invalid mixed mode. The type of the expression is not permitted.

- If in line 15 *PRINT* was misspelled as *PIRNT*, the compiler listing would appear as:

```
7:   006dh          PIRNT ANSWER
                              ^ 30
                              ^ 51
                              ^ 33
                              ^ 27
```

The error messages from Appendix D read as follows:

30   Invalid symbol follows a variable, constant, or function reference.
51   An equal sign is missing in an assignment statement. An equal sign is inserted.
33   Invalid symbol encountered in an expression. The symbol is ignored.
27   Invalid mixed mode. The type of expression is not permitted.

The compiler is not designed to detect spelling errors and as a result several errors messages are printed. Each is a possible cause for a syntax error. However, the programmer would have to examine the line and discover specifically what is wrong.

- Even an entry error of *PIRNT* on a line by itself [line 11] would produce:

```
3:   001ah           PIRNT
                      ^  51
                      ^  33
```

Two contradictory messages are given, and again the line must be examined to discover the actual error. Despite a list of more than 200 possible compiling errors, it is often necessary for the programmer to hunt for the real error in a specific line or sometimes in a preceding line.

Compiler Directives

The programmer can alter the normal compiler process by using:

- Source code **compiler directives** that are included as part of the source program, and/or
- **Command line toggles** that are entered as part of the line after the program name. [See **Figure 12-2** for a list of toggles and their functions.]

There are six source code compiler directives under the compiler version of CBASIC. Four control the listing of the program and the other two perform specialized functions.

- **%LIST** and **%NOLIST** are used to control the listing of the program during compile time. %NOLIST suppresses the listing and %LIST resumes the listing. They can be used any number of times within a program.
- **%EJECT** works only when the listing is directed to the printer. It calls for starting a new page in the listing. However, if it is preceded by the %NOLIST directive, it is ignored.
- **%PAGE** is used to limit the number of printed lines on a 66-line page. This is the only compiler directive which must be accompanied by a parameter, a positive integer indicating the maximum number of lines on the printed page. The number of lines is included on the same line with a blank space between the directive and the number:

```
%PAGE 51
```

limits the printed output to 51 lines which includes the compiler heading and a blank line immediately after.

- **%INCLUDE** has already been used in Chapter 11 in the section on cursor control. This directive tells the compiler to include the code from a specified source file in the program in which the directive is inserted. The control assumes that the file is on the default drive unless otherwise specified, and it is a .BAS filetype.
- **%DEBUG** is used in conjunction with one or more of three command line toggles, I, N, and V, which may be turned on or off at different points during the program. This directive is used by advanced programmers and can be an aid in learning assembly language. You can try compiling Program 1-2 and inserting the %DEBUG statement in place of the first REM. It should read %DEBUG I; the I toggle will produce the assembly language code.

This is the assembly language translation of line 3 of the program which reads PRINT.

```
3:    001ah              PRINT
      001ah CALL    ?PCNL
```

Command-Line Toggles

Command-line toggles are single-letter directives that are specified in the command line instead of in the source program. Once the toggle is set, it remains in effect during the entire compilation except for Toggles I, N, and V, which can be altered by the source program when used in conjunction with the source code directive %DEBUG.

A toggle directive is invoked in the command line following the filename specification and is enclosed within brackets. More than one can be used at a time and may be entered in any of three forms:

```
CB86 <filename>   [ BU ]    or
CB86 <filename>   [B] [U]    or
CB86 <filename>   [ B, U ]
```

The 15 toggles which can be used are shown in **Figure 12-2**. They may be entered in either upper case or lower case. If conflicting toggles are entered, the last one read takes effect. Some of the toggles require additional parameters which must be enclosed within parentheses, for example:

```
CB86 <Filename> [B, L(51)]
```

Again using Program 1-2, if we wish to obtain the symbol table with the program listing, we would enter after the system prompt:

```
A:   ANSWER [T]   <CR>
```

TOGGLE	APPLICATION
B	Supresses the listing of the source code
C	Changes the default drive with the %INCLUDE directive
F	Writes the source listing on the same disk on which the source file is located
I	Lists each source code line with its assembly language translation
L	Sets page length for printing; must be followed by the number of lines within parenthesis: e.g., L(51)
N	Generates code for the line numbers
O	Supresses the generation of an .OBJ [object] file; used to save time and disk space when one expects a number of compile-time errors to occur
P	Produces hardcopy by listing the source file on the printer
R	Changes the disk to which the .OBJ file is written; if the program is on drive B and the .OBJ file is to be placed on drive A, enter: [R(A)] after the filename
S	Includes symbol name information in the .OBJ file
T	Lists the symbol table following the source listing
U	Generates error messages for undeclared variables; useful when the INTEGER, REAL, and STRING statements are used in the source program
V	Places source code line numbers into the .SYM [symbol table] file
W	Sets page width for printing; must be followed by the number of columns within parenthesis: e.g., W(110)
X	Changes the disk used for the work or intermediate files; if the source program is on drive B and the work files go on drive A, enter [X(A)]

FIGURE 12-2   Compiler Command-Line Toggles

This would produce a listing of the source program as before and the symbol table as follows:

```
                    symbol table information
no variables in common

program contains no functions

global variables:

        name                  type           class     address    # subscrp

HN                        simple variable     real      0000h
AGE                       simple variable     real      0008h
ANSWER                    simple variable     real      0010h
```

This would be followed by the storage allocation data that accompanies the compilation of a program.

Linking Files with the Link Editor

Before you can run a source program that has been compiled under a CBASIC Compiler, it is necessary to use the **link editor**. This combines the object file generated by the compiler with object modules from the run-time **Subroutine Library**, for example, CB86.L86. By linking you create an executable program; you may also create overlays if required.

To link the object file with the subroutine library, enter:

```
A:   LINK86 <filename>   <CR>
```

or

```
A:   LK80 <filename>     <CR>
```

This produces the following output:

```
------------------------------------------------
LINK-86  Linkage Editor            Version 1.0
Serial No. XXX 000-00013    All rights reserved
Copyright (C) 1982,1983  Digital Research, Inc.
------------------------------------------------
CODE      017A7
DATA      005B4

USE FACTOR:  .05%
```

The link editor generates three different output files, namely:

- An executable program file of filetype .EXE, .CMD, or .COM depending upon the specific compiler used
- A symbol table file, filename.SYM
- An optional information file, filename.MAP if the appropriate command line option has been used

The .SYM file is used with the Digital Research symbolic debugging program, **SID-86**. The .MAP file contains information about segments and groups. Both are more advanced programming techniques and are not covered in this book.

Link-Editor Command Lines and Toggles

There is a set of link-editor command lines and command-line toggles comparable to the set of compiler command-line toggles. Many are advanced programming techniques and will not be included here; the essential and elementary ones will be explained. The executable file has the same filename as the .OBJ file and is placed on the same disk by the computer, unless otherwise directed.

The following are some of the link-editor command lines which you may find useful:

APPLICATION	LINK-EDITOR COMMAND
Rename executable file	LINK86 <new filename> = <old filename>
Assign disk drive for executable program which is different from the drive on which the .OBJ file resides. The name can be changed at the same time.	LINK86 A:<new filename> = B:<old filename>
Link several files into one executable program	LINK86 <filename.one>, <filename.two>

Similarly, there are command-line toggles which can be used with the link editor. There are 5 link editor toggles for CB80 and 14 toggles for CB86. **Figure 12-3** lists the toggles for CB80 and **Figure 12-4** lists those for CB86.

The structure when using a toggle during the linking phase follows the form:

```
A:   LINK86 <filename> [ <toggle> ] {[ <toggle> ]}
```

TOGGLE	APPLICATION
L	Redirect console output from LK80 to printer
M	List all module names followed by an absolute starting address for each
O	Write output file to a drive other than the default drive
Q	Place all symbols beginning with a question mark into the .SYM file
S	Save linking information for the overlays in a file for future shortlinks

FIGURE 12-3 LK80 Toggles

To Run a Program under CBASIC Compiler

Once a program has been compiled without errors and link edited, an executable file is produced and stored as follows:

<filename>.EXE   with the PC-DOS or MS-DOS compiler
<filename>.CMD   with the CP/M86 compiler
<filename>.COM   with the CP/M80 or CP/M3 or earlier compiler

To execute the program enter its filename immediately after the system prompt and press the return or enter key as shown below.

```
A: <filename>   <CR>
```

If an error occurs during the execution of the program refer to the run-time error listing in Appendix D and to Chapter 13, which covers debugging techniques.

USING THE NON-COMPILER VERSION OF CBASIC

At the beginning of this book we included a short program, Program 1-2, just for introductory experience in entering and executing a program. It was suggested that all notations resulting from the compiling of the program be disregarded except for the errors.

We are now advanced enough to interpret all notations and to use a set

TOGGLE	APPLICATION
FILL [F]	Zero fill and include uninitialized data in CMD file
NOFILL [NOF]	Do not include uninitialized data in .CMD file
INPUT [I]	Read command line from disk file
LIBSYMS [LI]	Include symbols from library files in .SYM file
NOLIBSYMS [NOLI]	Do not include symbols from library files in .SYM file
LOCALS [LO]	Include local symbols in .SYM file
NOLOCALS [NOLO]	Do not include local symbols in .SYM file
MAP [M]	Generate a .MAP file
SEARCH [S]	Search library and link only referenced modules
$C	Specify .CMD file destination
$L	Specify .L86 file location for libraries linked automatically, such as CB86.L86
$M	Specify .MAP destination
$O	Specify .OBJ or .L86 file location for files linked in the command line
$S	Specify .SYM file destination

FIGURE 12-4   LINK86 Command-Line Options

of compiler commands which control the compile process. Compiling is the first step in running a program. When the process is complete an intermediate language file with the file extension .INT has been created.

To illustrate the output of a compiled program, Program 1-2 will be compiled again but with an error, as shown in **Program 12-1**.

PROGRAM 12-1   **ERROR.BAS**   **[Non-Compiler]**

PROGRAM 1-2 with a Mixed Mode Error

Copyright 1985, Compulit, Inc.

```
\         Program contains an ERROR; it will not compile properly.
\
10        INPUT "ENTER YOUR HOUSE NUMBER.........."; HN
          PRINT
          INPUT "ENTER YOUR AGE IN YEARS.........."; AGE$
          PRINT
\             HN is real; AGE$ is a string. They cannot be added
          ANSWER = (2* HN + 5)* 50 + AGE$ + 365 - 615
          PRINT ANSWER
          PRINT
          PRINT "HOUSE NUMBER IS ON THE LEFT; AGE IS ON THE RIGHT."
          END
```

In compiling and running programs in this section we have used the latest non-compiler versions of CBASIC available at the time of writing. Check your disk to verify which version of CBASIC you are using.

In response to the compile command:

```
CBAS86 ERROR
```

the copy shown in **Figure 12-5** would appear on the screen.

```
    1:         REM   PROGRAM 12-1        ANSWER1.BAS
    2*  10     INPUT "ENTER YOUR HOUSE NUMBER.........."; HN
    3:         PRINT
    4:         INPUT "ENTER YOUR AGE IN YEARS.........."; AGE$
    5:         PRINT
    6:         ANSWER = (2* HN + 5)* 50 + AGE$ + 365 - 615
ERROR MM IN LINE    6 AT POSITION    38
    7:         PRINT ANSWER
    8:         PRINT
    9:         PRINT "HOUSE NUMBER IS ON THE LEFT; AGE IS ON THE RIGHT."
   10:         END
     1 ERROR DETECTED
CONSTANT AREA:       8
CODE SIZE:         170
DATA STMT AREA:      0
VARIABLE AREA:      24
```

FIGURE 12-5   Compiler Output of Program 12-1 Showing Errors

Note that:

1. Each line of code has been numbered by the compiler. These numbers are completely independent of any line numbers used in the program.
2. The asterisk [*] in line 11 indicates that the line label [10] used in the program is not referenced by any branching statement and should be omitted. It is not an error but all unnecessary code makes the program more difficult to follow.

3. An error, **MM**, has been found in line 6 at position 38. If you refer to the list of error messages for the non-compiler versions in Appendix E, you will find that MM stands for mixed mode. It is the error introduced in the program for this illustration. AGE$ defines a string which cannot be added to a numeric value. The INPUT statement for AGE$ did not produce an error because a string may contain any alphanumeric characters. Counting from the beginning of the source code, line position 38 brings us to the $.

4. The four lines after the error message indicate the size of the areas reserved real constants, program code, data statements, and variables. In this illustration, for example, there are no data statements and the third line, DATA STMT AREA, is zero [0].

Compile-Time Toggles for Non-Compiler CBASIC

Where and how the compiled program is listed can be controlled by a set of commands called **toggles** which are part of the compiler command line. The name dates back to the early days of computing when this kind of control was accomplished by setting a toggle switch; now the computer sets the appropriate switch in response to a command which begins with $. All toggles are off unless included in the command which starts the compile process. **Figure 12-6** contains a summary of the compile-time toggles.

1. *To suppress listing of compiled program on the console screen* use **Toggle B**.

Toggle B only suppresses the listing on the screen, not on the printer or disk if these have been indicated by other toggle commands. An error message will be printed if an error is detected.

2. *To suppress generation of INT file* use **Toggle C**.

The use of Toggle C permits the programmer to check the syntax of a program without taking computer time to create the INT file. Errors are common in initial program coding and can be corrected before the INT file is generated.

3. *To suppress translation of lower case letters to upper case* use **Toggle D**.

With Toggle D set, all key words (PRINT, INPUT, etc.) must be entered in capitals, but this toggle permits the use of an identifier in upper and lower case as two different variables; for example, MONEY and money.

4. *To aid run-time debugging* use **Toggle E**.

With Toggle E set, any *run-time* error message will be accompanied by the compiler line number where the error occurs. Without it program execution stops and an error message appears but only the type of error is indicated, not the line in which it occurs. Toggle E must be set to use the TRACE option as discussed in Chapter 13. This toggle should not be used with a program which has been debugged since that would unnecessarily increase the size of the INT file.

5. *To print compiled program on printer and console* use **Toggle F**.

Toggle F causes the compiled program to be printed as hard copy even if Toggle B has been used to suppress the listing on the console screen. The printing is in pages of 64 lines, 132 characters wide. Each page is numbered and has a title.

6. *To write the compiled program to a disk* use **Toggle G**.

Toggle G causes the compiled program to be written to a disk. The file of the compiled program will have the same name as the source program with the suffix .LST. Even if the listing on the screen has been suppressed by Toggle B it will be complete on the disk. The disk listing will be on the same drive as the source program unless another drive is specified in the command. For example:

```
CBAS2 ANSWER $G(B:)
```

will put the compiled program on the disk in drive B although the source program is on the disk in drive A.

The toggles may be used together as shown in the following illustrations.

1. **CBAS2   ANSWER $BG** will cause the compiled program to be listed completely on the disk but will suppress the listing on the console except for error messages.
2. **CBAS2   ANSWER $BGF** will have the same effect as CBAS2 ANSWER $BG but in addition, the compiled program will be printed as hard copy.
3. **CBAS2   B:DEPRECIATION $CG** will stop the generation of an INT file and record the compiled program on the disk in drive B.

ACTION	TOGGLE
Suppress listing on console	B
Suppress generation of INT file	C
Suppress translation of lower to upper case	D
Obtain line numbers with run-time error messages	E
Print listing as hard copy	F
Write compiled output to disk	G

FIGURE 12-6   Summary of Compile-Time Toggles

Compiler Directives for Non-Compiler CBASIC

There are six special commands, **compiler directives**, that are used *within a program* to control the processing of the compiler. Each begins with a percent sign [%] entered in the first column [no indent] and should be by itself on the line. Anything following a directive will be ignored.

* * To list selected parts of a program* use **%LIST** and **%NOLIST**

%LIST turns the compiler listing on and **%NOLIST** turns the compiler listing off. They may be used together repeatedly in a program and can affect listings on the console, printer, or disk. %NOLIST by itself will suppress the listing of any code that follows.

* * To specify the number of printed lines on a page of output* use **%PAGE**.

%PAGE must be followed by a constant which specifies the number of lines which are to be printed on a 66-line page. In addition to the program output, allowance must be made for the compiler heading line and the blank line immediately after it. The directive for a 55-line printout is:

```
%PAGE 55
```

The page length is always set at 66 lines. All the directive will do is change the number of lines printed on this size page.

> * *To print compiler output at the top of the next blank page* use
> **%EJECT**

%EJECT can be used to separate parts of the compiled program on individual pages. Be sure your printer is on and Toggle F has been set if this directive is used.

> * *To insert one program into another to be compiled together* use
> **%INCLUDE**.

%INCLUDE is a very useful directive if a library of frequently used routines has been established. It assumes that the file to be included is a .BAS type and only one file may be specified on a line. The use of %INCLUDE is illustrated in the next section of this chapter.

> * *When using the CHAIN statement also* use **%CHAIN**.

Used together the CHAIN statement and the %CHAIN directive attach one program to another for execution. This procedure is discussed and illustrated later in this chapter in the section "How to Combine and Run Multiple Programs."

To Run a Program under CBASIC Non-Compiler

To run a program enter:

    CRUN238 <Filename>   for 8-bit machines
    CBAS86 <Filename>   for 16-bit machines

If an error occurs refer to the run-time error listing in Appendix E and to Chapter 13.

HOW TO COMBINE AND RUN MULTIPLE PROGRAMS

There are two ways in which to combine two or more programs for a single run-time execution.

- The programs can be combined into a single program when compiled and then executed by a single run instruction. This is done by using the **%INCLUDE** compiler directive.
- The programs can be interconnected to be executed individually and successively by a single run instruction by using the **CHAIN** statement and the **%CHAIN** compiler directive.

In the first method the programs are combined into one large program which is stored in memory. In the second method, only one program is in memory at a time. In non-compiler CBASIC each subsequent part is read from a disk and overlaid in memory over the preceding program as it is needed. With the compiler version the first or **root program** remains in memory and the overlays displace each other as they are called. This CHAINing method is especially useful when the combined programs occupy more computer memory than is normally allocated to a program by the operating system.

Combining Programs Using %INCLUDE

For this illustration we will use Program 5-4, which created a file on a disk and permitted data entry, and Program 5-6, which read the file from a disk and printed it on the console screen. Modifications in both programs are necessary. First, let us examine the modified Program 5-4, which is shown in **Program 12-2**, written for the compiler version of CBASIC.

PROGRAM 12-2   **INCLUDE.BAS**   **[Compiler]**

PROGRAM 5-4 Modified to Include %INCLUDE Compiler Directive

Copyright 1985, Compulit, Inc.

```
\              Declaration of variables
          STRING PROD.NO, PROD.DESC, NOF, AN
          INTEGER ON.HAND, INDEX
          REAL PROD.COST
          PRINT: PRINT: PRINT
          INPUT "ENTER NAME OF FILE.........";NOF: PRINT
          CREATE "B:"+ NOF RECL 128 AS 1
          INDEX = 1
10        PRINT: PRINT: INDEX = INDEX + 1
          INPUT "Enter product number..........."; PROD.NO    :PRINT
          INPUT "Enter product description......"; PROD.DESC :PRINT
          INPUT "Enter number of units on hand.."; ON.HAND    :PRINT
          INPUT "Enter product cost ............"; PROD.COST :PRINT
          PRINT #1,INDEX; PROD.NO, PROD.DESC, ON.HAND, PROD.COST
          PRINT #1,1; INDEX
          PRINT: PRINT
          INPUT "Another entry?  Yes or No?     ";AN
          IF UCASE$(AN) = "YES" THEN 10
          CLOSE 1
\              Include second program
          %INCLUDE PRINTOUT.BAS
          PRINT: PRINT: PRINT "Normal termination of program"
          END
```

Aside from the addition of the STRING, INTEGER, and REAL statements at the beginning of the program, the major change is the third line from the end, %INCLUDE PRINTOUT.BAS. It is, however, necessary to modify any independent .BAS program that is to be inserted by the %INCLUDE statement so that:

• The END statement of any "included" program is removed.

- Declaration statements [STRING, INTEGER, REAL] are not repeated in succeeding programs if the compiler version is used.
- There is no duplication of line labels [numeric or alphanumeric] in the programs to be compiled together.

LANGUAGE CODING RULE

The compiler directive, **%INCLUDE**, is used to add other source code, such as a program, subroutine, or multi-line function, within a source program.

%INCLUDE <file specification>

- For example:

%INCLUDE PCSCRN.DEF   to include cursor control functions
%INCLUDE PRINTOUT   to include a program called
                                 PRINTOUT.BAS

- A maximum of six %INCLUDE statements may be used within any combination of attached programs and routines. A .BAS filetype on the default drive is assumed unless otherwise specified.

Program 5-6 has been modified to meet these restrictions. The END statement has been removed and no declaration statements are included. In addition, the original label 10 has been changed to 100. The modified program is shown in **Program 12-3**

PROGRAM 12-3   PRINTOUT.BAS   [Compiler]

PROGRAM 5-6 Modified for Inclusion in PROGRAM 12-2

Copyright 1985, Compulit, Inc.

```
\      Program is part of an INCLUDE segment; it cannot be used by itself.
\      The declaration of variables must be combined with Program 12-2.
\      This program cannot be compiled by itself without the removal
\      of the backslashes \ before the declaration of the variables.
\      Even if it is compiled, it will not execute; it must be included
\      as part of Program 12-2.
\
\      STRING NOF, PROD.NO, PROD.DESC
\      INTEGER K, ON.HAND
\      REAL PROD.COST
\
       PRINT: PRINT: PRINT
       PRINT "PRODUCT #", "DESCRIPTION", "UNITS ON HAND", "COST" :PRINT
       IF END #1 THEN 50
       OPEN "B:"+ NOF RECL 128 AS 1
       K = 2
100    READ #1,K; PROD.NO, PROD.DESC, ON.HAND, PROD.COST
       PRINT PROD.NO, PROD.DESC, ON.HAND, PROD.COST
       K = K + 1
       GOTO 100
50     CLOSE 1
```

The %INCLUDE statement joins the two programs into one when they are compiled using CBASIC in either the non-compiler or compiler versions. From the computer's viewpoint, there is only a single program with the filename the same as the "source" or root program in which the first %INCLUDE appears. **Figure 12-7** shows the compiler listing of the two programs. Note that the included program is indicated by **a** after the compiler line numbers.

```
  1:   0000h \         PROGRAM 12-2    INCLUDE.BAS
  2:   0000h           STRING PROD.NO, PROD.DESC, INDEX%, NOF, AN
  3:   0000h           INTEGER ON.HAND, INDEX
  4:   0000h           REAL PROD.COST
  5:   0000h           PRINT: PRINT: PRINT
  6:   0012h           INPUT "ENTER NAME OF FILE........";NOF: PRINT
  7:   0026h           CREATE "B:"+ NOF RECL 128 AS 1
  8:   0041h           INDEX = 1
  9:   0047h 10        PRINT: PRINT: INDEX = INDEX + 1
 10:   0054h           INPUT "Enter product number........."; PROD.NO    :PRINT
 11:   0068h           INPUT "Enter product description......"; PROD.DESC :PRINT
 12:   007ch           INPUT "Enter number of units on hand.."; ON.HAND   :PRINT
 13:   0090h           INPUT "Enter product cost ............"; PROD.COST :PRINT
 14:   00a4h           PRINT #1,INDEX; PROD.NO, PROD.DESC, ON.HAND, PROD.COST
 15:   00cfh           PRINT #1,1; INDEX
 16:   00e2h           PRINT: PRINT
 17:   00e8h           INPUT "Another entry?  Yes or No?        ";AN
 18:   00f9h           IF UCASE$(AN) = "YES" THEN 10
 19:   010dh           CLOSE 1
 20:   0113h           %INCLUDE PRINTOUT
 21=a  0113h \         PROGRAM 12-3    PRINTOUT.BAS
 22=a  0113h           PRINT: PRINT: PRINT
 23=a  011ch           PRINT "PRODUCT #", "DESCRIPTION", "UNITS ON HAND", "COST"
>:PRINT
 24=a  0137h           IF END #1 THEN 50
 25=a  0141h           OPEN "B:"+ NOF RECL 128 AS 1
 26=a  015ch           K = 2
 27=a  0168h 100       READ #1,K; PROD.NO, PROD.DESC, ON.HAND, PROD.COST
 28=a  0194h           PRINT PROD.NO, PROD.DESC, ON.HAND, PROD.COST
 29=a  01b2h           K = K + 1
 30=a  01c4h           GOTO 100
 31=a  01c6h 50        CLOSE 1
 32:   01cch           PRINT: PRINT: PRINT "Normal termination of program"
 33:   01deh           END
end of compilation
no errors detected
code area size:    478        01deh
data area size:    314        013ah
```

```
common area size:  0          0000h
symbol table space remaining: 40956
```

FIGURE 12-7   Compiler Output for %INCLUDE Program 12-3

Chaining Programs with Common Storage

Several programs can be chained together by using both the CHAIN and the COMMON statements, and the %CHAIN compiler directive for the non-compiler version, under the following conditions:

- If a set of related programs to be executed sequentially is too large to fit the computer's memory, we can join them so that they are executed successively and data needed by one program remains stored in the computer for the next.
- If a single program to be executed is too large for the memory allocated by the operating system, the program can be written in modules and then chained for execution.

The CHAIN statement is part of the source program in the same way as the compiler directive, %INCLUDE. The COMMON statement specifies which variables are to be retained in memory for use by chained programs. The COMMON statement *must* appear in all the programs that are linked by the CHAIN statement.

LANGUAGE CODING RULE

The **CHAIN** statement transfers control to another program. Although its syntax is the same for the non-compiler and compiler versions, there are other differences.

CHAIN " [disk specification:] <filename> "

or

CHAIN [disk specification :] <string expression>

where the expression is previously defined as the filename.

- With the non-compiler version, the file or files to be chained must be the .INT filetype. No disk specification is needed if the file is on the default disk. Furthermore, a %CHAIN directive [illustrated later in this chapter] is required.
- With the compiler version, two filetypes may be used; the program to be chained may be an .OVL filetype for CB80 and .OVR for CB86 or any directly executable file. It is therefore possible to chain files generated from languages other than CBASIC. The filetype is assumed to be .OVL or .OVR unless specified with the filename.

How to Chain Programs with the Non-Compiler Version

We will again use variations of Program 5-4 and Program 5-6 to illustrate the CHAIN and COMMON statements when using the non-compiler version of CBASIC. In this example, we have the CBASIC compiler on drive A and the two programs, called INFILE.BAS and OUTFILE.BAS, on drive B.

LANGUAGE CODING RULE

The **COMMON** statement specifies the program variables that are common to the main program and all other programs executed by CHAIN·statements. They are retained in memory throughout the execution of all the programs.

COMMON <variable> {, <variable>}

The COMMON statement must appear early in the programs and only REM statements [or in the case of the compiler version, data type declaration statements] may precede it.

When using arrays, only the first program should contain the DIM statement. Subsequent programs will be able to access the common array without any DIM statement; in fact, if a DIM statement is executed later, the original data will be lost. However, when using arrays with the COMMON statement, the size of the array is indicated within parentheses. For example:

COMMON X, Y, A(20), B(31,12)

---

1. The only data which is required by both programs is the name of the data file that is created by Program 5-4. To provide for this transfer of data between the programs, we place a COMMON statement at the beginning of both programs immediately after the remarks:

```
COMMON NOF$
```

To chain the programs:

2. Include the CHAIN statement in the main program immediately before the END statement as shown in **Program 12-4**. In this case we have used:

```
CHAIN "OUTFILE"
```

3. Compile both programs separately in order to obtain the program and data storage requirements. These are:

	MAIN PROGRAM	CHAINED PROGRAM
CONSTANT AREA:	8	8
CODE SIZE:	354	145
DATA STMT AREA:	0	0
VARIABLE AREA:	56	48

4. Edit the main program to include the %CHAIN directive which is followed by four unsigned values separated by commas. These numbers specify the maximum space that will be required for each of the four areas. If any of the storage values exceed 32,767 they must be entered as real values in hexadecimal format in place of integers. In this case the maximum size of each of the four is found in the main program and these values are included in the compiler directive as shown in **Program 12-4**.

PROGRAM 12-4   **INFILE.BAS**   **[Non-Compiler]**

Use of %CHAIN Directive and COMMON

Copyright 1985, Compulit, Inc.

```
%CHAIN 8,354,0,56
        COMMON NOF$
        PRINT: PRINT: PRINT
        INPUT "ENTER NAME OF FILE........";NOF$ :PRINT
        CREATE "A:"+ NOF$ RECL 128 AS 1
        INDEX% = 1
10      PRINT: PRINT: INDEX% = INDEX% + 1
        INPUT "Enter product number..........."; PROD.NO$  :PRINT
        INPUT "Enter product description......"; PROD.DESC$:PRINT
        INPUT "Enter number of units on hand.."; ON.HAND%  :PRINT
        INPUT "Enter product cost ............"; PROD.COST :PRINT
        PRINT #1,INDEX%; PROD.NO$, PROD.DESC$, ON.HAND%, PROD.COST
        PRINT #1,1; INDEX%
        PRINT: PRINT
        INPUT "Another entry?  Yes or No?      ";ANS
        IF UCASE$(AN$) = "YES" THEN 10
        CLOSE 1
\               Include second program
        CHAIN "OUTFILE"
        END
```

The program to produce the output, **Program 12-5**, would also include a COMMON statement.

PROGRAM 12-5   **OUTFILE.BAS**   **[Non-Compiler]**

PROGRAM 5-6 Modified for Inclusion in PROGRAM 12-4

Copyright 1985, Compulit, Inc.

```
        COMMON NOF$
        PRINT: PRINT: PRINT
        PRINT "PRODUCT #", "DESCRIPTION", "UNITS ON HAND", "COST" :PRINT
```

(continues)

```
         IF END #1 THEN 50
         OPEN "A:"+ NOF$ RECL 128 AS 1
         K% = 2
10       READ #1,K%; PROD.NO$, PROD.DESC$, ON.HAND%, PROD.COST
         PRINT PROD.NO$, PROD.DESC$, ON.HAND%, PROD.COST
         K% = K% + 1
         GOTO 10
50       CLOSE 1
         PRINT "End of program:  Close of overlay"
         END
```

5. Recompile the programs after you have added the %CHAIN directive, and the CHAIN and COMMON statements. This does not
   affect the storage allocation areas.
6. You are now ready to run the chained programs. When the CHAIN
   statement in the main program is encountered, the computer will
   overlay the next program in the memory space allocated by the
   %CHAIN directive, where the main program was originally stored.

Saving Space for a Machine Language Subroutine

Memory space for a machine language subroutine can be saved and the file
loaded during execution when using the non-compiler version by in-
corporating the **SAVEMEM** statement in the program.

LANGUAGE CODING RULE

The **SAVEMEM** statement in the non-compiler version reserves space for a
machine language subroutine and loads that file during execution.

SAVEMEM <numeric constant> , <file specification>

- The numeric constant specifies the number of bytes to save for a
  machine language subroutine. The file specification is entered as a
  string variable or a string constant.
- The constant should be at least 128 or nothing will be read from a
  disk although the space is saved.
- Only one SAVEMEM statement may be used in a program.
- When programs are chained, the main and subsequent chained
  programs must contain a SAVEMEM statement with the *identical
  size* numeric constant although it is possible to designate different
  files.

This is an advanced statement which requires a knowledge of assembly
language or how to modify an assembly program and recompile it as well as

the use of PEEKs and POKEs to permit the execution of the statement. This is necessary because the saved space is at the top of the Transient Program Area [TPA] in memory and the starting address of the subroutine must be calculated. A CALL statement is used to access the routines loaded by the SAVEMEM statement.

How to Chain Programs with the Compiler Version

Again, we will start with the original Program 5-4 and Program 5-6 to illustrate this procedure. The modified Program 5-4 is shown as **Program 12-6**. We have set NOF as COMMON to both programs and included a CHAIN statement in which the program to be linked is indicated; the drive is included within quotation marks if it is not the default drive.

PROGRAM 12-6   **INFILE2.BAS**   **[Compiler]**

Use of CHAIN and COMMON

Copyright 1985, Compulit, Inc.

```
  \           Declaration of variables
            STRING PROD.NO, PROD.DESC, INDEX%, NOF, AN
            INTEGER ON.HAND, INDEX
            REAL PROD.COST
            COMMON NOF
            PRINT: PRINT: PRINT
            INPUT "ENTER NAME OF FILE........";NOF: PRINT
            CREATE "B:"+ NOF RECL 128 AS 1
            INDEX = 1
  10        PRINT: PRINT: INDEX = INDEX + 1
            INPUT "Enter product number..........."; PROD.NO    :PRINT
            INPUT "Enter product description......"; PROD.DESC :PRINT
            INPUT "Enter number of units on hand.."; ON.HAND   :PRINT
            INPUT "Enter product cost ..........."; PROD.COST :PRINT
            PRINT #1,INDEX; PROD.NO, PROD.DESC, ON.HAND, PROD.COST
            PRINT #1,1; INDEX
            PRINT: PRINT
            INPUT "Another entry?  Yes or No?      ";AN
            IF UCASE$(AN) = "YES" THEN 10
            CLOSE 1
  \            Include second program
            CHAIN "OUTFILE2"
            END
```

Program 5-6 has also been modified to include the COMMON statement as shown in **Program 12-7**. However, unlike Program 12-3 which was "included," it is not necessary to alter duplicate line labels or remove the data type declaration statements. Furthermore, since an .OBJ file had to be created so that the programs can be chained, the END statement is retained.

PROGRAM 12-7   **OUTFILE2.BAS**   **[Compiler]**

PROGRAM 5-6 Modified for Inclusion in PROGRAM 12-6

Copyright 1985, Compulit, Inc.

```
\               Declaration of variables
        STRING PROD.NO, PROD.DESC, NOF
        INTEGER ON.HAND, K
        REAL PROD.COST
        COMMON NOF
        PRINT: PRINT: PRINT
        PRINT "PRODUCT #", "DESCRIPTION", "UNITS ON HAND", "COST" :PRINT
        IF END #1 THEN 50
        OPEN "B:"+ NOF RECL 128 AS 1
        K = 2
10      READ #1,K; PROD.NO, PROD.DESC, ON.HAND, PROD.COST
        PRINT PROD.NO, PROD.DESC, ON.HAND, PROD.COST
        K = K + 1
        GOTO 10
50      CLOSE 1
        PRINT "Close of overlay"
        END
```

To link the programs for single run-time execution, compile each program independently with the CB86 or CB80 compiler and use the link editor to create an overlay and chain the programs as explained in the next section.

How to Create an Overlay

To chain CBASIC programs when using the compiler version it is necessary to create an **overlay** filetype, .OVL or .OVR, during the linking stage of compiling. The programs to be chained or overlaid need not be on the same disk, although many programmers find it more convenient. To illustrate this procedure we will use two programs:

- The first or **root program** we have named INFILE2.BAS [Program 12-6].
- The second program to be chained to the first we have named OUTFILE2.BAS [Program 12-7].

The first step is to compile both programs successfully in order that INFILE2.OBJ and OUTFILE2.OBJ are on the disk. If they are on the same disk as the link editor, they are linked by entering, after the system prompt:

```
A: LINK86 INFILE2 (OUTFILE2)  <CR>
```

That is, after the link command enter the basic or root program followed by the program we wish to overlay in parentheses. This will produce a program, OUTFILE2.OVL or OUTFILE2.OVR, which can then be called by the root program.

If the two .OBJ files are *not* on the same disk as the link editor, the disk drive must be included. For example, if INFILE2.OBJ and OUTFILE2. OBJ are on disk B and the link editor is on drive A, enter:

```
A:   LINK86 B:INFILE2 (B:OUTFILE2)   <CR>
```

SUMMARY OF PROCEDURES TO JOIN/CHAIN PROGRAMS

Three sets of programs which must be processed as pairs have been included in this section; they illustrate the sequential execution of related programs. Each of the three sets is an example of the different chaining or overlay procedures when using CBASIC.

In each case related pair of .BAS programs must be on the same disk.

1. The %INCLUDE technique is used to join Program 12-2, INCLUDE.BAS, with Program 12-3, PRINTOUT.BAS, using the CBASIC CB86 Compiler. PRINTOUT.BAS *cannot* be compiled or executed by itself. To process the two programs:

- Compile INCLUDE.BAS by entering: A> CB86 INCLUDE <CR>. The compiled listing will include *both* programs.
- Then link INCLUDE to produce an executable program.

2. The %CHAIN technique is used to join Program 12-4, INFILE.BAS, with Program 12-5, OUTFILE.BAS, using CBASIC [non-compiler version]. To chain the two programs compile each program separately so that the .INT files are on the same disk. Then execute INFILE.BAS and the programs will execute sequentially.

3. The CHAIN technique using CBASIC CB86 Compiler joins Program 12-6, INFILE2.BAS, with Program 12-7, OUTFILE2.BAS. To compile and produce an overlay program:

- Compile each program separately.
- Then produce the overlay file during linking by entering:

A> LINK86 INFILE2 (OUTFILE2) <CR>

4. Two new files, INFILE2.EXE and OUTFILE2.OVR, will now be on the disk. The two are executed sequentially by entering: A> INFILE2.

If OUTFILE2.OBJ is on drive B and INFILE2.OBJ and the link editor are on drive A, the entry would be:

```
A:  LINK86 INFILE2 (B:OUTFILE2)  <CR>
```

More than one overlay can be created with a root program. To link a third program, NEWFILE.OBJ, enter:

```
A:  LINK86 INFILE2 (OUTFILE2) (NEWFILE)  <CR>
```

This assumes that the link editor and all three programs are on drive A. A different drive may be specified for any of the three programs.

# CHAPTER 13

Improving Your
Debugging Techniques

Errors in computer programming have been called **bugs** since the early days of computing. The story goes that Commodore Grace Murray Hopper of the USNR, the First Lady of computing, in attempting to discover why a program failed to run on one of the old, massive, tube and relay computers, found that a flying insect had been crushed inside a relay and had interrupted the electrical circuit. **Debugging** is probably the most tedious and mentally taxing part of programming. It's generally done under pressure, either self-induced or actual.

Many types of bugs can creep into a program and even the most experienced programmer is not immune. Programming errors can be divided into several major types:

- Syntax errors
- Unusual typing errors
- Misuse of key or reserved words
- Data mismatch errors
- Logic or procedural errors

Experienced programmers have developed efficient procedures to locate the bugs. Some of these techniques are common sense procedures while others require extra programming and entry time. In the long run, except for short, simple programs, that extra entry time saves debugging time.

SYNTAX ERRORS

Syntax errors are probably the most common bugs of all. They are most easily detected and generally are easily corrected. When you compile a program under any version of CBASIC, the compiler will first scan for syntax errors. We will use **Program 13-1** to illustrate how syntax errors are trapped by the compiler. There are two errors in this program: First, a comma has been used in place of a semicolon with an INPUT statement, and second, the word PRINT has been misspelled as *PRNIT*.

PROGRAM 13-1   **SYNTAX.BAS**   **[Compiler]**

Compilation with Syntax Errors

Copyright 1985, Compulit, Inc.

```
\       Syntax error in program; for demonstration only
\
\              Declaration of variable
        STRING NAME
\              Syntax errors in next two lines
        INPUT "Enter your name  ", NAME
        PRNIT  NAME
        END
```

Compiler versions of CBASIC would produce the output, shown in **Figure 13-1**, during the first phase of the compile process.

```
    1:          \        PROGRAM 13-1
    2:                   STRING NAME
    3:                   INPUT "Enter you name  ", NAME
*** error                                      ^72
*** error                                      ^15
    4:                   PRNIT NAME
*** error                ^30
*** error                ^51
*** error                ^33
*** error                ^27
    5:          END
end of compilation
6 errors detected
symbol table space remaining: 41129
```

FIGURE 13-1   Compiler Output of Syntax Errors in Program 13-1

By checking the error message listing in Appendix D, we find that the two error messages in line 13 are:

72   A semicolon is missing in an INPUT statement.
15   A variable is missing.

The compiler was uncertain as to what the programmer wished to do and produced both messages. In reviewing the statement, it is obvious that the semicolon had not been used.

Again, in checking line 14 in which there was a misspelling of the PRINT statement, the error messages produced are:

30   Invalid symbol follows a variable, constant, or function reference.

51 An equal sign is missing in an assignment. An equal sign is inserted.

33 Invalid symbol encountered in an expression.

27 Invalid mixed mode; the type of expression is not permitted.

None of these errors applies. It is assumed that spelling errors have been detected when the program is read prior to compilation. *It is good programming practice to read the entire program, preferably from a printout, before it is compiled.* In this case, when the programmer finds that none of the error messages applies, the obvious next step is to reread the line and look for a spelling error.

The **non-compiler versions** of CBASIC would produce the output shown in **Figure 13-2** when Program 13-1, revised for the non-compiler CBASIC, is compiled.

```
CBASIC COMPILER VER 2.08
    1: REM      PROGRAM 13-0
    2:          INPUT "Enter your name ", NAME$
ERROR SE IN LINE     2 AT POSITION    33
    3:          PRNIT NAME$
ERROR SE IN LINE     3 AT POSITION    17
    4:          END
    2 ERRORS DETECTED
CONSTANT AREA:       8
CODE SIZE:          19
DATA STMT AREA:      0
VARIABLE AREA:       8
```

FIGURE 13-2   Non-Compiler Output of Syntax Errors in Program 13-1

ERROR SE [syntax error] appears for both lines [see Appendix E]. This means that a statement is not properly formed or a keyword is misspelled. These apply to the two errors respectively. The location of the error is also given. However, this is not always applicable; the location of the error may point to the wrong position.

UNREFERENCED VARIABLES

The second most common error is a typing error made when writing a variable name. A typing error in a **reserved word** is generally caught although not identified by the compiler; a similar error in a variable name is often not caught by the compiler. These errors are more frequently encountered in the non-compiler versions than in the compiler versions.

For example, in writing a program using a non-compiler version of CBASIC the variable NAME$ may, in another part of the program, be listed as NAME or NAME%. With a compiler version this mixed-mode error would not occur if declaration statements are used, but misspelling is a possibility—*NAEM* in place of *NAME*, for example.

If your program has been successfully compiled but fails to work, obtain a listing of all variables used in the program. This is especially necessary in a long program. The procedure to do this is different for the compiler and non-compiler versions.

SPECIAL PROGRAMMING NOTE

Use REM or comment statements frequently in a program such as those found in Program 2-2. These comments help when you are writing the statements in an algorithm, are helpful if you have to debug the program, and can be used by someone else to follow the logic.

At a later date you may find the REMs useful when updating the program or using part of it in another program. When the program has been successfully compiled and tested and you are certain that it works, you can save that copy as a source back-up and remove the REM statements from the working copy.

SPECIAL PROGRAMMING NOTE

When writing a program, particularly a long one, it is good programming practice to include a series of REM statements at the beginning of the program to identify each variable name. Using Program 7-4, for example, the variable list would be placed immediately after the first line as:

```
REM   VARIABLE              DEFINITION
REM
REM   ANNUAL.DEPRECIATION   Annual depreciation of the equipment
REM   AN$                   String variable to rerun new data
REM   CLEAR$                String variable to clear console screen
REM   COST                  Original cost of the equipment
REM   CUM.DEP               Cumulative depreciation to date
REM   I%                    Index used in control loop
REM   YEARS%                Total useful life of equipment
```

Cross-Reference Lister for Non-Compiler Versions

The cross-reference list of identifiers is valuable both for debugging and for documentation. It is an alphabetical list of all identifiers used in a program giving the usage [function, parameter, global] and the lines in which they are used. The functions are listed first, the parameters second, and the global identifiers last. The list is produced as a disk file on the same drive as the source program unless otherwise directed; it has the same name as the source with the file extension **.XRF**.

To obtain this list for a program named FUNC.BAS:

1. Include Toggle E in the compile command.

A: CBAS86 FUNC $E <CR>

2. Enter the XREF command.

A: XREF FUNC <CR>

To change the disk drive, add it after the filename. If FUNC.BAS is on drive B and the XREF listing should be written to drive A the command is:

A: XREF FUNC A: <CR>

The disk file FUNC.XRF can be read on the screen with a text editor. It can also be printed as hardcopy by using Toggle A [**$A**] in the XREF command. If it is to be read on the screen, include Toggle D [**$D**] in the XREF command. This will cause the output to be produced in 80 columns instead of 132 columns which is the default width.

We have used **Program 13-2**, FUNC.BAS, that determines the smaller of two values, to illustrate the output of the XREF command. The two commands just given will produce the XREF listing which follows the program.

PROGRAM 13-2   **FUNC.BAS**   **[Non-Compiler]**

Program Determines the Smaller of Two Values

Copyright 1985, Compulit, Inc.

```
\             Defining CLEAR.SCREEN for PC-DOS and MS-DOS
       CLEAR.SCREEN$ = CHR$(27) + "[2J"
\             Define function to determine smaller of values X and Y
       DEF FN.SMALLER (X, Y) = ( X + Y - ABS ( X - Y )) / 2
   10  PRINT CLEAR.SCREEN$
       INPUT "Enter the first value ....... "; FV
       INPUT "Enter the second value ...... "; SV
       LV = FN.SMALLER (FV,SV)
       PRINT
       PRINT "The first value entered was ....... "; FV
       PRINT "The second value entered was ...... "; SV
       PRINT "The smaller of the two values is .. "; LV
       PRINT: INPUT "Another test?  Yes or No?   "; ANS
       IF UCASE$(ANS) = "YES" THEN 10
       PRINT "Normal termination of program"
       END
```

The cross reference listing which is part of the compiled printout is shown in **Figure 13-3**.

```
CBASIC XREF LISTING OF A:FUNC.BAS                           PAGE NO 1

            NAME                        TYPE

     FN.SMALLER                     FUNCTION    3,    7
     X                              PARAMETER   3
     Y                              PARAMETER   3
     AN$                            GLOBAL     12,   13
     CLEAR$                         GLOBAL      2,    4
     FV                             GLOBAL      5,    7,    9
     LV                             GLOBAL      7,   11
     SV                             GLOBAL      6,    7,   10
```

FIGURE 13-3   Cross Reference Listing with XREF

Although the debugging of such a short program would ordinarily present no problem, in a much longer program with a very long list of identifiers the XREF listing may make obvious the kind of error which is easily overlooked, does not cause a run-time error, but produces incorrect output. For example, if the list contained, in addition to AN$, an identifier AN% it would be quickly apparent to the programmer that an entry error was causing the problem.

The list is an aid in documentation if Toggle E is included in the XREF command. Toggle E suppresses the listing of the line numbers; only the identifiers and their usage are listed. The purpose of each identifier can be added to the list; for example:

```
FV        GLOBAL    First value entered.
```

Cross-Reference Lister Toggles

There are eight **toggles** that may be used with the XREF command.

1. *To produce hardcopy in addition to the disk file* use **Toggle A**.
2. *To suppress output to the disk* use **Toggle B**. Toggle B used alone would produce no output. Use it with Toggle A to get a hardcopy listing with no disk file. However, Toggle C by itself produces the same result.
3. *To print the listing and suppress the disk file* use **Toggle C**.
4. *To produce the listing in 80 columns instead of 132* use **Toggle D**.
5. *To suppress the line numbers in the output* use **Toggle E**.
6. *To change the page length from the default value of 60 lines* use **Toggle F**.

The page length is enclosed in parentheses and must follow Toggle F. If additional toggles are used, list them before Toggle F as in:

```
XREF FUNC $DF(45)
```

The page length would be 45 lines and the width would be 80 columns.

7. *To suppress printing of heading lines and all form-feeds* use **Toggle G**. Toggle G will cause the disk file to be written with no page length set; this can be determined by the user if the file is printed later.

8. *To suppress translation of lower case letters to upper case* use **Toggle H**. Toggle H performs the same function as compiler toggle D. If the translation is suppressed when the program is compiled it should be suppressed in the XREF listing as well.

The use of these toggles is summarized in **Table 13-1**.

TABLE 13-1   Cross-Reference Toggle Functions

FUNCTION	TOGGLE
To print hardcopy	A
To suppress output to disk	B
To print hardcopy and suppress listing on disk	C
To change output width to 80 columns	D
To suppress line numbers	E
To change default page length of 60 lines	F
To suppress headings and form-feeds	G
To suppress translation of lower case to upper case	H

XREF is invoked by the following command:

XREF <filename> [disk assignment] [$toggles] ["title"]

In this language coding format:

• The filename, <filename>, must be a CBASIC source program with the filetype .BAS.

- The XREF file can be assigned to any disk drive, [disk assignment]. If this option is not used then the XREF listing is placed on the same drive as the source program.
- Toggles A through H, [$ toggles], shown in Table 13-1 may be used; leave at least one blank space before the $ used to denote toggles.
- The optional title, ["title"], is printed on the heading line of each page of hardcopy output and is written within a set of quotation marks. The title is limited to 30 characters if a 132 column listing is used. However, if toggle D, which limits output to 80 columns is used, the title may not exceed 20 characters.

For example:

```
A:   XREF FUNC.BAS C $A 'Version 3 - 8/13/85'   <CR>
```

would produce an XREF listing on disk drive C and cause the output to be listed by the printer with the title "Version 3 - 8/13/85."

Variable Table for Compiler Version Programs

Using the same program as we had for the non-compiler versions, Program 13-2, we can produce a table of variables during the compilation of the program. To do this we use toggle T and enter, for example:

```
A:   CB86 FUNC [T]   <CR>
```

The **symbol table** would be listed after the program as shown in **Figure 13-4**. The form is different from that available with the non-compiler versions. In addition to noting the type of variable, the output also includes the class and variable address and returns line labels with addresses.

The symbol table, however, does not provide a listing of the line numbers in which the variable is used. The last column, # subscrp, would list the number of subscripts in an array variable. For example, if the program included the variable AR(50,4,2) the number in the last column would be 3.

Using the U Toggle and Declare Statements

Unreferenced variables can also be detected with a compiler version by using the variable declaration statements, STRING, INTEGER, and REAL, and compiling the program using the U toggle. This toggle generates error messages for each undeclared variable.

```
                          symbol table information

        no variables in common

              function: FN.SMALLER                 at 0026h    returns real

                   name                 type        class     address    # subscrp

    X                            parameter          real      0012h
    Y                            parameter          real      000ah

              global variables:

                   name                 type        class     address    # subscrp

    CLEAR$                       simple variable     string    0000h
    10                           label                         005ch
    FV                           simple variable     real      001ah
    LV                           simple variable     real      002ah
    SV                           simple variable     real      0022h
    AN$                          simple variable     string    0032h

    end of compilation
    no errors detected
    code area size:     254      00feh
    data area size:     301      012dh
    common area size:   0        0000h
    symbol table space remaining: 41001
```

FIGURE 13-4   Compiler Version Variable Table

Again if we use Program 13-2 and insert the declaration lines after the first line as:

```
STRING   CLEAR,SCREEN
REAL     LV
```

we would have "accidentally" left out several of the variables. Therefore, if we compile the program as:

```
A:   CB86 FUNC [F, U]   <CR>
```

we would obtain the output with the error messages shown in **Figure 13-5**.

The U toggle would trap the real variables FV and SV as well as the string variable AN.

MISUSE OF RESERVED WORDS

Another possible error encountered when compiling a program is the inadvertent use of a reserved or key word. Although this list is relatively small [see Appendix A] it is common for a beginning programmer to over-look some words in this list especially when selecting a variable name which has a specific meaning to the user.

```
    1:              REM FUNC.BAS - DETERMINES SMALLER OF TWO VALUES
    2:              STRING CLEAR.SCREEN
    3:              REAL   LV
    4:              CLEAR.SCREEN = CHR$(27) + CHR$(69)
    5:              DEF FN.SMALLER (X, Y) = ( X + Y - ABS ( X - Y )) / 2
    6:          10  PRINT CLEAR.SCREEN
    7:              INPUT "Enter the first value ........ "; FV
*** error                                                      ^8
    8:              INPUT "Enter the second value ...... "; SV
*** error                                                    ^8
    9:              LV = FN.SMALLER (FV,SV)
   10:              PRINT
   11:              PRINT "The first value entered was ....... "; FV
   12:              PRINT "The second value entered was ...... "; SV
   13:              PRINT "The smaller of the two values is .. "; LV
   14:              PRINT:  INPUT "Another test?  Yes or No?   "; AN
*** error                                                        ^8
   15:              IF UCASE$(AN) = "YES" THEN 10
*** error                         ^27
   16:              PRINT "Normal termination of program"
   17:              END
end of compilation
4 errors detected
```

FIGURE 13-5 U Toggle Compiler Output for Modified Compiler Version of Program 13-2

In this example, **Figure 13-6**, we have written a program to compute compound interest for one year and have obtained the following compiled output:

```
    1:       \    PROGRAM 13-3
    2:       \    AMT     Amount of deposit
    3:       \    R       Annual rate of interest
    4:       \    FRE     Frequency of compounding during the year
    5:       \    I       Interest rate for each compounding period
    6:       \    SUM     Sum of amount deposited plus interest received
    7:            INPUT "Enter the amount of deposit ........ "; AMT
    8:            INPUT "Enter annual rate of interest ...... "; R
    9:            INPUT "Enter frequency of compounding ..... "; FRE
*** error                                                       ^15
*** error                                                       ^30
   10:            I = R / FRE
   11:            SUM = AMT * ( 1.0 + I ) ^ FRE
   12:            PRINT "Sum at the end of a year is "; SUM
   13:            END
```

FIGURE 13-6 Error Output When Using Reserved Word as Variable

Checking Appendix D, we find the following error messages:

15   A variable is missing.
30   Invalid symbol follows a variable, constant, or function reference.

Neither of the two error messages appears to be valid. We would then recompile the program to obtain a list of variable names and would find:

```
                    symbol table information

    no variables in common

    program contains no functions

    global variables:
```

name	type	class	address	# subscrp
AMT	simple variable	real	0000h	
R	simple variable	real	0008h	
I	simple variable	real	0010h	
SUM	simple variable	real	0018h	

```
end of compilation
2 errors detected
symbol table space remaining: 41108
```

FRE is *not* included in this list of variables. The cause of the program error is the use of a reserved word. FRE is a function and neither statement words nor function identifiers may be used as variable names in a program. If you encounter an error for which you cannot determine the cause, check the reserved word list.

Another example of this type of error occurs when using Program 13-2 with declaration statements for the variables:

```
\   PROGRAM 13-2     FUNC.BAS - DETERMINES SMALLER OF TWO VALUES
    STRING CLEAR, AN
    REAL X, Y, FV, SV, LV
    CLEAR = CHR$(27) + CHR$(69)
    DEF FN.SMALLER (X, Y) = ( X + Y - ABS ( X - Y )) / 2
    .....................................
    .....................................
```

The compiled version of this program, shown in **Figure 13-7**, contains three errors.

```
    2:                STRING CLEAR, AN
*** error                      ^41
    3:                REAL X, Y, FV, SV, GV
    4:                CLEAR = CHR$(27) + CHR$(69)
*** error                  ^53
    5:                DEF FN.LARGER (X, Y) = ( X + Y + ABS ( X - Y )) / 2
    6:        10      PRINT CLEAR
*** error                      ^53
```

FIGURE 13-7 Compiler Error Output for Program 13-2

- Error #41 indicates that a carriage return is missing in a declaration statement.
- Error #53 specifies that an unexpected symbol follows a simple statement. Again, neither of these two statement errors would appear to apply.

Even after checking the list of reserved words, it would be difficult to discover the real cause of the error. We used CLEAR as the string variable to clear the console screen. The word *CLEAR* is not now in the reserved word list of the older versions, but has been reserved since it is a statement in the GSX Graphics Extention to CBASIC.

Changing the string, CLEAR, to CLEAR.SCREEN would solve the problem and eliminate this compiler error. The clue to the solution is the fact that CLEAR is in all the statements where the error appears. This suggests a change in the variable name to see if the error is eliminated.

DEBUGGING METHODS DURING EXECUTION

Even after a program is compiled successfully there is no assurance that it will execute properly. The syntax may be correct, but a **procedural** or **logic error** may be present. These errors occur when a statement is asked, during

---

SPECIAL PROGRAMMING NOTE

You can reduce debugging time when preparing lengthy, complex programs by using a modular approach to programming before joining all the modules into a single program.

If the first module which creates a file, compiles successfully, run the program. To determine if the file has been properly written to the disk, use a text editor or the debugger utility of the compiler to examine the contents of the new file. If you use a text editor, do *not* make any changes in the file and exit from the file so that the structure is unaltered.

Next code the "add to a file" module. If it compiles successfully, execute the program and add to the existing file created by the first module. The contents of the new file can be examined to ascertain that the new data has been successfully added.

If you encounter difficulty at this phase, rerun the first module to create a new file and use the second module to add to it. If after examining the file with a text editor or debugger utility, you find that you were unable to add the new entries into the existing file, you have localized your problem in the second module. The difficult task now begins since somewhere within the module is a logical or procedural error. You may have failed to increase the counter in a relative file before writing the new records or you may have failed to close the file after data entry.

This step-by-step procedure is followed until each module has been written and tested. Only after all the modules have been completely tested are you ready to write the menu portion of the program, add the branching instructions in an ON-GOTO statement, and remove those statements in the modules that were used solely to test the module and are not needed as an integral part of the program.

Remember that it is a safe programming practice to close a file before returning to the menu and then to reopen it before each module is invoked. In this way the file is saved if there is a power outage during the use of the program or the user inadvertently fails to close the file with the menu selection after the work is done.

execution, to do something it cannot do or when the logic-flow of the program is incorrect. These errors are often more difficult to detect.

If an execution time error message occurs, you can localize the error's location by:

- Using the **TRACE** option with the non-compiler versions
- Including the **ON ERROR** statement and the **ERR** and **ERRL** functions with the compiler versions

If no execution time error message occurs and if the answer or program output is incorrect, you should:

- Verify that all the variables in the program have been properly defined and that there is no "illegal" variable that has been caused by a spelling error. This is done by recompiling the program and obtaining a list of variables as discussed earlier in this chapter.
- Perform a bench check of the program. This means taking a printout of the program and preparing a test run with sample data. Insert print lines at various test points in the program to verify data input and computations.

TRACE Option for Non-Compiler CBASIC

The TRACE option is very useful in run-time debugging. Combined with the compiler Toggle E, it prints the line number of each statement as it is executed so that when execution stops because an error has been encountered, the programmer can tell just how far execution has gone and in what line the error occurred. TRACE can be used for the entire program or for only a part.

A short program with obvious errors, **Program 13-3**, is used to illustrate the result of using Toggle E and TRACE.

PROGRAM 13-3   **TEST.BAS**   **[Non-Compiler]**

Illustration of TRACE Option

Copyright 1985, Compulit, Inc.

```
       OPEN "TRACE.FIL" AS 1
10     READ NAME$
       PRINT #1; NAME$
       GOTO 10
       DATA MARY, JANE
       CLOSE 1
       END
```

Compile the program without the program header, that is, starting with the line, OPEN "TRACE.FIL" AS 1, by entering:

```
A>    CBAS2 TEST $E   <CR>
```

To run the program enter:

```
A>    CRUN238 TEST TRACE   <CR>
```

Program execution will stop when the first error is encountered, the OPEN statement for a file which does not exist. The screen output is shown below.

```
CRUN VER 2.38
COPYRIGHT 1981 COMPILER SYSTEMS INC.

ERROR OE IN LINE 0001
```

The execution of the program started with line 1 where an error was detected; an attempt was made to open a file that did not exist. If this error is corrected by changing OPEN to CREATE and the program is again compiled with CBAS2, running the program with a trace option would result in the following output on the console screen:

```
AT LINE 0001
AT LINE 0002
AT LINE 0003
AT LINE 0004
AT LINE 0002
AT LINE 0003
AT LINE 0004
AT LINE 0002

ERROR OD IN LINE 0002
```

The programmer can now follow the complete program execution until the final OD (out of data) error is encountered in the READ line.

In a longer program it is often preferable to TRACE only part of the program. This is done by the addition of one or two parameters, the line number at which the TRACE should begin separated by a comma [,] from the line number at which the TRACE should end. If only the first parameter is used, the TRACE will continue from that line to the end. Toggle E must still be used in the compile command.

```
A>    CRUN238 MERGE TRACE 10, 21   <CR>
```

would TRACE between lines 10 and 21 of Program MERGE.BAS. If only 10 is used, TRACE continues through the end of the program.

LANGUAGE CODING RULE

The syntax for the TRACE option is:

CRUN238 <filename> **TRACE** [1st line, [, 2nd line]]

- The filename must be an .INT file.
- The 1st line is the first line number in the source program at which the trace begins.
- The 2nd line is the last line number in the source program at which the trace ends.

Error Detection with Compiler Versions

If Program 13-3 is compiled and linked with any of the compiler versions, we would encounter no difficulties. However, an attempt to execute the program if the file TRACE.FIL is not on the disk would produce the following message on the console screen:

```
ERROR OE AT IP 001EH
```

Checking the execution error message in Appendix D, we find that OE states that an attempt was made to OPEN a file that does not exist and for which no IF END statement is in effect. If we change OPEN to CREATE, recompile and relink the program, and then execute it, the following error message would appear on the screen:

```
ERROR OD AT IP 0024H
```

The OD run-time error message notifies us that a READ statement is executed but there are no DATA statements in the program, or all data items in all DATA statements have been read. In examining the program, we find that we have failed to provide for any orderly conclusion of the READ statement.

This is a comparatively easy error to detect because the program is short and not complex. The hexadecimal location of the error does not help the beginning programmer; most need to know the line number at which the error occurred. This is available to the programmer by using a statement and two functions.

The **ON ERROR** statement is used in conjunction with the **ERR** and **ERRL** functions. Program control reverts to an ON ERROR statement when an execution error is encountered. *The N toggle is used during program compilation* to save the line numbers in the source program and to enable the ERRL function to return the line number when an execution error occurs. **Program 13-4** illustrates the use of this statement.

PROGRAM 13-4 **TESTER.BAS** **[Compiler]**

Use of ON ERROR, ERR, and ERRL

Copyright 1985, Compulit, Inc.

```
\              Declaration of variables
        STRING NAME, ERROR.CODE
        INTEGER LINE.NUMBER
        ON ERROR GOTO 100
        CREATE "TRACE.FIL" AS 1
10      READ NAME
        PRINT #1; NAME
        GOTO 10
        DATA MARY, JANE
        CLOSE 1
\              Procedure for defining and printing the error
100     ERROR.CODE  = ERR
        LINE.NUMBER = ERRL
        PRINT: PRINT
        PRINT "Error "; ERROR.CODE; " has occurred at line number"; LINE.NUMBER
        STOP
        END
```

Remember to use the N toggle during the compiling of the program; for example:

```
A:  CB86  TESTER  [N]  <CR>
```

When using the ON ERROR statement within this program, when the program runs out of data to read, the following message is printed:

```
Error 0D has occurred at line 15
```

LANGUAGE CODING RULE

ON ERROR statement is used in the compiler versions to indicate the type and location of an execution time error. It is used in conjunction with the ERR and ERRL functions.

ON ERROR GOTO <line label>

- The ON ERROR statement should not be used in a multi-line function. The return address is lost because of the resetting of the stack.

LANGUAGE CODING RULE

The **ERR** function in the compiler versions returns a two-character string to indicate the error code when an error occurs in a program.

<string variable> = **ERR**

- The ERR function is used in conjunction with the ERRL function and the ON ERROR statement.

LANGUAGE CODING RULE

The **ERRL** function specifies the line number at which an execution error has taken place.

<integer variable> = **ERRL**

- This function is used with the ERR function and the ON ERROR statement.

LANGUAGE CODING RULE

The **STOP** statement terminates the execution of the program, closes all open files and returns control to the operating system.

STOP

- Any number of STOP statements can be used within a program. It should *not* be used in place of the END statement.

SAMPLE DATA FOR TEST RUNS

One of the most common errors in execution results from improper data entry. The individual who wrote the program is fully aware of the required input and too often not aware of how the input commands can be misinterpreted by the user.

A User-Generated Data Error

As a simple illustration of possible user error, we will use a program in which a negative cost value results when the program is executed. The programmer would determine sample input values and perform the actual computations listed in the successive statements, noting the values at each step of the program.

In searching for where the error may occur, it is best to start with a check of the data input. Let us take as a sample, a program which includes the statements:

LINE	STATEMENT
1	`INPUT "Enter cost per item ........ "; COST.PER.ITEM:    PRINT`
2	`INPUT "Enter number of units sold . "; UNITS.SOLD:    PRINT`
3	`INPUT "Enter discount ............. "; DISCOUNT:    PRINT`
4	`COST = (1.0 - DISCOUNT) * (COST.PER.ITEM * UNITS.SOLD): PRINT`

Since the programmer is not certain if this is the actual location of the error, a statement is included immediately after the computation of cost in line 4. To keep the test short and simple, it is decided to test for one item for which we would enter $12.00 for the cost per unit, 6 for the number of units sold, and take a 10% discount. The following line of code would be added as a possible *trap* immediately after line 4. The program is recompiled and run again.

```
IF COST <> 64.8 THEN PRINT "Error at cost computation"
```

To make the test more realistic, have a data entry clerk or someone other than the programmer enter the data. If the error occurs at this point, the programmer has localized the difficulty. The coding can be examined and the arithmetic statement checked.

If the error is not obvious, insert a PRINT line after each of the first three lines to print exactly what data has been entered. The program would appear as:

```
INPUT "Enter cost per item ........ "; COST.PER.ITEM:    PRINT
PRINT "Cost per item ............. "; COST.PER.ITEM:    PRINT
INPUT "Enter number of units sold . "; UNITS.SOLD:    PRINT
PRINT "Number of units sold ...... "; UNITS.SOLD:    PRINT
INPUT "Enter discount ............."; DISCOUNT:    PRINT
PRINT "Discount .................. "; DISCOUNT:    PRINT
COST = (1.0 - DISCOUNT) * (COST.PER.ITEM * UNITS.SOLD): PRINT
```

Again it is best to have a data entry clerk enter the required data. A review of the PRINT lines in this program may reveal the following:

Cost per item 12

Number of units sold 6

Discount 10

It is obvious that whoever entered the data failed to include a decimal point before the 10 entered as the discount. The programmer can then decide whether to:

• Change the input instructions to read:

```
INPUT "Enter discount as a decimal ....... "; DISCOUNT
```

or else

• Leave the instructions as written and insert the following code immediately following line 4:

```
IF DISCOUNT > 1 THEN \
        DISCOUNT = DISCOUNT / 100
```

Generating Test Data

Because the program worked with one set of sample data there is no guarantee that some bugs may not exist. After the program has been successfully executed, many programmers prefer to check the program with sets of random data. One way is to type values at random but in programs with a considerable number of values, this takes too much data entry time. The **RND** function may be used to generate values. It produces a series of random values, the same series each time it is started.

LANGUAGE CODING RULE

The **RND** function returns a series of random decimal values.

<real variable> = **RND**

• A uniform series of random values between 0 and 1 is generated by this function. Each is a 13-digit decimal real value.

To understand this function more fully we have **Program 13-5** that illustrates how you can obtain integer as well as large decimal values suitable for business applications.

PROGRAM 13-5   **RANDOM.BAS**   **[Compiler]**

Use of RND Function to Generate Random Numbers

Copyright 1985, Compulit, Inc.

```
\            Declaration of variables
        REAL X, A
        INTEGER Y, Z
        X = RND
        PRINT "Random variable ......... "; X:    PRINT
\            Y and Z are integers
        Y = INT( X * 10)
        PRINT "Random variable * 10 ..... "; Y:    PRINT
        Z = INT( X * 1000)
        PRINT "Random variable * 1000 ... "; Z:    PRINT
\            A is a real value with two decimal places
        A = INT( X * 1000000) / 100
        PRINT "Random varialbe  ......... "; A:    PRINT
        END
```

The values printed by this program would be:

- 0.592179098877—the first random variable generated by the computer
- 5—the integer value of the random variable multiplied by 10
- 592—the integer value of the random variable multiplied by 1000
- 5921.79—a real value obtained by multiplying the random variable by 1,000,000, converting it to an integer, and then dividing that value by 100

The RND function always produces the same series of random variables. The first 10 values produced by this generator are:

```
0.592179098877
0.0611468194856
0.608322177992
0.958523765684
0.468553352486
0.808302493007
0.423235445449
0.0155021838618
0.868074046565
0.529621660648
```

To obtain a different set of random values, we can either generate a given number of random variables which we discard and start using the next available one or use the RANDOMIZE statement.

To prime or pump the generator, the procedure is to produce and discard a preselected number of values. Insert the following after declaring the integer values in Program 13-6.

```
FOR I% = 1 TO 700
   X = RND
NEXT
```

We may select any value as the upper limit of the FOR-NEXT loop to generate and discard random values. However, a very large value for the upper limit takes too much computer time. The faster way is to use the RANDOMIZE statement, but if you do you will find it difficult to replicate the random series, unless you save it on a disk.

LANGUAGE CODING RULE

The **RANDOMIZE** statement *seeds* the built-in random generator and is used with the RND function.

RANDOMIZE

It is necessary to place a dummy INPUT statement immediately before the RANDOMIZE statement unless your system supports a time-of-day function. During the execution of the RANDOMIZE statement the computer uses either the time-of-day or the time it takes the user to respond to the dummy INPUT statement as a "seed" to prime the generator.

Assume we wished to run a more exhaustive test of the function FN.SMALLER as used in Program 13-2. A simple way is to create two arrays, which we will call array A and array B and fill each with 20 random numbers. When we call the functions, the smaller of the two numbers in each row of array A and array B is stored in the same row in array C. Examining the printout on the console screen we can verify the output from this program.

Program 13-6 illustrates the use of the dummy INPUT statement and the RANDOMIZE statement. Try it! But remember the earlier warning about the size of the largest integer digit the microcomputer can store.

PROGRAM 13-6   **RANDOM2.BAS**   [Compiler]

Use of RANDOMIZE Statement to "Seed" the Random Generator

Copyright 1985, Compulit, Inc.

```
\               Declaration of variables
        STRING CLEAR.SCREEN, AN
        REAL X, Y, A, B, C, V, W
        INTEGER I, RAN.KEY
        DIM A(20), B(20), C(20)
\               Defining CLEAR.SCREEN for PC-DOS and MS-DOS
        CLEAR.SCREEN = CHR$(27) + "[2J"
        DEF FN.SMALLER (X, Y) = ( X + Y - ABS ( X - Y )) / 2
10      PRINT CLEAR.SCREEN
\               Initialize the Random Generator
        INPUT "Enter any character ........ "; RAN.KEY
        RANDOMIZE
\               Fill array B with random values
        FOR I = 1 TO 20
                V = RND
                W = INT%(V * 1000) / 10
                A(I) = W
        NEXT
\               Fill array B with random values
        FOR I = 1 TO 20
                V = RND
                W = INT%(V * 1000) / 10
                B(I) = W
        NEXT
\               Fill C array with smaller of the two values, A and B
        FOR I = 1 TO 20
                C(I) = FN.SMALLER (A(I), B(I))
        NEXT
\               Print arrays A, B and C
        FOR I = 1 TO 20
                PRINT A(I), B(I), C(I)
        NEXT
        PRINT:  INPUT "Another run?  Yes or No?   "; AN
        IF UCASE$(AN) = "YES" THEN 10
        PRINT "Normal termination of program"
        END
```

The variable table information obtained when the program is compiled using Toggle T is shown in **Figure 13-8**. All variables were declared in this compiler version. The addresses of X and Y under global variables is a series of asterisks [*****] since their addresses are noted earlier under the location map of the function. Also the variable list informs us that A, B, and C are single [1] subscripted variables.

ADVANCED TECHNIQUES FOR COMPILER DEBUGGING

Because many compiled programs are lengthy, an advanced programmer tries to avoid recompiling and relinking a program if an execution error is detected. It is possible to make minor corrections directly in the hexadecimal coding of the program. It is also possible to verify the generated code of the entire program, or more often, an especially difficult section. Four techniques are available: the %DEBUG compiler directive, the creation of a

```
                        symbol table information

      no variables in common

            function: FN.SMALLER                at 005ch   returns real
                 name                 type            class  address   # subscrp

X                                 parameter               real    002eh
Y                                 parameter               real    0026h

      global variables:

                 name                 type            class   address   # subscrp

CLEAR.SCREEN                    simple variable     string   0000h
AN                              simple variable     string   0002h
X                                                   real     *****
Y                                                   real     *****
A                               subscripted variable real    0004h      1
B                               subscripted variable real    0006h      1
C                               subscripted variable real    0008h      1
V                               simple variable     real     000ah
W                               simple variable     real     0012h
I                               simple variable     integer  001ah
RAN.KEY                         simple variable     integer  001ch
10                              label                        0092h
```

FIGURE 13-8   Toggle T Symbol Table Output

.MAP file, an enhanced .SYM file, and the Symbolic Instruction Debugger [SID].

%DEBUG Compiler Directive

This compiler directive is used with three command line toggles:

- **Toggle I** interlists the generated code with the source file.
- **Toggle N** generates code for each of the line numbers.
- **Toggle V** places source code line numbers into the .SYM file.

All three toggles can be switched on or off at different points of the program. To switch the toggle on, it is included immediately after the compiler directive, for example:

```
%DEBUG I
```

To switch the toggle off, the toggle is listed but preceded by a minus sign, **%DEBUG −I**. The use of this directive is shown in **Figure 13-9**.

The .MAP File

The .MAP file is created during the linking phase when using the compiler versions and contains information about the segments and groups of the program. This is done by entering:

```
LINK86   TEST [MAP]
```

or

```
LINK86   TEST [M]
```

Figure 13-10 is a sample of the **.MAP file** that would be created for Program 13-3.

```
        Compiled version of Program 13-5 using %DEBUG I and %DEBUG -I


 1:   0000h \                Declaration of variables
 2:   0000h          REAL X, A
 3:   0000h          INTEGER Y, Z
 4:   0000h          X = RND
 5:   0012h          PRINT "Random variable ......... "; X:    PRINT
 6:   0024h \               Y and Z are integers
 7:   0024h %DEBUG I
 8:   0024h             Y = INT( X * 10)
      0024h MOV    BX,10
      0027h CALL   ?CRSH
      002ah MOV    BX,OFFSET(X)                    DATA SEG RELATIVE
      002dh CALL   ?MRSM
      0030h CALL   ?RINT
      0033h CALL   ?CIHS
      0036h MOV    Y,AX
 9:   0039h          PRINT "Random variable * 10 ..... "; Y:    PRINT
      0039h MOV    BX,29                         RCDATA SEG RELATIVE
      003ch CALL   ?PCSS
      003fh MOV    BX,Y
      0043h CALL   ?PCIN
      0046h CALL   ?PCNL
10:   0049h %DEBUG -I
11:   0049h          Z = INT( X * 1000)
12:   005eh          PRINT "Random variable * 1000 ... "; Z:    PRINT
13:   006eh \           A is a real value with two decimal places
14:   006eh          A = INT( X * 1000000) / 100
15:   0089h          PRINT "Random varialbe ......... "; A:    PRINT
16:   009eh          END
```

FIGURE 13-9   Compiler Output Using %DEBUG I

The .SYM File

A .SYM file is produced automatically after a program has been compiled and linked. For Program 13-2, the .SYM file would appear as:

```
0000 VARIABLES   0225 DATA
03F6 UCOMON
```

This file provides a memory map of the program, but a *more detailed map* may be obtained by using the **S toggle** during the compiling phase. The .SYM file would then appear as:

```
0000 VARIABLES   0207 DATA
0488 UCOMON
0000 LABELS      0040 CODE
002B FN.SMALLER  0061 10
0000 VARIABLES   0207 DATA
0488 CLEAR$      049A X         0492Y      04A2 FV      04AA SV
04B2 GV          04BA LV        04C2 AN$
```

A more comprehensive memory map which includes the library files can be obtained during the link edit stage. To do this, the program would first be compiled using the S toggle. Then during the link edit phase, we would use a command line option:

A: LINK86   TEST   [LIBSYMS]   <CR>

The Use of the Symbolic Instruction Debugger

The S toggle during compiling is used to put all information about the variables and the line labels into the .OBJ file, which is required before you can link the object module with the program library. At the time of linking, the link editor places this information into the .SYM file. This file can be used with a special debugging tool, **SID** [Symbolic Instruction Debugger] which is a special package produced by Digital Research. Specifically this

```
Map for file:   TEST.CMD

Segments
--------

Length    Start       Stop    Align Comb  Name           Class

1AE9   (0000:0005-1AED)   BYTE  PUB   CODE           CODE
005D   (0000:0100-015C)   WORD  PUB   IDATA          DATA
00F4   (0000:015E-0251)   WORD  PUB   RCDATA         DATA
0000                      WORD  PUB   DSDATA         DATA
0000                      WORD  COM   UCOMON         DATA
01DC   (0000:0252-042D)   WORD  PUB   DATA           DATA

Groups          Segments
------          --------

CGROUP          CODE
DGROUP          IDATA           RCDATA        DSDATA        UCOMON
                DATA

map for module:   TEST

00FE   (0000:0005-0102)   CODE
0003   (0000:0100-0102)   IDATA
00F4   (0000:015E-0251)   RCDATA
0034   (0000:0252-0285)   DATA
```

FIGURE 13-10   MAP File Output

package includes real-time breakpoints, fully monitored execution, symbolic disassembler, assembly, and other functions. This is an advanced procedure that is beyond the scope of this book.

SPECIAL PROGRAMMING NOTE

The compiling and linking phases using the compiler versions take much longer than compiling with the non-compiler versions. Some intermediate and advanced programmers use *both* the non-compiler and compiler versions when preparing a program. They take advantage of the debugging facilities available in both versions of the CBASIC compiler.

Once the program has been thoroughly tested, a compiled version of the program is created using the compiler version. The .EXE, .CMD, or the .COM version executes more quickly. Another advantage is that it is also easier to use by the non-professional since only the program name is entered to run the program. Possibly the greatest advantage is the increased security offerred by the executable program; it cannot be read or altered by the average user.

One problem does arise in this procedure of using the non-compiler and compiler versions. Most compiler users prefer to use the declaration statements, STRING, INTEGER, and REAL, which the non-compiler versions do not accept. Therefore the original writing is done using the $ to identify strings and % for integers. However, once a final operating version of the program is obtained, the global search-and-replace feature of a good text editor can be used to eliminate the $ and % symbols.

CHAPTER 14

Advanced Statements, Functions, and Techniques

There are several advanced and specialized statements and functions in the compiler versions of CBASIC which can be used:

- When operating under concurrent CP/M
- In a multi-user system operating under MP/M
- In advanced programming

These functions and statements are used after one has mastered the fundamental structure of CBASIC and has become proficient in programming techniques. In this chapter we emphasize the language coding of these functions and statements since the experienced programmer should encounter little difficulty in using any of the commands.

We have also included some more complex programs which illustrate more advanced programming techniques and which are useful additions to a program library.

CONCURRENT AND MULTI-USER OPERATING SYSTEMS

Several compiler version CBASIC statements and functions can be used either with concurrent CP/M on a single microcomputer or under MP/M in a multi-user environment. There are six commands in this category:

- **ATTACH** and **DETACH** are used to provide information about the status of the printer.
- **ERRX** is similar to the ERR function explained earlier but it is used with MP/M.
- **LOCK**, **UNLOCK**, and **MODE** provide some security for programs and data files.

Attaching a Printer

With a concurrent or multi-user operating system, the ATTACH statement is used to determine the availability of a printer and attaches the program to the printer if it is not in use. The DETACH statement is used to free the printer once the printing is completed. With some versions of CBASIC Compiler there is a bug in that the DETACH command does not operate when included in an overlay.

LANGUAGE CODING RULE

The **ATTACH** function is used to determine whether or not a specific printer is available for use.

    <integer variable> = **ATTACH** <number of specific printer>

- A Boolean integer value is returned depending upon the status of the printer. If the printer is available, a logical false, 0, is returned and the function attaches it to the program. If the printer is not available, a logical true, 1, is returned.

LANGUAGE CODING RULE

The **DETACH** statement is used in conjunction with the ATTACH statement and deactivates the printer from program access.

    DETACH

The following is an illustration of a program segment in which these functions are used.

```
\    Procedure to verify availability of the printer
50   IF ATTACH(PRINTER,ONE) = FALSE THEN 100
     CALL CLS:   PRINT BELL
     PRINT "Printer is not available"
     INPUT "Try again?  Yes or No?  "; AN
     IF UCASE$(AN) = "YES" THEN 50
     STOP
```

```
100 LPRINTER
    ----------
    ----------
    ----------
    DETACH
```

To Obtain the Error Code Using MP/M

The **ERRX** function is used with MP/M just as the ERR function was used with the single-user compiler version to locate an execution error. It is used with the ON ERROR statement as shown in the following illustration.

```
\     Use of ERRX with an ON ERROR statement
ON ERROR  GOTO ERROR.DISPLAY
    -----------
    -----------
    -----------
    -----------
ERROR.DISPLAY:
    IF ERRX = "EX" THEN \
    PRINT "MP/M II Extended Error ,,,, "; ERRX
    CLOSE 1
    END
```

LANGUAGE CODING RULE

The **ERRX** function returns a 16-bit MP/M II extended error code.

<integer variable> = **ERRX**

- The EX execution error under MP/M II indicates that an extended error has taken place. The ERRX function returns an integer corresponding to the extended error code listed in the MP/M Programmer's Guide.

The Security of Files and Records

There are two ways to protect a file when using a concurrent or multi-user operating system. The first is by using the **MODE** option in the CREATE and/or OPEN statements. The mode option controls an entire file. An individual record or several specific records within a file can be secured by the use of the **LOCK** function.

CBASIC Compiler supports three modes for accessing files: LOCK-ED, UNLOCKED, and READONLY. The *MODE* option is the last portion of either a CREATE or OPEN statement, for example:

```
CREATE "B:MASTER.FIL" RECL 128 AS 1 LOCKED
```

A file created in **LOCKED** mode is not accessible to any other user or program. On the other hand, a file in *unlocked* mode is accessible to any user or program. If you wish to create an unlocked file, there is no need to include the mode option.

The **READONLY** mode is used only with an OPEN statement; it *cannot* be used with the CREATE statement. When a file is opened in *READONLY* mode, any user or program may use the file but cannot modify data within that file. It would appear in a program as:

```
OPEN "B:PRODUCT.PRICE.LIST"  RECL 196 AS 2 READONLY
```

Individual records within a file may be locked by using the LOCK function. This prevents anyone from modifying the data in a specific record.

LANGUAGE CODING RULE

To prevent the modification of data in any record use the **LOCK** function.

<integer variable> = **LOCK** (<file number> , <record number>)

- The integer variable returned is zero [0] if the record has been locked.
- A record can be locked only if the *file* is in UNLOCKED mode.

LANGUAGE CODING RULE

The **UNLOCK** function is used to unlock a locked record so that the data can be modified.

<integer variable> = **UNLOCK** (<file number> , <record number>)

- To unlock a record the *file* must be in the UNLOCKED mode. The integer variable that is returned equals zero [0] when the record is unlocked.

A FOR-NEXT loop can be used to lock a series of records as shown in the following program segment.

```
\  To lock records 5 through 13 in an unlocked file
\  LOCK.CODE% is printed as each record is locked and
\  must be equal to zero to show that the record was locked
   --------------
   --------------
   FOR J% = 5 TO 13
       LOCK.CODE% = LOCK (2, J%)
       PRINT "Record #"; J%, "Status ="; LOCK.CODE%
   NEXT J%
   ---------------
   ---------------
```

Program security is possible with CBASIC even with a single-user system. This method will be shown later in this chapter in the section, "How to Provide Password Security for a Program."

MODIFICATION AND LOCATION OF DATA IN MEMORY

Several statements and functions are available to modify data in memory and to determine the size of memory available during the execution of a program. A memory map of your computer is required if one is to use these statements properly without possible damage to stored data in memory. Unless you are thoroughly familiar with the memory structure, it would be unwise to use some of these memory statements and functions. Some sample programs to illustrate these statements and functions are included. These programs may be safely used in order to obtain a better understanding of how the statements and functions work.

The computer's memory is used to store data and instructions. The main memory is directly addressable by the processor. Although the ROM BIOS provides a complete interface between the program and the hardware, there are times when a program, for efficiency of operation, may communicate directly with the hardware.

Most computer manuals contain a memory map. **Figure 14-1** is an example of such a map for the Columbia Data Products MPC 1600 series.

Memory allocation for program and data areas is part of the output when a CBASIC program is compiled. Both the CS or CGROUP [code group storage] and the DS or DGROUP [data group storage] are noted.

Availability of Memory Space

One pair of these memory-application functions is **FRE** and **MFRE**. The former is used to obtain the amount of space available in the FSA, the Free

Storage Area. The latter has the same purpose but provides the largest *contiguous* area of available memory space in the Free Storage Area.

ADDRESS RANGE	FUNCTION
00000–00400	Interrupt vectors for the 8088 CPU
00400–0047F	Reserved for ROM BIOS variables
00480–0050F	Reserved for ROM monitor variables
00510–1FFFF	User program/ operating system area

FIGURE 14-1   Main Circuit Board Memory Map

Program 14-1 is a short demonstration program showing the use of both the FRE and MFRE functions.

LANGUAGE CODING RULE

The FRE function returns the total amount of space available in the Free Storage Area.

    <integer variable> = **FRE**

LANGUAGE CODING RULE

The MFRE function returns the size of the largest contiguous memory space in the Free Storage Area.

    <integer variable> = **MFRE**

PROGRAM 14-1   **STORAGE.BAS**   **[Compiler]**

Demonstation of FRE and MFRE Functions

Copyright 1985, Compulit, Inc.

```
       STRING CLEAR.SCREEN
       INTEGER X, I
\               Defining CLEAR.SCREEN for PC-DOS and MS-DOS
       CLEAR.SCREEN = CHR$(27) + "[2J"
       PRINT CLEAR.SCREEN
       X = FRE
       I% = MFRE
       PRINT "Free Storage Area .............. "; X
       PRINT
       PRINT "Contiguous Free Storage Area .... "; I%
       PRINT: PRINT
       PRINT "Both the FRE and MFRE functions return an integer value."
       PRINT "When that value is greater than 32,767, CBASIC treats "
       PRINT "the larger value as a negative number.  A large amount of"
       PRINT "space remaining returns a negative value."
       END
```

Since the output of both functions is an integer value, the greatest positive integer obtainable is 32,767. If a greater amount of storage space is available, the output would be negative and incorrect. To avoid this problem use the FRE and MFRE statements within a program combined with statements such as:

```
       INTEGER  H, I
       I = FRE
       IF SGN(I)  > 0 THEN 100
       IF SGN(I)  = 0 THEN 150
       PRINT "FSA memory space available exceeds 32,767 bytes."
       H = INKEY
       GOTO 200
100    PRINT "FSA memory space available equals"; I; " bytes."
       H = INKEY
       GOTO 200
150    PRINT "FSA memory space is full."
       H = INKEY
200    -------
       -------
```

When Program 14-1 was run on our Columbia MPC, which has 832K memory, the output was:

Free Storage Area .... −15398

Contiguous Free Storage Area .... −15398

The amount of Free Storage Area was in excess of 32,767 bytes.

Locating Variables in Memory and Changing Their Value

There are two ways to determine the location of a variable in memory. The first is the **PEEK** function which presupposes a knowledge of the address of the variable. The **VARPTR** and **SADD** functions, which do not presuppose this knowledge, are used to obtain the address of a numeric variable and a string variable respectively.

Program 14-2 illustrates the use of the **VARPTR**, the VARiable PoinTeR, to obtain the address of an integer variable.

PROGRAM 14-2   **VARPTER.BAS**   **[Compiler]**

Use of VARPTR to Obtain Address of an Integer Variable

Copyright 1985, Compulit, Inc.

```
\            Declaration of variables
         INTEGER LOC, X
         STRING  AN
10       INPUT "Enter a value ....... "; X
         LOC = VARPTR (X)
         PRINT
         PRINT LOC
         PRINT
         PRINT "The original value is "; PEEK (LOC + 1) * 256 + PEEK (LOC)
         PRINT
         INPUT "Another try?  Yes or No? "; AN
         IF UCASE$(AN) = "YES" THEN 10
         PRINT "Normal termination of program"
         END
```

We use the VARPTR function to locate the *address* of a numeric variable, X, and later use the PEEK function to *recover* that value. An integer variable, we know from the language structure, is stored as two bytes. The address given by LOC is the least significant byte [LSB] and the next address, LOC + 1, holds the most significant byte [MSB]. We can reconstruct the integer value when using the VARPTR function by setting it equal to 256 * MSB + LSB.

Figure 14-2 is a sample output from the VARPTR function used in Program 14-2.

The **PEEK** function is used to obtain the contents at a specific memory address, while the **POKE** statement is used to store a single byte of data in a specific memory location. **Program 14-3** is a simple demonstration of the use of this function and statement.

Enter a value 7

7329

The original value is 7

Another try? Yes or No? YES

Enter a value 932

7329

The original value is 932

Another try? Yes or No? NO

Normal termination of program

FIGURE 14-2   Sample Output of VARPTR Function

LANGUAGE CODING RULE

The **VARPTR** function locates the address of a numeric variable.

<integer variable> = **VARPTR (** <variable> **)**

- This function works with unsubscripted numeric variables. For subscripted variables, the function returns the address of a pointer to an array in the Free Storage Area.

LANGUAGE CODING RULE

The **SADD** function is used to locate the address of a string variable.

<integer variable> = **SADD (** <string variable> **)**

- Strings are stored as a sequential list of ASCII characters. The first two bytes contain the length of the string, and the remainder contains the string itself.
- The function returns a zero [0] if the string variable is a null string.

PROGRAM 14-3   **PEEKPOKE.BAS**   [Compiler]

Demonstration of PEEK Function and POKE Statement

Copyright 1985, Compulit, Inc.

```
\               Declaration of variables
        INTEGER FA, I, LA, Y
        REAL    X
        STRING  AN
\               Note to check manual
        PRINT "Check your computer's manual for memory location areas"
        PRINT "before using this program.":        PRINT
10      INPUT "Enter starting address ..... "; FA:    PRINT
        INPUT "Enter final address ........ "; LA      PRINT
        PRINT "Enter an ASCII value between 0 and 255"
        PRINT "when asked to enter a value.":        PRINT
\               Place values in memory between two addresses
        FOR I = FA TO LA
                PRINT
                INPUT "Enter a value ....... "; X
                POKE I, X
        NEXT
\               Display contents of memory between two addresses
        FOR I = FA TO LA
                Y = PEEK (I)
                PRINT Y
        NEXT
        INPUT "Another run?  Yes or No? .... "; AN
        IF UCASE$(AN) = "YES" THEN 10
        PRINT:   PRINT "Normal termination of program"
        END
```

LANGUAGE CODING RULE

The **PEEK** function is used to obtain the contents of a specific address in computer memory.

<integer variable> = **PEEK (** <numeric expression> **)**

- The numeric expression is the integer value of the address. If a real value is specified, it is converted into an integer.
- There is no check of the validity of the address. Specifying a value outside of the address available within the computer will result in erroneous information.

Both the PEEK function and the POKE statement do *not* validate the address entered by the user. If the address is outside the range of the computer's memory, an error will occur. With some computers a flicker will appear on the screen and move down line by line. With others, the user will be unaware of the use of an illegal address. Also if the address selected is within the areas reserved for interrupt vectors, the BIOS, video board, or monitor controls, it will be impossible to proceed safely with the program and the system must be rebooted.

LANGUAGE CODING RULE

The **POKE** statement stores one byte in a specific memory location.

POKE <numeric expression> , <numeric expression>

- The first numeric expression is the absolute memory address of the computer you are using.
- The second numeric expression is the value to be stored. The statement converts the value into a one-byte integer, ranging between 0 and 255 and corresponding to the ASCII code.

A sample output of Program 14-3 is shown in **Figure 14-3**.

Enter starting address 11000

Enter final address 11004

Enter a value 7

Enter a value 13

Enter a value 26

Enter a value 113

Enter a value 255

7
13
26
113
255

FIGURE 14-3   Sample Output of Program 14-3

The values that may be poked into specific memory locations must be integers ranging between 0 and 255. These values correspond to the ASCII code for keyboard characters. For example:

VALUE POKED	CHARACTER STORED IN MEMORY
36	$
51	3
72	H
93	]
106	j
158	Pt
255	[blank]

If 256 is entered, the value will be zero, a null character in ASCII. Any greater value that is entered will be transformed by the computer so that the value stored is equal to the difference between the value entered and 256. Thus if you enter 300, the result would be 40, which is the ASCII for (.

OTHER BYTE MANIPULATION FUNCTIONS

There are four additional statements and functions which are byte-oriented and which can be used in more advanced programming in CBASIC.

- **GET** reads a single byte of data from a specified disk file.
- **PUT** writes a single byte of data to a disk file.
- **INP** reads a single byte from an input or output port of the CPU.
- **OUT** sends a single byte to a specified input or output port.

Those that read from a disk file or input/output port are functions in the language; those that write or send a byte to a disk file or input/output port are language statements. In each case the single byte is an integer value between 0 and 255 corresponding to the ASCII code.

LANGUAGE CODING RULE

The GET function reads a single byte, an ASCII 0 through 255, from a specified disk file.

<integer variable> = **GET** <file number>

- The file number is unique and has been assigned in a CREATE or OPEN statement.

LANGUAGE CODING RULE

The **PUT** statement writes a single byte to a specified disk file.

PUT <file number> <integer variable>

- The integer variable ranges from 0 to 255 to correspond to the ASCII code.

INP and **OUT** perform comparable operations but instead of accessing a specified disk file, they access a specified input or output port of the computer. The INP function and the OUT statement are *hardware dependent* and may not work with a specific computer. Furthermore, there is no check of the validity of the port address under CBASIC.

Program 14-4 is an example of the use of the INP function. In this program the final address is the starting address plus seven.

PROGRAM 14-4   **INPBYTE.BAS**   **[Compiler]**

Use of INP to Read a Single ASCII Byte from Input or Output Port

Copyright 1985, Compulit, Inc.

```
\           Declaration of variables
        INTEGER FV, I, SV
        STRING  AN, CLEAR.SCREEN
\           Defining CLEAR.SCREEN for PC-DOS and MS-DOS
        CLEAR.SCREEN = CHR$(27) + "[2J"
10      PRINT CLEAR.SCREEN
        INPUT "Enter starting value ....... "; FV
        PRINT
        SV = FV + 7
        PRINT
        FOR I = FV TO SV
            PRINT TAB(10); "Port #"; I; " has a byte value of "; INP(I)
        NEXT
        INPUT "Try another series?  Yes or No?  "; AN
        IF UCASE$(AN) = "YES" THEN 10
        PRINT "Normal termination of program"
        END
```

The output of this program, which lists the ASCII code, is shown in **Figure 14-4**. Two series have been run for this test. The first is from 0 through 7 and the second from 50 to 57.

Program 14-4 showed the byte value is ASCII code. To obtain the actual characters in these locations, you can use **Program 14-5**.

Enter starting value .... <u>0</u>

       Port # 0 has a byte value of 95
       Port # 1 has a byte value of 93
       Port # 2 has a byte value of 30
       Port # 3 has a byte value of 127
       Port # 4 has a byte value of 29
       Port # 5 has a byte value of 93
       Port # 6 has a byte value of 30
       Port # 7 has a byte value of 31

Try another series? Yes or No?   <u>YES</u>

Enter starting value .... <u>50</u>

       Port # 50 has a byte value of 51
       Port # 51 has a byte value of 51
       Port # 52 has a byte value of 55
       Port # 53 has a byte value of 53
       Port # 54 has a byte value of 54
       Port # 55 has a byte value of 55
       Port # 56 has a byte value of 59
       Port # 57 has a byte value of 57

Try another series? Yes or No?   <u>NO</u>

Normal termination of program

FIGURE 14-4   Sample Output of Program 14-4

PROGRAM 14-5   BYTECHAR.BAS   [Compiler]

INP Function with Byte Value and Character Equivalent

Copyright 1985, Compulit, Inc.

```
\            Declaration of variables
        INTEGER FV, I, SV, M
        STRING  AN, CLEAR.SCREEN, MM
\            Defining CLEAR.SCREEN for PC-DOS and MS-DOS
        CLEAR.SCREEN = CHR$(27) + "[2J"
10      PRINT CLEAR.SCREEN
        INPUT "Enter starting value ....... "; FV:    PRINT
        INPUT "Enter stopping value ....... "; SV:    PRINT
        PRINT TAB(7); "Port #"; TAB(15); "Binary Value"; TAB(28); "Symbol"
        PRINT
```

       (continues)

```
FOR I = FV TO SV
        M = INP(I)
        MM = CHR$(M)
        PRINT TAB(10); I; TAB(20); M; TAB(30); MM
NEXT
INPUT "Try another series?  Yes or No?  "; AN
IF UCASE$(AN) = "YES" THEN 10
PRINT "Normal termination of program"
END
```

Figure 14-5 illustrates the output of Program 14-5. In addition to printing the ASCII value at the port it also prints the actual character.

Enter starting value .... <u>0</u>

Enter stopping value .... <u>2</u>

Port #	Binary Value	Symbol
0	13	[carriage return]
1	93	]
2	126	˜

Try another series? Yes or No?   <u>YES</u>

Enter starting value .... <u>50</u>

Enter stopping value .... <u>60</u>

Port #	Binary Value	Symbol
50	51	3
51	51	3
52	53	5
53	53	5
54	55	7
55	55	7
56	57	9
57	123	{
58	59	;
59	123	{
60	63	?

Try another series? Yes or No?   <u>NO</u>

Normal termination of program

FIGURE 14-5   Sample Output of Program 14-5

LANGUAGE CODING RULE

The **INP** function returns a single ASCII byte from a valid input/output port.

<integer variable> = **INP** <numeric expression>

- The numeric expression is an integer value from a port and the returned value ranges from 0 to 255, corresponding to the ASCII code.

LANGUAGE CODING RULE

The **OUT** statement sends an integer value to a specified port.

OUT <numeric expression> , <numeric expression>

- The first numeric expression must be a valid port number.
- The second numeric expression is an eight-bit integer between 0 and 255 and may be sent in decimal form, the appropriate level in hexadecimal or even a string in the form of: OUT 1, ASC("#").

ADVANCED SPECIAL FUNCTIONS

The two remaining specialized functions for the advanced programmer are **COMMAND$** and **SHIFT**. The former returns a string containing the command tail used to execute a program, and the latter is a shift arithmetic function.

The COMMAND$ function can be used anywhere and any number of times in a CBASIC program. It can also be used in a program that has been loaded with a CHAIN command. A command line is one that is entered to execute a program; it consists of the command keyword and an optional tail. The keyword indentifies the program to be executed and the tail contains added information such as a filename, option, or a parameter. This function returns the command tail used to execute a program.

The SHIFT function returns an integer value that has been arithmetically manipulated. For example:

```
VALUE% = SHIFT(4096,4)
```

LANGUAGE CODING RULE

The **COMMAND$** function returns a string containing the tail of the command used to execute the program.

<string variable> = **COMMAND$**

---

would result in VALUE% = 256. The 4096 is divided by 2 raised to the power of 4 or 16. Any second value [enclosed in the parentheses after the comma] greater than 15 will result in a fatal run-time error.

Program 14-6 is a demonstration of the use of the SHIFT function.

PROGRAM 14-6   **SHIFTVAL.BAS**   **[Non-Compiler]**

Illustration of Use of SHIFT Function

Copyright 1985, Compulit, Inc.

```
\           Examples of SHIFT function with decimal values
     I% = SHIFT(256,1):      PRINT I%
     I% = SHIFT(256,2):      PRINT I%
     I% = SHIFT(256,3):      PRINT I%
     I% = SHIFT(256,4):      PRINT I%
     I% = SHIFT(-256,1):     PRINT I%
     I% = SHIFT(-256,2):     PRINT I%
\           Example of SHIFT function with hexadecimal value
     I% = SHIFT(10H, 4):     PRINT I%
\           Example of SHIFT function with binary value
     I% = SHIFT(1100100B, 2):    PRINT I%
     END
```

The value to be manipulated may be entered in decimal, hexadecimal, or binary form and may be either negative or positive. The output of Program 14-6 is shown in **Figure 14-6**.

LANGUAGE CODING RULE

The **SHIFT** function returns an integer that has been arithmetically shifted a specified number of positions to the right, that is, divided by powers of 2.

<integer variable> = **SHIFT(**<numeric expression> , <numeric expression>**)**

- The first expression is the value to be divided by some power of 2 and may be entered in decimal, hexadecimal, or binary form.
- The second numeric expression is the power of 2 by which the first value is divided. It must be a positive value but may not exceed 15; a negative value will result in zero [0].

SHIFT STATEMENT	ARITHMETIC FORM	OUTPUT
I = SHIFT(256,1)	I = 256 / 2^1	128
I = SHIFT(256,2)	I = 256 / 2^2	64
I = SHIFT(256,3)	I = 256 / 2^3	32
I = SHIFT(256,4)	I = 256 / 2^4	16
I = SHIFT($-$256,1)	I = $-$256/ 2^1	$-$128
I = SHIFT($-$256,2)	I = $-$256/ 2^2	$-$64
I = SHIFT(10H, 4)	I = 16 / 2^4	1
I = SHIFT(1100100B, 2)	I = 100 / 2^2	25

FIGURE 14-6   Sample Output of Program 14-6

PROVIDING PASSWORD SECURITY FOR A PROGRAM

Even if you are not using a concurrent or multi-user operating system, you may want to provide for program security and prevent any unauthorized user from reading, altering, or executing a program. To do this, you must:

- Make certain that the source program with the .BAS file extension does *not* appear on the work disk.
- Use an .INT filetype with non-compiler or .EXE filetype with the compiler version of CBASIC on the work disk.
- Start the program with a **password procedure**.

PASSWORD.BAS, that appears on the supplementary disk accompanying this volume, can be modified and used as a preamble for any protected program. It is self-contained so that you can understand its construction. To use the program, you must enter the correct password. Failure to do so will cause the computer's bell to ring for about one minute and make it impossible to use the keyboard until a correction-password is entered. If the correct password is entered, the user must answer three questions. Failure to answer any question correctly causes the program to branch to the alarm bell routine and the keyboard is locked.

Preparing Passwords, Access Questions, and Answers

The program contains two passwords, three questions, and their answers in the definition of variables:

```
\           Storage of password, questions and answers
   PASSWORD    = "Orion, the hunter"
   BOSS.NAME = "Betelgeuse"
   QUESTION1 = "What is the Northern Cross?"
   QUESTION2 = "Who is Draco's nearest neighbor?"
   QUESTION3 = "What is the belt? "
   ANSWER1    = "Cygnus"
   ANSWER2    = "Cepheus"
   ANSWER3    = "Alnitak, Alnilam and Mintaka"
```

The first password, "Orion, the hunter," is used to gain access to the questions, which can be eliminated, reduced, or increased in number. The second password, "Betelgeuse," is needed only if the incorrect password is entered or the wrong answer is given to any of the questions. It is obvious that astronomical terms are used; you may substitute any passwords and change the questions and answers to meet your needs.

The Procedure Routine

A series of statements is used to print each question, accept the reply, and compare the input with the answer stored in the program. If the reply to the question is incorrect, the program branches to the alarm sequence. Only by entering "Betelgeuse" is it possible to branch back to start the program.

```
FIRST.ENTRY:     \ Request for user entry of password
      PRINT CLEAR.SCREEN
      PRINT "What is your password?     ": PRINT
      INPUT ""; PASSWORD.IN
      IF PASSWORD.IN <> PASSWORD THEN GOSUB ALARM
\             Requests for answers to three questions
      PRINT CLEAR.SCREEN
      PRINT QUESTION1: PRINT
      INPUT ""; REPLY1
      IF REPLY1 <> ANSWER1 THEN GOSUB ALARM
      PRINT CLEAR.SCREEN
      PRINT QUESTION2: PRINT
      INPUT ""; REPLY2
      IF REPLY 2 <>ANSWER2 THEN GOSUB ALARM
```
                                                      (continues)

```
          PRINT CLEAR,SCREEN
          PRINT QUESTION3: PRINT
          INPUT ""; REPLY3
          IF REPLY3 <> ANSWER3 THEN GOSUB ALARM
```

Acceptance Procedure

If the correct password is entered and the reply to each of the question is correct, the program permits the user to enter the system, or the protected program if it is inserted at this point. The statements include:

```
     PRINT CLEAR,SCREEN
     PRINT "You are authorized to use this disk and microcomputer."
     PRINT
     INPUT "Press space bar and return key to get to system."; AN
     GOTO PROGRAM,TERMINATION
     ──[Alarm Routine is located here]──
PROGRAM,TERMINATION:
     PRINT CLEAR,SCREEN
     PRINT "Normal termination of program"
```

The last line above may be replaced with the start of the program that is to be protected.

The Alarm Routine

If an incorrect password or answer is entered, the program branches to the alarm routine. In addition to the message printed on the screen, the bell will sound for about one minute. The routine is:

```
ALARM:             \Subroutine to sound bell for illegal entry
     PRINT CLEAR,SCREEN
\              Command to print "You are an illegal user" 80 times
     WARNING = STRING$ (80, "You are an illegal user!      ")
REPEAT,WARNING:    \ Print warning on screen and ring bell
     PRINT WARNING
\              Bell will sound for about one minute
     FOR K = 1 TO 450
          PRINT BELL
     NEXT
     PRINT CLEAR,SCREEN
     PRINT "Keyboard is locked until you enter the proper password."
```

```
PRINT
INPUT ""; HELP.NAME
IF HELP.NAME = BOSS.NAME THEN GOTO FIRST.ENTRY
GOTO REPEAT.WARNING
RETURN
```

The time the bell alarm sounds is determined by the FOR-NEXT loop which has been set to 450. If you wish the alarm to sound for a shorter time interval change the 450 to a smaller value. Furthermore, the program is easily modified so that the user is given more than one chance to enter a reply to any question. However, it is good security practice not to allow more than three chances before setting off the alarm.

AN INCOME/EXPENDITURE ANALYSIS PACKAGE

FUNDS.BAS, which is available on the supplementary disk for this book, is written for CBASIC Compiler CB86 and executable under PC-DOS and MS-DOS. It illustrates:

- The use of many of the statements and functions as well as techniques covered in this book
- A user-friendly console screen for data input
- The integration of several procedures into a menu-directed program

It is a simple income and expenditure program to provide a rapid overview of a small business operation. Expenditures are itemized into 15 categories each with an identification number (IDN) as follows:

```
IDN(1)="Wages"
IDN(2)="Office supplies"
IDN(3)="Printing"
IDN(4)="Messenger Service"
IDN(5)="Legal/Accounting/Banking"
IDN(6)="Rent"
IDN(7)="Telephone"
IDN(8)="Postage"
IDN(9)="Publications"
IDN(10)="Rentals and Repairs"
IDN(11)="Entertainment"
IDN(12)="Travel"
IDN(13)="Advertising"
IDN(14)="Equipment"
IDN(15)="Miscellaneous"
```

Changes in the IDN descriptions can be made by replacing copy between quotation marks with one with your choice. *No other change has to be made in the program.* However, if you want to add categories, several minor changes will be necessary, including changing the DIM statement for the array and modifying the loop controls in program segments 7 and 8.

The program is menu-directed. It is an integration of nine procedures somewhat similar to the MENUPRO programs presented earlier. The program menu appears on the console screen as follows:

What do you want to do?
[1] Exit from program
[2] Create a NEW file
[3] Add to an existing file
[4] Search by IDN or name
[5] Change part of a record
[6] Delete a record
[7] Accumulate amount by IDN or name
[8] Accumulate all expenses and income
[9] Print file from record to record

There are eight subroutines, each of which can be used directly in any program where appropriate without modification. However, with some a declaration of variables, such as BELL = CHR$(07), is needed in the program. [A copy of this lengthy program is included on the supplementary disk for this book.]

CHAPTER 15

Introduction to
Graphics Programming

You can incorporate graphics into your CBASIC programs by using Digital Research's *GSX-86 Graphics Extension*. It is available only with the Compiler version, CB86, in either 8-bit or 16-bit for CP/M and in 16-bit for PC-DOS. This latter version will work on many of the compatibles under MS-DOS. It is designed to be used with a monochromatic or color monitor, several models of matrix dot printers and the HP 7470 plotter. Special **device drivers**, a software package that interfaces the graphics package and the output device, can be developed by an experienced user or a professional programmer.

Graphics is exciting and a complete book can be written on this topic itself. This chapter is only an introduction to the graphics part of CBASIC. There are 15 programs included in order to explain and demonstrate the use of 25 graphics statements. Before you can execute the programs in this chapter, you must have both ASSIGN.SYS and GSX.EXE files and the device drivers as required by the ASSIGN.SYS file on the default drive.

The ASSIGN.SYS file, which you can create with a text editor, contains a list of the device drivers needed for your system. Specific drivers and the rules for listing in the ASSIGN.SYS file are contained in the *GSX-86 User's Guide*.

The GSX.EXE file is part of the graphics extension package.

To avoid possible run-time errors, such as "ERROR GX" because the GSX.EXE file has not been loaded, create an AUTOEXEC.BAT file for each disk containing the executable graphics programs. This batch file would include:

gsx.exe

> The programs in this chapter were created and executed using PC-DOS on a Columbia Data Products MPC 1600-1 and a PGS [Princeton Graphics System] HX-12RGB monitor. The device driver, IBMCM1P1.SYS, appeared on a single line as <u>01 IBMCM1P1</u> in the ASSIGN.SYS file.

Many of the graphics statements, aside from those used for output, start with **SET**. These are directives to the computer. Some of the statements, however, can start with **ASK** in which case they are queries to the computer to obtain specific information. For example, SET COLOR 2 instructs the computer to use color 2 for output, but ASK COLOR I returns the number of the color being used by the output device as the integer variable I, which you can then print or display.

OPENING AND CLOSING A GRAPHICS PROGRAM

Two statements contained in every graphics program are designed to:

- Initialize the graphics system and select the output device.
- Close the graphics output device, terminate the graphics system, and return to the normal operating system.

GRAPHIC OPEN should be used at the start of the graphics program and **GRAPHIC CLOSE** at the end of the graphics program. Failure to use the GRAPHIC CLOSE statement will result in a 40-column screen when the systems prompt appears.

GRAPHIC OPEN 1	will initialize the graphics system and select the console terminal as the output device if the terminal has been defined as device driver 1 in the ASSIGN.SYS file.
GRAPHIC CLOSE	will close the currently active graphic device and return the system to normal operating mode.

One device may be closed during the program and another opened with a GRAPHIC OPEN statement. In this way you are able to observe the program output on the console screen and then obtain a hardcopy output from a printer or plotter.

Since graphics are available only with CBASIC Compiler versions, we have avoided the use of the $ and % to identify specific variables. Instead we have declared the variables as REAL, INTEGER, and/or STRING at the

---

LANGUAGE CODING RULE

The **GRAPHIC OPEN** statement initializes the graphics system and selects the output device.

GRAPHIC OPEN <integer variable or constant>

- The device number range recommend is: 1–10 for monitors, 11–20 for plotters, and 21–30 for matrix dot printers.
- This statement initializes the BOUNDS, VIEWPORT, and WINDOW statements at 0,1,0,1. [See section on viewing area.]

---

beginning of the program. These declaration statements must be the *first* set of statements in the program just as they are placed in programs that do not contain graphics. In a stand-alone graphics program placing them *after* a GRAPHIC OPEN statement will result in a compile-time error.

LANGUAGE CODING RULE

The **GRAPHIC CLOSE** statement closes the current graphics output device.

GRAPHIC CLOSE

- No assignment variable follows the command. Another device may be opened with a GRAPHIC OPEN statement but only one device should be activated at a time.
- The GRAPHIC CLOSE statement followed by the END statement deactivates the graphics system and returns the console screen to its normal 80 columns.

UNDERSTANDING THE VIEWING AREA

Any graphics output — on the console screen, from a plotter or from the matrix dot printer — is defined in terms of its X- and Y-coordinates. As in traditional graphs, the X-axis is the horizontal axis and the Y-axis is the vertical axis. Both scales begin at 0,0 which is the lower left-hand corner of the device. The GRAPHIC OPEN statement initializes the system so that the coordinates range from 0.0 to 1.0 for both axes, regardless of the physical dimensions of the device. **Figure 15-1** illustrates the coordinate system used under GSX-86.

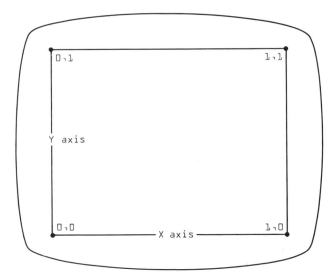

FIGURE 15-1   Coordinate System Used by GSX

A Sample Plot

Before discussing any of the statements that control the viewing area, let us first examine the specification of coordinate positions. We will do so with a simple plot program, **Program 15-1**, PLOT1.BAS. We will define a box along the outside of the viewing area of the console screen.

- The first line will be drawn along the left side of the screen and will connect coordinates 0,0 [the lower left corner] with 0,1 [the upper left corner].
- The line across the top of the screen joins coordinates 0,1 [the upper left corner] with 1,1 [the upper right corner].
- The line down the right side of the screen connects coordinates 1,1 [the upper right corner] with 1,0 [the lower right corner].
- The final line, across the bottom, joins coordinates 1,0 with 0,0.

To draw these four lines we use the statement:

```
PLOT   (0,0), (0,1), (1,1), (1,0), (0,0)
```

In PLOT1.BAS we have used the graphics CLEAR statement to start with a blank screen and the INKEY statement to hold the plotted box on the screen. We will cover the PLOT statement in more detail later in the chapter.

PROGRAM 15-1   **PLOT1.BAS**   **[Compiler: Graphics]**

Use of the PLOT Command

Copyright 1984, 1985, Compulit, Inc.

```
        INTEGER  H
\                Opening of graphics system
        GRAPHIC OPEN 1
\                Clearing the screen
        CLEAR
\                Plot of box on the screen
        PLOT (0,0),(0,1),(1,1),(1,0),(0,0)
\                Use of INKEY to hold copy on screen until key is depressed
        H = INKEY
\                Terminating graphics program
        GRAPHIC CLOSE
        END
```

You can draw this box in slow motion and study the specific coordinate statements by using **Program 15-2**, PLOT2.BAS. Forgetting for the moment the meaning of some of the graphics statements in the program, try entering and executing Program 15-2. You can reduce entry time when writing the program by creating a file with your text editor which can be repeatedly inserted in the program at appropriate locations. This file contains the following statements:

```
CLEAR
SET COLOR 1
PLOT (0,0),(0,1),(1,1),(1,0),(0,0)
PLOT (.1,.1),(.1,.9),(.9,.9),(.9,.1),(.1,.1)
SET COLOR 2
GRAPHIC PRINT AT (.1,.75): \
        " --------- copy goes here --------- "
GRAPHIC PRINT AT (.1,.55): \
        " ----------copy goes here --------- "
H = INKEY
```

PROGRAM 15-2   **PLOT2.BAS**   **[Compiler: Graphics]**

Analysis of the Use of the PLOT Command

Copyright 1984, 1985, Compulit, Inc.

```
        INTEGER  H
        GRAPHIC OPEN 1
        CLEAR
\                Procedure to print the instruction screen
        PLOT (0,0),(0,1),(1,1),(1,0),(0,0)
        PLOT (.1,.1),(.1,.9),(.9,.9),(.9,.1),(.1,.1)
        SET COLOR 2
        GRAPHIC PRINT AT (.05,.75): \
                "THIS PROGRAM DISPLAYS SEVERAL SCREENS"
        GRAPHIC PRINT AT (.15,.55): \
                "PRESS ANY LETTER TO CONTINUE"
```

(continues)

```
           GRAPHIC PRINT AT (.25,.35): \
                   "TO THE NEXT SCREEN"
           H = INKEY
\                   Instructions for first display
           CLEAR
           SET COLOR 1
           PLOT (0,0),(0,1),(1,1),(1,0),(0,0)
           SET COLOR 2
           GRAPHIC PRINT AT (.1,.75): \
                   "THIS PROCEDURE WILL PLOT A VERTICAL"
           GRAPHIC PRINT AT (.1,.55): \
                   "LINE FROM 0,0 TO 0,1"
           H = INKEY
           CLEAR
           PLOT (0,0),(0,1)
           H = INKEY
\                   Instructions for second display
           CLEAR
           PLOT (0,0),(0,1),(1,1),(1,0),(0,0)
           SET COLOR 2
           GRAPHIC PRINT AT (.1,.75): \
                   "THIS PROCEDURE WILL CONTINUE PLOT"
           GRAPHIC PRINT AT (.1,.55): \
                   "FROM 0,1 TO 1,1"
           H = INKEY
           CLEAR
           SET COLOR 1
           PLOT (0,0),(0,1)
           SET COLOR 2
           PLOT (0,1),(1,1)
           H = INKEY
\                   Instructions for third display
           CLEAR
           PLOT (0,0),(0,1),(1,1),(1,0),(0,0)
           SET COLOR 3
           GRAPHIC PRINT AT (.1,.75): \
                   "THIS PROCEDURE WILL CONTINUE PLOT"
           GRAPHIC PRINT AT (.1,.55): \
                   "FROM 1,1 DOWN TO 0,1"
           H = INKEY
           CLEAR
           SET COLOR 1
           PLOT (0,0),(0,1),(1,1)
           SET COLOR 2
           PLOT (1,1),(1,0)
           H = INKEY
\                   Instructions for fourth display
           CLEAR
           PLOT (0,0),(0,1),(1,1),(1,0),(0,0)
           SET COLOR 4
           GRAPHIC PRINT AT (.1,.75): \
                   "THIS PROCEDURE WILL COMPLETE PLOT"
           GRAPHIC PRINT AT (.1,.55): \
                   "ACROSS BOTTOM OF SCREEN TO 0,0"
           H = INKEY
           CLEAR
           SET COLOR 1
           PLOT (0,0),(0,1),(1,1),(1,0)
           SET COLOR 2
           PLOT (1,0),(0,0)
           H = INKEY
\                   Reprint of the box on the screen
           SET COLOR 1
           PLOT (0,0),(0,1),(1,1),(1,0),(0,0)
           H = INKEY
           GRAPHIC CLOSE
           END
```

Four statements can be used to control and/or obtain information about the viewing area. They include: **DEVICE**, **BOUNDS**, **VIEWPORT**, and **WINDOW**. All *except* the DEVICE statement can be used to control the viewing area.

The DEVICE Statement

The **DEVICE** statement obtains the physical limits of the output device. For example, **ASK DEVICE HV, WV** will produce the device height and width. When used with our monitor, the program, GRAFDATA.BAS [used later in this chapter], produced the following output:

```
Device height:   0.739644970414
Device width:     1
The veritcal axis is 73.9644970414% of the horizontal.
```

This ratio between the vertical axis and horizontal axes is known as the **aspect ratio**. In this illustration the aspect ratio is about 74 to 100. Knowing this relationship it is possible to modify the viewing area by using the BOUNDS statement to form a square.

LANGUAGE CODING RULE

The **DEVICE** statement obtains the height and width of the graphics output device.

ASK DEVICE <height variable> , <width variable>

- Both the height and width variables must be declared as *real*.

BOUNDS Statement

The **BOUNDS** statement establishes the aspect ratio of an output device, that is, the ratio of the Y-axis to the X-axis. The BOUNDS of each axis ranges from 0.0 to 1.0 whether the actual device height and width are measured in inches or pixels.

The GRAPHIC OPEN statement sets the bounds of both axes from 0.0 to 1.0 and since the height of the console screen is less than the width, a line from 0.0 to 1.0 is longer along the X-axis than along the Y-axis. If we want the two lines to be the same length, we change the bounds after we have determined the aspect ratio with the ASK DEVICE statement. Thus, to obtain a square output on the screen we would use the statement:

```
SET BOUNDS  1,  .74
```

This is helpful in retaining the shape of figures, such as circles, as you move from one graphics output device to another. The aspect ratio can also be controlled with the WINDOW statement.

LANGUAGE CODING RULE

The **BOUNDS** statement determines the aspect ratio [Y-axis to X-axis] of a graphics output device.

    SET BOUNDS <height> , <width>

sets the X- and Y-axes of the output device with a range anywhere between 0.0 and 1.0; if variables are used they must be declared as *real*.

    ASK BOUNDS <height variable> , <width variable>

requests the computer to return the current heights of both axes. Since they range between 0.0 and 1.0 both variables must be *real*.

The VIEWPORT and WINDOW Statements

The **VIEWPORT** statement sets the area within the BOUNDS in which the graphics output is printed. The VIEWPORT may be defined anywhere within the area established by the BOUNDS; see **Figure 15-2**. The limits of the VIEWPORT are between 0.0 and 1.0 similar to those of the BOUNDS statement.

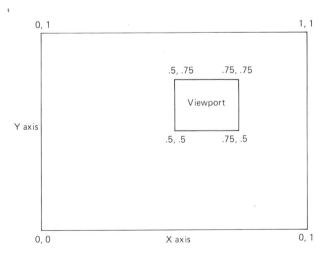

FIGURE 15-2   BOUNDS and VIEWPORT Parameters

Changing the dimensions of the VIEWPORT does not affect any graphics currently displayed on the screen unless the screen is cleared *before* changing the VIEWPORT statement. If variable names are used to set the coordinates with this statement, they must be *real*.

LANGUAGE CODING RULE

The **VIEWPORT** statement sets the boundaries of the graphics output area in which printed output may appear.

 SET VIEWPORT <X-axis left limit> , <X-axis right limit> ,
       <Y-axis lower limit> , <Y-axis upper limit>

The coordinates of the viewport currently in use may be requested by:

 ASK VIEWPORT <X-axis left variable> , <X-axis right variable> ,
       <Y-axis lower variable> , <Y-axis upper variable>

• All four variables should be declared as *real*.

The **WINDOW** statement defines the coordinate scale within the viewport. In Figure 15-2 we defined the Viewport with coordinates of 0.1,0.1 for the lower left corner, 0.1,0.6 for the upper left, 0.6,0.1 for the lower right and 0.6,0.6 for the upper right. In effect we have a viewport that is one-fourth of the total area. To simplify placing graphics output within the viewport, we can designate the X-axis as 100 units and the Y-axis as 100 units with the statements:

```
VIEWPORT  .1,.6,1,.6
WINDOW    0,100,0,100
```

This would permit us, for the X-axis, to designate the .1,.1 [lower left corner] of the viewport as 0,0 for our graphics output and the .6,.1 [lower right corner] as 100,0 for output. Similarly, the Y-axis would range from 0 to 100. See **Figure 15-3**.

The **BOUNDS, VIEWPORT, and WINDOW** statements automatically default to **0,1,0,1 unless otherwise declared**. It is not necessary to follow the GRAPHIC OPEN statement with BOUNDS, VIEWPORT, or WINDOW statements unless you wish to declare other limits. To make programming easier for the location of graphics output, we have used the statement

```
WINDOW 0,100,0,100
```

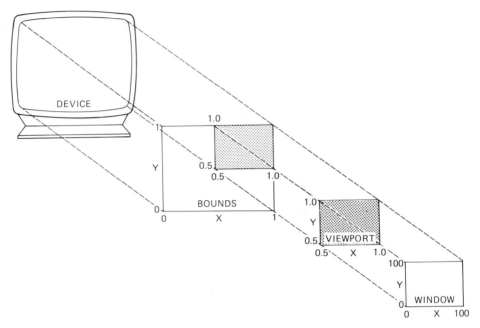

FIGURE 15-3   DEVICE, BOUNDS, VIEWPORT, and WINDOW Parameters

---

LANGUAGE CODING RULE

The **WINDOW** statement sets the scale of the X- and Y-axes within the BOUNDS and **VIEWPORT** statement.

SET WINDOW <X-axis left limit> , <X-axis right limit>,
            <Y-axis lower limit> , <Y-axis upper limit>

The coordinates of the window currently in use may be requested by:

ASK WINDOW <X-axis left variable> , <X-axis right variable> ,
            <Y-axis lower variable> , <Y-axis upper variable>

• All four variables should be declared as *real*.

---

in some of the programs that follow in this chapter. Several demonstration programs will help explain the relationship between VIEWPORT and WINDOW.

Program 15-3, VUPORT1.BAS, demonstrates 10 viewport statements. Starting with a complete console screen, the viewport is redefined to plot the same box as used in Program 15-2 with different viewports:

VIEWPORT STATEMENT	POSITION OF PLOT
SET VIEWPORT 0,1,0,1	Full screen printout
SET VIEWPORT 0,.5,0,.5	Lower left quadrant of the screen
SET VIEWPORT .5,1,0,.5	Lower right quadrant of the screen
SET VIEWPORT 0,.5,.5,1	Upper left quadrant of the screen
SET VIEWPORT .5,1,.5,1	Upper right quadrant of the screen
SET VIEWPORT .25,.75,.25,.75	Centered half-screen size
SET VIEWPORT .4,.6,.4,.6	Smaller section in center of screen
SET VIEWPORT .45,.55,0,1	Wide box across center of the screen
SET VIEWPORT 0,1,.45,.55	Narrow vertical box down center of screen
SET VIEWPORT .48,.52,.48,.52	Very small box in center of the screen

PROGRAM 15-3   VUPORT1.BAS   [Compiler: Graphics]

Demonstration of the VIEWPORT Statement

Copyright 1984, 1985, Compulit, Inc.

```
        INTEGER  H
        GRAPHIC OPEN 1
        CLEAR
\                Printout of the instruction screen
        PLOT (0,0),(0,1),(1,1),(1,0),(0,0)
        PLOT (.1,.1),(.1,.9),(.9,.9),(.9,.1),(.1,.1)
        SET COLOR 2
        GRAPHIC PRINT AT (.04,.75): \
                "THIS PROGRAM DISPLAYS SEVERAL SCREENS"
        GRAPHIC PRINT AT (.15,.55): \
                "PRESS ANY LETTER TO CONTINUE"
        GRAPHIC PRINT AT (.25,.35): \
                "TO THE NEXT SCREEN"
        H = INKEY
\                Set viewport for full screen
        CLEAR
        SET VIEWPORT 0,1,0,1
        PLOT (0,0),(0,1),(1,1),(1,0),(0,0)
        H = INKEY
\                Set viewport for lower left part of screen
        CLEAR
        SET VIEWPORT 0,.5,0,.5
        PLOT (0,0),(0,1),(1,1),(1,0),(0,0)
        H = INKEY
\                Set viewport for lower right part of screen
        CLEAR
        SET VIEWPORT .5,1,0,.5
        PLOT (0,0),(0,1),(1,1),(1,0),(0,0)
```

(continues)

```
         H = INKEY
\                Set viewport for upper left part of the screen
         CLEAR
         SET VIEWPORT 0,.5,.5,1
         PLOT (0,0),(0,1),(1,1),(1,0),(0,0)
         H = INKEY
\                Set viewport for upper right part of the screen
         CLEAR
         SET VIEWPORT .5,1,.5,1
         PLOT (0,0),(0,1),(1,1),(1,0),(0,0)
         H = INKEY
\                Set viewport for center of the screen
         CLEAR
         SET VIEWPORT .25,.75,.25,.75
         PLOT (0,0),(0,1),(1,1),(1,0),(0,0)
         H = INKEY
\                Set viewport for smaller center screen
         CLEAR
         SET VIEWPORT .4,.6,.4,.6
         PLOT (0,0),(0,1),(1,1),(1,0),(0,0)
         H = INKEY
\                Set viewport for x-center vertical screen
         CLEAR
         SET VIEWPORT .45,.55,0,1
         PLOT (0,0),(0,1),(1,1),(1,0),(0,0)
         H = INKEY
\                Set viewport for y-center vertical screen
         CLEAR
         SET VIEWPORT 0,1,.45,.55
         PLOT (0,0),(0,1),(1,1),(1,0),(0,0)
         H = INKEY
\                Set viewport for a minium screen
         CLEAR
         SET VIEWPORT .48,.52,.48,.52
         PLOT (0,0),(0,1),(1,1),(1,0),(0,0)
         H = INKEY
         GRAPHIC CLOSE
         END
```

Program 15-4, VUPORT2.BAS, illustrates 20 successively smaller viewports starting with a full-sized console screen and terminating with a viewport in the upper right corner of the screen. This has been done by using a real variable, K, within a FOR-NEXT loop:

```
FOR K = 0 TO .95 STEP 0.05
    SET VIEWPORT K, 1, K, 1
    SET WINDOW   0, 1, 0, 1
    PLOT (0,0), (0,1), (1,1), (1,0), (0,0)
    H = INKEY
NEXT
```

The WINDOW and PLOT statement parameters remain unchanged as only the VIEWPORT is altered during this loop. The INKEY statement is used to permit you to view each plot individually as it is drawn on the console screen.

PROGRAM 15-4   **VUPORT2.BAS**   **[Compiler: Graphics]**

Applications of VIEWPORT and WINDOW Statements

Copyright 1984, 1985, Compulit, Inc.

```
        INTEGER  H
        REAL K
        GRAPHIC OPEN 1
        CLEAR
\               Procedure for the instruction screen
        SET WINDOW 0,100,0,100
        SET CHARACTER HEIGHT 0
        PLOT (0,0),(0,100),(100,100),(100,0),(0,0)
        PLOT (10,10),(10,90),(90,90),(90,10),(10,10)
        SET COLOR 2
        GRAPHIC PRINT AT (4,75): \
               "THIS PROGRAM DISPLAYS SEVERAL SCREENS"
        GRAPHIC PRINT AT (15,55): \
               "PRESS ANY LETTER TO CONTINUE"
        GRAPHIC PRINT AT (25,35): \
               "TO THE NEXT SCREEN"
        H = INKEY
\               Main program
        CLEAR
        FOR K = 0 TO .95 STEP 0.05
               SET VIEWPORT K,1,K,1
               SET WINDOW 0,1,0,1
               PLOT (0,0),(0,1),(1,1),(1,0),(0,0)
               H = INKEY
        NEXT
        GRAPHIC CLOSE
        END
```

The output of VUPORT2.BAS would appear on the console screen or hardcopy output as shown in **Figure 15-4**.

Program 15-5, VUPORT3.BAS, is another example of the use of VIEWPORT statement to produce a small viewing area terminating at the center of the screen. In this program real variables are used for the lower and upper limits of the X- and Y-axes. K is set for the lower limit of both axes and initialized at 0; M is initialized as 1, the upper limit of both axes.

```
K = 0          \ Lower limit of each axis
M = 1          \ Upper limit of each axis
FOR I = 1 TO 13
    SET VIEWPORT K, M, K, M
    SET WINDOW   0, 1, 0, 1
    PLOT (0,0), (0,1), (1,1), (1,0), (0,0)
    M = M - 0.04          \ Upper limit decreased by 0.04
    K = K + 0.04          \ Lower limit increased by 0.04
NEXT
```

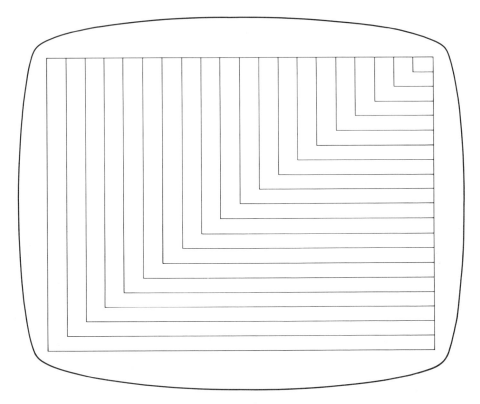

FIGURE 15-4   VUPORT2.BAS Output Showing Successive Viewports

PROGRAM 15-5   **VUPORT3.BAS**   **[Compiler: Graphics]**

Additional Applications of VIEWPORT and WINDOW Statements

Copyright 1984, 1985, Compulit, Inc.

```
       INTEGER  H, I
       REAL K, M
       GRAPHIC OPEN 1
       CLEAR
\              Procedure for the instruction screen
       SET WINDOW 0,100,0,100
       SET CHARACTER HEIGHT 0
       PLOT (0,0),(0,100),(100,100),(100,0),(0,0)
       PLOT (10,10),(10,90),(90,90),(90,10),(10,10)
       SET COLOR 2
       GRAPHIC PRINT AT (4,75): \
               "THIS PROGRAM DISPLAYS SEVERAL SCREENS"
       GRAPHIC PRINT AT (15,55): \
               "PRESS ANY LETTER TO CONTINUE"
       GRAPHIC PRINT AT (25,35): \
               "TO THE NEXT SCREEN"
       H = INKEY
\              Main program
       CLEAR
       M = 1:    K = 0
       FOR I = 1 TO 13
```

(continues)

```
        SET VIEWPORT K,M,K,M
        SET WINDOW 0,1,0,1
        PLOT (0,0),(0,1),(1,1),(1,0),(0,0)
        H = INKEY
        M = M - 0.04
        K = K + 0.04
    NEXT
    H = INKEY
    GRAPHIC CLOSE
    END
```

The output of this program is shown in **Figure 15-5**.

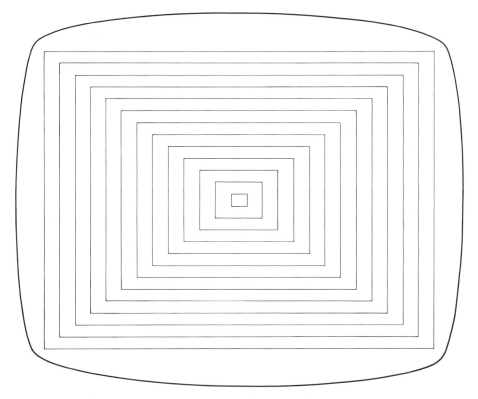

FIGURE 15-5 VUPORT3.BAS Output Showing Alternate Viewports

CLEAR, BEAM, AND PLOT STATEMENTS

Setting up the viewing area is the first step in writing a graphics program. Until you are more proficient, you may wish to use the default options as noted earlier. However, at this point it is necessary to distinguish between the **cursor** and the **graphic cursor** in graphics programming.

- **Cursor** refers to the current print position for any non-graphics output.
- The **graphic cursor** is displayed on the console screen only when the GRAPHIC INPUT statement is being executed.

The BEAM Statement

The BEAM statement is similar to PEN UP/PEN DOWN when using a plotter. It is generally used in conjunction with the PLOT statement and it can be set "ON" or "OFF" with the **SET BEAM** command. A more extensive analysis of this statement will be included in the discussion of the PLOT statement which follows later.

LANGUAGE CODING RULE

The **BEAM** statement is used to turn the drawing beam or a plotter pen on or off.

SET BEAM "ON"

or

SET BEAM "OFF"

You can determine the current status of the BEAM by using the ASK version of this statement:

ASK BEAM <string variable>

The CLEAR Statement

Anything we print or plot on the console screen will remain on the screen until a CLEAR statement is encountered in the program. With graphics programming special attention must be paid to clearing the screen at appropriate times or the new graphics copy will overlay the previous screen.

The **CLEAR** statement clears the screen and returns the graphic cursor and BEAM to home (0,0), the lower left corner of the screen, not to the conventional upper left corner. It *also* resets the VIEWPORT statement to 0,1,0,1.

The PLOT Statement

The **PLOT** statement is used to draw a line and figures; each point is designated by a pair of X- and Y-coordinates. To make graphics programming simpler we recommend two procedures.

LANGUAGE CODING RULE

The **CLEAR** statement clears the screen and returns the graphic cursor and BEAM to the graphics home position 0,0, the *lower* left corner of the console screen.

CLEAR

- The VIEWPORT is reset to 0,1,0,1 by this statement.

---

1. It is easier for most people to visualize scales in unit from 0 to 100 than in decimal parts between 0.0 and 1.0; also there is less chance of forgetting the decimal point before a value when entering data. Therefore, we recommend that the 0 to 100 scale be invoked by using the statement:

```
SET WINDOW 0, 100, 0, 100
```

2. In the Graphics Extension package, the BEAM may be set *on* prior to a PLOT statement; to draw a line from the lower left corner of the screen to the upper left corner, the coding would be:

```
SET BEAM "ON"
PLOT (0,1)
```

With the BEAM *on* the computer would connect point 0,0 [the *home* position of the BEAM] with 0,1 in the PLOT statement.

LANGUAGE CODING RULE

The **PLOT** statement connects a pair or series of coordinate points.

PLOT $<X1,Y1>$, $<X2,Y2>$ [,$<Xn,Yn>$] [;]

- If the BEAM is *on* before the PLOT statement, the graphics system draws a line from the current location of the beam to the first point.
- If the list ends with a semicolon [;], the beam stays on and the last position is the starting point of the next PLOT statement.

To keep the BEAM *on* for further drawing place a semicolon [;] at the end of the PLOT statement. To draw a box around the screen and continue drawing we would have:

```
SET BEAM "ON"
PLOT (0,1), (1,1), (1,0), (0,0) ;
```

The programmer would have to be continually aware of whether the BEAM was on or off and the last location of the BEAM. On the other hand, only one additional pair of coordinates is needed if we *ignore* the BEAM statement when the console screen is the graphics output device. The same box could be drawn, as we did earlier in this chapter, by writing:

```
PLOT (0,0), (0,1), (1,1), (1,0), (0,0)
```

However, it is helpful to use the BEAM statement when using any hardcopy graphics output device such as a plotter. This should be used in conjunction with the POSITION statement which sets the beam at a specific pair of X- and Y-coordinates before starting the plot. The beam is positioned to the starting coordinates with BEAM "OFF" and POSITION statements.

LANGUAGE CODING RULE

The **POSITION** statement sets the beam position to a specific X- and Y-coordinate position on the screen.

SET POSITION <X-coordinate> , <Y-coordinate>

• The two coordinates are specific, numeric real values.

To determine the current position of the BEAM use:

ASK POSITION <X-coordinate variable> , <Y-coordinate variable>

• Both of the coordinate variables are *real*.

Program 15-6, PLOT3.BAS, illustrates the use of the PLOT statement.

PROGRAM 15-6   **PLOT3.BAS**   **[Compiler: Graphics]**

Use of Multiple PLOT Statements

Copyright 1984, 1985, Compulit, Inc.

```
INTEGER  H, I, L, M
GRAPHIC OPEN 1
```

(continues)

```
CLEAR
SET WINDOW 0,100,0,100
SET COLOR 3
L = 0:   H = 100
FOR I = 1 TO 9
         PLOT (L,L),(L,H),(H,H),(H,L),(L,L)
         L = L + 5
         H = H - 5
NEXT
M = INKEY
GRAPHIC CLOSE
END
```

The output, **Figure 15-6**, is similar to that shown in Figure 15-5, the output for the VUPORT3.BAS program.

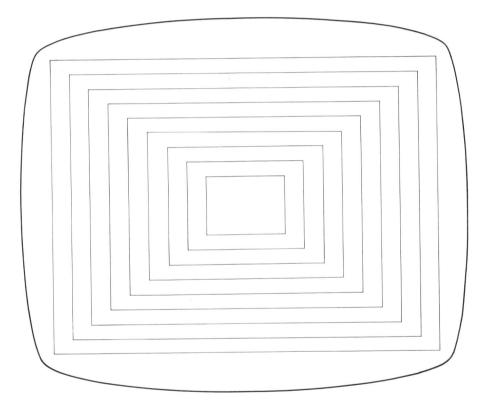

FIGURE 15-6   Output of PLOT3.BAS

PRINTING TEXT COPY IN A GRAPHICS PROGRAM

Text copy in a graphics program can be printed by using the conventional PRINT statement or the **GRAPHIC PRINT** statement. In either case the size of the characters is that found in a 40-column screen.

The GRAPHIC PRINT statement is used to print a *string* at a given pair of coordinates on the console screen or graphics output device. The coordinates must be scaled to fit the current window ranges. The string may be either a constant or a variable. Using SET WINDOW 0, 100, 0, 100 we would find that:

GRAPHIC PRINT AT (50,50): "HERE"   The lower left corner of the H in HERE begins at coordinates 50,50 or the center of the screen.

GRAPHIC PRINT AT (0,50): "NOW"   The lower left corner of the N in NOW would be at the center of the screen along the bottom edge at coordinates 0,50.

Multiple GRAPHIC PRINT lines may be used but be careful to avoid printing one output line over another. With my PGS color monitor and a Y-axis scale from 0 to 100, a difference of 5 units is necessary to avoid having one line overwrite another; one unit of space is left between lines. Also, if there is insufficient space for the output string, it will be truncated.

LANGUAGE CODING RULE

The GRAPHIC PRINT statement prints a string starting at a given point.

GRAPHIC PRINT AT (\<X\> , \<Y\>) : \<string variable or constant\>

- The X- and Y-coordinates are *real* values and are scaled by the ranges of the current window.
- The coordinates must be separated by a comma, enclosed in parentheses and followed by a colon [:].
- The material to be printed must be a string, either a constant or variable.

The conventional PRINT statement may also be used in a graphics program but with some versions of the graphics compiler it is not possible to reposition the first PRINT statement after a CLEAR so that it occupies the first line at the top of the console screen. If you wish to print a variable in response to an *ASK* graphics command and want to position it on the screen, use the GRAPHIC PRINT statement.

If the variable is a string:

```
STRING PEN, LINE.OUT
ASK BEAM   PEN
LINE.OUT = "The Beam is " + PEN
GRAPHIC PRINT AT (10,40): LINE.OUT
```

If the variable is an integer:

```
INTEGER NO.COL
STRING  LINE.OUT
ASK COLOR NO.COL
LINE.OUT = "The current color is #" + STR$(NO.COL)
GRAPHIC PRINT AT (10,40): LINE.OUT
```

CHANGING COLORS, LINE STYLE, AND DIRECTION

The variety of colors and line styles available under the Graphics Extension package depends on the graphics output device. You can determine the number of line styles and colors available by using the *ASK* form of the statements. You can change the color and/or line styles by using the *SET* form of the statements. In addition, there is a graphics statement which permits the programmer to alter the angle of a text string.

The COLOR Statement

Program 15-7, COLOR.BAS, demonstrates the **ASK COLOR COUNT** and **SET COLOR** statements. After the introductory prompt screen, the program determines the number of colors available from the graphics output device and then displays each color and its associated number.

PROGRAM 15-7   **COLOR.BAS**   **[Compiler: Graphics]**

Test of COLOR and COLOR COUNT Statements

Copyright 1984, 1985, Compulit, Inc.

```
      INTEGER H, I, CT
      STRING  COL.NO
      GRAPHIC OPEN 1
      CLEAR
      SET WINDOW 0,100,0,100
      SET CHARACTER HEIGHT 0
  \          Instruction screen routine
      PLOT (0,0),(0,100),(100,100),(100,0),(0,0)
      PLOT (10,10),(10,90),(90,90),(90,10),(10,10)
      SET COLOR 2
      GRAPHIC PRINT AT (4,75): \
             "THIS PROGRAM DISPLAYS SEVERAL SCREENS"
      GRAPHIC PRINT AT (15,55): \
             "PRESS ANY LETTER TO CONTINUE"
      GRAPHIC PRINT AT (25,35): \
             "TO THE NEXT SCREEN"
      H = INKEY
  \          Request number of colors from computer system
      CLEAR
```

(continues)

```
        ASK COLOR COUNT CT
\               Display color number and borders
        FOR I = 1 TO CT
                SET COLOR I
                CLEAR
                COL.NO = "COLOR " + STR$(I)
                GRAPHIC PRINT AT (45,50): COL.NO
                PLOT (0,0),(0,100),(100,100),(100,0),(0,0)
                PLOT (10,10),(10,90),(90,90),(90,10),(10,10)
                H = INKEY
        NEXT
        GRAPHIC CLOSE
        END
```

LANGUAGE CODING RULE

The **COLOR** statement sets the foreground color or indicates the foreground color in use. Color is defined by integer.

SET COLOR <integer>

• The integer is the number of the color for the foreground color.

To obtain the numeric value of the foreground color now in effect, the statement is:

ASK COLOR <integer variable>

LANGUAGE CODING RULE

The **COLOR COUNT** statement is an *ASK* form used to determine the number of foreground colors available with a specific graphics output device.

ASK COLOR COUNT <integer variable>

The LINE Statement

We can vary the style of the line to solid, dashed, dotted, dash-dotted, etc. The graphics output device determines the number of line styles available. With the Princeton Graphics System color monitor there are seven line styles from which to select. To change the line style a **SET LINE STYLE** statement is used; for example, with a SET WINDOW 0,100,0,100 scale for the viewport, four different line styles can be used to draw a box around the inside of the console screen [the default line style is always 1].

```
PLOT (0,0), (0,100)
SET LINE STYLE 2
PLOT (0,100), (100,100)
SET LINE STYLE 3
PLOT (100,100), (100,0)
SET LINE STYLE 4
PLOT (100,0), (0,0)
```

Program 15-8, LINE.BAS, plots an X–Y grid in seven different line styles. Two sets of PLOT statements are used in the program to draw the horizontal and vertical lines. A more compact way to program the grid is with nested FOR-NEXT loops.

```
REAL  K
- - - - - - - - - -
- - - - - - - - - -
SET WINDOW 0, 1, 0, 1
FOR I = 1 TO 7
    FOR K = 0.2 TO 1.0 STEP 0.2
        PLOT (0.0, K), (1.0, K)
        PLOT (K, 0.0), (K, 1.0)
    NEXT
    H = INKEY
    CLEAR
NEXT
```

PROGRAM 15-8   **LINE.BAS**   **[Compiler: Graphics]**

Demonstration of Various Line Styles

Copyright 1984, 1985, Compulit, Inc.

```
INTEGER  H, I
GRAPHIC OPEN 1
CLEAR
\           Instruction screen routine
SET WINDOW 0,100,0,100
SET CHARACTER HEIGHT 0
PLOT (0,0),(0,100),(100,100),(100,0),(0,0)
PLOT (10,10),(10,90),(90,90),(90,10),(10,10)
SET COLOR 2
GRAPHIC PRINT AT (4,75): \
    "THIS PROGRAM DISPLAYS SEVERAL SCREENS"
GRAPHIC PRINT AT (15,55): \
    "PRESS ANY LETTER TO CONTINUE"
```

                                    (*continues*)

```
          GRAPHIC PRINT AT (25,35): \
                  "TO THE NEXT SCREEN"
          H = INKEY
   \              Main program
          CLEAR
          SET WINDOW 0,1,0,1
          FOR I = 1 TO 7
                  SET LINE STYLE I
   \              Horizontal line plot
                  PLOT (0.0,1.0), (1.0,1.0)
                  PLOT (0.0,0.8), (1.0,0.8)
                  PLOT (0.0,0.6), (1.0,0.6)
                  PLOT (0.0,0.4), (1.0,0.4)
                  PLOT (0.0,0.2), (1.0,0.2)
   \              Vertical line plot
                  PLOT (0.0,0.0), (1.0,0.0)
                  PLOT (0.0,0.0), (0.0,1.0)
                  PLOT (0.2,0.0), (0.2,1.0)
                  PLOT (0.4,0.0), (0.4,1.0)
                  PLOT (0.6,0.0), (0.6,1.0)
                  PLOT (0.8,0.0), (0.8,1.0)
                  PLOT (1.0,0.0), (1.0,1.0)
                  H = INKEY
                  CLEAR
          NEXT
          GRAPHIC CLOSE
          END
```

The TEXT ANGLE Statement

The **TEXT ANGLE** statement permits the programmer to print a string at any angle to the horizontal within the limitations of the graphics output device. The most limited device is the console screen.

This statement is defined in radians and since most of us do not think in terms of radians, it is preferable to convert the radians to degrees. This is done in **Program 15-9**, ROTATE.BAS by using:

```
PI = 3.1415926535897
DEGREE = PI * 2 / 360
```

The large number of decimal places in the value of PI is used to obtain greater accuracy. A substitute for the two-statement arithmetic operation is:

```
DEGREE = 0.0174532925199
```

This would speed operations by avoiding the multiplication and division in the former method.

PROGRAM 15-9   ROTATE.BAS   [Compiler: Graphics]

Print Copy in Rotated Positions

Copyright 1984, 1985, Compulit, Inc.

```
          INTEGER H, I
          REAL    PI, DEG
          STRING  COPY
```

```
          GRAPHIC OPEN 1
          SET COLOR 3
10        CLEAR
          PRINT "Limit string to 10 characters":    PRINT
          INPUT "Enter a string ....... "; COPY
          IF LEN (COPY) > 10 THEN 10
          CLEAR
          SET WINDOW 0,100,0,100
          SET CHARACTER HEIGHT 0
          PI = 3.1415926535897:    DEG = PI * 2 / 360
          FOR I = 0 TO 360 STEP 90
                SET TEXT ANGLE I * DEG
                GRAPHIC PRINT AT (50,50): COPY
          NEXT
          H = INKEY
          GRAPHIC CLOSE
          END
```

If * REBECCA * is entered in response to the input prompt in Program 15-9, the output on the console screen is shown in **Figure 15-7**. In printing the output the angle is measured counterclockwise from a horizontal line across the screen and a vertical line through the center of the string.

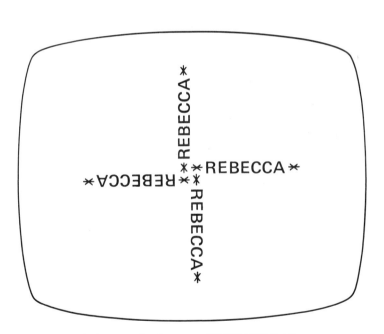

FIGURE 15-7   Sample Output of ROTATE.BAS

CHECKING PARAMETERS OF GRAPHICS OUTPUT DEVICE

What is the character height of a GRAPHIC PRINT output? What is the aspect ratio of your output device? These and other questions can be answered by using a utility program, GRAFDATA.BAS, that is included on the program disk available for this book.

LANGUAGE CODING RULE

The **TEXT ANGLE** statement prints string text at a specific angle to the horizontal.

SET TEXT ANGLE <angle in radians>

- The angle can be specified in degrees by entering the number of degrees desired and multiplying it by 0.0174532925199 [the number of radians in one degree]. Rotation from the horizontal is counter-clockwise.

To determine the existing text angle of the graphics output device:

ASK TEXT ANGLE <angle variable>

- The angle variable is *real* and in radians.

This program provides you with the answers to 18 questions about your graphics system. As you become more familiar with graphics programming, you may alter some of these program statements and note the difference in results.

Various character and marker heights can be set with the appropriate statements. However, the graphic compilers available during the preparation of this copy could support only the minimum height.

LANGUAGE CODING RULE

The **CHARACTER HEIGHT** statement sets the height of the printed graphics text or obtains the current height setting from the computer.

SET CHARACTER HEIGHT <numeric expression>

- The numeric expression, variable, or constant must be *real*.

To determine the character height currently in use, the *ASK* version is:

ASK CHARACTER HEIGHT <real variable>

LANGUAGE CODING RULE

The **MARKER HEIGHT** statement sets the height of the printed graphics marker or obtains the current height setting from the computer.

> **SET MARKER HEIGHT** <real value or variable>

To obtain the current marker height setting:

> **ASK MARKER HEIGHT** <real variable>

HOW TO PLOT A CHART

There are many demonstration programs that are part of the CBASIC graphics package to enable you to draw different types of charts. To provide a fuller explanation of how to prepare a chart we have included several CHART programs. It is best to use graph paper with X- and Y-axes ranging from 0 to 100 to design the output.

The Initial Chart Program and the JUSTIFY Statement

Program 15-10, CHART1.BAS, plots the X- and Y-axes, places the tick marks, the legends for both axes, the title of the graph [sales of the Vuilnis Fast Food Company], and the legend for estimated sales for 1986.

- With a SET WINDOW 0, 100, 0, 100 statement, the two axes are defined to run from 20 to 90. They are graphed with the statement:

```
PLOT (20,90), (20,20), (90,20)
```

- The tick marks for both scales of the graph are 2 plot-units long and are added with a FOR-NEXT loop:

```
FOR I = 30 TO 90 STEP 10
    PLOT (18,I), (20,I)
    PLOT (I,18), (I,20)
NEXT
```

The first plot statement places the tick marks along the Y-axis and the second plot statement places the tick marks along the X-axis.

- To place the scale along the Y-axis [sales in millions of dollars] we again use a FOR-NEXT loop:

```
FOR I = 20 TO 80 STEP 10
    K = I / 10 - 2
    VALUE = STR$(K)
    GRAPHIC PRINT AT (13,I): VALUE
NEXT
```

The dollar values printed range from 0 [when $I = 20$ and $K = 20/10 - 2$] to 6. Since we wish to place the values so that they are centered at the tick marks on the graph, we use the **JUSTIFY** statement. In the GRAPHIC PRINT statement the lower left corner of the letter was positioned at the X- and Y-coordinates; the JUSTIFY statement adjusts the position of the output by modifying the X- and/or Y-coordinates. In this case we need to adjust the lettering along the Y-axis. Therefore, the statement preceding the FOR-NEXT loop would read:

```
SET JUSTIFY 1, .5
```

LANGUAGE CODING RULE

The **JUSTIFY** statement positions alphanumeric strings for the GRAPH PRINT statement relative to either or both the X- and Y-axes.

SET JUSTIFY <horizontal numeric value> , <vertical numeric value>

- Both the horizontal and vertical values are *real,* ranging from 0.0 to 1.0

To determine the current justification setting we use:

ASK JUSTIFY <horizontal variable> , <vertical variable>

- The returned variables are both *real.*

- The years are placed along the X-axis with a FOR-NEXT loop and an apostrophe is inserted before each abbreviated year that is printed.

```
SET JUSTIFY .5, 1
YEAR = 80
```

```
FOR I = 30 TO 90 STEP 20
    VALUE = "'" + STR$(YEAR)
    GRAPHIC PRINT AT (I-5,12): VALUE
    YEAR = YEAR + 2
NEXT
```

The X-coordinate in the GRAPHIC PRINT statement has been further adjusted since we plan to plot a bar chart and the year should be printed *between* the tick marks. See **Figure 15-8**.

PROGRAM 15-10   **CHART1.BAS**   **[Compiler: Graphics]**
Creation of Basic Chart Using JUSTIFY Statement

Copyright 1984, 1985, Compulit, Inc.

```
      INTEGER  H, I, K
      STRING   VALUE
      REAL     YEAR
      GRAPHIC OPEN 1
      CLEAR
      SET WINDOW 0,100,0,100
\           Printout of title, heading and footnote
      SET CHARACTER HEIGHT 0
      GRAPHIC PRINT AT (25,95): "VUILNIS Fast Food Sales"
      GRAPHIC PRINT AT (0,90):  "Million"
      GRAPHIC PRINT AT (82,2):  "Est."
\           Plot of X-axis and Y-axis
      PLOT (20,90),(20,20),(90,20)
\           Placement of tick marks on graph
      FOR I = 30 TO 90 STEP 10
            PLOT (18,I),(20,I)
            PLOT (I,18),(I,20)
      NEXT
\           Creation of Y-scale labels
      SET JUSTIFY 1, .5
      FOR I = 20 TO 80 STEP 20
            K = I / 10 - 2
            VALUE = STR$(K)
            GRAPHIC PRINT AT (13,I): VALUE
      NEXT
\           Creation of X-scale labels
      SET JUSTIFY .5, 1
      YEAR = 80
      FOR I = 30 TO 90 STEP 20
            VALUE = "'" + STR$(YEAR)
            GRAPHIC PRINT AT (I-5,12): VALUE
            YEAR = YEAR + 2
      NEXT
      H = INKEY
      GRAPHIC CLOSE
      END
```

The MARKER Statement

Markers are available for several purposes; they can:

- Indicate the nodes of a graph *without* showing the actual lines.
- Outline an area which will later be filled with color.
- Designate the points in a correlation scattergram.

Most graphics systems have at least five types of markers; our system with the PGS color monitor has seven. Unlike many other graphics statements, there is no ASK counterpart to the **SET MARKER** statement. **Program 15-11**, MARKER.BAS, displays the different markers on the console screen. It is set for seven with the statement:

```
FOR J = 1 TO 7
```

If there are no more than five marker types, the sixth and seventh markers displayed will be a repeat of the first marker. To test your system change the 7 to a larger value; however, modify the printing of the markers in the program so that the output does not exceed the limits of the screen.

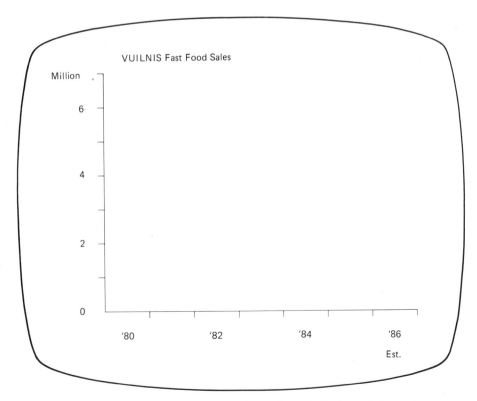

FIGURE 15-8   CHART1.BAS Output of Graph with Scale and Lettering

PROGRAM 15-11 **MARKER.BAS** **[Compiler: Graphics]**

Display of Marker Types Available

Copyright 1984, 1985, Compulit, Inc.

```
        INTEGER  H, J
        REAL MX, MY
        GRAPHIC OPEN 1
        CLEAR
        SET COLOR 2
        SET WINDOW 0,100,0,100
\                Initial position for marker
        DIM MX(0), MY(0)
        MX(0) = 15:  MY(0) = 15
        FOR J = 1 TO 7
                SET MARKER TYPE J
                MAT MARKER 0: MX,MY
\                Shift marker print position up and to the right
                MX(0) = MX(0) + 10
                MY(0) = MY(0) + 10
        NEXT
        H = INKEY
        GRAPHIC CLOSE
        END
```

LANGUAGE CODING RULE

The **MARKER TYPE** statement sets the marker type to be used by a graphics program.

    SET MARKER TYPE <integer expression>

    The integer expression can also be an integer constant or integer variable.

The Chart Program with MAT MARKER and MAT PLOT Statements

For this and succeeding illustrations, we will use annual sales data for the Vuilinis Fast Food Company. The sales data to be plotted includes actual sales from 1980 through 1985 and estimated sales for 1986; the data is:

YEAR	DOLLAR SALES
1980	500,000
1981	1,310,000
1982	2,195,000
1983	3,330,000
1984	4,525,000
1985	5,625,000
1986	7,000,000

First determine the position of these annual sales values on the grid in Program 15-11. The point of origin of the grid, the lower left corner, was placed at 20,20 and each axis continued to 90. The sales tick marks were placed at 10 units apart [STEP 10] to represent one million dollars. To convert the sales figures into coordinate points:

- Round each year's sales to millions with one decimal place so that sales in 1985 would be 5.6 compared with 2.2 in 1982.
- Multiply the annual sales by 10 and add 20 to each to obtain the Y-coordinate for each year.

Now we can set the coordinates for 1980, the first year. 1980 is represented on the X-axis by the line between 20 and 30. 1980 sales, $500,000, is at 25 on the Y-axis. The coordinates for 1980 would be:

20,25   30,25   [The upper limits of the bar]

20,20   30,20   [The lower limits of the bar]

The coordinates for the second year, 1981, range from 30 to 40 along the X-axis and reach 33 [1.3 * 10 + 20] along the Y-axis. The coordinates for 1981 would be:

30,33   40,33   [The upper limits of the bar]

30,20   40,20   [The lower limits of the bar]

We could do this for each year, but there is a shorter way to obtain these data. We could plot only the upper boundary of each bar. These would be:

20,20		point of origin of the graph
20,25	30,25	1980 sales
30,33	40,33	1981 sales
40,42	50,42	1982 sales
50,53	60,53	1983 sales
60,65	70,65	1984 sales
70,76	80,76	1985 sales

Because we plan to use a different color to indicate estimated sales, we will postpone designating the coordinates for 1986. To define the sales area completely, plot the vertical line for 1985 which runs from 80,76 down to the X-axis at 80,20. Also define the left portion of each bar that connects one year with the next. For example, the top of the 1980 sales bar extends from 20,25 to 30,25. The top of the 1981 sales bar extends from 30,33 to 40,33. The part from 30,25 to 30,33 must be specified in the arrays. Therefore we have a total of 14 coordinate points, XP and YP, that must be included in the program as:

```
DIM XP(13), YP(13)
XP(0)  = 20:   YP(0)  = 20
XP(1)  = 20:   YP(1)  = 25
XP(2)  = 30:   YP(2)  = 25
XP(3)  = 30:   YP(3)  = 33
XP(4)  = 40:   YP(4)  = 33
XP(5)  = 40:   YP(5)  = 42
XP(6)  = 50:   YP(6)  = 42
XP(7)  = 50:   YP(7)  = 53
XP(8)  = 60:   YP(8)  = 53
XP(9)  = 60:   YP(9)  = 65
XP(10) = 70:   YP(10) = 65
XP(11) = 70:   YP(11) = 76
XP(12) = 80:   YP(12) = 76
XP(13) = 80:   YP(13) = 20
```

In all arrays used in graphics programming the zero subscript must be used. Otherwise, both the X- and Y-coordinates in this position of the array will be set to zero and used as the starting point for any MAT PLOT, MAT FILL, or MAT MARKER statement.

Similarly, we can establish the coordinates for the 1986 estimated sales at 80,90 and 90,90 as the top of the bar. We need to add the two sides; the coordinates of the four points to be connected are:

```
DIM XE(3), YE(3)
XE(0)  = 80:   YE(0)  = 20
XE(1)  = 80:   YE(1)  = 90
XE(2)  = 90:   YE(2)  = 90
XE(3)  = 90:   YE(3)  = 20
```

Program 15-12, CHART2.BAS, uses the **MAT MARKER** and **MAT PLOT** statements to plot these sales data. Different colors were used to separate the markers for estimated and actual sales.

PROGRAM 15-12   **CHART2.BAS**   [Compiler: Graphics]

Test of Basic Chart Using MAT MARKER and MAT PLOT Statements

Copyright 1984, 1985, Compulit, Inc.

```
      INTEGER  H, I, J, K, FLAG
      STRING   VALUE
      REAL     YEAR, XP, YP, XE, YE
      FLAG = 0
      GRAPHIC OPEN 1
      CLEAR
      SET WINDOW 0,100,0,100
            Procedure for the instruction screen
```

\

(continues)

```
            SET CHARACTER HEIGHT Ø
            PLOT (Ø,Ø),(Ø,1ØØ),(1ØØ,1ØØ),(1ØØ,Ø),(Ø,Ø)
            PLOT (1Ø,1Ø),(1Ø,9Ø),(9Ø,9Ø),(9Ø,1Ø),(1Ø,1Ø)
            SET COLOR 2
            GRAPHIC PRINT AT (4,75): \
                    "THIS PROGRAM DISPLAYS SEVERAL SCREENS"
            GRAPHIC PRINT AT (15,55): \
                    "PRESS ANY LETTER TO CONTINUE"
            GRAPHIC PRINT AT (25,35): \
                    "TO THE NEXT SCREEN"
            H = INKEY
10          CLEAR
            SET COLOR 1
  \                 Printout of title, heading and footnote
            GRAPHIC PRINT AT (25,95): "VUILNIS Fast Food Sales"
            GRAPHIC PRINT AT (Ø,9Ø):  "Million"
            GRAPHIC PRINT AT (82,2):  "Est."
  \                 Plot of x-axis and y-axis
            PLOT (2Ø,9Ø),(2Ø,2Ø),(9Ø,2Ø)
  \                 Place tick marks on graph
            FOR I = 3Ø TO 9Ø STEP 1Ø
                    PLOT (18,I),(2Ø,I)
                    PLOT (I,18),(I,2Ø)
            NEXT
  \                 Create y-scale labels
            SET JUSTIFY 1, .5
            FOR I = 2Ø TO 8Ø STEP 2Ø
                    K = I / 1Ø - 2
                    VALUE = STR$(K)
                    GRAPHIC PRINT AT (13,I): VALUE
            NEXT
  \                 Create x-scale labels
            SET JUSTIFY .5, 1
            YEAR = 8Ø
            FOR I = 3Ø TO 9Ø STEP 2Ø
                    VALUE = "'" + STR$(YEAR)
                    GRAPHIC PRINT AT (I-5,12): VALUE
                    YEAR = YEAR + 2
            NEXT
  \                 Restore justifification
            SET JUSTIFY Ø,Ø
  \                 Data for existing sales
            DIM XP(14), YP(14)
            XP(Ø)  = 2Ø:  YP(Ø)  = 2Ø
            XP(1)  = 2Ø:  YP(1)  = 25
            XP(2)  = 3Ø:  YP(2)  = 25
            XP(3)  = 3Ø:  YP(3)  = 33
            XP(4)  = 4Ø:  YP(4)  = 33
            XP(5)  = 4Ø:  YP(5)  = 42
            XP(6)  = 5Ø:  YP(6)  = 42
            XP(7)  = 5Ø:  YP(7)  = 53
            XP(8)  = 6Ø:  YP(8)  = 53
            XP(9)  = 6Ø:  YP(9)  = 65
            XP(1Ø) = 7Ø:  YP(1Ø) = 65
            XP(11) = 7Ø:  YP(11) = 76
            XP(12) = 8Ø:  YP(12) = 76
            XP(13) = 8Ø:  YP(13) = 2Ø
  \                 Data for estimated sales
            DIM XE(3), YE(3)
            XE(Ø)  = 8Ø:  YE(Ø)  = 2Ø
            XE(1)  = 8Ø:  YE(1)  = 9Ø
            XE(2)  = 9Ø:  YE(2)  = 9Ø
            XE(3)  = 9Ø:  YE(3)  = 2Ø
  \                 Test to display final screens
            IF FLAG = 1 THEN 77
  \                 Set markers for existing sales
            SET COLOR 3
            SET MARKER TYPE 3
            MAT MARKER 13: XP, YP
            H = INKEY
  \                 Set markers for estimated sales
            SET COLOR 2
            SET MARKER TYPE 5
            MAT MARKER 3: XE, YE
            H = INKEY
```

```
\               Test to print MAT PLOT statements
        IF FLAG = 0 THEN FLAG = 1: GOTO 10
\               Plot matrix for existing sales
77      SET COLOR 3
        MAT PLOT 13: XP, YP
        H = INKEY
\               Plot matrix for estimated sales
        SET COLOR 2
        MAT PLOT 3: XE, YE
        H = INKEY
        GRAPHIC CLOSE
        END
```

The output when the MAT MARKER statement is used is shown in **Figure 15-9**. One type of marker is used for existing data and a different type of marker is used for estimated data.

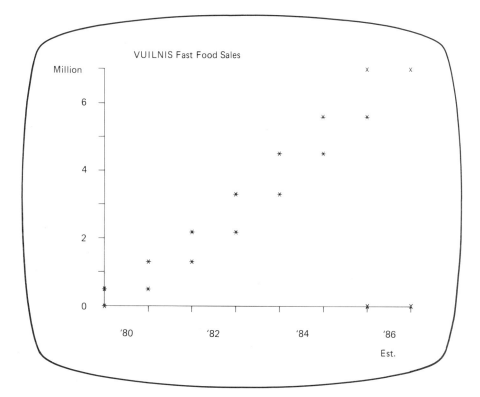

FIGURE 15-9   MAT MARKER Output of CHART2.BAS

The same chart produced by Program 15-12 and using the MAT PLOT statement is shown in **Figure 15-10**.

The Bar Chart Program and the MAT FILL Statement

The completed bar chart is produced by **Program 15-13**, CHART3.BAS, which fills the area for actual sales with one color or pattern and the area for

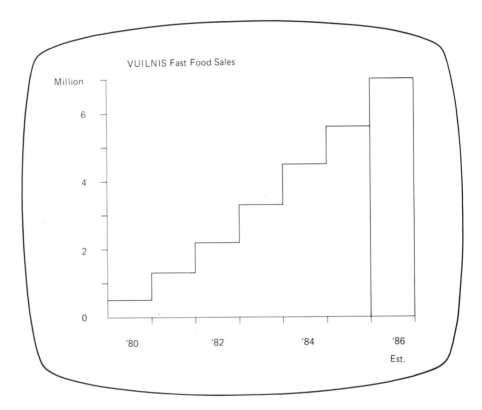

FIGURE 15-10 MAT PLOT Output of CHART2.BAS

LANGUAGE CODING RULE

The **MAT MARKER** graphics statement plots markers at an array of X and Y coordinates.

MAT MARKER <maximum array subscript> : <X array>, <Y array>

- Both the X and Y *array* variables must be *real.*
- The markers may be specified with a SET COLOR statement.
- The statement begins with the X(0),Y(0) element. Any single array is limited to 72 elements so that the maximum array subscript cannot exceed 71. If more points are required, additional arrays must be used.

LANGUAGE CODING RULE

The **MAT PLOT** graphics statement connects the points defined in an X-Y matrix with lines.

MAT PLOT <maximum array subscript> : <X array> , <Y array>

- The *array* variables must be *real*.
- The line may be specified with a SET LINE STYLE statement and/or SET COLOR statement.
- The statement begins with the X(0),Y(0) element. Any single array is limited to 72 elements so that the maximum array subscript cannot exceed 71. If more points are required, additional arrays must be used.

---

estimated sales with another. In it we use the MAT FILL statement which is similar to the MAT MARKER and MAT PLOT statements but which fills in the area defined by the matrix.

PROGRAM 15-13   **CHART3.BAS**   **[Compiler: Graphics]**

Final Bar Chart in Three Colors

Copyright 1984, 1985, Compulit, Inc.

```
        INTEGER   H, I, J, K
        STRING    VALUE
        REAL      YEAR, XP, YP, XE, YE
        GRAPHIC OPEN 1
        CLEAR
        SET WINDOW 0,100,0,100
\               Procedure for the instruction screen
        SET CHARACTER HEIGHT 0
        PLOT (0,0),(0,100),(100,100),(100,0),(0,0)
        PLOT (10,10),(10,90),(90,90),(90,10),(10,10)
        SET COLOR 2
        GRAPHIC PRINT AT (4,75): \
            "THIS PROGRAM DISPLAYS SEVERAL SCREENS"
        GRAPHIC PRINT AT (15,55): \
            "PRESS ANY LETTER TO CONTINUE"
        GRAPHIC PRINT AT (25,35): \
            "TO THE NEXT SCREEN"
        H = INKEY
\               Printout of title, heading and footnote
        CLEAR
        SET COLOR 1
        GRAPHIC PRINT AT (25,95): "VUILNIS Fast Food Sales"
        GRAPHIC PRINT AT (0,90):  "Million"
        GRAPHIC PRINT AT (82,2):  "Est."
\               Plot of x-axis and y-axis
        PLOT (20,90),(20,20),(90,20)
\               Placement of tick marks on graph
        FOR I = 30 TO 90 STEP 10
            PLOT (18,I),(20,I)
            PLOT (I,18),(I,20)
```

(continues)

```
      NEXT
\              Creation of y-scale labels
      SET JUSTIFY 1, .5
      FOR I = 20 TO 80 STEP 20
            K = I / 10 - 2
            VALUE = STR$(K)
            GRAPHIC PRINT AT (13,I): VALUE
      NEXT
\              Creation of x-scale labels
      SET JUSTIFY .5, 1
      YEAR = 80
      FOR I = 30 TO 90 STEP 20
            VALUE = "'" + STR$(YEAR)
            GRAPHIC PRINT AT (I-5,12): VALUE
            YEAR = YEAR + 2
      NEXT
      SET JUSTIFY 0, 0
\              Data for existing sales
      DIM XP(14), YP(14)
      XP(0)  = 20:   YP(0)  = 20
      XP(1)  = 20:   YP(1)  = 25
      XP(2)  = 30:   YP(2)  = 25
      XP(3)  = 30:   YP(3)  = 33
      XP(4)  = 40:   YP(4)  = 33
      XP(5)  = 40:   YP(5)  = 42
      XP(6)  = 50:   YP(6)  = 42
      XP(7)  = 50:   YP(7)  = 53
      XP(8)  = 60:   YP(8)  = 53
      XP(9)  = 60:   YP(9)  = 65
      XP(10) = 70:   YP(10) = 65
      XP(11) = 70:   YP(11) = 76
      XP(12) = 80:   YP(12) = 76
      XP(13) = 80:   YP(13) = 20
\              Data for estimated sales
      DIM XE(3), YE(3)
      XE(0)  = 80:   YE(0)  = 20
      XE(1)  = 80:   YE(1)  = 90
      XE(2)  = 90:   YE(2)  = 90
      XE(3)  = 90:   YE(3)  = 20
\              Fill-in of existing sales bars in color
      SET COLOR 3
      MAT FILL 13: XP, YP
\              Change color and fill-in estimated sales
      SET COLOR 2
      MAT FILL  3: XE, YE
      H = INKEY
      GRAPHIC CLOSE
      END
```

The filled area would appear in color on the console screen with a color monitor or can be plotted in color with a plotter. Matrix dot printers that support 12 character sizes from 7 to 84 pixels in height can support six hatch patterns as shown in **Figure 15-11**:

- Vertical lines
- Horizontal lines
- +45 degree lines
- −45 degree lines
- Both vertical and horizontal crosshatch
- Both +45 and −45 degree crosshatch

The output from Program 15-13 would be a bar chart and would appear as shown in **Figure 15-12**. We have used hatch patterns since the printing is in black-and-white.

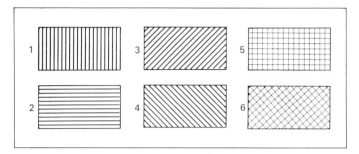

FIGURE 15-11 Six Hatch Patterns for Black-and-White Matrix Dot Output

---

LANGUAGE CODING RULE

The **MAT FILL** graphics statement draws a filled polygon using X and Y array coordinates.

> **MAT FILL** <maximum array subscript> : <X array> , <Y array>

- The values used in the array are *real*.
- The color of the filled polygon can be changed by using a SET COLOR statement.
- The statement begins with the X(0),Y(0) element. Any single array is limited to 72 elements so that the maximum array subscript cannot exceed 71. If more points are required, additional arrays must be used.

Changing Chart Shapes

Changing the ratio between the lengths of the X- and Y-axes often creates a different view of the same chart. **Program 15-14**, CHART4.BAS, permits the user to obtain different size X- and Y-scales by using the VIEWPORT statement.

The inputs into this program are the variables that are part of the VIEWPORT statement, namely, the lower and upper limits of the X-axis and the lower and upper limits of the Y-axis. The statement is

```
SET VIEWPORT XL, XH, YL, YH
```

where:

    XL   is the lower limit of the X-axis or left side of the screen
    XH   is the upper limit of the X-axis or right side of the screen

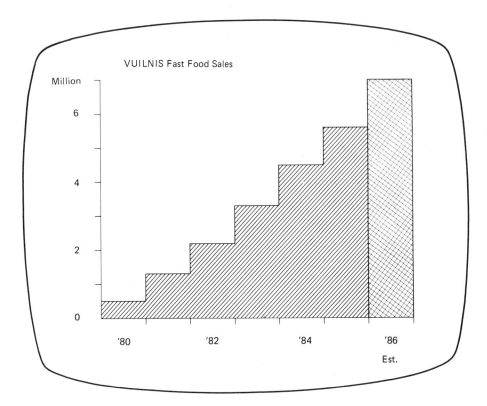

FIGURE 15-12   Final Chart Output of CHART3.BAS

YL   is the lower limit of the Y-axis or bottom of the screen
YH   is the upper limit of the Y-axis or top of the screen

Since these values must range between 0.0 and 1.0 and an entry error would result in aborting the program, two verification lines have been included in the program:

```
IF XL < 0 OR XH > 1 OR YL < 0 OR YH > 1 THEN \
        PRINT BELL:   GOTO 26
IF XL > XH OR YL > YH THEN \
        PRINT BELL:   GOTO 26
```

The first IF statement verifies that neither XL nor YL is less than zero and neither XH nor YH is greater than one. The second IF line checks to see that the lower limits of X and Y are below their respective upper limits.

PROGRAM 15-14   **CHART4.BAS**   **[Compiler: Graphics]**

Final Bar Chart with Different Viewports

Copyright 1984, 1985, Compulit, Inc.

```
        INTEGER  H, I, J, K
        STRING   VALUE, AN, BELL
        REAL     YEAR, XL, XH, YL, YH, XP, YP, XE, YE
        BELL = CHR$(07)
        GRAPHIC OPEN 1
        CLEAR
        SET WINDOW 0,100,0,100
\            Procedure for the instruction screen
        SET CHARACTER HEIGHT 0
        PLOT (0,0),(0,100),(100,100),(100,0),(0,0)
        PLOT (10,10),(10,90),(90,90),(90,10),(10,10)
        SET COLOR 2
        GRAPHIC PRINT AT (4,75): \
            "THIS PROGRAM DISPLAYS SEVERAL SCREENS"
        GRAPHIC PRINT AT (15,55): \
            "PRESS ANY LETTER TO CONTINUE"
        GRAPHIC PRINT AT (25,35): \
            "TO THE NEXT SCREEN"
        H = INKEY
\            Input of viewport limits
26      CLEAR
        PRINT "      INPUT VIEWPORT LIMITS": PRINT
        PRINT "Decimal data between 0.0 and 1.0": PRINT
        INPUT "LEFT:    Lower  X-value   "; XL
        INPUT "RIGHT:   Higher X-value   "; XH
        INPUT "BOTTOM:  Lower  Y-value   "; YL
        INPUT "TOP:     Higher Y-value   "; YH
        IF XL > 1 OR XH > 1 OR YL > 1 OR YH > 1 THEN \
            PRINT BELL:   GOTO 26
        IF XL < 0 OR XH < 0 OR YL < 0 OR YH < 0 THEN \
            PRINT BELL:   GOTO 26
        SET VIEWPORT  XL, XH, YL, YH
        CLEAR
        SET COLOR 1
\            Plot of x-axis and y-axis
        SET JUSTIFY 0, 0
        PLOT (20,90),(20,20),(90,20)
\            Place tick marks on graph
        FOR I = 30 TO 90 STEP 10
            PLOT (18,I),(20,I)
            PLOT (I,18),(I,20)
        NEXT
\            Restore justify and change color
        SET JUSTIFY 0,0
        SET COLOR 3
\            Data for existing sales
        DIM XP(13), YP(13)
        XP(0)  = 20:  YP(0)  = 20
        XP(1)  = 20:  YP(1)  = 25
        XP(2)  = 30:  YP(2)  = 25
        XP(3)  = 30:  YP(3)  = 33
        XP(4)  = 40:  YP(4)  = 33
        XP(5)  = 40:  YP(5)  = 42
        XP(6)  = 50:  YP(6)  = 42
        XP(7)  = 50:  YP(7)  = 53
        XP(8)  = 60:  YP(8)  = 53
        XP(9)  = 60:  YP(9)  = 65
        XP(10) = 70:  YP(10) = 65
        XP(11) = 70:  YP(11) = 76
        XP(12) = 80:  YP(12) = 76
        XP(13) = 80:  YP(13) = 20
\            Plot of matrix of existing sales
        MAT FILL 13: XP, YP
\            Data for estimated sales
        SET COLOR 2
```

(continues)

```
DIM XE(3), YE(3)
XE(Ø)  = 8Ø:  YE(Ø)  = 2Ø
XE(1)  = 8Ø:  YE(1)  = 9Ø
XE(2)  = 9Ø:  YE(2)  = 9Ø
XE(3)  = 9Ø:  YE(3)  = 2Ø
\              Plot of matrix of estimated sales
MAT FILL 3: XE, YE
H = INKEY
CLEAR
PRINT "     ANOTHER VIEWPORT TEST?"
INPUT "Answer YES or NO    "; AN
IF UCASE$(AN) = "YES" THEN 26
GRAPHIC CLOSE
END
```

If the VIEWPORT is set with XL and YL equal to 0.25 and XH and YH equal to 0.75, the program produces a graph in the center of the console screen that is one-half the size of that produced by Program 15-14. With the X-axis set at 0 and 1 and the Y-axis at 0.3 and 0.7, the program produces a short elongated graph of the same data. Conversely, with the X-axis set at 0.3 and 0.7 and the Y-axis at 0 and 1, the graph displayed is tall and narrow. **Figure 15-13** and **Figure 15-14** are sample output from the program CHART4.BAS. The former is a squat, elongated graph of the data used in Figure 15-12 whereas the latter, using the same data, produces a compact, tall graph.

The **CLIP** statement can be used to remove graphic segments that would extend outside the limits of the current window. Since only part of the copy would have been removed from the CHART program, we decided to delete the head and the legends from Program 15-14 for this demonstration.

FUN AND GAMES WITH THE GRAPHIC INPUT STATEMENT

The **GRAPHIC INPUT** statement is a powerful tool in graphics programming and it is also useful for fun and games. This statement permits the user to position the graphic cursor on the console screen and store the pair of coordinates as part of the program. Instead of using graph paper to de-

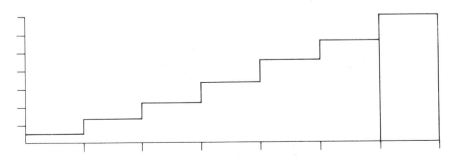

FIGURE 15-13   CHART4.BAS Output: Compact Vertical and Expanded Horizontal Scales

termine the coordinates for the bar chart in Program 15-13, it would have been possible to plot a grid scale as part of the graph and enter the sales values with a GRAPHIC INPUT statement.

Invoking the statement permits the user to move the graphics cursor to

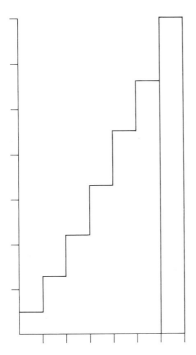

FIGURE 15-14   CHART4.BAS Output: Expanded Vertical and Compact
Horizontal   Scales

LANGUAGE CODING RULE

The **CLIP** statement in graphics edits portions of line segments that extend outside the range of the WINDOW.

SET CLIP "ON"

or

SET CLIP "OFF"

- To determine the current status of CLIP we use this statement:

ASK CLIP <string variable>

- If you set the CLIP "ON" you will avoid possible overlays of graphic data that the software and/or hardware requires to operate.

any part of the screen. For small incremental movements, the NUM LOCK key should be depressed. Otherwise, each press of an arrow key moves the cursor about 5 units with a WINDOW defined at 0, 100, 0, 100. When the user depresses any key other than the arrow keys or the "home" key, the computer records the X- and Y-coordinates of the graphics cursor.

LANGUAGE CODING RULE

The **GRAPHIC INPUT** statement permits the user to position the graphics cursor and the computer then stores the X- and Y-coordinates of that position in its memory.

GRAPHIC INPUT <X variable> , <Y variable> , <string variable>

- The X variable represents the X-coordinate and the Y variable, the Y-coordinate. Both must be *real* variables. Once the graphics cursor is positioned, striking any key will send that key's character code as the necessary string variable for this statement.
- To limit the movement of the graphics cursor to small increments, lock the NUM LOCK key.

Program 15-15, TARGET.BAS, illustrates the use of the GRAPHIC INPUT statement. Instead of the conventional business programs used in this book, we have included a small game, **"Spaceship and Clones."** The object of the game is to position the graphics cursor over the target in order to destroy it. There are three problems:

1. In addition to the spaceship target there are 20 clones so that the player is not certain which one is the target.
2. If the player hits a clone, its explosion is great enough to destroy the player's spaceship.
3. The target is "hidden" in a complex matrix marker which extends beyond its assigned X- and Y-coordinates; there are 25 pixel points in the target and only one is the assigned coordinate.

If the target or clone is not hit, the X- and Y-coordinates are displayed on the screen. Using X for the X-coordinate and Y for the Y-coordinate of the GRAPHIC INPUT statement, we can display their values with the following statements:

```
GRAPHIC PRINT AT (10,50): "YOU WERE AT: "
LOCATION = "X-coordinate: " + STR$(X)
GRAPHIC PRINT AT (10,40): LOCATION
LOCATION = "Y-coordinate: " + STR$(Y)
GRAPHIC PRINT AT (10,30): LOCATION
```

LOCATION has to be defined as a string and X and Y are real variables.

When the GRAPHIC INPUT statement is used the cursor position will most often be a decimal value with a fractional part. Since whole numbers are used to place markers with a SET WINDOW 0, 100, 0, 100 the fractional part must be removed with an INT function:

```
X = INT (X + 0.5)
Y = INT (Y + 0.5)
```

This is true even with a SET WINDOW of 0, 1, 0, 1 where the marker position would be given in decimal form, for example as 0.15,0.82 for a marker. Using the GRAPHIC INPUT statement it is possible to obtain an X-coordinate of 0.149982761. An IF statement comparison with 0.15 would indicate that the two values were *not* equal. Therefore, always transform the X and Y values from a GRAPHIC INPUT statement so that they are usable in the program.

The program illustrates how the moving cursor can be used to select items in a program menu. Even with SET WINDOW 0, 100, 0, 100 it is possible to create a box one-unit square which is easily covered by the graphics cursor. Instead of turning the screen red, ringing the bell, and notifying the player that the player's spaceship has been destroyed, the program can branch to any procedure desired.

PROGRAM 15-15   TARGET.BAS   [Compiler: Graphics]

Spaceship and Clone Game: GRAPHIC INPUT Statement

Copyright 1984, 1985, Compulit, Inc.

```
      INTEGER  H, I
      STRING   TK, AN, BELL, LOCATION
      REAL     X, Y, TARX, TARY, XO, YO, XE, YE, TACX, TACY, TADX, TADY
      BELL = CHR$(07)
      GRAPHIC OPEN 1
      SET WINDOW 0,100,0,100
\            Array for hit/explode screen display
      DIM XO(4), YO(4)
      XO(0) = 0  : YO(0) = 0  : XO(1) = 0  : YO(1) = 100
      XO(2) = 100: YO(2) = 100: XO(3) = 100: YO(3) = 0
      XO(4) = 0  :  YO(4) = 0
\            Procedure for the opening screen
      SET COLOR 2
      CLEAR
      GRAPHIC PRINT AT (10,95): "WELCOME  TO"
      GRAPHIC PRINT AT (5,85): "SPACESHIP  AND  CLONE"
      GRAPHIC PRINT AT (5,65): "Only one is an enemy spaceship;"
      GRAPHIC PRINT AT (5,55): "the others are clones.  If you"
      GRAPHIC PRINT AT (5,45): "hit a clone your spaceship"
      GRAPHIC PRINT AT (5,35): "will explode.  The spaceship and"
      GRAPHIC PRINT AT (5,25): "the clones are hidden in clouds."
      GRAPHIC PRINT AT (5,05): "Press any letter to continue."
      H = INKEY
\            Procedure for the instruction screen
      CLEAR
      GRAPHIC PRINT AT (5,95): "THE GRAPHIC INPUT STATEMENT"
      GRAPHIC PRINT AT (5,80): "Use cursor arrows to move"
```

(continues)

```
            GRAPHIC PRINT AT (5,70): "cursor to hit the target."
            GRAPHIC PRINT AT (5,60): "Press the letter H when the"
            GRAPHIC PRINT AT (5,50): "cursor is in proper position."
            GRAPHIC PRINT AT (5,20): "Press any letter to continue."
            H = INKEY
            CLEAR
            GRAPHIC PRINT AT (5,95): "TO CONTROL CURSOR MOVEMENT:"
            GRAPHIC PRINT AT (5,80): "1. Use cursor arrows on keyboard."
            GRAPHIC PRINT AT (5,65): "2. To make small incremental"
            GRAPHIC PRINT AT (5,55): "movements use NUM LOCK key."
            GRAPHIC PRINT AT (5,20): "Press any letter to continue."
            H = INKEY
\                   Arrays for target and clones
10          CLEAR
            DIM TARX(6), TARY(6), TACX(6), TACY(6), TADX(6), TADY(6)
            TARX(0) = 30: TARY(0) = 32:   TARX(1) = 43: TARY(1) = 82
            TARX(2) = 52: TARY(2) = 21:   TARX(3) = 71: TARY(3) = 69
            TARX(4) = 83: TARY(4) = 39:   TARX(5) = 17: TARY(5) = 40
            TARX(6) = 65: TARY(6) = 71:   TACX(0) = 20: TACY(0) = 61
            TACX(1) = 30: TACY(1) = 52:   TACX(2) = 45: TACY(2) = 60
            TACX(3) = 40: TACY(3) = 18:   TACX(4) = 55: TACY(4) = 60
            TACX(5) = 91: TACY(5) = 67:   TACX(6) = 88: TACY(6) = 88
            TADX(0) = 40: TADY(0) = 40:   TADX(1) = 55: TADY(1) = 42
            TADX(2) = 65: TADY(2) = 18:   TADX(3) = 40: TADY(3) = 70
            TADX(4) = 52: TADY(4) = 48:   TADX(5) = 95: TADY(5) = 95
            TADX(6) = 50: TADY(6) = 25
\                   Place target and clones on screen
            SET MARKER TYPE 7
            SET COLOR 1
            MAT MARKER 6: TARX, TARY
            SET COLOR 2
            MAT MARKER 6: TACX, TACY
            SET COLOR 3
            MAT MARKER 6: TADX, TADY
\                   Graphic input statement to control cursor movement
            SET COLOR 4
            GRAPHIC INPUT X, Y, TK
\                   Truncation of X and Y variables
            X = INT(X + 0.05)
            Y = INT(Y + 0.05)
\                   Verification of target strike
            IF X = 52 AND Y = 21 THEN 20
            IF X = 30 AND Y = 32 OR X = 43 AND Y = 82 THEN 30
            IF X = 71 AND Y = 69 OR X = 83 AND Y = 39 THEN 30
            IF X = 17 AND Y = 40 OR X = 75 AND Y = 71 THEN 30
            IF X = 20 AND Y = 61 OR X = 30 AND Y = 52 THEN 30
            IF X = 45 AND Y = 60 OR X = 40 AND Y = 18 THEN 30
            IF X = 91 AND Y = 67 OR X = 88 AND Y = 88 THEN 30
            IF X = 55 AND Y = 60 OR X = 40 AND Y = 40 THEN 30
            IF X = 55 AND Y = 42 OR X = 65 AND Y = 18 THEN 30
            IF X = 40 AND Y = 70 OR X = 52 AND Y = 48 THEN 30
            IF X = 95 AND Y = 95 OR X = 50 AND Y = 25 THEN 30
            GOTO 40
\                   Procedure if target is hit
20          CLEAR
            PRINT BELL
            SET COLOR 2
            MAT FILL 4: XO, YO
            SET COLOR 3
            GRAPHIC PRINT AT (10,50): "HIT .... YOU HIT IT .... HIT"
            GOTO 50
\                   Procedure if a clone is hit
30          CLEAR
            FOR I = 1 TO 10
                    PRINT BELL
            NEXT
            SET COLOR 1
            MAT FILL 4: XO, YO
            SET COLOR 3
            GRAPHIC PRINT AT (10,55): "YOU HIT A CLONE - YOUR"
            GRAPHIC PRINT AT (10,45): "SPACESHIP IS DESTROYED"
            GOTO 50
\                   Procedure if target is missed
```

```
40       SET COLOR 2
         GRAPHIC PRINT AT (10,95): "YOU MISSED THE TARGET"
         GRAPHIC PRINT AT (10,50): "YOU WERE AT:"
         LOCATION = "X-COORDINATE: " + STR$(X)
         GRAPHIC PRINT AT (10,40): LOCATION
         LOCATION = "Y-COORDINATE: " + STR$(Y)
         GRAPHIC PRINT AT (10,30): LOCATION
\              Restart procedure
50       SET COLOR 3
         GRAPHIC PRINT AT (5,5): "Another try?   YES or NO?"
         INPUT ""; AN
         IF UCASE$(AN) = "YES" THEN 10
         GRAPHIC CLOSE
         END
```

Figure 15-15 shows three of the console screens produced by this program for the game. The actual target screen is shown in Figure 15-16.

This program is static in that the target position has been defined. If you have located the target, try a simple modification. Use the random generator function, RDN, to create the pairs of coordinates for the clones and to select the coordinates for the target spaceship. Remember to include in the

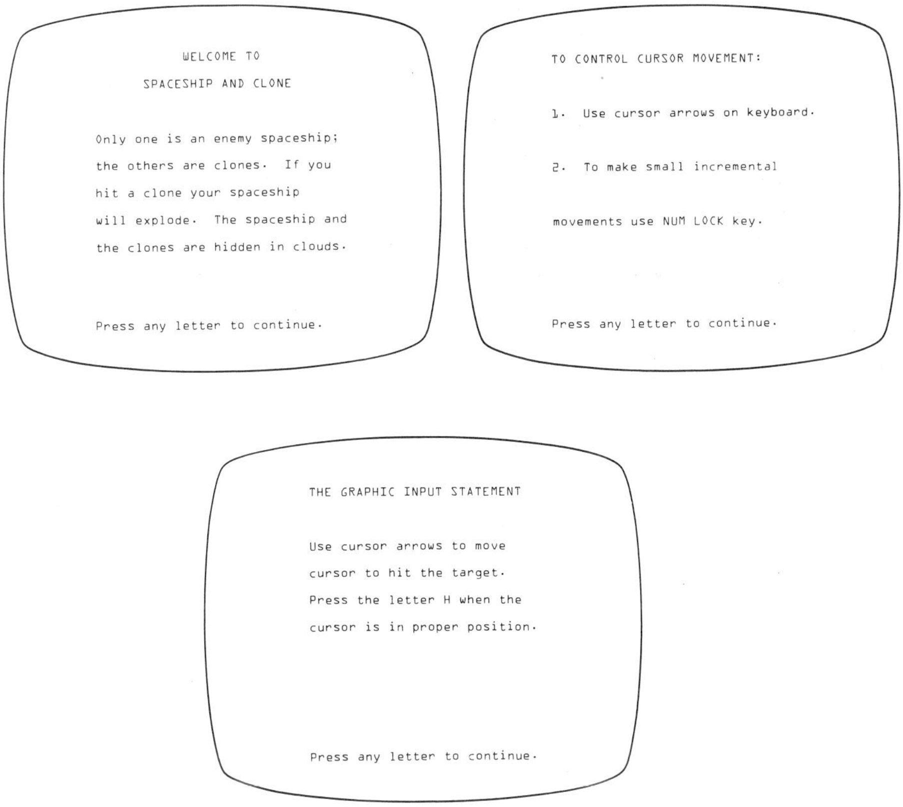

FIGURE 15-15   Three Screens from Game Program, TARGET.BAS

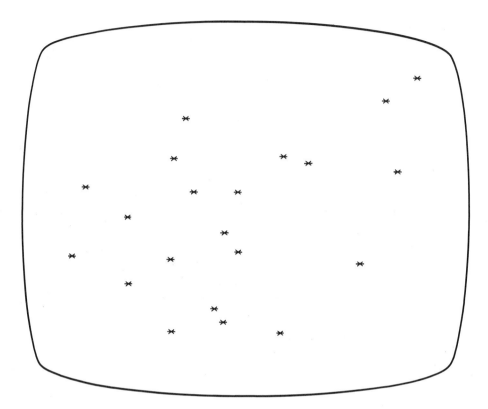

FIGURE 15-16 Spaceship and Clones Screen from TARGET.BAS

program a verification routine to determine if any clone overlaps another clone or the target, which is randomly assigned. There are many games you can program with GSX-86. Let the games begin!

APPENDIX A

Reserved Word List

It is recognized that a program may *not* contain a reserved word used as a variable name. However, the list of reserved words for the non-compiler version of CBASIC is different from that for the compiler versions, CB80 and CB86. Even among the compiler versions, there are differences depending upon the release number and whether the graphics extention routines are included.

To permit portability from one system to another and from non-compiler to compiler version, we recommend that none of the reserved words in this extended list be used as variable names.

ABS	CLIP	DIM	GET
AND	CLOSE	ELSE	GO
ANGLE	COLOR	END	GOSUB
AS	COMMAND$	ERR	GOTO
ASC	COMMON	ERRL	GRAPHIC
ASK	CONCHAR%	ERROR	GT
AT	CONSOLE	ERRX	HEIGHT
ATTACH	CONSTAT%	EQ	IF
ATN	COS	EXP	INITIALIZE
BEAM	COUNT	EXTERNAL	INKEY
BOUNDS	CREATE	FEND	INP
BUFF	DATA	FILE	INPUT
CALL	DATE$	FILL	INT
CHAIN	DEF	FLOAT	INT%
CHARACTER	DELETE	FOR	INTEGER
CHR$	DETACH	FRE	JUSTIFY
CLEAR	DEVICE	GE	LE

(continues)

LEFT$	ON	REMARK	TAB
LEN	OPEN	RENAME	TAN
LET	OR	RESTORE	TEXT
LINE	OUT	RETURN	THEN
LOCK	PEEK	RIGHT$	TIME$
LOCKED	PLOT	RND	TO
LOG	POKE	SADD	TYPE
LPRINTER	POS	SET	UCASE$
LT	POSITION	SGN	UNLOCK
MARKER	PRINT	SHIFT	UNLOCKED
MAT	PUBLIC	SIN	USING
MATCH	PUT	SQR	VAL
MFRE	RANDOMIZE	STEP	VARPTR
MID$	READ	STOP	VIEWPORT
MOD	READONLY	STR$	WEND
MODE	REAL	STRING	WHILE
NE	RECL	STRING$	WIDTH
NEXT	RECS	STYLE	WINDOW
NOT	REM	SUB	XOR

APPENDIX B

Mathematical Functions and Their Application

Some functions have not been fully explained in the text since they are used primarily for mathematical manipulation. A concise overview of these function is included in this Appendix.

NOTE: In examples of statements under Structure, **N** is either a numeric value or a numeric expression.

FUNCTION	STRUCTURE	COMMENTS
ABS	X = ABS(N)	Returns the absolute value of a real number or expression. Integers are converted into real.
ATN	Y = ATN(N)	N is the tangent of an angle. Function returns the arctangent or inverse of the tangent in radians.
COS	Z = COS(N)	N must be expressed in radians. Function returns the cosine of N as a real value.
EXP	C = EXP(N)	Returns the constant *e* raised to an exponent, expressed as a real value.
FLOAT	H = FLOAT(N)	Converts an integer value or expression to a floating-point or real value. Caution: when used with a real value, it first converts the value to an integer and then to a real.

(continues)

FUNCTION	STRUCTURE	COMMENTS
INT	U = INT(N)	Returns the integer portion of a number as a real value, truncating the fractional portion of the number or expression.
INT%	K = INT%(N)	Returns the integer portion of a number as an integer, truncating the fractional portion if N is a real number or real expression.
LOG	Q = LOG(N)	Returns the natural logarithm of either an integer or real number or expression. Caution: N must be positive and greater than zero. [See note below.]
MOD	D = MOD(N,M)	Function divides N by M and returns the remainder as an integer value. Real values convert to integers.
RND	R = RND	Function generates and returns a random value that is a decimal uniformly distributed between zero and one.
SIN	E = SIN(N)	N must be expressed in radians. Function returns the sine of N as a real value.
TAN	F = TAN(N)	N must be expressed in radians. Function returns the tangent of N as a real value.

To convert a *natural* logarithm to a *common* logarithm, multiply the natural logarithm by 0.4342944819; for example, COM.LOG.N = LOG(N) * 0.4342944819.

APPENDIX C

ASCII Code Table

The following table contains the full ASCII character set, a total of 256 that are available for systems capable of handling graphics.

The first 31 characters are **Control Characters** that can be used for communications and control functions. They are produced by simultaneously pressing the *control* key [CTRL] and the corresponding key shown in the control character column. They can also be produced by entering the ASCII decimal value in a CBASIC program after a PRINT statement in the following form:

```
PRINT CHR$( <decimal ASCII value> )
```

Control characters are used by the CPU to communicate with peripherals, such as a monitor or printer, and for communications via a modem. In communications, for example, some of the abbreviations noted have the following meaning:

ACK   Acknowledge
STX   Start of the text
ETX   End of the text
EOT   End of transmission
DC1   X-ON communications protocol
DC3   X-OFF communications protocol
NAK   Negative acknowledge

From a control function viewpoint, some of the abbreviations are defined as:

VT   Home [move cursor to upper left corner of screen]
HT   Horizontal tab
FF   Form feed [start a new page]
CR   Carriage return [start a new line]

BS   Backspace
FS   Cursor right [move cursor one position to the right]
BEL   Beep [sound bell]

The next 94 characters are used to produce all the digits, the alphabetic characters in both capitals and lower case and the special symbols, such as a blank space, +, #, (, :, <, /, $, etc.

The remaining 130 characters produce graphics characters and special symbols. These include, for example, ¢, £, ∞, √, Σ, ä, and ö.

ASCII CHARACTER	CONTROL CHARACTER	ASCII DECIMAL	BINARY VALUE	HEXADECIMAL VALUE
(null)	NUL [@]	000	00000000	00
☺	SOH [A]	001	00000001	01
☻	STX [B]	002	00000010	02
♥	ETX [C]	003	00000011	03
♦	EOT [D]	004	00000100	04
♣	ENQ [E]	005	00000101	05
♠	ACK [F]	006	00000110	06
(beep)	BEL [G]	007	00000111	07
■	BS [H]	008	00001000	08
(tab)	HT [I]	009	00001001	09
(line feed)	LF [J]	010	00001010	0A
(home)	VT [K]	011	00001011	0B
(form feed)	FF [L]	012	00001100	0C
(carriage return)	CR [M]	013	00001101	0D
♫	SO [N]	014	00001110	0E
☼	SI [O]	015	00001111	0F
▶	DLE [P]	016	00010000	10
◀	DC1 [Q]	017	00010001	11
↕	DC2 [R]	018	00010010	12
‼	DC3 [S]	019	00010011	13
¶	DC4 [T]	020	00010100	14
§	NAK [U]	021	00010101	15
▬	SYN [V]	022	00010110	16
↕	ETB [W]	023	00010111	17
↑	CAN [X]	024	00011000	18
↓	EM [Y]	025	00011001	19
→	SUB [Z]	026	00011010	1A
←	ESC [[]	027	00011011	1B
(cursor right)	FS [\]	028	00011100	1C
(cursor left)	GS []]	029	00011101	1D
(cursor up)	RS [^]	030	00011110	1E
(cursor down)	US [-]	031	00011111	1F

(continues)

ASCII CHARACTER	ASCII DECIMAL	BINARY VALUE	HEXADECIMAL VALUE
\<space\>	32	0100000	20
!	33	0100001	21
"	34	0100010	22
#	35	0100011	23
$	36	0100100	24
%	37	0100101	25
&	38	0100110	26
'	39	0100111	27
(	40	0101000	28
)	41	0101001	29
*	42	0101010	2A
+	43	0101011	2B
,	44	0101100	2C
−	45	0101101	2D
.	46	0101110	2E
/	47	0101111	2F
0	48	0110000	30
1	49	0110001	31
2	50	0110010	32
3	51	0110011	33
4	52	0110100	34
5	53	0110101	35
6	54	0110110	36
7	55	0110111	37
8	56	0111000	38
9	57	0111001	39
:	58	0111010	3A
;	59	0111011	3B
<	60	0111100	3C
=	61	0111101	3D
>	62	0111110	3E
?	63	0111111	3F
@	64	01000000	40
A	65	01000001	41
B	66	01000010	42
C	67	01000011	43
D	68	01000100	44
E	69	01000101	45
F	70	01000110	46
G	71	01000111	47
H	72	01001000	48
I	73	01001001	49
J	74	01001010	4A
K	75	01001011	4B

(continues)

ASCII CHARACTER	ASCII DECIMAL	BINARY VALUE	HEXADECIMAL VALUE
L	76	01001100	4C
M	77	01001101	4D
N	78	01001110	4E
O	79	01001111	4F
P	80	01010000	50
Q	81	01010001	51
R	82	01010010	52
S	83	01010011	53
T	84	01010100	54
U	85	01010101	55
V	86	01010110	56
W	87	01010111	57
X	88	01011000	58
Y	89	01011001	59
Z	90	01011010	5A
[	91	01011011	5B
\	92	01011100	5C
]	93	01011101	5D
^	94	01011110	5E
_	95	01011111	5F
`	96	01100000	60
a	97	01100001	61
b	98	01100010	62
c	99	01100011	63
d	100	01100100	64
e	101	01100101	65
f	102	01100110	66
g	103	01100111	67
h	104	01101000	68
i	105	01101001	69
j	106	01101010	6A
k	107	01101011	6B
l	108	01101100	6C
m	109	01101101	6D
n	110	01101110	6E
o	111	01101111	6F
p	112	01110000	70
q	113	01110001	71
r	114	01110010	72
s	115	01110011	73
t	116	01110100	74
u	117	01110101	75
v	118	01110110	76
w	119	01110111	77

(continues)

ASCII CHARACTER	ASCII DECIMAL	BINARY VALUE	HEXADECIMAL VALUE
x	120	01111000	78
y	121	01111001	79
z	122	01111010	7A
{	123	01111011	7B
|	124	01111100	7C
}	125	01111101	7D
~	126	01111110	7E
⌂	127	01111111	7F

ASCII CHARACTER	ASCII DECIMAL	BINARY VALUE	HEXADECIMAL VALUE
Ç	128	10000000	80
ü	129	10000001	81
é	130	10000010	82
â	131	10000011	83
ä	132	10000100	84
à	133	10000101	85
å	134	10000110	86
ç	135	10000111	87
ê	136	10001000	88
ë	137	10001001	89
è	138	10001010	8A
ï	139	10001011	8B
î	140	10001100	8C
ì	141	10001101	8D
Ä	142	10001110	8E
Å	143	10001111	8F
É	144	10010000	90
æ	145	10010001	91
Æ	146	10010010	92
ô	147	10010011	93
ö	148	10010100	94
ò	149	10010101	95
û	150	10010110	96
ù	151	10010111	97
ÿ	152	10011000	98
Ö	153	10011001	99
Ü	154	10011010	9A
¢	155	10011011	9B
£	156	10011100	9C
¥	157	10011101	9D

(continues)

ASCII CHARACTER	ASCII DECIMAL	BINARY VALUE	HEXADECIMAL VALUE
Pt	158	10011110	9E
∫	159	10011111	9F
á	160	10100000	A0
í	161	10100001	A1
ó	162	10100010	A2
ú	163	10100011	A3
ñ	164	10100100	A4
Ñ	165	10100101	A5
a	166	10100110	A6
o	167	10100111	A7
¿	168	10101000	A8
⌐	169	10101001	A9
¬	170	10101010	AA
½	171	10101011	AB
¼	172	10101100	AC
¡	173	10101101	AD
<<	174	10101110	AE
>>	175	10101111	AF
░	176	10110000	B0
▒	177	10110001	B1
▓	178	10110010	B2
│	179	10110011	B3
┤	180	10110100	B4
╡	181	10110101	B5
╢	182	10110110	B6
╖	183	10110111	B7
╕	184	10111000	B8
╣	185	10111001	B9
║	186	10111010	BA
╗	187	10111011	BB
╝	188	10111100	BC
╜	189	10111101	BD
╛	190	10111110	BE
┐	191	10111111	BF
└	192	11000000	C0
┴	193	11000001	C1
┬	194	11000010	C2
├	195	11000011	C3
─	196	11000100	C4
+	197	11000101	C5
╞	198	11000110	C6
╟	199	11000111	C7
╚	200	11001000	C8
╔	201	11001001	C9

(continues)

ASCII CHARACTER	ASCII DECIMAL	BINARY VALUE	HEXADECIMAL VALUE
⊥	202	11001010	CA
⊤	203	11001011	CB
╟	204	11001100	CC
=	205	11001101	CD
╬	206	11001110	CE
⊥	207	11001111	CF
⊥	208	11010000	D0
⊤	209	11010001	D1
╥	210	11010010	D2
╙	211	11010011	D3
╘	212	11010100	D4
╒	213	11010101	D5
╓	214	11010110	D6
╫	215	11010111	D7
╪	216	11011000	D8
┘	217	11011001	D9
┌	218	11011010	DA
█	219	11011011	DB
▄	220	11011100	DC
▌	221	11011101	DD
▐	222	11011110	DE
▀	223	11011111	DF
α	224	11100000	E0
ß	225	11100001	E1
Γ	226	11100010	E2
π	227	11100011	E3
Σ	228	11100100	E4
σ	229	11100101	E5
μ	230	11100110	E6
τ	231	11100111	E7
Φ	232	11101000	E8
θ	233	11101001	E9
Ω	234	11101010	EA
δ	235	11101011	EB
∞	236	11101100	EC
∅	237	11101101	ED
∈	238	11101110	EE
∩	239	11101111	EF
≡	240	11110000	F0
±	241	11110001	F1
≥	242	11110010	F2
≤	243	11110011	F3
⌠	244	11110100	F4
⌡	245	11110101	F5

(continues)

ASCII CHARACTER	ASCII DECIMAL	BINARY VALUE	HEXADECIMAL VALUE
$\div$	246	11110110	F6
$\approx$	247	11110111	F7
$^\circ$	248	11111000	F8
$\bullet$	249	11111001	F9
$\cdot$	250	11111010	FA
$\sqrt{}$	251	11111011	FB
^{n}	252	11111100	FC
^{2}	253	11111101	FD
$\blacksquare$	254	11111110	FE
(blank 'FF')	255	11111111	FF

APPENDIX D

Compiler Version:
Error Messages

D-1   FILE SYSTEM AND MEMORY SPACE ERRORS

The compiler prints the following messages when a file system error or memory space error occurs. In each case, control returns to the operating system.

ERROR	MEANING
COULD NOT OPEN FILE: <filename>	The filename cannot be found in the file system directory.
%INCLUDES NESTED TOO DEEP: <filename>	The filename occurs in an %INCLUDE directive that exceeds the allowed nesting of %INCLUDE directives.
SYMBOL TABLE OVER-FLOW	The available memory for symbol table space has been exceeded. Break the program into modules or use shorter symbol names.
INVALID FILENAME: <filename>	The filename is not valid for your operating system.
DISK READ ERROR	The operating system reports a disk read error.
CREATE ERROR: <filename>	The file cannot be created. Normally this means there is no directory space on the disk.
DISK FULL	The operating system reports that no additional space is available to write temporary or output files. The directory is full or the disk is out of space.
INVALID COMMAND LINE	The command line is incorrect. The compiler prints a greater-than sign, >, one blank space, and all command line characters beginning with the first character in error. If no characters remain in the command line when an error occurs, the compiler does not print the > or the space.
MISSING SOURCE FILE-NAME	The command line processor reports that you did not specify a source file.
CLOSE OR DELETE ERROR	The operating system reports that it cannot close a file. This occurs if disks are switched during compilation.

If the compiler detects an internal failure, the following error message appears:

```
FATAL COMPILER ERROR XXX
NEAR SOURCE LINE ZZZZ
```

where XXX is a three-digit number. If the preceding error message occurs during compilation of your CBASIC program, contact the Digital Research Technical Support Center. Please report the three-digit number and the circumstances under which it occurs.

D-2   COMPILE-TIME ERRORS

The following error messages indicate the occurrence of compilation errors. Compilation error messages display within the source code listing. CB86 does not create the object file if a compilation error occurs.

ERROR	MEANING
1	Invalid character in the source program. The character is ignored.
2	Invalid string constant. The string is too long or contains a carriage return.
3	Invalid numeric constant. An integer constant of zero is assumed.
4	Undefined compiler directive. This source line is ignored.
5	The %INCLUDE directive is missing a filename. This source line is ignored.
6	Statements found after an END.
7	The program attempts to divide-by-zero in the evaluation of an integer constant expression, such as $I\% = 7/0$.
8	Variable used without being defined, and the U toggle used during compilation.
9	The DEF statement is not terminated by a carriage return. A carriage return is inserted.
10	A right parenthesis is missing from the parameter list. A right parenthesis is inserted.
11	A comma is missing in the parameter list. A comma is inserted.
12	An identifier is missing in the parameter list.
13	The same name is used twice in a parameter list.
14	A DEF statement occurs within a multiple-line function. Multiple-line functions cannot be nested. The statement is ignored.
15	A variable is missing.
16	The function name is missing following the keyword DEF. The DEF statement is ignored.

(continues)

ERROR	MEANING
17	A function name is used previously. The DEF statement is ignored.
18	A FEND statement is missing. A FEND is inserted.
19	There are too many parameters in a multiple-line function.
20	Inconsistent identifier usage. An identifier cannot be used as both a label and a variable.
21	Additional data exists in the source file following an END statement. This is the logical end of the program.
22	Data statements must begin on a new line. The remainder of this statement is treated as a remark.
23	There are no variables or function names in a declaration statement, or a reserved word appears in the list of identifiers.
24	A function name appears in a declaration within a multiple-line function other than the multiple-line function that defines this function name.
25	A function call has incorrect number of parameters.
26	A left parenthesis is missing. A left parenthesis is inserted.
27	Invalid mixed mode. The type of the expression is not permitted.
28	Unary operator cannot be used with this operand.
29	Function call has improper type of parameter.
30	Invalid symbol follows a variable, constant, or function reference.
31	This symbol cannot occur at this location in an expression. The symbol is ignored.
32	Operator is missing. Multiplication operator inserted.
33	Invalid symbol encountered in an expression. The symbol is ignored.
34	A right parenthesis is missing. A right parenthesis is inserted.
35	A subscripted variable is used with the incorrect number of subscripts.

(continues)

ERROR	MEANING
36	An identifier is used as a simple variable with previous usage as a subscripted variable.
37	An identifier is used as a subscripted variable with previous usage as an unsubscripted variable.
38	A string expression is used as a subscript in an array reference.
39	A constant is missing.
40	Invalid symbol found in declaration list. The symbol is skipped.
41	A carriage return is missing in a declaration statement. A carriage return is inserted.
42	A comma is missing in declaration list. A comma is inserted.
43	A common declaration cannot occur in a multiple-line function. The statement is ignored.
44	An identifier appears in a declaration twice in the main program or within the same multiple-line function.
45	The number of dimensions specified for an array exceeds the maximum number allowed. A value of one is used. This might generate additional errors in the program.
46	Right parenthesis is missing in the dimension specification within a declaration. A right parenthesis is inserted.
47	The same identifier is placed in COMMON twice.
48	An invalid subscripted variable reference encountered in a declaration statement. An integer constant is required. A value of 1 is used.
49	An invalid symbol found following a declaration, or the symbol in the first statement in the program is invalid. The symbol is ignored.
50	An invalid symbol encountered at the beginning of a statement or following a label.
51	An equal sign is missing in an assignment. An equal sign is inserted.
52	A name used as a label previously used at this level as either a label or variable.

(*continues*)

ERROR	MEANING
53	Unexpected symbol follows a simple statement. The symbol is ignored.
54	A statement is not terminated with a carriage return. Text is ignored until the next carriage return.
55	A function name is used in the left part of an assignment statement outside of a multiple-line function. Only when the function is being compiled can its name appear on the left of an assignment statement.
56	A predefined function name is used as the left part of an assignment statement.
57	In an IF statement, a THEN is missing. A THEN is inserted.
58	A WEND statement is missing. A WEND is inserted.
59	A carriage return or colon is missing at the end of a WHILE loop header.
60	In a FOR loop header, the index is missing. The compiler skips to end of this statement.
61	In a FOR loop header, a TO is missing. A TO is inserted.
62	An equal sign is missing in a FOR loop header assignment. An equal sign is inserted.
63	Carriage return or colon is missing at end of FOR loop header.
64	A NEXT statement is missing. A NEXT is inserted.
65	Not used.
66	The variable that follows NEXT does not match the FOR loop index.
67	NEXT statement encountered without a corresponding FOR loop header.
68	WEND statement encountered without a corresponding WHILE loop header.
69	FEND statement encountered without a corresponding DEF statement. This error indicates that the end of the source program was detected while within a multiple-line function.

(continues)

ERROR	MEANING
70	The PRINT USING string is not of type string.
71	A delimiter is missing in a PRINT statement. A comma is inserted.
72	A semicolon is missing in an INPUT prompt. A semicolon is inserted.
73	A delimiter is missing in an INPUT statement. A comma is inserted.
74	A semicolon is missing following a file reference. A semicolon is inserted.
75	The prompt in an INPUT statement is not of type string.
76	In an INPUT LINE statement, the variable following the keyword LINE is not a string variable.
77	In an INPUT statement, a comma is missing between variables. A comma is inserted.
78	The keyword AS is missing in an OPEN or CREATE statement. AS is inserted.
79	The filename in an OPEN or CREATE statement is not a string expression.
80	A delimiter is missing in a READ statement. A comma is inserted.
81	In a GOTO, GOSUB, or ON statement, a label is missing. This token can be an identifier previously used as a variable.
82	The label in a GOTO statement is not defined. If the label is used in a function, it must be defined in that function.
83	A delimiter is missing in a file READ statement. A comma is inserted.
84	In a READ LINE statement, the variable following the keyword LINE is not a string variable.
85	The label in an IF END statement is not defined.
86	A pound sign, #, is missing in an IF END statement. A pound sign is inserted.
87	A THEN is missing in an IF END statement. A THEN is inserted.

(continues)

ERROR	MEANING
88	In a PRINT statement, the semicolon is missing following a USING string. A semicolon is inserted.
89	In an ON statement, a GOTO or GOSUB is missing. A GOTO is assumed.
90	The index of a FOR loop header is of type string. The index must be an integer or real number.
91	The expression following the keyword TO in a FOR loop header is of type string. The expression must be an integer or real value.
92	The expression following the keyword STEP in a FOR loop header is of type string. The expression must be an integer or real value.
93	A variable in a DIM statement is defined previously as other than a subscripted variable.
94	An identifier is missing as an array name in a DIM statement. The entire statement is ignored.
95	A left parenthesis is missing in a DIM statement. A left parenthesis is inserted.
96	A right parenthesis is missing in a DIM statement. A right parenthesis is inserted.
97	The maximum number of dimensions allowed with a subscripted variable is exceeded.
98	A comma is missing in a POKE statement. A comma is inserted.
99	The index of a FOR loop header is not a simple variable.
100	In a CALL statement, a multiple-line function name is missing.
101	A file PRINT statement is terminated with a comma or semicolon.
102	A DIM statement is missing for this subscripted variable.
103	A comma is missing in the label list associated with an ON GOTO or ON GOSUB statement. A comma is inserted.
104	A GOTO is missing in an ON ERROR statement. A GOTO is inserted.

(continues)

ERROR	MEANING
105	A comma is missing in a PUT statement. A comma is inserted.
106	The expression in an IF statement is of type string. An integer or real expression is required.
107	The expression in a WHILE loop header is of type string. An integer or real expression is required.
108	In an OPEN or CREATE statement, the filename is missing.
109	In an OPEN or CREATE statement, the expression following the reserved word AS is missing.
110	A multiple-line function calls itself.
111	A semicolon separates expressions in a file PRINT statement. A comma is substituted for the semicolon.
112	A file PRINT statement does not have an expression list.
113	A TAB function is used in a file PRINT statement expression list.
114	Label used as a variable in a list of expressions.
115	A GO not followed by a TO or SUB. GOTO is assumed.
116	An OPEN or CREATE statement specifies both UNLOCKED and LOCKED access control.
117	A CREATE statement uses the READ-ONLY access control.

CBASIC Graphics Extension Error Messages

The following error messages indicate compilation errors that can occur during compilation of a graphics statement in a program. Compilation continues after the error is recorded. Errors 180 to 240 are reserved for use with the CBASIC Compiler graphics extension.

ERROR	MEANING
180	A left parenthesis is missing. A left parenthesis is inserted.
181	A right parenthesis is missing. A right parenthesis is inserted.
182	A comma is missing in a PLOT statement. A comma is inserted.
183	The keyword STYLE is missing in a SET or ASK statement. STYLE is inserted.
184	A comma is missing in a SET statement. A comma is inserted.
185	The keyword HEIGHT is missing in a SET or ASK CHARACTER statement. HEIGHT is inserted.
186	The keyword ANGLE is missing in a SET or ASK TEXT statement. ANGLE is inserted.
187	A comma is missing in a SET or ASK WINDOW statement. A comma is inserted.
188	A comma is missing in a SET or ASK VIEWPORT statement. A comma is inserted.
189	The keyword PAGE is missing in a SET statement. PAGE is inserted.
190	Not used.
191	The keyword COUNT is missing in a ASK STYLE statement. COUNT is inserted.
192	A comma is missing in an ASK statement. A comma is inserted.
193	Not used.
194	Not used.
195	The keyword COUNT is missing in a SET COLOR statement. COLOR is inserted.
196	Not used.
197	Not used.
198	Not used.
199	Not used.

(continues)

ERROR	MEANING
200	Not used.
201	Not used.
202	Not used.
203	A comma is missing in a GRAPHIC statement. A comma is inserted.
204	The keyword following GRAPHIC is unexpected. INPUT is inserted.
205	A left parenthesis is missing in a GRAPHIC statement. A left parenthesis is inserted.
206	A right parenthesis is missing in a GRAPHIC statement. A right parenthesis is inserted.
207	A colon is missing in a GRAPHIC statement. A colon is inserted.
208	The variable in an ASK statement is of type real or string. An integer variable is required.
209	The variable in an ASK statement is of type integer or string. A real variable is required.
210	The variable in an ASK statement is of type integer or real. A string variable is required.
211	Not used.
212	Not used.
213	Not used.
214	Not used.
215	Not used.
216	A comma is missing in a GRAPHIC statement. A comma is inserted.
217	The variable in a MAT statement is of type integer or string. A real variable is required.
218	Not used.

(continues)

ERROR	MEANING
219	Not used.
220	Not used.
221	The keyword following MAT is unexpected. FILL is inserted.
222	A colon is missing in a MAT statement. A colon is inserted.
223	An identifier is missing in a MAT statement. An identifier is inserted.
224	A comma is missing in a MAT statement. A comma is inserted.

D-3   LINK86 ERROR MESSAGES

MESSAGE	MEANING
CANNOT CLOSE	An output file cannot be closed. The disk might be write-protected.
COMMAND TOO LONG	Too many characters in a command line INPUT [INP] file.
DIRECTORY FULL	There is no directory space for the output files or intermediate files.
DISK READ ERROR	A file cannot be read properly.
DISK WRITE ERROR	A file cannot be written properly, probably due to a full disk.
GROUP OVER 64K	LINK86 attempted to put more than 64K bytes into a single group. This can occur in either the code or data group.
LINK86 ERROR	Internal LINK86 error.
MORE THAN ONE MAIN PROGRAM	There is more than one main program among the files being linked. When linking multiple CBASIC object files, only one file [the main program] can contain executable statements. All other files must contain only multiple-line functions.
MULTIPLE DEFINITION	The specified symbol is defined in more than one of the modules being linked.
NO FILE	The indicated file cannot be found.
NO STACK SEGMENT	There is no stack segment defined for the .EXE file created by LINK86.
OBJECT FILE ERROR	LINK86 detected an error in the object file. This is caused by a translator error or by a bad disk file. Try regenerating the file.

(continues)

MESSAGE	MEANING
SEGMENT ATTRIBUTE ERROR	The align type or combine type of the indicated segment is not the same as the type of the segment in a previously linked file. Regenerate the object file after changing the segment attributes as needed.
SEGMENT COMBINATION ERROR	Attempt to combine segments that cannot be combined, such as LOCAL segments. Change the segment attributes and relink.
SEGMENT OVER 64K	LINK86 attempted to put more than 64K bytes in a single segment.
SYMBOL TABLE OVERFLOW	LINK86 ran out of symbol table space. Reduce the number and/or length of symbols in the program, or relink on a system with more memory available.
TARGET OUT OF RANGE	LINK86 attempts to resolve a reference made to a symbol outside the acceptable referencing range.
UNDEFINED SYMBOLS	The symbols following this message are referenced but not defined in any of the modules being linked.

D-4 COMPILER VERSION EXECUTION ERROR MESSAGES

The following warning message might be printed during execution of a CB86 program:

```
IMPROPER INPUT - REENTER
```

This message occurs when the fields you enter from the console do not match the fields specified in the INPUT statement. Following this message, you must reenter all values required by the input statement.

Execution errors cause a two-letter code to be printed. The following table contains valid CB86 error codes.

If an error occurs with a code consisting of an asterisk followed by a letter, such as *R, a CB86 library has failed. Please notify Digital Research of the circumstances under which the error occurs.

CODE	ERROR
AC	The argument in an ASC function is a null string.
BN	The value following the BUFF option in an OPEN or CREATE statement is less than 1 or greater than 128.
CE	The file being closed cannot be found in the directory. This occurs if the file has been changed by the RENAME function.
CM	The file specified in a CHAIN statement cannot be found in the selected directory. If no filetype is present, the compiler assumes a type of .OVR.
CT	The filetype of the file specified in a CHAIN statement is not .EXE or .OVR.
CU	A CLOSE statement specifies a file identification number that is not active.
CX	Overlay does not fit in overlay area.
CY	DISK read error during loading of overlay.
DE	File to delete cannot be found in the directory.
DF	An OPEN or CREATE statement uses a file identification number that is already used.

(continues)

CODE	ERROR
DU	A DELETE statement specifies a file identification number that is not active.
DW	The operating system reports that there is no disk or directory space available for the file being written to, and no IF END statement is in effect for the file identification number.
DZ	Division by zero is attempted.
EF	Attempt to read past the end-of-file, and no IF END statement is in effect for the file identification number.
ER	Attempt to write a record of length greater than the maximum record size specified in the OPEN or CREATE statement for this file.
FR	Attempt to rename a file to a filename that already exists.
FU	Attempt to access a file that was not open.
GX	GRAPHIC OPEN statement was attempted with GSX-86 not installed.
IF	A filename in an OPEN or CREATE statement, or with the RENAME function, is invalid for your operating system.
IR	A record number of zero is specified in a READ or PRINT statement.
LN	The argument in the LOG function is zero or negative.
ME	The operating system reports an error during an attempt to create or extend a file. Normally, this means the disk directory is full.
MP	The third parameter in a MATCH function is zero or negative.
NE	A negative value is specified for the operand to the left of the power operator.
NF	A file identification is less than 1 or greater than the maximum number of files allowed. See Appendix A, Table A-1.
NN	An attempt to print a numeric expression with a PRINT USING statement fails because there is not a numeric field in the USING string.

(continues)

CODE	ERROR
NS	An attempt to print a string expression with a PRINT USING statement fails because there is not a string field in the USING string.
OD	A READ statement is executed, but there are no DATA statements in the program, or all data items in all the DATA statements have been read.
OE	Attempt to OPEN a file that does not exist, and for which no IF END statement is in effect.
OF	An overflow occurs during a real arithmetic calculation.
OM	The program runs out of dynamically allocated memory during execution.
PO	Indicates polygon coordinate overflow. Clipping process computes additional coordinates required to plot a given polygon within current window. Therefore, the MAT FILL statement with CLIP set to "ON" can result in more than 72 coordinates.
PU	An attempt was made to nest PRINT USING. This can only happen if a multiple-line function that contains a PRINT USING statement is called in the output list of another PRINT USING statement.
RB	Random access is attempted to a file activated with the BUFF option specifying more than one buffer.
RE	Attempt to read past the end of a record in a fixed file.
RU	A random read or print is attempted to a stream file.
SL	A concatenation operation results in a string greater than the maximum allowed string length.
SQ	Attempt to calculate the square root of a negative number.
SS	The second parameter of a MID$ function is zero or negative, or the last parameter of a LEFT$, RIGHT$, or MID$ is negative.
TL	A tab statement contains a parameter less than 1.
UN	A PRINT USING statement is executed with a null edit string, or a backslash escape character, \, is the last character in an edit string.

(continues)

CODE	ERROR
WR	Attempt to write to a stream file after it is read, but before it is read to the end-of-file.
ZW	Indicates any of the following conditions. BOUNDS statement height or width argument has been set to a value less than 1.0E-05, greater than 1.0, or neither argument has been set to 1.0. The left/right or upper/lower bounds arguments of a VIEWPORT or WINDOW statement have been set to values that differ by less than 1.0E-05. The left, right, lower, or upper bound argument of a VIEWPORT statement has been set to a value less than 0 or greater than 1.0.

D-5   LIB86 ERROR MESSAGES

LIB86 can produce the following error messages during processing. With each message, LIB86 displays additional information appropriate to the error, such as the filename or module name, to help isolate the location of the problem.

ERROR	MEANING
CANNOT CLOSE	LIB86 cannot close an output file. Make sure the disk is not write-protected.
DIRECTORY FULL	There is not enough directory space for the output files. Erase unnecessary files or use a disk with more space.
DISK FULL	There is not enough disk space for the output files. Erase unnecessary files or use a disk with more space.
DISK READ ERROR	LIB86 detects a disk error while reading the indicated file. Try regenerating the file.
INVALID COMMAND SWITCH	LIB86 encounters an unrecognized switch in the command line. Retype the command line or edit the .INP file.
LIB86 ERROR n	Internal LIB86 error.
MODULE NOT FOUND	The indicated module name, which appeared in a REPLACE, SELECT, or DELETE switch, could not be found. Retype the command line, or edit the .INP file.
MULTIPLE DEFINITION	The indicated symbol is defined as PUBLIC in more than one module. Correct the problem in the source file.
NO FILE	LIB86 could not find the indicated file.
RENAME ERROR	LIB86 cannot rename a file. Check that the disk is not write-protected.
SYMBOL TABLE OVER-FLOW	There is not enough memory for the symbol table. Reduce the number of switches in the command line [MAP and XREF both use symbol table space], or use a system with more memory.
SYNTAX ERROR	LIB86 detected a syntax error in the command line, probably due to an improper filename or an invalid command option. LIB86 echoes the command line up to the point where it found the error. Retype the command line or edit the .INP file.

APPENDIX E

Non-Compiler Version:
Error Messages

E-1 FILE SYSTEM AND MEMORY SPACE ERRORS

The compiler prints the following messages when a file system error or memory space error occurs. In each case, control returns to the operating system.

ERROR	MEANING
NO SOURCE FILE: *file-name*.BAS	The compiler cannot locate a source file on the specified disk. This file was used in either the CBAS2 command or a %INCLUDE directive.
OUT OF DISK SPACE	The compiler has run out of disk space while attempting to write either the INT file or the LST file.
OUT OF DIRECTORY SPACE	The compiler has run out of directory entries while attempting to create or extend either the INT file or the LST file.
DISK ERROR	A disk error occurred while trying to read or write to a disk file. This message can vary slightly in form depending on the operating system used. See the CP/M documentation for the exact meaning of this message.
PROGRAM CONTAINS n UNMATCHED FOR STATEMENT(S)	There are n FOR statements for which a NEXT cannot be found.
PROGRAM CONTAINS n UNMATCHED WHILE STATEMENT(S)	There are n WHILE statements for which a WEND cannot be found.
PROGRAM CONTAINS 1 UNMATCHED DEF STATEMENT	A multiple line function was not terminated with a FEND statement. This causes other errors in the program.
WARNING INVALID CHARACTER IGNORED	The previous line contained an invalid character. The compiler ignores the character; a question mark is printed in its place.
INCLUDE NESTING TOO DEEP NEAR LINE n	An INCLUDE statement near line n in the source program exceeds the maximum level of nesting of INCLUDE files.

E-2 COMPILE-TIME ERROR MESSAGES

Other errors detected during compilation cause a two-letter error code to be printed with the line number and position of the error. The error message usually follows the line where the error occurred.

CODE	ERROR
BF	A branch into a multiple line function from outside the function was attempted.
BN	An invalid numeric constant was encountered.
CF	A COMMON statement must be in the first line.
CI	An invalid filename was detected in a %INCLUDE directive. The filename cannot contain a ?, *, or: [except as part of a disk reference where a colon can be the second character of the name].
CS	A COMMON statement, that was not the first statement in a program, was detected. Only a compiler directive such as %CHAIN, a REMARK statement, or blank lines can precede a COMMON statement.
CV	An improper definition of a subscripted variable in a COMMON statement was detected. The subscript count is possibly not a constant, or there is more than one constant. Only one constant can appear in parentheses. It specifies the number of subscripts in the defined array.
DL	The same line number was used on two different lines. Other compiler errors can cause a DL error message to be printed even if duplicate line numbers do not exist. Defining functions before use and, sometimes, if the DIM statement does not precede all references to an array, results in a DL error.
DP	A variable dimensioned by a DIM statement was previously defined. It either appears in another DIM statement or was used as a simple variable.
FA	A function name appears on the left side of an assignment statement but is not within that function. In other words, the only function name that can appear to the left of an equal sign is the name of the function currently compiled.
FD	The same function name is used in a second DEF statement.

(continues)

CODE	ERROR
FE	A mixed mode expression exists in a FOR statement that the compiler cannot correct. Probably the expression following the TO is of a different type than the index.
FI	An expression is a subscripted numeric variable being used as a FOR loop index.
FN	A function reference contains an incorrect number of parameters.
FP	A function reference parameter type does not match the parameter type used in the function's DEF statement.
FU	A function was referenced before it was defined, or the function was never defined.
IE	An expression immediately following an IF statement evaluates to type string. Only type numeric is permitted.
IF	A variable used in a FILE statement is of type numeric where type string is required.
IP	An input prompt string was not surrounded by quotes.
IS	A subscripted variable was referenced before dimensioned.
IT	An invalid compiler directive was encountered. A parameter required by the directive can be out of range or missing, or the directive was misspelled.
IU	A variable defined as an array in a DEF statement is used without subscripts.
MC	The same variable is defined more than once in a COMMON statement. Each variable can appear in only one COMMON statement.
MF	An expression evaluates to type string when an expression of type numeric is required.
MM	An invalid mixed mode was detected. Probably variables of type string and type numeric were combined in the same expression.
MS	A numeric expression was used where a string expression was required.

(continues)

CODE	ERROR
ND	A FEND statement was encountered without a corresponding DEF statement. This error could be the result of an improper DEF statement.
NI	A variable referenced by a NEXT statement does not match the variable referenced by the associated FOR statement.
NU	A NEXT statement occurs without an associated FOR statement.
OF	A branch out of a multiple line function from inside the function was attempted.
OO	More than 40 ON statements were used in the program. CBASIC has an arbitrary limit of 40 ON statements in a single program. Notify Digital Research if this limit causes problems.
PM	A DEF statement appeared within a multiple line function. Functions cannot be nested.
RF	A multiple line function cannot call itself.
SD	A second SAVEMEM statement was encountered. A program can have only one SAVEMEM statement.
SE	The source line contained a syntax error. This means that a statement is not properly formed or a keyword is misspelled.
SF	A SAVEMEM statement uses an expression of type numeric to specify the file to be loaded. The expression must be a string. Possibly, the quotation marks were left off a string constant.
SN	A subscripted variable contains an incorrect number of subscripts, or a variable in a DIM statement was previously used with a different number of dimensions.
SO	The statement is too complex to compile; simplify it. Consider making the expression into two or more expressions. Please send Digital Research a copy of the source statement.
TO	Symbol table overflow has occurred. This means that the program is too large for the system being used. The program must be simplified or the amount of available memory increased. Smaller variable names reduce the amount of symbol table space used. Please inform Digital Research if programs generate this error.

(continues)

CODE	ERROR
UL	A line number that does not exist was referenced.
US	A string was terminated by a carriage return rather than by quotes.
VO	Variable names are too long for one statement. This should not usually occur. If it does, please send a copy of the source statement to Digital Research. Reducing the length of variable names and reducing the complexity of the expression within the statement can eliminate the error.
WE	The expression immediately following a WHILE statement is not numeric.
WN	WHILE statements are nested to a depth greater than 12. CBASIC has an arbitrary limit of 12 for nesting WHILE statements.
WU	A WEND statement occurred without an associated WHILE statement.

E-3 RUN-TIME ERROR MESSAGES

The following warning messages might be printed during execution of a CBASIC program.

ERROR	MEANING
NO INTERMEDIATE FILE:*filename*	A filename was not specified with the CRUN2 command, or no file of type INT with the specified filename was found on the specified disk.
IMPROPER INPUT - REENTER	This message occurs when the fields entered from the console do not match the fields specified in the INPUT statement. This occurs when field types do not match or the number of fields entered differs from the number of fields specified. Following this message, all values required by the INPUT statement must be reentered.

Run-time errors cause a two-letter code to be printed. If the code is preceded by the word WARNING, execution continues. If the code is preceded by the word ERROR, execution terminates. If an error occurs with a code consisting of an * followed by a letter such as *R, the CBASIC run-time package has failed. Please notify Digital Research of the circumstances under which the error occurred.

The following are valid CBASIC *warning* codes.

CODE	ERROR
DZ	A number was divided by zero. The result is set to the largest valid CBASIC number.
FL	A field length greater than 255 bytes was encountered during a READ LINE statement. The first 255 characters of the record are retained; the other characters are ignored.
LN	The argument given in the LOG function was zero or negative. The value of the argument is returned.
NE	A negative number was specified before the raise to a power operator. The absolute value of the parameter is used in the calculation. When using real variables, a positive number can be raised to a negative power, but a negative number cannot be raised to a power.

(continues)

CODE	ERROR
OF	A calculation using real variables produced an overflow. The result is set to the largest valid CBASIC real number. Overflow is not detected with integer arithmetic.
SQ	A negative number was specified in the SQR function. The absolute value is used.

The following are valid CBASIC *error* codes.

CODE	ERROR
AC	The argument in an ASC function is a null string.
AE	An attempt was made to access an array element before the array DIM statement was executed.
BN	The value following the BUFF option in an OPEN or CREATE statement is less than one or greater than 52.
CC	A chained program's code area is larger than the main program's code area. Use a %CHAIN directive in the main program to adjust the size of the code area.
CD	A chained program's data area is larger than the main program's data area. Use a %CHAIN directive in the main program to adjust the size of the data area.
CE	The file being closed cannot be found in the directory. This occurs if the RENAME function has changed the file.
CF	A chained program's constant area is larger than the main program's constant area. Use a %CHAIN directive in the main program to adjust the size of the constant area.
CP	A chained program's variable storage area is larger than the main program's variable storage area. Use a %CHAIN directive in the main program to adjust the size of the variable storage area.
CS	A chained program reserved a different amount of memory, with a SAVEMEM statement, than the main program.
CU	A CLOSE statement specifies a file identification number that is not active.

(continues)

CODE	ERROR
DF	An OPEN or CREATE statement uses a file identification number that is already used.
DU	A DELETE statement specifies a file identification number that is not active.
DW	The operating system reports that there is no disk or directory space available for the file being written to, and no IF END statement is in effect for the file identification number.
EF	An attempt is made to read past the end of a file, and no IF END statement is in effect for the file identification number.
ER	An attempt was made to write a record of length greater than the maximum record size specified in the OPEN, CREATE, or FILE statement for this file.
FR	An attempt was made to rename a file to an existing filename.
FU	An attempt was made to access a file that was not open.
IF	A filename was invalid. Most likely, an invalid character was found in the filename. A colon can never appear embedded in the name proper. ? and * can only appear in ambiguous filenames. This error also results if the filename was a null string.
IR	A record number of zero was specified in a READ or PRINT statement.
IV	An attempt was made to execute an INT file created by a version one compiler. To use CRUN2, a program must be recompiled using the version two compiler, CBAS2. This error also results from attempting to execute an empty INT file.
IX	A FEND statement was encountered before executing a RETURN statement. All multiple line functions must exit with a RETURN statement.
ME	The operating system reports an error during an attempt to create or extend a file. Usually this means the disk directory is full.
MP	The third parameter in a MATCH function was zero or negative.
NC	The source program contains a real constant outside the range of CBASIC real numbers.

(continues)

CODE	ERROR
NF	A file identification number is less than one or greater than 20, or a FILE statement was executed when 20 files were already active.
NM	There was insufficient memory to load the program.
NN	An attempt to print a numeric expression with a PRINT USING statement fails because there is not a numeric field in the USING string.
NS	An attempt to print a string expression with a PRINT USING statement fails because there is not a string field in the USING string.
OD	A READ statement was executed, but there are no DATA statements in the program, or all data items in all DATA statements were already read.
OE	An attempt was made to OPEN a file that does not exist and for which no IF END statement was in effect.
OI	The expression specified in an ON . . . GOSUB or an ON . . . GOTO statement evaluated to a number less than one or greater than the number of line numbers contained in the statement.
OM	The program ran out of dynamically allocated memory during execution. Space can be conserved by closing files when no longer needed and by setting strings to a null string when no longer required. Also, by not using DATA statements, but reading the constant information from a file, space is saved. Large arrays can be dimensioned with smaller subscripts when the array is no longer required.
QE	An attempt was made to print a string containing a quotation mark to a file. Quotation marks can only be written to files when using the PRINT USING option of the PRINT statement.
RB	Random access was attempted to a file activated with the BUFF option specifying more than one buffer.
RE	An attempt was made to read past the end of a record in a fixed file.
RF	A recursive function call was attempted; CBASIC does not support recursion.
RG	A RETURN statement occurred for which there was no GOSUB statement.

(continues)

CODE	ERROR
RU	A random read or print was attempted to a stream file.
SB	An array subscript was used which exceeds the boundaries for which the array was defined.
SL	A concatenation operation resulted in a string greater than the maximum allowed string length.
SO	The file specified in a SAVEMEM statement cannot be located on the referenced disk. The expression specifying the filename must include the filetype if one is present. A filetype of COM is not forced.
SS	The second parameter of a MID$ function was zero or negative, or the last parameter of a LEFT$, RIGHT$, or MID$ function was negative.
TL	A TAB statement contains a parameter less than one.
UN	A PRINT USING statement was executed with a null edit string, or an escape character is the last character in an edit string.
WR	An attempt was made to write to a stream file after it was read, but before it was read to the end of the file.

APPENDIX F

Quick Guide to Number-String and Other Conversions

There are several sets of functions that can be used to convert data from one form to another. They can be classified into several categories among which are:

- Numeric value to string and digit string to numeric value
- Real to integer and integer to real
- String to ASCII decimal value and ASCII code to string

Converting numbers to strings and digit string expressions [those containing only numeric characters] to numbers is often an efficient method of manipulating data during programming. An example is a file including a product number, a product description, its price, number of units on hand, and dollar value of the item's inventory. It is easier in programming to store and manipulate each record as part of a matrix than to use five arrays, but it is not possible to multiply the unit price by the number of units on hand to obtain the dollar value of the item's inventory if the values are strings.

CONVERSION FUNCTIONS

Number ⟶ String

To convert a numeric value or expression to a string, use STR$:

<string> = **STR$(** <numeric value> **)**

String ⟶ Number

To transform a digit string to a numeric value, use VAL:

<numeric variable> = **VAL(** <digit string expression> **)**

ASCII Value of the First Character of a String

To obtain the ASCII decimal value of the first character of a string, use the ASC function:

<integer value> = **ASC(** <string> **)**

Character for an ASCII Value

To obtain a one-character string for a given ASCII decimal value, between 0 and 255, use CHR$:

<string> = **CHR$(** <ASCII decimal value> **)**

Integer ⟶ Real

To convert an integer value to a real value, use FLOAT:

<real numeric value> = **FLOAT(** <integer numeric value> **)**

Real ⟶ Integer

To convert a real value to an integer value and truncate the fractional portion of the real value, use INT%:

<integer numeric value> = **INT%(** <real numeric value> **)**

Index

NOW AVAILABLE!

Save the time it takes to type in all the data for the data files that are used in this book. Avoid keying errors in your programs that may require recompiling or result in runtime errors often difficult to trace. Over 100 programs, subroutines, and data files listed in the CBASIC/CB86 WITH GRAPHICS book are available on disk (IBM PC version).

SPECIAL FEATURES only available on disk: Useful CBASIC programs and subroutines are included that are not listed in the book, such as a program to maintain income and expenditure records and produce summary reports, a subroutine to determine the color graphics capability of your system, a passwording program that controls access to a disk or to a program, and much more.

PUT ALL THE SOFTWARE PROGRAMS AND UTILITIES TO WORK FOR YOU IMMEDIATELY. FILL OUT AND MAIL YOUR ORDER IN **TODAY** !

PUT YOUR IBM PC TO WORK TODAY

CBASIC/CB86 WITH GRAPHICS: PROGRAMMING FOR BUSINESS software is now available for IBM PC computers.

Buy the $5\frac{1}{4}$ inch disk at your favorite computer store, or order from Wiley:

In the United States: John Wiley & Sons
1 Wiley Drive
Somerset, NJ 08873
or call: 212-850-6788.
In the United Kingdom John Wiley & Sons, Ltd.
and Europe: Baffins Lane, Chichester
Sussex PO 19 IUD UNITED KINGDOM
In Canada: John Wiley & Sons Canada, Ltd.
22 Worcester Road
Rexdale, Ontario M9W 1L1 CANADA
In Australia: Jacaranda Wiley, Ltd.
GPO Box 859
Brisbane, Queensland AUSTRALIA

Highland – CBASIC/CB86 WITH GRAPHICS 1-82604-9

NO POSTAGE
NECESSARY
IF MAILED
IN THE
UNITED STATES

BUSINESS REPLY MAIL

FIRST CLASS   PERMIT NO. 2277   NEW YORK, NY

Postage will be paid by addressee:

JOHN WILEY & SONS, Inc.
1 Wiley Drive
Somerset, N.J. 08873

Attn: CBASIC/CB86 Software